Partisan Hostility and American Democracy

Chicago Studies in American Politics

*A series edited by Susan Herbst, Lawrence R. Jacobs, Adam J. Berinsky,
and Frances Lee; Benjamin I. Page, editor emeritus*

Also in the series:

*Respect and Loathing in
American Democracy:
Polarization, Moralization,
and the Undermining
of Equality*
by Jeff Spinner-Halev and
Elizabeth Theiss-Morse

*Countermobilization: Policy
Feedback and Backlash
in a Polarized Age*
by Eric M. Patashnik

*Race, Rights, and Rifles:
The Origins of the NRA
and Contemporary Gun
Culture*
by Alexandra Filindra

*Accountability in State
Legislatures*
by Steven Rogers

*Dynamic Democracy:
Public Opinion, Elections,
and Policymaking in the
American States*
by Devin Caughey and
Christopher Warshaw

*Persuasion in Parallel: How
Information Changes Minds
about Politics*
by Alexander Coppock

*Radical American
Partisanship: Mapping
Violent Hostility, Its Causes,
and the Consequences for
Democracy*
by Nathan P. Kalmoe and
Lilliana Mason

*The Obligation Mosaic:
Race and Social Norms in
U.S. Political Participation*
by Allison P. Anoll

*A Troubled Birth:
The 1930s and American
Public Opinion*
by Susan Herbst

*Power Shifts: Congress and
Presidential Representation*
by John A. Dearborn

*Prisms of the People: Power
and Organizing in Twenty-
First-Century America*
by Hahrie Han, Elizabeth
McKenna, and Michelle
Oyakawa

*Democracy Declined:
The Failed Politics of
Consumer Financial
Protection*
by Mallory E. SoRelle

*Race to the Bottom: How
Racial Appeals Work in
American Politics*
by LaFleur Stephens-Dougan

*The Limits of Party:
Congress and Lawmaking
in a Polarized Era*
by James M. Curry and
Frances E. Lee

America's Inequality Trap
by Nathan J. Kelly

*Good Enough for Government
Work: The Public Reputation
Crisis in America (And What
We Can Do to Fix It)*
by Amy E. Lerman

*Who Wants to Run? How
the Devaluing of Political
Office Drives Polarization*
by Andrew B. Hall

*From Politics to the Pews:
How Partisanship and the
Political Environment Shape
Religious Identity*
by Michele F. Margolis

*The Increasingly United States:
How and Why American
Political Behavior Nationalized*
by Daniel J. Hopkins

Partisan Hostility and American Democracy

Explaining Political Divisions and When They Matter

JAMES N. DRUCKMAN,
SAMARA KLAR,
YANNA KRUPNIKOV,
MATTHEW LEVENDUSKY,
AND JOHN BARRY RYAN

The University of Chicago Press
Chicago and London

The University of Chicago Press, Chicago 60637
The University of Chicago Press, Ltd., London
Published 2024
Printed in the United States of America

33 32 31 30 29 28 27 26 25 24   1 2 3 4 5

ISBN-13: 978-0-226-83365-1 (cloth)
ISBN-13: 978-0-226-83367-5 (paper)
ISBN-13: 978-0-226-83366-8 (e-book)
DOI: https://doi.org/10.7208/chicago/9780226833668.001.0001

Library of Congress Cataloging-in-Publication Data
Names: Druckman, James N., 1971- author. | Klar, Samara, author. | Krupnikov,
    Yanna, author. | Levendusky, Matthew, author. | Ryan, John Barry, 1979- author.
Title: Partisan hostility and American democracy : explaining political divisions
    and when they matter / James N. Druckman, Samara Klar, Yanna Krupnikov,
    Matthew Levendusky, and John Barry Ryan.
Other titles: Chicago studies in American politics.
Description: Chicago ; London : The University of Chicago Press, 2024. |
    Series: Chicago studies in American politics | Includes bibliographical
    references and index.
Identifiers: LCCN 2023050767 | ISBN 9780226833651 (cloth) |
    ISBN 9780226833675 (paperback) | ISBN 9780226833668 (ebook)
Subjects: LCSH: Polarization (Social sciences)—United States. | Political culture—
    United States. | United States—Politics and government—2017–2021. |
    BISAC: POLITICAL SCIENCE / Political Ideologies / Conservatism & Liberalism |
    POLITICAL SCIENCE / Political Ideologies / Democracy
Classification: LCC JK1726 .D78 2024 | DDC 306.20973—dc23/eng/20231219
LC record available at https://lccn.loc.gov/2023050767

♾ This paper meets the requirements of ANSI/NISO Z39.48-1992 (Permanence of Paper).

Contents

1 Partisan Hostility in America 1

2 Partisan Animosity in American Politics 24

3 Analyzing the Impact of Partisan Animosity 39

4 How Partisan Animosity Can Fuel Issue Polarization 62

5 A Political Virus: How Partisan Animosity Polarized
Voters' Responses to the COVID-19 Pandemic 74

6 Partisan Animosity and Evaluations of Political Leaders 96

7 Partisan Animosity and Political Compromise 122

8 A Democratic Paradox: Opposing the Practices and Norms
That Uphold a Popular Democracy 138
With Jon Kingzette

9 The Challenges of Partisan Hostility for American Democracy 158

Acknowledgments 179
Appendixes 183
Notes 217
References 229
Index 257

Partisan Hostility in America

On December 12, 2000, the United States Supreme Court ruled 5 to 4 to end the recount of contested presidential votes in the state of Florida. This meant that Republican nominee George W. Bush won the state of Florida by 537 votes out of a total of 5,963,110 votes cast in the state, a margin of victory of .009 percent. Bush subsequently received 271 total Electoral College votes, one more than the 270 required for victory. He thus defeated Democratic nominee Al Gore even though nationally, more voters had preferred Gore (by 543,895 votes, roughly one-half of a percentage point more than Bush). That election introduced many voters to the U.S. Constitution's rules for selecting the president: the Electoral College, not the national popular vote, elects the president. Such inversions, where the loser of the popular vote wins the Electoral College, were rare—2000 marked only the third time this had occurred in the nation's history. As such, most voters likely assumed that it was a one-off political fluke and stable politics would return.

Alas, the challenges of that election were a harbinger of subsequent decades. Since the 2000 election, America experienced (among many other events) the terrorist attack of 9/11, the wars in Iraq and Afghanistan, the most severe financial crisis since the Great Depression, the legalization of gay marriage and the overturning of the right to an abortion by the Supreme Court, foreign meddling in a presidential election, another presidential election where the winner received a minority of the popular vote, a polarizing pandemic, the country's largest protest movement ever, two presidential impeachments, and an insurrection at the U.S. Capitol. And, of course, at the same time, technological and demographic changes continued apace, with demographers now projecting that white Americans will become the numerical minority by midcentury and artificial intelligence threatening to transform the global economy. Instability and change have characterized the politics of the past two decades.

Such an eventful period belies a simple characterization. Yet, if there has been one political through line to this period, it is polarization. For instance, a 2014 Pew Research Center report summed up the conventional wisdom by noting that "political polarization is the defining feature of early 21st century American politics" (Doherty 2014). Few people would disagree. While research was first focused on ideological polarization among elected officials, such as members of Congress (McCarty, Poole, and Rosenthal 2006), scholars soon turned their attention to determining whether the mass public was, or was not, similarly polarized (cf. Fiorina 2017; Abramowitz 2010). More recently, scholars have focused on an arguably more alarming trend—the dramatic rise of partisan hostility. "A new type of division has emerged in the mass public in recent years: Ordinary Americans increasingly dislike and distrust those from the other party. . . . Democrats and Republicans both say that the other party's members are hypocritical, selfish, and closed-minded, and they are unwilling to socialize across party lines, or even to partner with opponents in a variety of other activities" (Iyengar et al. 2019, 130; also see Stone 2023). The rise of partisan hostility has concerned not just scholars, but also journalists and citizens. *New York Times* columnist David Brooks (2021) put it succinctly in stating that it became clear in this "age of affective polarization" that we "didn't disagree more, we just hated each other more."

Concern about partisans hating one another is far from new. In his famous defense of the Constitution, James Madison expressed a fearful scenario where elites had "divided mankind into parties, inflamed them with mutual animosity, and rendered them much more disposed to vex and oppress each other than to co-operate for their common good" (Hamilton, Madison, and Jay [1787–1788] 1961, *Federalist* 10, 79).

The country's first president, George Washington, in 1796, echoed these concerns in his farewell address, focusing on the danger posed by nascent political parties: "The alternating domination of one faction over another, sharpened by the spirit of revenge, natural to party dissention. . . . [S]ooner or later the chief of some prevailing faction, more able or more fortunate than his competitors, turns this disposition to the purposes of his own elevation, on the ruins of public liberty."

For many, the twenty-first century—thanks to demographic shifts, technological change, and incorrigible elites, inter alia—has elevated partisan hostility to such a level that the despotism Madison and Washington warned against seems to be inevitable. Partisans refuse to work with, befriend, or even talk to those from the other party (Iyengar et al. 2019). They also excuse or dismiss key constitutional norms such as checks and balances, freedom to protest, and equal voting access if it benefits their party at the expense of the other (Bartels 2020; Graham and Svolik 2020; Kingzette et al. 2021). Hostility toward the other party has become so intense that it is likened to a sect involving a "poisonous cocktail of othering, aversion, and moralization" that "poses a threat to democracy" (Finkel et al. 2020, 533).

Despite these real and significant concerns, there continues to be scant empirical evidence of the broader *political* consequences of partisan hostility. Do partisan tensions and hostility alter political opinions? Does partisan hostility actually pose a threat to democracy, and if so, how? The lack of evidence concerning political consequences of hostility has enabled some researchers to raise the question of whether there is much to worry about at all (e.g., A. Fowler 2020) or whether this is just a case of omitted variable bias such that other factors dwarf hostility in affecting politics (Broockman, Kalla, and Westwood 2023; Voelkel et al., "Interventions," 2023). On the other hand, it has led others to conclude, without clear evidence, that the country is imperiled, with no way out (Drutman 2020; Finkel et al. 2020). We see merit in each perspective, but we believe that more work is necessary to clarify them. We aim to do just that in this book. We offer a new theory of *when* hostility—which we term *partisan animosity* (for reasons we will soon explain)—affects political beliefs and behaviors. We then test the theory's predictions with a data set that encompasses three of the most eventful years of politics in recent American history: 2019, 2020, and 2021. Using these data, we document a wide range of effects of animosity, while also showing various null effects. Jointly, these patterns highlight that the role of animosity in politics is conditional and varies across settings.

To preview our findings, we conclude that partisan hostility (i.e., animosity) is unlikely to directly lead to democratic breakdown or collapse; however, it does have deleterious effects on democracy that could contribute to erosion over time. In particular, we find the following:

- *Democratic Functioning versus Democratic Collapse.* We find broad-ranging effects of animosity on policy positions, responses to the COVID-19 pandemic, evaluations of public figures, support for political compromise, and support for undemocratic practices (e.g., gerrymandering, challenging close elections). In each of these cases, animosity polarizes individuals: as animosity increases, so do the partisan gaps in issue positions, collectively beneficial behaviors (e.g., mask wearing during COVID-19), evaluations of ostensibly nonpolitical figures (e.g., Dr. Anthony Fauci), willingness to compromise, and the privileging of party over democratic processes. This can make democratic functioning difficult and, over time, could contribute to erosion, particularly when nefarious elites exploit these gaps. However, when it comes to outcomes that pose a more proximate threat to democratic governance—including beliefs in fundamental norms such as checks and balances and support for illicit political activities or partisan violence—animosity has an extremely small, or in some cases null, effect. These findings highlight the importance of varying the outcomes under study and carefully considering their implications. Our findings also strike a middle ground between researchers who claim that animosity has few important effects (e.g., Broockman, Kalla, and Westwood 2023) and those who claim that it is unraveling democracy (e.g., Finkel et al. 2020).

- *Availability of Party Cues.* Citizens can take positions consistent with their party only if they know or can impute where their party stands. While partisan elites typically clarify their positions on highly salient issues, they fail to do so on many other topics. Without these signals, even partisans with extreme animus will not know what position to take. On such topics, animosity has little to no impact.

- *Personalization versus Politicization.* The impact of animosity depends on partisans' motivations. When individuals have a reason to seek the most accurate possible outcome—because the costs of a mistake are high—the relationship between animosity and beliefs is severed. For example, we show how the salience of COVID-19 changed the behavior of even the highest-animus Republicans. Normally, these individuals took few precautions to protect themselves from this potentially lethal virus. Yet if the virus severely affected them or their friends or family, they took more steps to prevent themselves from becoming infected (or reinfected). On the other hand, as a topic becomes more politicized, animus becomes more relevant to evaluations (e.g., animosity affects views on politicized policies like the Affordable Care Act (ACA) but not less politicized policies such as economic relocation incentives for businesses). Moreover, individuals who are higher in animus politicize nonpolitical actors and entities (such as scientists during the COVID-19 pandemic), which further contributes to polarization (A. Lee 2021). In short, animosity goes hand in hand with politicization but has much smaller effects when the decision has direct personal consequences.

- *Hateful Partisans.* We find that when animosity does have effects, they appear to be largely monotonic: higher animosity correlates with larger partisan gaps in opinions. However, the divisions (on outcomes such as policy beliefs or COVID-19 behaviors) become notably larger at higher levels of animus (e.g., over the 50th percentile, and particularly over the 67th). If these individuals have undue impact on other voters or elected officials, it could exacerbate the negative effects of animosity on democracy. Thus, partisans who exhibit the highest levels of animosity toward the other party likely constitute the most sizable threat in terms of undermining democratic functioning.

These findings make clear that Madison and Washington had good reason to worry about the rise of factions with hostility toward one another. Yet animosity does not invariably lead to despotism. As with most political phenomena, the exact effect depends on the broader context. In this case, it depends on the outcomes under consideration, the availability of party cues, the extent of personalization and politicization, and the influence of the most hateful partisans. Animosity likely has contributed to the downgrading of the functioning of American democracy according to many international metrics (e.g., Repucci and Slipowitz 2021; Boese et al. 2022), but, as Dahl (1971) made clear more than a half-century ago, democracy is far from a dichotomous variable, and conclusions about collapse are often overly simplistic (see, for example, Little and Meng 2023). This book introduces nuance to the debate about the effects of animosity and provides a framework for understanding when it matters and what variables to focus on. That said, we do not mean to minimize the impact of partisan animosity—indeed, as we will discuss, its effects on democratic functioning can create opportunities for elites to exploit divisions in their quest to gain power, which can lead in turn to subtle, but substantial, democratic backsliding.

The book also offers a more focused contribution: the data come from an original four-wave panel survey that enveloped one of the most consequential periods in American history, one that captured some of the significant events noted earlier in the chapter. Over twenty-one months, the survey covered the COVID-19 lockdowns and ensuing economic downturn, George Floyd's murder and the subsequent nationwide protests, the 2020 presidential election (including President Donald Trump's electoral conspiracies), the January 6th Capitol insurrection, two presidential impeachment trials, a shift in the congressional majority, and the mass distribution of the COVID-19 vaccines.

In what follows in this chapter, we both broaden and focus the discussion of animosity. We begin in the next section by taking a step back and discussing conceptions of political polarization and, specifically, the rise of partisan animosity in the twenty-first century. We then briefly discuss the potential consequences of partisan animosity. Next, we turn to how we study the effects of animosity, and we present our theoretic and empirical approach. We detail the

timeline of events over the course of our data collection and the types of outcomes we study. This foregrounds the presentation of our theory in chapter 2.
We conclude this introductory chapter with a brief overview of the book that
provides readers with a roadmap of our entire argument.

Political Polarization and Partisan Animosity
in Contemporary America

Polarization is a word that has become so ubiquitous that it has almost lost
its meaning. Scholars of American politics invoke it to refer to the growing
ideological disagreement between Republicans and Democrats in Congress
(McCarty 2019), residential partisan sorting (Martin and Webster 2020), issue-
based partisan divides (Abramowitz and Saunders 2008), and increasing hostility between Republicans and Democrats in the mass public (Iyengar et al.
2019). The unifying theme concerns increased disagreement or divergence between the parties, whether at the elite or the mass level. Perhaps the most common instantiation is so-called ideological polarization such that, over time,
Democratic preferences have become more liberal and Republican preferences
more conservative. This shift appears most clearly among members of Congress, where since the 1960s, the two parties have become more internally homogenous and have drifted further apart from each other, driven mostly by a
Republican rightward shift (McCarty 2019).

The evidence of ideological polarization among the mass public remains
notably murkier. Some researchers argue that the public consists of moderates
rather than ideologues (Fiorina 2017), while others show that the mass public
has become ideologically more divided over time (Abramowitz 2010). Data
tend to support the first position of moderation, though strong partisans exhibit greater divergence (Lelkes 2016; also see DellaPosta 2020; Groenendyk,
Kimbrough, and Pickup 2023).[1]

Regardless, scholars have recognized a new type of polarization emerging
in the mass public, one not fully attributable to ideology. Even when Democrats and Republicans agree on specific policies (and hence are not ideologically polarized), they often dislike and distrust one another (Iyengar, Sood,
and Lelkes 2012; Mason 2018). Study after study confirms striking levels of
this dislike and distrust: roughly 8 in 10 partisans report negative feelings (as
opposed to neutral or positive feelings) toward those from the other party,
and majorities describe their partisan opponents with a variety of pejorative
adjectives like "hypocritical," "closed-minded," and "immoral" (Pew Research
Center 2019b). More than three-quarters say that they "fundamentally disagree about core American values" with those from the other party (Gramlich

2020), and similar numbers say that those from the other party are "a clear and present danger to the American way of life" (Robinson 2021). Rather than being polarized over policy issues, partisans seem polarized in the way they view the other side.

Scholars call this phenomenon *affective polarization*, where *affective* refers to the way one feels about something—in this case, the opposing party. Unlike the case of ideological polarization among the public, scholars agree that affective polarization—the gap between individuals' positive feelings toward their own political party and negative feelings toward the opposing party—has grown over time. Indeed, in the next section, we will show these over-time changes (also see Iyengar et al. 2019). While *polarization* traditionally refers to a shifting distribution of opinions or beliefs, the term now also includes how individual partisans feel toward their own party and the opposing one.

Of course, as with any academic concept, scholars have used a host of labels to refer to affective polarization or analogous concepts, including pernicious polarization (McCoy and Somer 2019), partyism (Sunstein 2015), partisanism (Pope 2021), social polarization (Mason 2018; Webster, Connors, and Sinclair 2022), partisan animus/antipathy (Pew Research Center 2019b), moral polarization (Tappin and McKay 2019), partisan prejudice (Lelkes and Westwood 2017), negative partisanship (Abramowitz and Webster 2018; Bankert 2021), sectarianism (Finkel et al. 2020), and no doubt many more. Throughout the book, we primarily refer to this concept as partisan animus or partisan animosity. We do so for theoretical and practical reasons. In terms of the former, as we will discuss in chapter 2, we argue that animus toward the opposing party, more than warmth toward one's own party, shapes how partisans react to politics and form political opinions (also see Rudolph and Hetherington 2021; Bankert 2023). In terms of the latter, we view an advantage to not invoking *polarization*, given its aforementioned broad and inconsistent usage (see, e.g., Jost, Baldassarri, and Druckman 2022). That said, readers who prefer to use another term, such as *affective polarization*, can substitute it without any loss of generality. They also can freely use *hostility*, the term with which we opened the book. Animosity denotes more intense dislike than hostility, and, as we show in the next section, the dislike often appears to be quite intense. Further, we opt for *animosity* throughout to be consistent with academic discussions that employ that term more frequently than *hostility*.

Such animosity reflects identity and group attachment considerations. Iyengar (2021) explains that it is "rooted in social psychology. . . . Once people adopt a partisan identity, they immediately categorize the world into an ingroup (their own party), and an out group (the opposing party) . . . This sense of partisan identity elicits strong feelings of hostility toward political opponents." Put another way, the construct's foundation lies in group attachments and involves negative intergroup evaluations based largely, though not entirely, on affect (although see Orr and Huber 2020).

How Do We Know Partisan Animosity When We See It?

While we empirically focus on a snippet of American politics from 2019 through 2021, we want to contextualize how animosity has evolved over time. Measurement is pivotal to any such exercise, and we will have more to say about the way scholars capture animosity in chapter 3; for now, however, we note that the best over-time data come from the American National Election Studies (ANES; online at https://electionstudies.org/). Since 1978, the ANES has asked people to rate the "Democratic Party" and the "Republican Party" on a 101-point scale depicted visually on a thermometer; hence, this instrument is called a feeling thermometer scale. A feeling thermometer rating of 0 degrees (the lowest point) implies that someone feels very negatively toward that party, a rating of 50 degrees means that someone is neutral toward it, and a rating of 100 degrees (the highest point) means that someone feels very warmly toward it. We cannot know why one assigns a party a given rating, but we can use these ratings as an over-time measure of the overall affect that people have for both their own party and the other party.[2] The feeling thermometer also is the canonical measure of partisan animosity, whether used by itself or with other items, as done in virtually every study of animosity or affective polarization. Figure 1.1 plots the average feeling thermometer for the in-party and out-party ratings over time.

Figure 1.1 displays in-party ratings in black and out-party ratings in gray. The two different line types (solid and dotted) correspond to the different interview modes used by the ANES. Traditionally, the ANES interviewed respondents face-to-face, with the interviewer sitting across from the respondent in their home; we plot these respondents with the solid lines. But beginning in 2012, the ANES began to interview some respondents online in preparation for the day when the study would shift fully online; their responses are plotted with the dotted lines. That shift arrived in 2020, when the COVID-19 pandemic made lengthy face-to-face interviews impossible, given the potential hazards of in-person contact. While the levels across modes differed (i.e., online respondents rated *both* their own party and the other party more negatively), the trends were similar across modes.[3]

We begin with the in-party ratings. Clearly, respondents like their own party. They have rated it consistently at around 70 degrees, a quite positive rating.[4] As Levendusky (2023) shows, this is one of the highest average thermometer

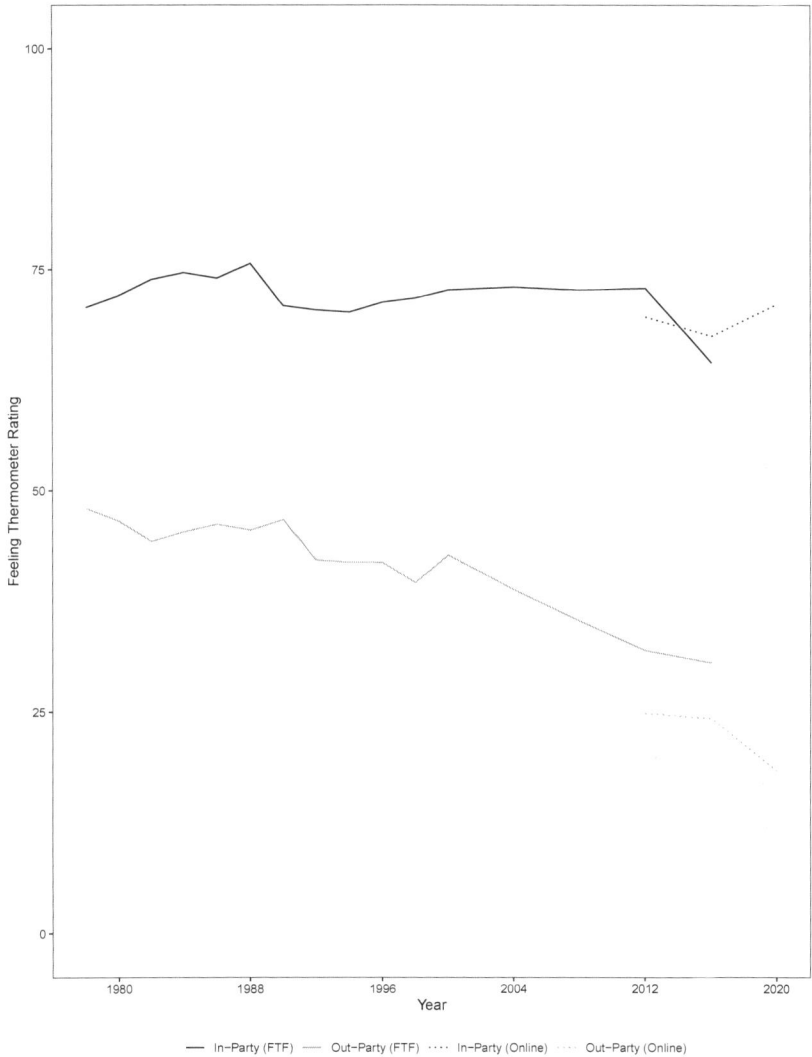

FIGURE 1.1. Over-Time Trends in Feeling Thermometer Ratings, American National Election Studies Data
Note: In-party ratings are displayed in black and out-party ratings in gray. Face-to-face (FTF) interviews are solid lines and online interviews are dotted lines.

ratings in American politics over time, trailing only groups like the military and middle-class people. The trend has remained consistent, albeit with an aberrational drop in 2016. In that year, both Hillary Clinton and Donald Trump were uniquely unpopular, even among their own party's supporters. Since presidential candidates serve as the symbols of their parties in the minds of most voters (G. Jacobson 2019), Americans' poor ratings of Clinton and Trump dragged down the in-party ratings. But this was the exception that proved the rule; overall, people like their own party, as revealed by the 2020 data, which returned to the previous high levels. In sum, looking at these patterns alone would suggest little dramatic change in recent years, but rather a period of, mostly, stability.

The same point about stability cannot be said for ratings of the opposing party. Here, while the rating for the opposition used to be relatively neutral— the average rating for the out-party was 47 degrees in 1980—more recently it has become strikingly negative, hovering at a chilly 19 degrees in 2020. Looking at the online data, the rating in 2020 was fully 40 percent lower than it was in 2012—in just eight short years, dislike for the other side increased markedly. Rather than being akin to lauded groups such as the military, feelings about the other party look similar to those about stigmatized groups from the past such as radical students. This is a much grimmer outlook.

If we were to look at the difference between in-party and out-party ratings, as some scholars do in constructing affective polarization scores (see, e.g., Lelkes and Westwood 2017; Klar, Krupnikov, and Ryan 2018), we would see the same pattern. In the 1980s, the gap was roughly 25 degrees, but by the end of our series, it had ballooned to 53 degrees, more than half the scale. Individuals have consistently liked their own party, but even relative to just eight or ten years ago, they dislike the other party much more now.

Why Has Partisan Animosity Increased?

Scholars have identified a host of sources behind the trends displayed in figure 1.1. While the causes of increasing polarization are not the focus of this book (for discussion, see Iyengar et al. 2019; Druckman and Levy 2022), we nevertheless consider one of the most critical factors to provide context—that is, the sorting of the electorate. Beginning with a party alignment often attributed to the civil rights era in the 1960s, partisans have become more ideologically sorted so that Democrats are more likely to be liberals and Republicans are more likely to be conservatives. This sorting stems at least in part from elite ideological polarization; greater divisions among the elites have made for clearer cues connecting party to ideology. In turn, these cues facilitated partisans switching their ideological identification accordingly (Levendusky 2009): conservative Democrats became liberal and liberal Republicans became conservative. Indeed, the ANES data indicate that in 2000, 78 percent of Democrats identified as liberal while 67 percent of Republicans identified as conservative. Those numbers increased to 90 percent and 88 percent, respectively, in 2020.

This sorting suggests the possibility that in part, individuals dislike and distrust those from the other party because they disagree with their issue positions (Bougher 2017; Orr and Huber 2020) and because policy preferences signal partisan identity (N. Dias and Lelkes 2022).[5] As Fiorina (2017, 60) notes, "nothing . . . allows us to separate the affective from the cognitive"; in other words, issue differences inform partisan animosity.

Beyond ideology, public sorting occurred on demographic characteristics—racial, religious, and geographic identities have all become more aligned with partisanship (Mason 2018). For instance, since the 1960s, Black Americans have become more likely to be Democrats while white Americans have become more likely to be Republicans; those who regularly attend church have increasingly aligned with the Republican Party and nonreligious individuals have affiliated with the Democratic Party. Partisan and demographic sorting can beneficially provide clearer political information to voters (Levendusky 2009). However, they also turn partisanship into a "mega-identity" (Mason 2018). Consequently, fewer individuals in the mass public experience the social cross-pressures that allow the political system to adjust to changing dynamics on the ground. Individuals become more involved in "real and invented conflicts" (Mason 2018, 13), which affects party evaluations, anger, and activism "independent of a person's policy opinions" (Mason 2018, 15). Mason (2016) provides experimental evidence that such social sorting produces anger more consistently than policy attitudes or partisan identity alone. Put another way, the parties have become socially distinctive and homogenous, leading people to harbor more animus toward the other party, which looks less and less like them. Sorting in the electorate may now be so complete that partisanship and race are enmeshed in the public mind. As Westwood and Peterson (2022) show, for example, priming one such identity triggers positive-or-negative affect toward the other. Drutman (2020, 2) states, "America now has a genuine, fully sorted, two-party system" (also see Klein 2020).[6]

In this sense, the rise of out-party animosity reflects, in part, ideological and demographic sorting, which has changed the composition of the parties and what partisans think of one another. It represents a fundamental challenge to the pluralism that underpins some visions of American democracy. Cross-cutting cleavages (e.g., the presence of liberal Republicans and conservative Democrats) across the parties have shrunk, replaced by two ideologically homogenous parties representing distinct groups whose leaders have very different visions of the country. The consequence could be Madison's greatest fear: a situation where elites have "divided mankind into parties, inflamed them with *mutual animosity*, and rendered them much more disposed to vex and oppress each other than to co-operate for their common good"

(Hamilton, Madison, and Jay [1787–1788] 1961, *Federalist* 10; italics added). Many modern social scientists and commentators have put forth renditions of Madison's worry—in contemporary terms, that partisan animosity (and the ensuing partisan bias it generates) are a vital threat to democracy. For instance, fleshing out his aforementioned discussion of the sorted party system, Drutman (2020, 25) suggests that toxic politics have created a "doom loop" where "partisan fighting . . . beget[s] more partisan fighting, until self-governance collapse[s] into authoritarianism." Democracy becomes demagoguery, which reinforces the binary of good versus evil, and ends (i.e., winning) over means (Roberts-Miller 2017) and gives credence to Finkel et al.'s (2020, 533) description of polarization as a "poisonous cocktail . . . [that] poses a threat to democracy."

The logic reflects a presumption that animosity reflects expressive partisanship such that people seek to affirm their commitment to partisanship because of a "team" mindset (e.g., D. Green, Palmquist, and Schickler 2002, 21; Mason 2018, 4). In turn, the connection to issue positions or other experiences becomes less salient, even though they play some role in the increase in animosity via ideological sorting. The ultimate worry, then, is that as animosity increases, partisans become more willing to "do what it takes" for their team to win; team loyalty blinds them (Pope 2021).[7] Hence we have the "doom loop," or demagoguery, whereby pluralism across parties ostensibly ceases to exist and defeating the other party becomes the ultimate goal.

Studying Partisan Animosity

Given the extensive normative concerns, it is no surprise that so many scholars have investigated the effects of animosity on a wide variety of behaviors. Overall, those studies have typically found evidence of partisan bias: that is, individuals discriminate against those from the other party (relative to those from their party) in a wide variety of economic and social settings (see Iyengar et al. 2019; Druckman and Levy 2022). A smaller, but still robust, set of studies has also explored the effects of animosity on a range of more direct political outcomes, such as trust in government, prejudice, political participation, and fake news sharing (Hetherington and Rudolph 2015; Lelkes and Westwood 2017; Iyengar and Krupenkin 2018; Osmundsen et al. 2021). Animosity drives many of these outcomes, which underscores why scholars have focused so much attention on this topic.

Some authors also have studied how animosity contributes to support for undemocratic politicians (or undemocratic processes) or the erosion of key democratic norms; they have found mixed results (e.g., Bartels 2020; Kingzette et al. 2021; Orhan 2022; Broockman, Kalla, and Westwood 2023; Harteveld et al.

2022; Voelkel et al., "Interventions," 2023; Voelkel et al., "Megastudy," 2023). Even more importantly, this literature has done little to offer a theoretical framework that provides predictions about *when* animosity will and will not *affect* a particular belief or behavior, and hence it is difficult to know how to reconcile these conflicting studies. That is the framework we offer in the next chapter and then test in the remainder of the book.

But any effort to test such a theory requires using data from a particular point in time. Our study is no different. Our data come from the twenty-one months between July 2019 and April 2021, and we now discuss the implications of this timing for our efforts to generalize from our study.

2019–2021: Tumultuous Politics in the United States and Its Implications

Our data come from a four-wave panel survey during a remarkable period in the United States. The first wave, in July 2019, measured partisan animosity and various background variables; and later waves—in April 2020, October 2020, and April 2021—measured a host of outcome variables that that we expected, under certain conditions, to correlate with animosity. These include policy positions, evaluations of public figures, willingness to compromise with the other party, and support for undemocratic practices and democratic norms. So, for instance, does animosity correlate with the positions partisans take, how they evaluate political actors, whether they advocate for undemocratic practices, and so on?

For now, we describe the timing of each wave by detailing relevant political events, as well as events related to the COVID-19 pandemic, in table 1.1. Much happened between our initial July 2019 wave and our second wave in April 2020, including President Trump's first impeachment trial, Joe Biden's (unofficial) securing of the Democratic nomination for president, and most notably, the emergence of the COVID-19 pandemic.[8] During this time, the country saw the first reported U.S. COVID-19 death, declarations of a global pandemic and a national emergency, and stay-at-home orders. The economy also collapsed in an unprecedented fashion, due in large part to the stay-at-home orders.

Our third wave, in October 2020, occurred during the confluence of events that may have been even more troubling. Over the summer, the country underwent a racial reckoning following the murder of George Floyd by Minneapolis police office Derek Chauvin, as millions of Americans took to the streets to protest centuries of discrimination against Black Americans (Simonson et al. 2024). While the inciting event focused on police brutality, the broader

TABLE 1.1. Timeline of Data Collection, Political Highlights, and COVID-19 Highlights

Date	Political highlight	COVID-19 highlight	Wave (dates)
July 2019	• Trump disparages four Democratic congresswomen	—	Wave 1 (July 9–August 2)
November 2019	• Trump impeachment 1 hearings	• First suspected COVID-19 case	
February 2020	• Trump impeachment 1 acquittal • Democratic primaries begin	• U.S. bans travel from China • U.S. declares public health emergency • First U.S. COVID-19 fatality	
March 2020	• Super Tuesday Primaries	• WHO declares pandemic • U.S. bans travel from Europe • U.S. declares national emergency • Stay-at-home orders issued	
April 2020	• Biden becomes presumptive Democratic nominee	• First states reopen	Wave 2 (April 6–16)
May 2020	• George Floyd murder and protests	• U.S. COVID-19 deaths >100,000	
October 2020	• Early voting in Texas surpasses total 2016 state turnout	• Trump gets COVID-19 • U.S. COVID-19 deaths >200,000	Wave 3 (October 20–November 3)
November 2020	• Election Day	• U.S. reports 100,000 cases in a day for first time	
December 2020	• Biden wins Electoral College	• FDA approves vaccines (emergency use authorization)	
January 2021	• Capitol insurrection • Trump impeachment 2 hearings	• U.S. COVID-19 deaths >400,000	
February 2021	• Trump impeachment 2 acquitted	• Delta variant detected in U.S.	
March 2021	• Passage of first state voting restrictions	• First states lift all COVID-19 restrictions	
April 2021	• Legislators in 47 states introduced bills with voting restriction provisions	• All adults eligible for vaccinations in all states	Wave 4 (April 9–23)

Note: This timeline presents an abbreviated overview of some of the key events that took place during our study period.

Black Lives Matter movement directed the conversation more generally toward the nation's shameful legacy of slavery and racism. Still, by October 2020, the time of our third wave, aggregate support for the Black Lives Matter movement among white voters was already dropping (Chudy and Jefferson 2021). Further, following the protest, opinions about race and crime enforcement polarized (Reny and Newman 2021). The third wave also took place after early voting had begun across the country, heightening the partisan signals voters received, especially with respect to the legitimacy of the election.[9] In addition to the high-stakes election, the COVID-19 pandemic continued to rage across the country. Case counts had declined over the summer but, as Americans returned indoors in the fall, and as schools and universities in some places resumed in-person classes, the numbers began to rise again. At the time of our October 2020 wave, there had been nearly 8 million confirmed COVID-19 cases in the United States including more than 200,000 deaths, with both statistics trending sharply upward.[10]

The time between our third wave in October 2020 and our fourth and final wave in April 2021 saw still more historically significant events. This included the election of Biden as president and the Democrats' ascendence to control of the House and the Senate, giving them their first unified control of the federal government in a decade. Biden's election, however, also coincided with pervasive ongoing claims of a rigged election by Trump and his followers, the January 6th Capitol insurrection, and Trump's second impeachment for his role in that day's events. In the wake of the 2020 election, many state governments introduced and passed state-level voting restrictions (Brennan Center for Justice 2021). With regard to COVID-19, the Food and Drug Administration (FDA) approved vaccines and several states had fully reopened and lifted COVID-19–related restrictions, with many analysts thinking that the pandemic was coming to an end. Of course, few realized that the Delta variant (and then the Omicron variant) would soon spread across the nation, leading to yet another wave of the virus and more deaths and hospitalizations (while the Delta variant was first detected in the spring, it did not begin to spread widely until later that summer, well after our April 2021 wave).

The time period of our full data collection brings with it the intersection of three notable elements: high levels, on average, of animosity (as we see in figure 1.1); an extremely polarizing, twice-impeached president and a campaign that was framed as a fight over the "soul of democracy" (E. Dias 2020), whereby partisanship became "calcified" (Sides, Tausanovitch, and Vavreck 2022); and the COVID-19 pandemic as well as many other tumultuous events, including the Black Lives Matter protests and the January 6th Capitol insurrection (Annenberg IOD Collaborative 2023).

Such an eventful period allows us to explore an unusually broad array of outcomes: Does animosity relate to highly salient issues on which the parties take distinctive positions, such as efforts to limit assault rifles (whose sales surged during the pandemic; see Lacombe et al. forthcoming) or efforts to defund the police, which became a rallying cry for some activists in 2020? How does it affect issue positions on which the parties do not clearly differ, such as banning government officials from becoming lobbyists or campaign finance reform? Did animosity shape the now well-known partisan divides in how Americans responded to the COVID-19 pandemic (e.g., Gadarian, Goodman, and Pepinski 2022)? Did those effects depend on the severity of one's own experience with the virus? How did animosity shape how individuals evaluated leading political figures, ranging from clearly politicized figures such as Presidents Trump and Biden to those who, at least in theory, are apolitical, such as the staff at the Centers for Disease Control (CDC)? Does animosity change how individuals perceive political compromise? Perhaps more importantly, we also can explore the relationship between animosity and normatively salient behaviors, such as whether individuals support undemocratic practices (e.g., partisan gerrymandering, blocking court nominations), violations of fundamental democratic norms (e.g., eroding checks and balances), and even partisan violence. Our data enable us to explore these phenomena during a period of constitutional crisis, given the impeachment trials, the election lies, and the January 6th insurrection; we also can see whether attitudes change as power shifts in light of the transition from Trump to Biden.

While our unique time period allows us to examine a number of important events, it also comes with limitations. In particular, we recognize that the context of our data means we have three reasons for selecting a "most likely" case in terms of documenting a relationship between animosity and political beliefs. First, while levels of animosity in the United States match those in many other countries (Gidron, Adams, and Horne 2020), the rate of increase stands out (Boxell et al. 2022), making it salient. Second, the American media regularly discuss polarization (Levendusky and Malhotra 2016) and citizens view the parties as deeply divided (Silver, Fetterolf, and Connaughton 2021). Third, the two-party system makes partisan signaling very clear and undermines the possibility that coalitions could temper animus toward a particular party (Bassan-Nygate and Weiss 2022). Gerring (2001, 217) explains that selecting a likely case, though, offers "advantages in elucidating the mechanism at work in a causal relationship. . . . We can justify focusing our attention on this particular unit as an exemplar." That works well for us since our interest lies in a mechanism (i.e., animosity) existing between partisanship and opinions and we seek to establish whether such a relationship exists, even if generalizing from the context is constrained. In the end, as we will detail, we offer precise theoretical predictions, and our goal is to assess whether the data cohere with or falsify these hypotheses.

Overview of the Book

In the pages that follow, we explain and contextualize the effects of partisan animosity on political behavior. We begin in the next chapter by offering a novel theory of those effects. Our theoretical starting point is that people form political opinions with goals in mind. To simplify, sometimes people pursue partisan directional goals, which means they seek to affirm their partisan identities. At other times, people have nondirectional accuracy goals whereby they seek to form the attitudes that most positively impact their personal welfare. We argue that people are more likely to have partisan goals as their animosity toward the out-party (rather than toward the in-party) increases.[11] If party signals make it clear where a partisan "should stand," then those with high animus will be more likely to take such stances. Individuals who are high in animus and thus have strong directional goals also are incentivized to politicize entities with ambiguous political content (e.g., scientists); that is, they are more likely to approach evaluations from a political perspective, given the accessibility of partisan goals.

That said, if circumstances mean that a wrong decision would have dire consequences, then individuals (including those with high animus) are more likely to be motivated by accuracy, leading them to ignore partisan signals. Our theory predicts, then, that *animosity toward the other party shapes political goals and, subsequently, political preferences in the presence of clear party signals or an ambiguous target that can be politicized, and in the absence of a context in which an incorrect opinion carries significant consequences.*

In chapter 3, we present our empirical strategy for testing the hypotheses derived in chapter 2. In so doing, we also explain how we measured animosity and discuss its distribution within our sample and its stability over the time of our data collection. We also show how distinctive high-animus partisans are from others: while they are similar demographically, they hold stronger political identities and are more politically engaged, which has important normative implications for the findings we document throughout the book. Additionally, we describe our outcome variables and our approach to inferring relationships between animosity and those outcomes.

The subsequent five chapters test our predictions. In chapter 4, we explore the relationship between animosity and policy positions on three types of issues: symmetrically politicized issues, on which both parties take clear stances (e.g., the ACA, a fifteen-dollar minimum wage); asymmetrically politicized issues, on which one party takes a clear stance but the other does not (e.g., banning assault rifles, defunding police), and nonpoliticized issues, on which neither party takes a clear stance (e.g., banning government officials from becoming lobbyists, allowing organizations to make unlimited donations to parties or candidates). We expect that those with higher animosity will have a higher likelihood of taking party-consistent positions on the politicized issues, particularly when both parties offer unambiguous signals. On nonpoliticized issues, however, the lack of party signals means that even the most motivated partisans do not know where to stand, and hence, we do not expect to find a relationship. We find evidence consistent with our expectations, including that on the asymmetric issues, high-animus partisans polarize. This chapter reveals a political manifestation of partisan animosity (via policy cue-taking) and highlights the endogeneity of ideological polarization and partisan animosity (cf. Rogowski and Sutherland 2016; Webster and Abramowitz 2017).

Chapter 4 points to a relationship between issue positions and animosity but leaves open the possibility that people's perceptions of the parties' reputations on the issues could shape both levels of animosity and issue positions. An ideal strategy for disentangling reputation and positions involves exploring the effect of animosity on an entirely novel issue. This is what we do in chapter 5 by analyzing how animosity relates to COVID-19 attitudes and self-reported behaviors. Specifically, we leverage the fact that we first measured animosity in summer 2019—well before the pandemic, which began in early 2020. Therefore, when we use our summer 2019 measures to analyze COVID-19 beliefs, we can rule out the possibility that elites' positions on the pandemic affected animosity or the possibility that perceptions of parties' reputations on the pandemic shaped both animosity and positions. Moreover, COVID-19 allows for an additional test of partisan motivations given that after its emergence, the parties took clear and contrasting positions on pandemic policies and behaviors.

We use our prepandemic animosity measure to investigate how animosity relates to COVID-19 preventative behaviors (e.g., social distancing, wearing a mask), perceived safety of various activities (e.g., getting a haircut, traveling in an airplane), and support for policies aimed at stopping the spread of the virus (e.g., stay-at-home orders, the closure of nonessential businesses) over the course of the pandemic. We find robust relationships between animosity and these outcomes, showing that prepandemic animosity leads partisans to take more partisan-consistent positions. That is, as animus increases, Democrats become more oriented toward health safety actions and Republicans become less so.

Even so, the relationship vitiates or disappears when the COVID-19 threat becomes especially consequential—that is, when people themselves or someone they knew experienced a severe case of the virus or they worried about that occurring in the future. When the danger of the pandemic seems imminent, partisans shift to an accuracy goal, severing the animosity effect. In this case, high-animus Republicans took more preventative actions and low-animus Democrats did the same, making both groups similar to high-animus Democrats. We find that threat moderates the impact of animosity—the partisan gap at high levels of animus substantially shrinks in the presence of threat. This supports our prediction that animosity effects occur only when directional processes dwarf accuracy processes induced by threat.

Chapter 5 moves beyond the substantial evidence that Democrats and Republicans behaved differently during the pandemic (see, e.g., Allcott et al. 2020; Gadarian et al. 2022; Gollwitzer et al. 2020; Clinton et al. 2021; Graham and Singh 2023). It shows that animus drove these gaps, although only among those for whom the pandemic was not personally consequential (also see Constantino et al. 2022; A. Flores et al. 2022). The results also reinforce the power of elite signals, as polarized attitudes throughout the pandemic depended on whether elites took clear positions (also see Bisbee and Lee 2022).

In chapter 6, we turn to evaluations of political figures, a particularly intriguing topic given the growing tendency for partisanship, rather than a leader's performance, to drive how the public sees them (e.g., Donovan et al. 2020; Small and Eisinger 2020). Despite the academic and media attention to the topic, unanswered questions remain about the role of animosity in this process. Does animosity, for example, lead partisans to politicize even ostensibly nonpolitical figures? We again leverage our prepandemic animosity measures to explore people's evaluations of how various figures reacted to COVID-19. Here, we consider prominent partisan figures (e.g., Biden, Trump), less prominent political actors (e.g., state and local officials, including mayors), and nonpartisan actors directing the scientific response (e.g., the staff of the CDC and the FDA). The results show a clear relationship between animosity and evaluations of the parties' leaders (i.e., Trump and Biden), suggesting that the dominance of partisanship over substance occurred most strongly among people who had high animosity toward the other party. In contrast, the effect of animosity in evaluations of less prominent partisan figures (e.g., mayors) was largely absent, as these actors were much less politicized (i.e., the party signals were unclear).

Perhaps most interesting are the dynamics for scientific figures who, in theory, should not evoke partisan evaluations. Indeed, Dr. Fauci, head of the

National Institute of Allergy and Infectious Diseases (NIAID) and a key member of the president's Coronavirus Task Force, had largely evaded the development of a political profile throughout his lengthy career. He had served presidents of both parties dating back to the Reagan administration, but always in a behind-the-scenes, scientific capacity. After he was thrust into the spotlight during the pandemic and began to clash repeatedly with President Trump, he became embroiled in partisan politics. Reflective of this dynamic, we find that as the pandemic wore on and partisan rhetoric about Dr. Fauci increased, so did the role of animosity in partisans' evaluations of him. In this chapter, we see other notable patterns; for example, there are no animosity effects in the assessments of the CDC early in the pandemic, but a clear animosity effect emerges later in the pandemic when the CDC became entangled in partisan debate concerning its health and safety advice. The result particularly manifests among high-animus Republicans. We also find that high-animus members of both parties politicized the "United States" when asked about the country's response to the pandemic, viewing the term as synonymous with the presidential administration currently in power. This supports our expectation that individuals who are high in animus politicize targets.

Overall, chapter 6 makes clear that a trend toward evaluations that are *partisan* rather than event-based stems largely from people with high animus. This suggests that animosity toward the other party works to undermine political accountability since the actual behaviors become secondary to partisan signals. It also shows that no individual or entity—even those with long histories of bipartisanship—or even the nation itself can be immune from the snare of animosity. Finally, the results pinpoint the relative trade-off between personalization and politicization, with the former severing the effects of animosity and the latter intensifying it.

Chapters 4, 5, and 6 offer a range of evidence suggesting that partisan animosity impacts attitudes and evaluations in the presence of partisan signals and the absence of accuracy motivations. While these may be concerning dynamics that affect democratic functioning and collective actions, they do not necessarily constitute a proximate threat to democracy itself. In chapter 7, we turn to a key behavior underlining conceptions of pluralistic democracy: the tendency of groups, including parties, to compromise with one another to meet the needs of the polity overall. We look at support for abstract compromise and who partisans believe should compromise (e.g., their party, the other party, both), as well as compromise in the case of a specific spending bill where each party has an ideal point. We find animosity consistently matters; as animosity increases, so does the belief that the other party should compromise and, even more so, that their party should not. At the highest levels of animus, partisans reject the possibility of their party compromising from their ideal point toward the other party's preference on a spending bill.

In chapter 8, we continue this line of inquiry by moving from behavioral norms to institutional norms, including support for undemocratic practices, support or opposition to democratic norms, and support for illegal actions and partisan violence in the pursuit of political goals. We look at the extent to which partisans privilege their party over democratic processes—beliefs such as endorsing their party doing anything it can to block Supreme Court nominees from the other party, gerrymandering congressional districts to its advantage, and challenging a close election outcome in court. We find that animosity has clear, predictable effects on prioritizing party over process, with high-animus members of both parties endorsing undemocratic practices to favor their party. Others have shown that strong partisans are more likely to take such actions (e.g., Graham and Svolik 2020; Moore-Berg et al. 2020), but ours is the first demonstration of how *animosity* drives this process. That said, the effects are generally modest, and overall, partisans do not strongly support undemocratic practices. The only case that achieves strong support, on average, involves very high-animus partisans advocating for challenging an election outcome where their candidate loses in a key state by a tiny margin (one thousand votes). In this scenario, it actually seems quite reasonable to launch such a legal challenge.

One concern with any such scenarios is they are necessarily context dependent. To help alleviate that concern, we turn to data that we collected at two different points on support for more fundamental, underlying norms, such as checks and balances and separation of powers (e.g., McClosky 1964). Here, we leverage the panel nature of our data to, at least partially, alleviate concerns of confounding variables by exploiting the change in political power produced by the 2020 election. When we initially asked our norm battery in our July 2019 wave, the Republicans held control of both the presidency and the Senate, but when we asked it again during our April 2021 wave, Democrats had unified control of the government. We use this change in control to leverage a shift in party signals. In 2019, high-animus Republicans expressed weaker support for constitutional protections that would check the president's power, but they flipped in 2021 to be more supportive when such rules would block the Democratic administration. High-animus Democrats displayed the reverse pattern. These patterns suggest that support for democratic norms depends on context, and particularly the party in power. Equally important, however, are three other dynamics that we find. First, analogous to the lack of strong support for undemocratic practices, partisans generally support democratic norms, with the most notable exception being comfort with the executive taking actions to accomplish goals (likely reflecting frustration with gridlock). Second, the substantive effects of animus are *very* small, and even the basic party divides do not exhibit sizable gaps. Finally, we find no relationship between partisan animosity and willingness to break the law (e.g., defacing public property) or engage in partisan violence in the case of election defeat. Partisans express clear opposition to both these activities, suggesting clear limits to their willingness to break the rules of American politics.

We conclude in chapter 9 by discussing the implications of our findings. Our results paint a picture of animosity having deleterious effects on democratic functioning. High levels of animus polarize policy beliefs and evaluations and politicize the nonpolitical in ways that—as COVID-19 made clear—can undermine collective response in critical situations. High levels of animosity in the United States have harmful implications. The flip side, however, is that the effects work conditionally. They require the presence of party signals and the absence of significant personal consequences regarding the topic under consideration. Moreover, the consequences remain concentrated among those partisans with very high levels of animus, the most hateful ones. These caveats are essential as they provide a framework for understanding and studying the effects of hostility and highlight the need to isolate the supply dynamics of party cues, the motivational triggers for accuracy processes, and the relative influence of hateful partisans.

At first glance, our results may be reassuring in that the effects of animosity on proximate outcomes that directly undermine democracy—such as extreme opposition to norms and support for partisan violence—are either small or nonexistent. Alas, however, there are a few reasons why this could provide a false sense of optimism. First, as with COVID-19, party elites can quickly politicize topics and offer cues, and individuals do not always clearly perceive the costs of their actions. Second, animosity can be self-perpetuating; high-animus partisans are the most engaged and vocal partisans. Consequently, other partisans imagine these people when they think of the other party and come (themselves) to hold more animus toward the other party (Druckman et al. 2022). Animus thus can grow due to misperceptions (Ahler and Sood 2018; Moore-Berg et al. 2020) that are difficult to correct (Druckman 2023a). Over time, this could lead to more partisans supporting undemocratic practices or opposing democratic norms, which could undermine the democratic equilibrium whereby all voters believe the other side will punish democratic transgressions (Weingast 1997).

Third, by making democratic functioning more difficult via pushing partisans apart and undercutting compromise, even a small number of party leaders and elected officials can gradually but dangerously justify undemocratic actions as a response to the lack of compromise. In this sense, voters may hold attitudes that facilitate erosion even though they do not recognize them as such, either because they do not connect beliefs to macro-democratic outcomes (Ahmed 2023) or because they dismiss transgressions if they accord with their preferred policy outcomes (Krishnarajan 2023). Moreover, voters also may fail to punish elite democratic transgressions for reasons other than animosity, such as ethnic antagonism (Bartels 2020), ideological extremity (Graham and Svolik 2020), or antiestablishment orientations (Uscincki et al. 2021). In short, democratic decline often comes from elites, not citizens (Bartels 2023); elites who seek power may find any feasible path to obtain it. In a stable democracy such as the United States, citizens can, in theory, act as a check. But if animosity undermines functioning and even a few elites exploit frustrated citizens for a power grab—under the guise of getting things done, disingenuously attributing blame to other citizens, or referencing relatively less democratic outcomes in the past (Grillo and Prato 2023)—democracy becomes imperiled. In sum, even though animosity does not directly lead citizens to opt out of democratic practices, its contribution to dysfunction provides a potential, although not determinative, pathway to nefarious elites. As such, it is a phenomenon that warrants attention and should cause concern, much as Madison and Washington suggested at the founding.

Partisan Animosity in American Politics

Partisanship predicts Americans' political behaviors remarkably well. A preference for one political party over the other powerfully explains vote choice, political attitudes, and many other relevant outcomes. Indeed, no other variable offers such a parsimonious explanation of so many different dynamics. This makes understanding how people use their partisanship crucial to making sense of political outcomes in America.

Most prior work conceptualizes partisanship in one of two distinct ways. One tradition, rooted in Downs (1957), argues that partisanship comes from political beliefs: individuals choose the party closest to them on the issues, that best manages the country, or both. As Downs (1957, 38) states, "Each citizen . . . votes for the party he believes will provide him with a higher utility income than any other party during the coming election period." In this view, partisanship acts as a "running tally" of how well party performance matches one's own issue positions (Fiorina 1981). Citizens follow the advice of partisan elites because they trust them to offer useful guidance (Lupia and McCubbins 1998). Many scholars refer to this depiction of partisanship as the rational choice or instrumental approach.

Other scholars argue that partisanship acts as a social identity, which is grounded in individuals' group attachments and akin to religion or social class. Individuals form social attachments with a party, in part through socialization, and partisanship reflects a group belonging, more so than an assessment of the parties' policy positions (A. Campbell et al. 1960; D. Green, Palmquist, and Schickler 2002; Huddy, Mason, and Aarøe 2015).[1] From this perspective, people follow the advice of partisan elites not because they worry about what is "best" but because it affirms their group identities, and thus they are "defending valued pre-commitments" (Petersen et al. 2013, 833). Their policy positions are, much of the time, rationalizations of their partisan beliefs (Lenz 2012), and they often follow advice with little consideration of its content (Barber and Pope 2019). This model is less normatively appealing than Downs's approach since it sidelines most substantive considerations (e.g., policy performance) that underpin accountability (e.g., Huddy and Bankert 2017). Scholars often refer to this perspective as the social psychological or expressive approach.

After more than sixty years of debate, the answer as to which of these conceptualizations better depicts partisanship remains unclear. Indeed, as Lavine, Johnston, and Steenbergen (2012) show, both are true—in some settings, partisanship is a social identity (expressive), and in others, it is more of a running tally (rational or instrumental). Huddy and Bankert (2017, 3) make a similar point: "Partisanship likely is a mix of both instrumental and expressive factors, and the conditions under which one or the other model holds sway is worth future research investigation."

We agree that this debate calls for future research (even after more than six decades of work on this topic). To be clear, we do not contribute to debates about the origins and evolution of partisanship itself, as we treat it as exogenous in our theory and empirical analyses. We will provide evidence for the validity of this assumption in chapter 3. However, because we are looking at animus, which is closely linked to how partisanship works, our findings have implications for broader debates about the nature of partisanship. In particular, we show that in different settings, partisans sometimes behave more expressively, and at other points, they behave more instrumentally. Understanding the distinction requires specifying the *conditions* under which animosity affects preference formation, given partisanship and a particular level animosity. This is the task to which we turn our attention in this chapter.

A Motivational Theory of Political Decision-Making

We incorporate partisan animosity into theories of partisanship by building on the concept of motivated reasoning, which has become increasingly central to political psychology in recent decades (e.g., Lodge and Taber 2013; Bayes and Druckman 2021). Our theory has three main parts: (1) linking partisan animosity to a directional motivation, (2) specifying the role of party cues, and (3) recognizing the impact of an accuracy motivation. We assemble these parts to identify when we expect animosity to relate to policy positions, evaluations of public figures, willingness to compromise with the other party, or support for undemocratic practices and democratic norms.

Partisan Motivations and Partisan Animus

When people seek and assess information to make decisions (political or not), they do so with varying levels of effort and in the service of one or more motivations or goals (Kruglanski 1989; Fazio 1990, 2007; Leeper and Slothuus 2014). A motivation (or a goal) is a "cognitive representation of a desired endpoint that impacts evaluations, emotions and behaviors" (Fishbach and Ferguson 2007, 491). Striving to obtain a goal motivates actions perceived as best suited to bring about the desired endpoint. For example, a person motivated to buy the most environmentally friendly car possible will evaluate car features differently than a person motivated to select the car that feels most luxurious.

Scholars often distinguish between directional and nondirectional goals. Directional goals involve gathering and processing information to support or confirm a specific desired conclusion, such as when a climate skeptic rejects ostensibly compelling evidence of climate change in order to maintain their skepticism. In contrast, nondirectional goals involve gathering and processing information in a way that is independent from specific conclusions; nondirectional goals involve some broader objective, such as forming an accurate opinion or a clear and concise opinion (Kunda 1999; Molden and Higgins 2012; Dunning 2015; Molden, Bayes, and Druckman 2022). Political scientists have incorporated these distinctions into work on opinion formation (Lodge and Taber 2013) and partisanship (Lavine, Johnston, and Steenbergen 2012; Groenendyk 2013; Bolsen, Druckman, and Cook 2014; Leeper and Slothuus 2014). This work often falls under the umbrella of "motivated reasoning," which includes theories of *partisan* motivated reasoning—the idea that social identity protection goals shape reasoning; that is, people operate with a nondirectional goal to guard their partisan identity.

Key to partisan motivated reasoning is a goal that stems from people's concerns about their social connections with others (Baumeister and Leary 1995). They desire to maintain and protect their sense of identification with important social groups, and arguably in politics, no social grouping equals the importance of partisanship. People seek to maintain a sense of identification with their party to "protect their connection to others with whom they have important material and emotional ties" (Kahan 2015, 26). Partisan motivated reasoning aligns with the expressive portrayal of partisanship since it involves a social group attachment and adapting beliefs for noninstrumental purposes. This can lead partisans to seek out (avoid) information favorable to their party (the other party), view information from their (the other) party as strong (weak), and counterargue information contrary to their partisan interests (e.g., information from the other party) (Lodge and Taber 2013).[2] All these actions further the goal of affirming partisan identities. In other words, a Democrat (Republican) motivated by a desire to be like other Democrats (Republicans) may report supporting a political issue because they believe their support connects them to other copartisans rather than because they have researched the issue and determined it appealing to their ideological worldview.

Partisan goals do *not* constitute the only directional goal one could pursue (Bayes and Druckman 2021). Most notably, people may seek to confirm an existing belief, regardless of whether it conflicts with what one's party endorses. Mullinix (2016), for example, argues that on issues that are salient to them, people display a motivation to maintain their standing views regardless of what their party endorses: for example, a Democratic gun rights advocate may dismiss strong gun control arguments with the goal of affirming their standing view on guns, despite the partisan implications. Alternatively, some seek to protect their moral values. For example, Feinberg and Willer (2013) show that messages that frame environmental issues in terms of conservative values of purity and sanctity lead conservatives who typically oppose environmental legislation to become more supportive—here the argument resonates with cherished values (Feinberg and Willer 2019). Finally, citizens may prioritize consistency with a distinct social group; Klar (2013) shows that when their parental identity is threatened, Democratic parents express preferences counter to the party on social service spending and sentences for sex offenders in order to protect their parental identity. Indeed, partisanship tends to rank low in importance relative to other group identities (Druckman and Levendusky 2019), so we should not be surprised if people often pursue goals other than partisan ones as a general matter.[3]

OUT-PARTY ANIMUS

Given the various motivations that can drive people's political decisions, we focus on a particular question: when is someone more or less likely to pursue a partisan directional goal? We suggest that partisan animosity plays a role. The desire to protect one's connections to fellow partisans and differentiate oneself from those in the other party often stems from out-party animosity. As animus increases, it prompts a motivation to distinguish oneself from the other (disliked) group by doing things that affirm one's partisanship (and hence self-esteem). In short, the more an individual dislikes the other party, the more they will be motivated to arrive at conclusions that affirm their partisan identity.

Why do we focus on out-party animus, rather than in-party love? First, the well-known negativity bias means negative information has a stronger impact than positive information (Norris 2021). This would mean attending more to the negative feelings toward the out-party as compared to positive feelings toward the in-party. Second, over-time social and political developments have accentuated out-party animus (as shown in figure 1.1; see also Groenendyk 2018). Concomitant with those trends have been increases in negative campaigns (Lau et al. 2017) and partisan vitriolic rhetoric (W. Brady et al. 2017). In line with our argument, Rathje, Van Bavel, and van der Linden (2021) find that negative out-group language is the strongest predictor of partisan shares and retweets on social media (also see Yu, Wojcieszak, and Casas 2021). And, Pierce and Lau (2019, 9) argue that "strong affective reactions to a politician may themselves engender awareness of and like or dislike for certain policies. For instance, a visceral aversion to a candidate may lead a voter to reject positions associated with that politician" (also see Stone 2023). People do this when the out-party animus is so strong that they want to differentiate themselves from the party they so dislike.[4] Importantly, it follows that those with greater out-party animus (i.e., stronger affective reactions) will be the most motived to hold distinctive views, taking positions in line with those of their own party's politicians and opposite those put forth by politicians from the other party (Tajfel and Wilkes 1963; Armaly and Enders 2021). Finally, much of the normative concern focuses on out-party animosity, which, as Bankert (2023) shows, relates to attitudes that undermine democratic functioning and contributes to democratic erosion.

Notably, our theory treats animosity as exogenous—that is, we expect that individuals with more animus will be increasingly likely to follow their party, relative to those with less animus.[5] We will explore the validity of that assumption (for our analyses) with our data in chapter 3.

Party Cues

Of course, voters can only pursue partisan goals if they know what their party would do in a given situation. If the Democratic or Republican Party positions on a given issue are unclear, then even the strongest partisan motivation will have little effect. While party cues—by which we mean endorsements by party leaders—often appear in the contemporary media environment (Stecula 2018), they are not omnipresent. Milita, Ryan, and Simas (2014, 428) explain that "while candidates may mention the issues, they typically are not discussing those issues in a clear manner or giving specific policy proposals." For instance, most people may know where the parties stand on climate change, but they likely have scant knowledge of where they stand on the majority of other scientific issues such as medical x-rays, fluoridation, genetically modified foods, raw milk, nanotechnology, or synthetic beef hormones (Kahan

2015). Scholars who study party cue-taking find huge variation in the effect of such cues, ranging from 3 percent to 43 percent shifts on the policy opinion scale (Bullock 2011, 2020). And those are cases where respondents explicitly receive party positions. Tappin (2023) finds that much of the variance in the effectiveness of party cues stems from the use of different issues; clearly, the extent of politicization on a topic influences whether people can and do follow their parties (also see Druckman and Leeper 2012; Clifford, Leeper, and Rainey 2023).

The most straightforward scenario occurs when both parties take clear and distinct stances on a particular topic; here the cues come from both sides, leaving little ambiguity for a partisan reasoner on what to do. When only one side offers a clear perspective, partisan reasoning can still occur, but the likelihood may drop both because the information may be less available or because the incentives may decline. Even so, the impact can still be considerable. For example, Slothuus and Bisgaard (2021a) show that when a party suddenly shifts positions (on welfare programs), that party's supporters follow suit, regardless of their initially held opinions or other beliefs (also see Lenz 2012; Barber and Pope 2019). If only one party changes its stance, all partisans may react: while in-partisans will follow their party's lead, out-partisans will do the opposite, treating the change as a sort of anti-cue (Nicholson 2012; Goren, Federico, and Kittilson 2009; Bakker, Lelkes, and Malka 2020). In fact, we have reason to expect that an anti-cue may even be stronger than an in-party cue—partisans care more about doing the opposite of the other party than doing what their party suggests, in line with our argument about out-party animus trumping in-party love as a motivator. Thus, we anticipate animosity to correlate with opinions when parties take stances, particularly when both parties do so or the out-party does—although we do not dismiss the possibility of partisans following their party somewhat when only their party takes a stance.

When neither party takes a clear position, then we would, with one caveat, not expect to see a relationship between partisan animosity and opinions because motivated partisans will not know how to proceed (Bolsen, Druckman, and Cook 2014). The caveat involves the situation in which partisans evaluate an ambiguous target that *could* have political content. To take an example that we discuss later, consider what happens when partisans assess the performance of the "United States." For many Americans, the United States itself does not inherently have partisan content; in fact, it could sometimes counteract partisan urges (Levendusky 2018). Yet those with high levels of animus have partisan consideration chronically accessible in their mind (e.g., Bargh, Lombardi, and Higgins 1988). In other words, they view the world through a

partisan lens. As such, when asked about a topic that could possibly be politicized, they will invoke partisan considerations and, in this example, likely
view the "United States" as synonymous with the party in power (i.e., the
party that controls the presidency). It is this type of dynamic that explains
why people with high levels of animosity do not trust "government" when the
other side holds power (Hetherington and Rudolph 2015). A manifestation of
this type of "ambiguous politicization" is B. Lee and Bearman's (2020) finding that, over the last few decades, people have come to think of "important
matters" as political.[6]

In sum, individuals who are high in out-party animus and thus are more
likely to engage in partisan reasoning will do so when party stances are clear.[7]
Even partisans who profoundly dislike the opposing party typically need cues
about the best way to differentiate themselves from the other side. That said,
in the absence of explicit cues, if the target of evaluation is ambiguous, those
with high levels of animus will politicize it and impute partisan positions.

Accuracy Motivation

While protecting one's partisan identity is important to political decision-
making, it is not always central, as individuals can, and do, pursue other goals.
This includes not only the aforementioned alternative directional goals (e.g.,
value affirmation) but also, as referenced, nondirectional goals, the most notable of which is a desire to reach an accurate conclusion, namely, the "correct
or otherwise best conclusion" (Taber and Lodge 2006, 756).[8] In contrast to
those with directional goals, people with accuracy motivations do not begin
with a specific desired (partisan) conclusion (Kunda 1999; Molden and Higgins 2012; Dunning 2015). Instead, they strive for what they believe to be the
objective truth. They therefore dedicate a substantial amount of time and effort to gather information that could impact their opinions. They carefully
evaluate the provenance and strength of this information, and attempt to correct biases in how they might process it (e.g., see Hill 2017; Kahan 2016; Druckman and McGrath 2019).

What constitutes the "best," "most accurate," or "objective" truth is not always clear; being motivated by accuracy goals does not guarantee accurate
outcomes (Kunda 1999, 238). People can put forth a great amount of effort and
try to minimize biases but still have misplaced beliefs about the reliability of
information (Baron and Jost 2019). For example, a highly accuracy-motivated
Republican may have sought to figure out whether Iraq had stockpiled weapons of mass destruction in the 1990s and early 2000s. That Republican may
have perceived President George W. Bush to be a credible source of informa-

tion, along with most media outlets at the time, and thus believed that Iraq possessed such weapons. While most accuracy-motivated Republicans now believe this was untrue, at the time, believing Iraq possessed weapons was where an accuracy goal might have led. Moreover, relying on one's party for information can be consistent with accuracy motivations (Leeper and Slothuus 2014; Druckman and McGrath 2019). This coheres with an instrumental view of partisanship, whereby a rational thinker, motivated by their material well-being or specific issue positions, turns to credible party cues (Downs 1957; also see Kam 2007; Sniderman and Stiglitz 2012; Boudreau and MacKenzie 2014).[9] Differentiating when party cue-taking indicates directional or nondirectional reasoning (i.e., expressive or instrumental partisanship) is thus a difficult task, requiring scholars to manipulate or measure motivations (e.g., Petersen et al. 2013; Druckman and McGrath 2019; Tappin, Pennycook, and Rand 2020, 2021; Molden, Bayes, and Druckman 2022).

We focus, however, not on party cues per se but rather on the role of partisan animosity. In this case, *if* one engages in nondirectional accuracy processing, we have *no* reason to expect to find a relationship between animosity and one's opinions or decisions. This follows since we argued that animus aligns with an individual's motivation to engage in partisan reasoning—that is, animus drives whether directional (partisan) motives dominate. But absent a directional motivation, animus should not matter. Of course, party cues may still shape behavior—for example, people may perceive their party to be a more credible source of information than the opposing party (Lupia and McCubbins 1998)—but those effects will not be due to partisan animosity.[10]

WHAT PROMPTS ACCURACY PROCESSING?

Our discussion raises the question of what prompts accuracy processing. Extant work suggests that in contemporary political settings, individuals will, all else constant, engage in directional processing. Groenendyk and Krupnikov (2021, 181) explain that "in contexts deemed 'political' people are typically motivated to fight for their side with the goal of winning the argument, rather than seeking agreement and accepting counter-attitudinal information." Empirical work confirms that people tend to engage in directional reasoning in political contexts (Bolsen, Druckman, and Cook 2014; Bayes et al. 2020; also see Redlawsk 2001; Braman and Nelson 2007; Redlawsk, Civettini, and Emmerson 2010; Lodge and Taber 2013; Petersen et al. 2013)—though, as Coppock (2023) finds, people only successfully dismiss counter-attitudinal information when it comes with partisan group cues.[11] Most political decisions remain distant to individuals' immediate well-being, and thus there are no clear negative consequences from engaging in directional reasoning (Carpenter 2019, 11).

We draw on two lines of work to identify conditions that are likely to prompt accuracy processing. First, decades of scholarship on persuasion suggest that increased issue involvement or personal relevance lead individuals to engage in more systematic or elaborative thinking (Petty and Cacioppo 1986; Eagly and Chiaken 1993). That said, systematic processing may lower reliance on cues, but it does not necessitate accuracy motivation (Leeper and Slothuus 2014). Recall our earlier discussion of Mullinix's (2016) study, which showed that when people attach personal importance to a particular attitude (e.g., with regard to tax and education policies), they depart from partisan cues and rely on their prior positions with greater frequency, but in so doing they engage in belief-consistent directional processing.[12] Personal relevance then leads to more engagement and less partisan motivated reasoning, but another ingredient is needed to fully trigger accuracy.

This leads us to a second group of literature, which shows that accuracy goals emerge when people anticipate consequences for their actions: "accuracy goals are typically created by increasing the stakes involved in making a wrong judgment or in drawing the wrong conclusion, without increasing the attractiveness of any particular conclusion" (Kunda 1999, 481; also see Freund, Kruglanski, and Shpitzajzen 1985; Plaks 2011). This type of anticipation can come in distinct guises such as, for example, expecting to have to justify one's opinion later (e.g., Lord, Lepper, and Preston 1984; Tetlock 1985; Lerner and Tetlock 1999). Bolsen et al. (2014) and Bayes et al. (2020) provide evidence that inducing just such an expectation directly stimulates accuracy processing. Alternatively, if one anticipates that there will be clear personal or material consequences from the outcome of a decision, accuracy motivations can also materialize. For example, Jonas and Frey (2003) show that accuracy motivations and objective processing of evidence occur when study participants learn that they will receive a prize for a correct choice (also see B. Johnson and Eagly 1989; Albarracín 2002).[13] As W. Hart et al. (2009, 558) conclude, "One motivational variable linked to accuracy motivation is outcome relevant involvement . . . which refers to attitudes, beliefs, and decisions linked to an important outcome."

An example comes from Lerman and McCabe's (2017, 626) study of Medicare and the ACA. They explain that when individuals "detect imminent, clear, and personal benefits from a policy . . . self-interest is likely to be weighted more heavily than other group interests or partisan considerations." They show that indeed people with public insurance (and thus those with more experience and/or more at stake) report more support for the ACA and

Medicare (i.e., they oppose Medicare cuts); this is particularly true for Republicans, who might otherwise be inclined to hold the reverse attitudes. Further, opposition to cutting Medicare spending is particularly salient among people who are in poor health. The results suggest that experiences and the anticipated consequences of policies alter how people reason, countering partisan motivations.[14]

The challenge, of course, is to identify situations where, in Kunda's (1999, 236) words, "a lot rides on your decision. Chances are that you will have strong accuracy goals when you expect that a wrong decision could cost you" (also see Carpenter 2019, 11).[15] In our empirical analyses, we follow Lerman and McCabe by focusing on health consequences, specifically focusing on the COVID-19 pandemic—a situation with substantial heterogeneity in perceived consequences and threat. For those facing severe consequences from contracting COVID-19, we would expect the effects of animosity to wane. As Constantino et al. (2022, 3) explain in their discussion of the pandemic: "Experience is a powerful teacher and can change attitudes and actions. This is especially true when threats are immediate, concrete, and local."[16] Indeed, threats make the topic highly salient and the decision outcome highly consequential; hence, directional goals fade into the background. We discuss this idea in more detail in chapter 5.

Our framework envelopes both an expressive and an instrumental view of partisanship. When animus is high, cues are clear, and threats are low, partisans with high animus will operate as expressive partisans. When a threat is clear, partisans may still follow a cue from their party if they believe it to be credible, but they would do so for instrumental or rational purposes (see Slothuus and Bisgaard 2021b).

In sum, we posit that those with high levels of out-party animus will be particularly likely to pursue directional partisan goals, all else constant. When party signals are clear, then we expect a relationship between animus and the direction the party endorses. If party signals are not clear but the target of evaluation is politically ambiguous, partisans with high animus will politicize it and impute a partisan position. Finally, in situations where a person perceives the direct, personal consequences of a decision as both clear and severe, accuracy motivations will likely take hold. This dilutes or severs the relationship with partisan animosity.

Implications and Empirical Overview

These arguments imply a set of hypotheses about how and when partisan animosity will shape political attitudes (policy positions, evaluations of public figures, willingness to compromise, and support for undemocratic practices and norms). Specifically, we expect, all else constant, that (1) animus will be positively correlated with opinions in the presence of clear party cues, most notably if both parties take stances or if the out-party takes a stance (i.e., as partisan animus rises, respondents become more likely to take their party's position), (2) animus will be positively correlated with opinions in the absence of clear party cues if the target is politically ambiguous, (3) there will be no correlation in the absence of clear party cues when the target is not ambiguous, and (4) there will be a weaker correlation (or even no correlation) as the direct personal consequences of an opinion increase (as accuracy motivations replace directional ones).[17]

These predictions reveal the points we mentioned at the start of the book. That is, the impact of animus depends on the availability of party cues as well as whether the topic is politicized (i.e., cues are clear or an ambiguous target becomes political) or personalized (i.e., a wrong decision has significant personal consequences). Further, when the conditions for animus effects are met, it is the people with the most animus toward the other party who will display the greatest divergence in opinions and actions. These are the partisans who could potentially pose a threat to democracy, a topic to which we return in later chapters.

As our discussion makes clear, we also expect differences across sets of outcome variables. We look at four main types of outcome variables. First, we explore a range of policy views such as positions on various issues, behavioral intentions regarding COVID-19, and perceptions of the safety of various indoor activities during the COVID-19 pandemic. Second, we study evaluations of public actors, including very politicized actors such as Presidents Trump and Biden, less politicized actors such as governors or mayors, and—in theory—nonpoliticized actors, such as scientific advisers. We also look at how partisans evaluate the "United States" in terms of the country's reaction to COVID-19. Third, we analyze the relationship with another crucial construct—willingness to compromise with those from the other party, and in particular, who, exactly, should be compromising. Fourth, we investigate support for undemocratic practices where one privileges their party over democratic processes (e.g., blocking Supreme Court appointments from the other party), support for basic democratic norms such as checks and balances, and likelihood of engaging in illegal activities or partisan violence.[18] Contrasting these outcomes will allow us to better explore both the power of animus to shape attitudes and behaviors and also its limits.

As discussed in our chapter 1 overview, after describing our data further in chapter 3, in chapter 4 we test our predictions about the effects of animus on policy views. We explore a wide range of issues that vary on whether parties have taken clear positions (e.g., the ACA) or not (e.g., economic relocation incentives). We test the idea that on politicized issues (e.g., both parties take clear stances), animosity promotes cue-taking (e.g., Lavine et al. 2012; Lelkes 2018). We also look at issues where only one party takes a clear stand (e.g., the Green New Deal) to see whether partisans on both sides react, or if there is an asymmetric reaction with partisans reacting only to out-party cues.

In chapter 5, we turn to one of the most deeply polarized recent issues: the COVID-19 pandemic. Here, partisan elites—led by President Trump as well as many prominent governors and members of Congress—took very distinct stances (J. Green et al. 2020; Gollust, Nagler, and Fowler 2020), and the public followed suit (Druckman et al. 2021a; Gadarian et al. 2022). But our argument implies an important caveat to earlier studies. It is not just that Democrats and Republicans had divided, but rather, that those divisions were due to partisan animosity. Further, COVID-19 offers an excellent test case for our expectation that the effect of animosity will be dramatically weakened or even disappear when a belief has direct consequences for an individual—some Americans were directly affected/threatened by the pandemic, depending on geography and vulnerability. We investigate whether such threat vitiates the relationship between animus and COVID-19 policy positions, concern, and behaviors. Our findings in chapters 4 and 5 have a broader implication for debates about ideological polarization. One enduring question in this literature is why elites are so much more ideologically divided than voters, as this seems to defy theories of representation (Fiorina, Abrams, and Pope 2005). Our theory and results provide an answer to the question of why high levels of elite ideological polarization have produced voter sorting, but not large-scale voter polarization. The latter would require clear cues, the lack of clear personal consequences, and even then, high levels of partisan animosity in the electorate. Given these requirements, even while animosity has climbed ever higher in recent years (see figure 1.1), levels of mass polarization have remained modest, at best (Lelkes 2016).

We turn to evaluations of elite leaders in chapter 6. The theory has three implications when it comes to such actors. First, for highly partisan actors, such as the president and other prominent party leaders, we expect that animus will matter but its effect will not be particularly large, as all partisans, regardless of how much animosity they have for the other party, will pursue partisan motives. In effect, even those with low animus will pursue partisan motivations because the partisan cue is so strong. Nevertheless, as animus increases, so too will the approval gap, at least somewhat.

Second, with regard to ostensibly apolitical entities, our expectations match those for policy opinions sans accuracy motivation. If the figure is endorsed by a party, we expect evaluations to divide as animosity increases, but if not, then we anticipate no effect. So, for example, earlier in the pandemic, when both parties were more supportive of Dr. Anthony Fauci and his efforts, we should see little relationship between partisan animus and approval (as there is little to no political cue). But as Dr. Fauci clashed with President Trump—and, de facto, endorsed Biden shortly before the election—he takes on a more partisan cast for voters. Once this happens, we expect that partisan animus will strongly shape evaluations of him.

Third, we predict that animus shapes which ambiguous targets are seen as political. Individuals with strong motivations to arrive at a particular outcome will exploit uncertainty to do so (Kahan 2016; Carpenter 2019). Those who are high in animus will therefore come to see neutral or apolitical figures through a partisan lens (Groenendyk, Sances, and Zhirkov 2020). In essence, they politicize individuals.[19]

Chapter 7 takes up the topic of political compromise. It is no exaggeration to say that compromise is central to democracy: without it, a democracy—especially a large, pluralistic democracy—cannot function. Here, we expect that the effects of animus again will depend on *who* compromises: when one's own party is asked to compromise, high-animus individuals will be particularly opposed. as it undermines their identity. For these individuals, compromise means that the other party should be the one making the concessions, which arguably strains the definition of the term. We also expect partisans who are high in animosity to exhibit relatively more opposition to compromise generally (e.g., in cases in which both sides compromise) since, as with evaluations, they will politicize compromise, viewing it as an untenable sacrifice of their identity.

Finally, we turn to democratic attitudes in chapter 8, the final test of our theory. This includes undemocratic practices such as blocking Supreme Court nominees from the other party, engaging in partisan gerrymandering, and challenging election results where we expect partisans who are high in animus to follow their party's interest and support such actions. We also look at norms such as checks and balances, limits on executive power, and respect for institutions (e.g., news organizations). We again argue that animus interacts with partisan cues in driving support for these norms, especially norms surrounding constitutional protections that limit elites' power (through, for example, checks and balances). The twist here is that the cues stem from which party is in power. Elites who win and gain power—especially the presidency—push against democratic norms precisely because they tie their hands and limit their power. The opposing party, in contrast, will support these norms, as they would prefer that the president's power be limited (especially in the contemporary era of elite ideological polarization).[20] So voters receive a clear partisan cue about whether to support such norms based on which party controls the White House—to support them when the opposing party has the presidency, but not when one's own party does. The extent of these reactions, in turn, will depend on levels of animus.[21]

This partisan conditionality in support for core norms is among the most concerning dynamics that we study. Such norms are the fundamental rules of the game that make democracy stable, so if they become political footballs and not fundamental principles, the system collapses (McClosky 1964). Pluralistic democracy requires not just diverse perspectives but also a recognition of alternative value systems as legitimate and a consensus that some common good is worth pursuing (e.g., Weingast 1997). Without those conditions, one can justify taking any means to achieve their (partisan) ends. Along these lines, we also explore an even more salient threat to democracy—support for taking illegal actions on behalf of one's party or supporting partisan violence. These actions challenge the basic rule of law and the system itself. We investigate whether people who invest in a partisan identity, and thus the extant nature of partisan politics, would advocate for extrasystemic action.

Conclusion

The authors of the *Federalist Papers* famously feared factions because they foresaw the precarious relationship between parties and democracy (Hamilton, Madison, and Jay [1787–1788] 1961). Parties organize people to seek power; this works well when conditions prevent partisans from prioritizing winning over the maintenance of democracy itself. The hope is that a large pluralistic society ensures enough overlapping interests within a single party to preclude agreement on an end that justifies dispensing with democratic means. Yet American parties have evolved in the twenty-first century in a way that has dramatically shrunk conflicting interests and groups within parties. These sorted parties created an ostensibly toxic environment. This has led many people to worry that pluralism is failing and democracy is imperiled unless institutional checks are sufficiently strong to protect the system from would-be autocrats.

There is a wealth of evidence that the contemporary political climate has undermined social relationships (e.g., Chen and Rohla 2018; McConnell et al. 2018) and been defined by increasingly vitriolic rhetoric (Crockett 2017; Gentzkow et al. 2019; W. Brady, Crockett, and Van Bavel 2020). That said, despite these grave concerns, there is a lack of systematic evidence about whether and when hostility and animosity affect the polity across a range of beliefs. We address this gap by offering a novel theory of animosity and decision-making. Our theory has the advantage of recognizing multiple types of decision-making criteria and explaining how animosity shapes decision-making by heightening the effects of party cues. In what follows, we test these hypotheses to understand how animosity shapes political behavior.[22]

Analyzing the Impact of Partisan Animosity

As we noted in chapter 1, "political polarization" has gone mainstream and seeped into the zeitgeist. One need not look further than the titles of recent popular books, including those such as *Why We're Polarized* by *New York Times* columnist and podcast host Ezra Klein (2020), *Political Tribes* by Yale law professor Amy Chua (2018), *Divided We Fall* by political commentator David French (2020), and *Demagoguery and Democracy* by rhetoric professor Patricia Roberts-Miller (2017). But books are not the only sign of this trend: since 2012, 6,850 scholarly articles that mention the phrase "affective polarization" have been written.[1] Affective polarization has arrived, often through a focus on partisan animus and animosity.

All this attention reflects real evidence of unprecedented divisions between Democrats and Republicans and a growing fear of how these divisions might impact attitudes, behaviors, and day-to-day life for regular Americans. Yet documenting the actual effects of animosity is much more difficult than it may initially appear. In this chapter, we describe how we gathered data over the roughly two-year period we described in chapter 1, beginning prior to the COVID-19 pandemic and concluding in the first months of Biden's presidency. We show how studying animus over time—a unique contribution of this book—leads into the empirical strategy we will use throughout to understand the consequences of animosity. This sets the stage for the remainder of this book, in which we use these data to test our theories regarding the polarization of American politics and policies.

Measuring Animosity

We began the data collection for our study in summer 2019. The first wave of our data collection took place from July 9, 2019, through August 2, 2019. We asked respondents various demographic and political questions (e.g., political ideology, frequency of political talk). This included asking them to indicate their partisanship on a fully labeled and branched 7-point scale: Democrats and Republicans were asked whether they are strong or not-so-strong partisans and Independents were asked whether they leaned toward the Democratic or the Republican Party. We focus on partisans, including partisan leaners. Our hypotheses do not apply to pure Independents, who do not lean toward either party, given that they lack a clear out-party and have no reason to follow particular party signals, and hence we exclude them from our sample.

The centerpiece of this wave was our measure of partisan animosity. Indeed, when we designed the first wave, we did not think we would be conducting a panel study, but rather simply a single study of partisan animosity (i.e., we did not anticipate the evolution of politics, which made our panel study extremely valuable). Building on Druckman and Levendusky (2019), we included four related sets of items:

- Feeling thermometers that asked respondents to rate members of each party on a scale from 0 to 100, with 0 being the most unfavorable/coldest and 100 being the most favorable/warmest. As we noted in chapter 1, the feeling thermometer item is the canonical measure of partisan animosity and affective polarization. But because of the limitations of the thermometer scales (e.g., Wilcox, Sigelman, and Cook 1989), we included several other measures of animosity.

- Trait ratings that asked respondents to evaluate how well five positive traits (patriotic, intelligent, honest, open-minded, generous) and three negative traits (hypocritical, selfish, mean) describe members of each party, using 5-point scales from not at all to extremely well (Garrett et al. 2014). The negative traits were reversed coded so that all the scores indicated higher favorability.

- Trust questions that asked respondents how much of the time they could trust each party to do what is right for the country, using 5-point scales from almost never to almost always.

- Social distance questions (Bogardus 1959) that asked respondents how comfortable they are having close personal friends who are from the other party, having neighbors on their street from the other party, and having their child marry someone from the other party, using 4-point scales from not at all comfortable to extremely comfortable.[2]

Each of these items taps into a manifestation of affective evaluations of the other party. Simply put, animosity is a feeling of dislike toward the out-party. The feeling thermometer taps directly into that: lower scores reflect colder sentiments and hence more dislike, warmer scores mean the opposite and hence less dislike. Similarly, trait ratings tap various dimensions of sentiment toward a group: to say that Democrats are "selfish" is to express dislike toward them, to say that Republicans are "intelligent" expresses the opposite. Political trust gets at perhaps the most politically consequential dimension of this measure: do you trust the other party to act in the best interest of the nation (Hetherington and Rudolph 2015)? If one likes and feels warmly toward the party, then such trust is much easier to grant than if one dislikes them. Finally, the social distance measures gauge the social dimension of animosity. In everyday life, are people willing to interact with those from the other party as friends and neighbors? In short, these are different dimensions of animosity, but together, they provide a richer and fuller picture of how individuals feel toward the other party.

Because our predictions focus on negative feelings toward the out-party (see chapter 2), we combined the out-party items from these measures (i.e., the out-party feeling thermometer, out-party trait ratings, etc.). We then standardized them on a [0, 1] scale and took the overall mean, scored so that higher values indicate greater out-party animosity. Cronbach's alpha for the combined scale for partisans is 0.88. This forms the measure of animosity that we use for the duration of this book.

In appendix 3.1, we describe the data vendor with whom we contracted to collect these data (Bovitz Forthright), the number of participants across the four waves, some data exclusion rules, and various other details about our data collection. That appendix also presents the demographics of our full sample, including pure Independents, across all four waves and analyses of attrition.[3] The precise question wordings for all items used in our study, including the animosity items, appear in appendix 3.3, which can be accessed online at this book's page at the University of Chicago Press website (www.press.uchicago.edu).

To begin, first consider the distribution of animus in the initial wave. Figure 3.1 displays the density plot of partisan animosity scores both pooled across parties (in the left-hand panel) and separately by party (right-hand panel).

While animus was approximately normally distributed, the upper-tail was noticeably thicker than the lower one—there were more high-animus respondents than low-animus ones in our data. Further, contrary to what some might suspect, if anything, there were more high-animus *Democrats* than Republicans, as also reflected in their respective means of 0.57 and 0.52 (both with a standard deviation of 0.18).[4] However, in both parties there was

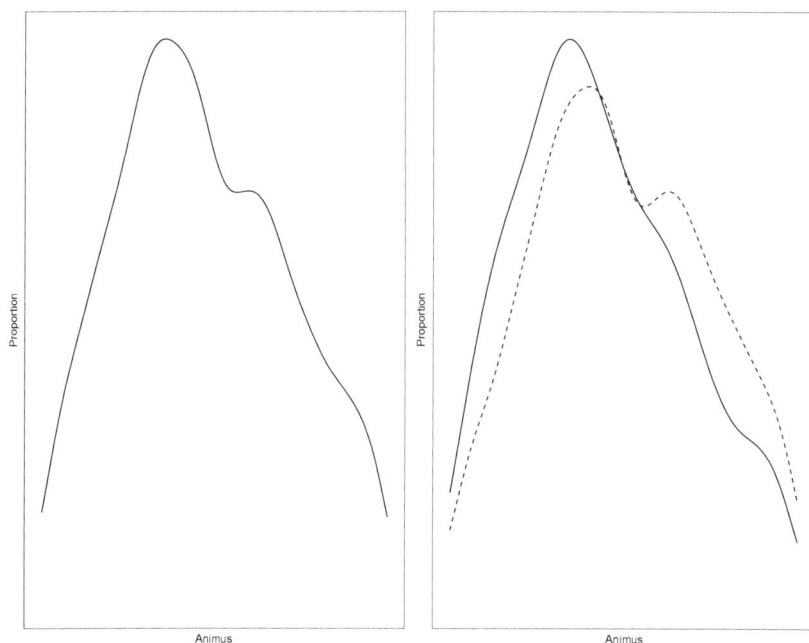

FIGURE 3.1. Distribution of Partisan Animosity

Note: The left-hand panel gives the overall distribution of partisan animosity; the right-hand panel gives the distribution for each party (with Democrats displayed with a dotted line and Republicans displayed with a solid line).

considerable variation in the level of animosity, which we will use to explore how animosity predicts our various outcome measures.

Is This a Valid Measure of Animosity?

By combining multiple different measures together, we improve the content and construct validity of our measure of animosity. In terms of predictive (convergent) validity, the measure should correlate with two associated, but distinct, outcomes: changing one's partisan identity across the waves of our panel and presidential vote choice in 2020. To take party switching first: approximately 6 percent of our sample switched parties (from Democrat to Republican or vice versa) across our study; this suggests our treatment of party identification as exogenous (as mentioned in chapter 2) is reasonable.

A valid measure of animosity should be strongly negatively correlated with party switching. The graphs we use to explore this correlation, as well as the graphs in later chapters, depict relationships with generalized additive models (Beck and Jackman 1998). These models fit a smooth response function (spline) between animus and our outcome measures, similar to a LOESS or other local regressions.[5] This allows us to map nonlinearities in our data, which, as we show throughout the book, occur with some frequency. That said, if we used OLS regression or other standard techniques, we would obtain substantively equivalent answers. Figure 3.2 presents the results for party

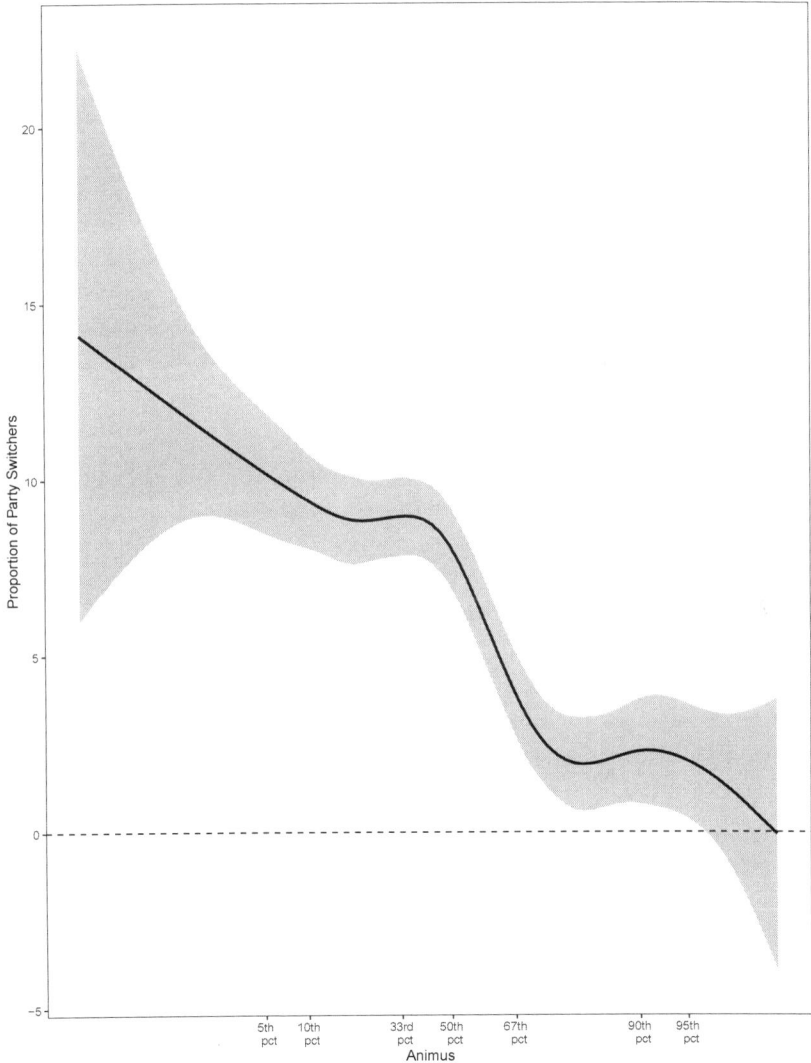

FIGURE 3.2. Party Animosity and Party Switching

Note: The solid black line shows the fraction of respondents who switched their partisanship during our panel as a function of animosity. Here and throughout subsequent figures (with the exception of figures 7.1, 7.3, and 7.4), the confidence intervals are shown shaded in gray.

switching. The x-axis depicts the percentile level of animus while the y-axis presents the proportion of party switchers.

These results strongly suggest we have a predictively valid measure. At low levels of animus, party switching was relatively common: among those with the lowest levels of animus, almost 15 percent switched parties during this twenty-one-month period. That percentage declined dramatically as animus increased. Indeed, above the median level of animosity, functionally no one switched parties. Only partisans with low levels of animus moved to the disliked opposition.

We expected a similarly strong relationship for 2020 presidential vote choice. In our October 2020 wave, we asked respondents which candidate they planned to support in the upcoming presidential election. Thus, technically this is vote intention rather than vote choice (except for some early voters), but given the closeness to the election and the stability of preferences in 2020, we are confident about the measure. We expected that as animus increased, Democrats should have become increasingly likely to vote for Biden, while the reverse should have been true of Republicans. In figure 3.3—which plots the percentages voting for Biden—we see exactly this pattern. The Democratic percentages appear in black and the Republican percentages in gray. Even most of the voters with the lowest levels of animus supported their party's nominee, consistent with claims of calcified preferences (Sides, Tausanovitch, and Vavreck 2022). Yet as animus increased, voters became even more likely to vote for their party's nominee. Indeed, for those scoring in the top one-third of the animosity scale, functionally all respondents supported their party's nominee, reaffirming—just as we would expect—that animosity strongly predicts vote choice. These analyses offer clear evidence for the predictive validity of our animus measure.

The figures in this chapter, particularly figure 3.1, also make clear that there are very few respondents at the lowest or highest levels of animus. This means any models we run necessarily do a lot of interpolation in that part of the data. We consequently excluded respondents with the highest and lowest 5 percent of animosity and focused on those in the 5th through 95th percentiles in our subsequent analyses throughout the book. Likewise, it is unclear what animosity in 2019 means for those who switched parties during our panel: at that point, one's animosity measure concerns their current party, so it becomes a different construct if they changed parties. We therefore excluded these individuals as well. Given the extreme stability of partisanship in recent time (e.g., D. Green and Platzman, forthcoming), this is not a significant limitation of our findings. In appendix 3.1 we also discuss some other minor exclusion criteria used in our data.

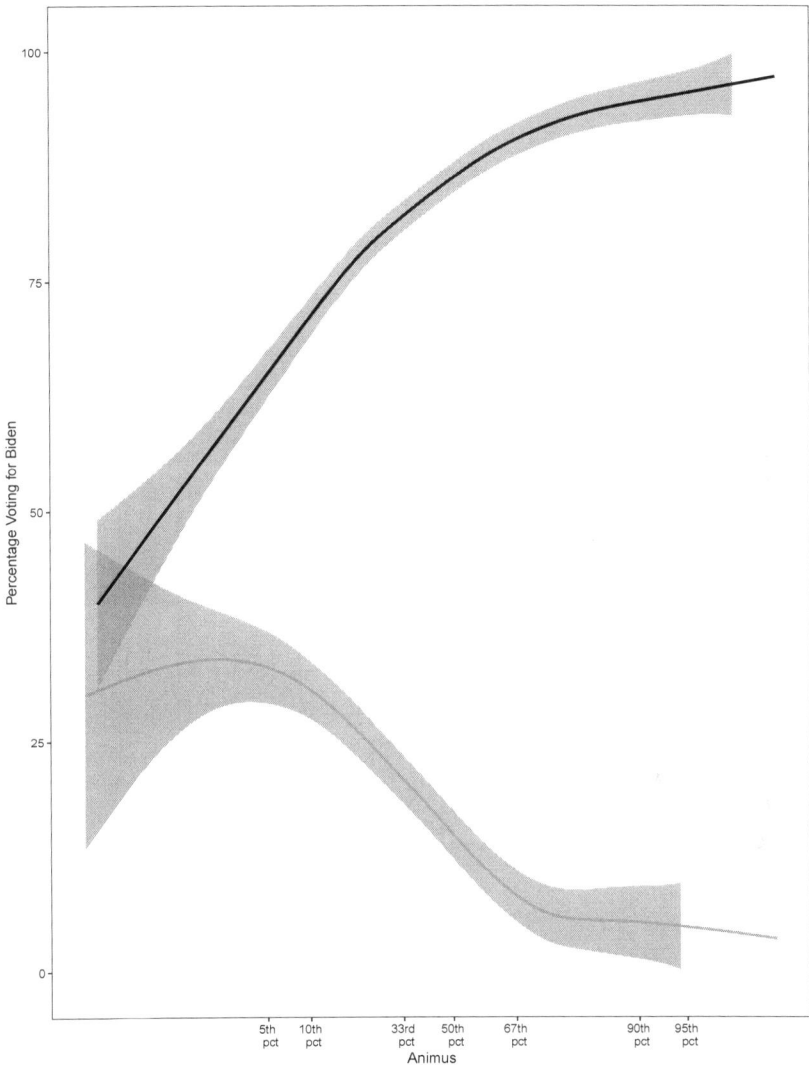

FIGURE 3.3. Presidential Vote Choice and Animosity

Note: The solid black (gray) line shows the fraction of Democratic (Republican) voters who balloted for Joe Biden in the 2020 election as a function of animosity.

Can We Treat Animus as Stable?

As we discussed in chapter 2, our theory treats animosity as exogenous, and we use our July 2019 measure (discussed earlier) as our measure of animus. We acknowledge that in the long run, animus changes: see, for example, the discussion of figure 1.1, which tracks the growth of animosity over the past

half-century. The key question for our analysis is whether animosity exhibited stability during our twenty-one-month study. In other words, how much
did voters' level of animosity change between July 2019 and April 2021?

We tested stability in two ways. First, we looked at the full battery of items
that we asked in July 2019 (the measure we use throughout the book) and
compared it to those same items from our final survey in April 2021. In that
last survey, we again asked our respondents the full set of items we used to
measure partisan animosity. In figure 3.4, we plot the July 2019 animus measure against the April 2021 version. We include the regression line (using July
2019 animosity to predict April 2021 animosity), shown in solid black, and the
45-degree line, in dashed gray; if no respondents changed, all of the points
would line up exactly on that 45-degree line. As one can see, there was little
change over time. The correlation is 0.79, and, if anything, we find some regression to the mean, as respondents with exceptionally high levels of animus
in July 2019 tended to have slightly lower levels of animosity in April 2021 and
vice versa. Stability, not change, is the norm in these data.

Second, we assessed stability by looking at the out-party thermometer
item across each wave. While we only included the full animus battery in
waves 1 and 4, we included the feeling thermometer items in every wave.[6]
Based on multiple observations per respondent, we calculated the Heise
(1969) reliability coefficient to be 0.65.[7] To put that into perspective, compare
it to the estimates from Hout and Hastings (2016), who calculated the reliability of a wide variety of items in the General Social Survey panel studies.
The reliability estimates we produced align with those for respondents' social class, vocabulary, and self-assessed health (see Hout and Hastings 2016,
table 2). While this is lower than the estimated reliability of partisanship
(which is usually estimated to be around 0.9, see D. Green and Palmquist
1990; D. Green and Platzman forthcoming), it exceeds the reliability of most
estimates of political attitudes (Erikson 1979). Our data suggest that animosity
acts more like a trait than an attitude that changes dramatically from wave to
wave, at least for the period of our data collection (also see Alwin 1997; Beam,
Hutchens, and Hmielowski 2018). Indeed, using different data, Boxell et al.
(2022) showed an analogous pattern for animosity during a similar time period (July 2019–February 2020), suggesting that our data are not anomalous.
Such results are reassuring in light of our theoretical and empirical argument
that we can use July 2019 animosity ratings to explain outcomes measured at
later waves; clearly, how people felt about the other party endured over the
time of our study.

This stability is particularly noteworthy given all that happened during
our panel study. During this time, the COVID-19 pandemic first emerged,

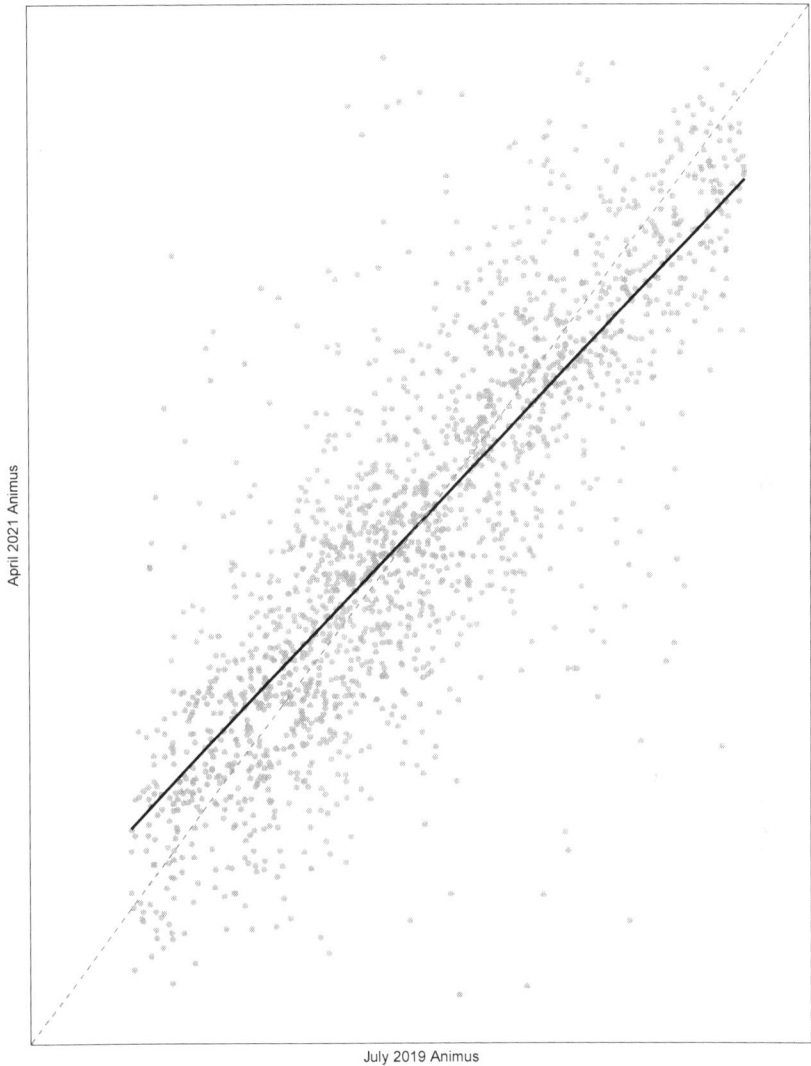

FIGURE 3.4. Stability of Animosity over Time

Note: Each point shows a respondent's level of animosity as measured in July 2019 (x-axis) and April 2021 (y-axis). The line of best fit (regression line) is displayed as a solid line; the 45-degree line is displayed as a dotted line.

then waned, and then waxed again at least three times; the economy collapsed due to lockdowns to fight the virus in spring 2020, and then very unevenly rebounded for those at the top and the bottom of the economic ladder; the Black Lives Matter movement sparked a national conversation about race and policing; the heated 2020 election campaign took place; the nation underwent a crisis of democratic legitimacy as a result of Donald Trump's refusal to accept his loss in the November 2020 presidential election; the January 6th insurrection at the Capitol occurred; and then some in the Republican Party attempted to downplay that event. Despite all this, animus over this period was largely stable. While animus clearly increases over longer periods of time (see figure 1.1), over our shorter period of time, it largely remained the same.

Correlates of Partisan Animosity

Before we turn to testing our theory in the next chapters, we consider what political and demographic factors correlate with animosity. Since there is no natural metric for animosity (i.e., what does it mean to have an animus score of 0.25 versus 0.15?), we use percentile benchmarks to demarcate those low in animosity (5th percentile, 10th percentile), those at middling levels (33rd percentile, 50th percentile, 67th percentile), and those with high animosity (90th percentile, 95th percentile). As we have shown in figures 3.2 and 3.3, this provides a way to discuss animus more sensibly and can show how behavior changes across these different levels of animosity.

In figure 3.5, we present the relationship between animus and indicators of political identity strength. More specifically, we show the percentage of the sample (merging both parties) that reported being (1) a strong partisan, (2) ideologically sorted (i.e., a liberal Democrat or a conservative Republican), and (3) in the top quartile of Huddy, Mason, and Aarøe's (2015) partisan social identity scale. We found that as animosity increased, so did all three of these measures. In other words, respondents with low levels of animosity were unlikely to be strong partisans, sorted, or strongly socially identified with their party. Those with higher levels of animus, however, were likely to report these beliefs and identities. Of those at the lowest level of animus, for example, roughly one-quarter reported being strong partisans and fewer than half were sorted. But at the highest end of our animosity scale, those figures jumped to about 50 percent and nearly 75 percent, respectively.

Clearly, partisan animus relates to these types of identity measures, but it also differs from them. Partisan animosity does not simply capture partisan strength, or sorting, or partisan social identity (also see Iyengar, Sood, and Lelkes 2012). The pairwise correlation between strong partisanship and animus in our data was 0.18, the parallel figure for sorting was 0.19, and that for partisan social identity was 0.15 (using polychoric/polyserial correlations where appropriate). People with higher animus have stronger attachments to their partisan identities, variously measured, but animus does not simply measure identity (West and Iyengar 2022).

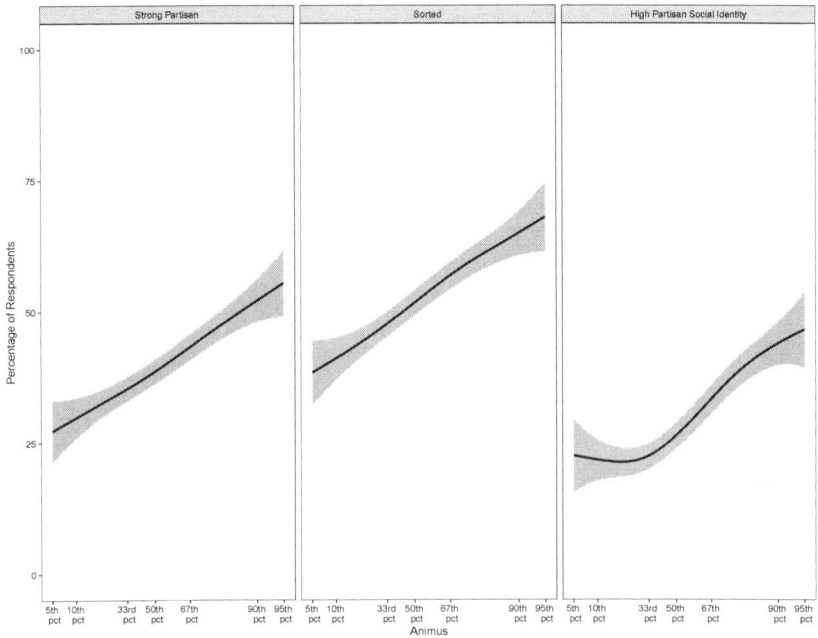

FIGURE 3.5. Political Identity and Animosity

Note: The figure panels depict the relationship between animosity and partisan strength (left-hand panel), partisan sorting (middle panel), and partisan social identity (right-hand panel).

Further, in figure 3.6, we plot animus against issue extremity (i.e., taking a position in the most extreme quartile on a range of policy issues) and then against ideological strength (i.e., being extremely liberal or extremely conservative on the liberal-conservative self-identification scale). As in figure 3.5, there is a clear relationship: respondents with higher animus were more likely to hold extreme positions and to identify as extremely liberal or conservative. But once again, these effects were modest, not massive, and a minority of respondents at even the highest levels of animus held such beliefs. Apparently, high-animus partisans are not necessarily those who consistently hold the most extreme positions.

In figure 3.7, we present analogous data with various measures of political engagement and knowledge. We saw increases in both engagement and knowledge as animus increased, albeit not quite as large as those in figure 3.5. Those who had more animosity discussed politics much more frequently, posted about politics on social media much more frequently, expressed greater interest in politics by stating they were extremely or very interested, and possessed substantially more political knowledge as captured by being in the top quartile of a scale of factual knowledge items.[8] High-animus respondents

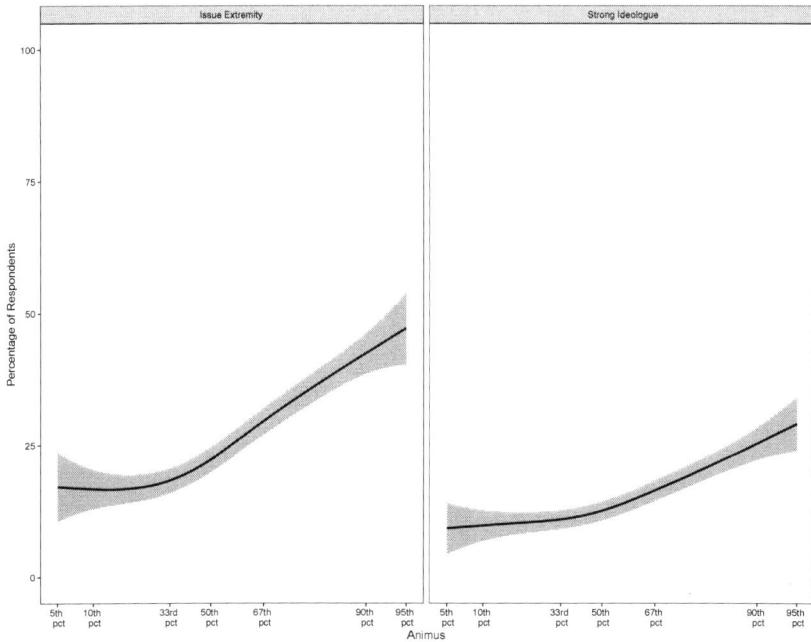

FIGURE 3.6. Issue Extremity and Animosity
Note: The figure panels depict the relationship between animosity and issue position extremity (left-hand panel) and strength of liberal-conservative self-identification (right-hand panel).

were thus not only much more politically identified with their party (fig-ure 3.5), and somewhat more ideologically extreme (figure 3.6), but they also were more politically knowledgeable, interested, and engaged.

We also investigated how a number of salient demographic features dif-fered across the range of animus. In figures 3.8 and 3.9, we explored how ed-ucation, income, religion, race, age, and gender varied as animus changes. Since, given social sorting, these demographics vary considerably by party, we separated Democrats (the darker line) and Republicans (the lighter line) in these analyses.[9] The panels in figure 3.8 show the mapping between ani-mus and education (those with a college degree), income (those who earn $100,000 or more per year), and religion (those who identify as Christian, including Catholics), and figure 3.9 shows the mapping between animus and race (percentage who identify as white), age (percentage over fifty years old), and gender (percentage who identify as female).

We begin with figure 3.8. The most striking finding is, generally speak-ing, the lack of clear relationships between demographics and animus. For education and income, there was basically no relationship with animus for either party. For religion (Christianity), the biggest effect was the intercept shift: Democrats were less likely to identify as Christians than Republicans at all levels of animosity (Margolis 2018; David Campbell, Layman, and Green 2020). But aside from that pattern, there was effectively no relationship between religion and animus in our data.

In figure 3.9, we see the parties' striking racial sorting (Mason 2018). Republicans of all levels of animus were much more likely to be white; this increased with animosity but then leveled off, as there is a ceiling effect. Democrats, on the other hand, were less likely to be white at all levels of animus, highlighting their more multiracial and multiethnic composition (and for Democrats, there was functionally no relationship between animosity and identifying as white). We also saw a positive relationship between age and animus for both parties (also see Boxell, Gentzkow, and Shapiro 2017; Phillips 2022), though again it was very modest and was stronger for Republicans. Finally, for both parties, we found no clear pattern in the relationship between gender and animus.

Pulling back, the overall implication of figures 3.8 and 3.9 is that demographic traits, unlike political identity or engagement, did little to consistently

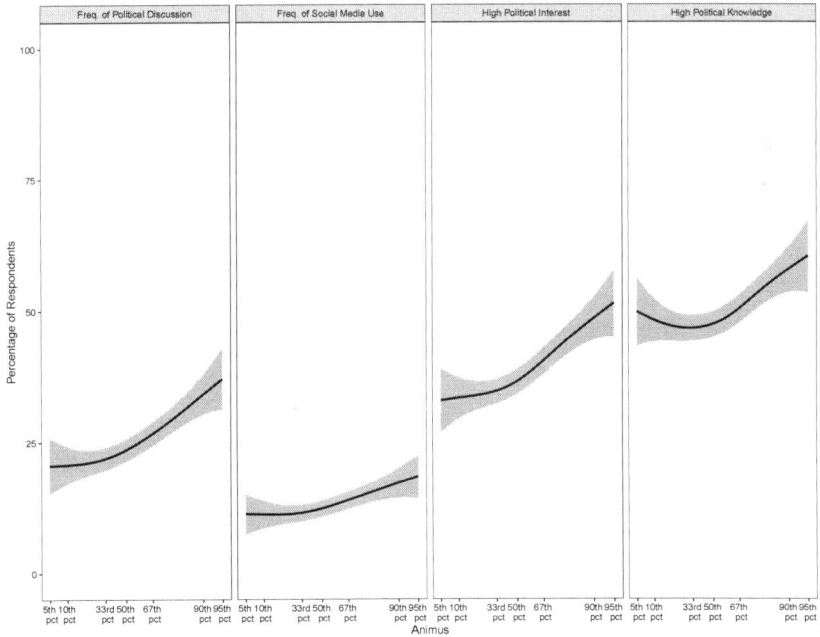

FIGURE 3.7. Political Engagement, Knowledge, and Animosity

Note: The figure panels depict the relationship between animosity and the frequency of political discussion (left-most panel), frequency of social media usage, political interest, and political knowledge (right-most panel).

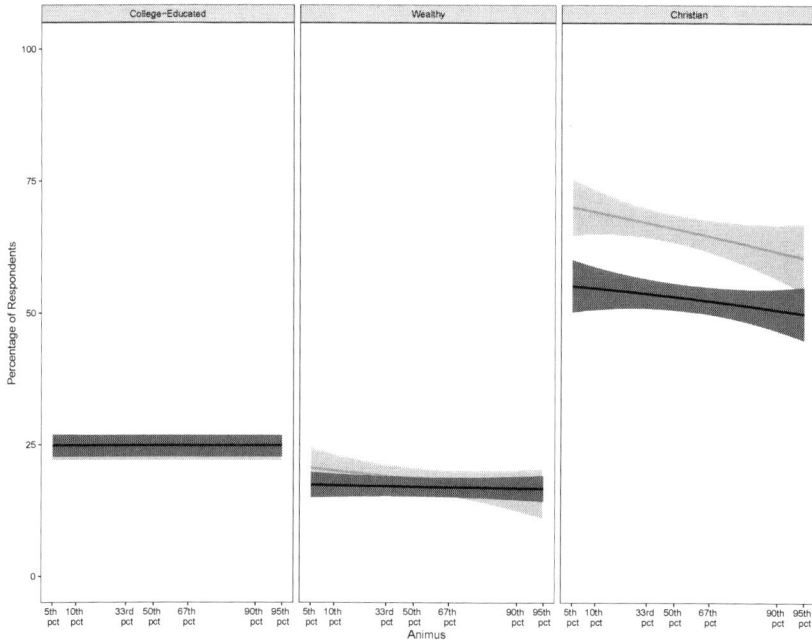

FIGURE 3.8. Education, Income, Religion, and Animosity

Note: The figure panels depict the relationship between animosity and having a college degree (left-hand panel), earning more than $100,000 per year (middle panel), and identifying as a Christian (right-hand panel). Democrats are displayed in black and Republicans are displayed in gray.

explain patterns in animus; the only partial exception was race, though even that was more of an intercept shift than a slope shift. The distinctive features of high-animus respondents were their political identities and engagement, much more so than their demographics.

The question motivating the remainder of the book is whether this class of high-animus partisans fundamentally differs from others when it comes to politically meaningful outcomes; we next turn to the specific manifestations of these outcomes.

What Outcomes Do We Study?

As explained in the first two chapters, we explored four broad classes of outcomes: policies, evaluations of public figures, political compromise, and support for various undemocratic practices and more fundamental norms. In table 3.1, we list the specific items we asked in order to measure each type of outcome and indicate when we asked them. We discuss the types of outcomes in the next several sections. Appendix 3.1 provides links to the preregistrations

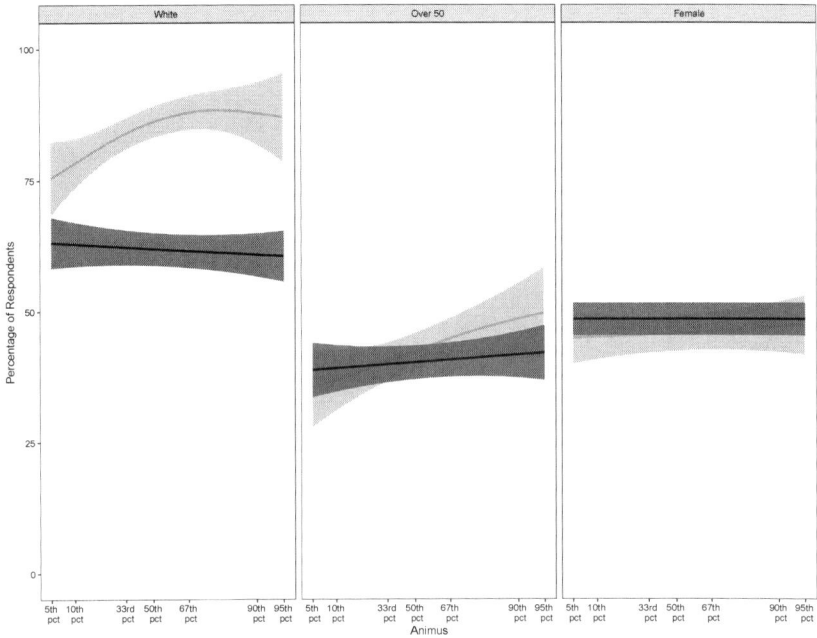

FIGURE 3.9. Race, Gender, Age, and Animosity

Note: The figure panels depict the relationship between animosity and identifying as white (left-most panel), being fifty years or older (middle panel), and identifying as female (right-most panel). Democrats are displayed in black and Republicans are displayed in gray.

TABLE 3.1. Outcome Measures Used throughout the Study

Construct	Measures	Waves
Policies (chapters 4 and 5)		
Public policy positions	• Politicized both party cues (e.g., Affordable Care Act, immigration)	April 2021
	• Nonpoliticized issues (e.g., campaign finance, economic incentives for business relocation)	
	• Politicized Democratic cues (e.g., assault rifles ban, paid family leave)	
	• Politicized Republican cues (e.g., Green New Deal, defunding the police)	
COVID-19 beliefs and behaviors	• Number of health protective behaviors taken (e.g., mask wearing, working from home, social distancing)	April 2020 October 2020
	• Opposition or support for policies (stay-at-home orders, closing nonessential businesses, fines for violating social distancing, requiring in-person school classes)	April 2021
	• Perception of safety of various indoor activities (e.g., socializing indoors, getting a haircut)[a]	
	• Likelihood of vaccination[b]	

(continued)

TABLE 3.1. (*continued*)

Construct	Measures	Waves
Evaluations of public figures (chapter 6)		
Trump and U.S. COVID-19 response	• Assessing the COVID-19 response of Trump or the U.S. (experimentally randomly assigned)	April 2020
Approval of handling of the COVID-19 pandemic	• Partisan figures (Biden, Trump)[c] • Political figures (members of Congress, state and local elected officials, respondent's mayor)[d] • Scientific advisers and agencies (Dr. Fauci, FDA, CDC)[e]	April 2020 October 2020 April 2021
Leader helping or hurting COVID-19 vaccine development and distribution	• President Trump, President Biden, respondent's state's governor	April 2021
Political compromise (chapter 7)		
Abstract compromise	• The importance of compromise and respect in general, by own party, or by other party (experimentally randomly assigned)	April 2021
Policy compromise	• Amount of hypothetical NASA budget cut (experimentally randomly varied) given parties' ideal points	April 2021
Democratic attitudes (chapter 8)		
Undemocratic practices	• Same-party senators blocking the other party's Supreme Court nominees, gerrymandering to benefit one's party, contesting an election with varying vote differences	October 2020
Democratic norms	• "Rules of the game" (e.g., separation of powers, checks and balances)	July 2019 April 2021
Breaking the law/ partisan violence	• Likelihood of breaking the law without engaging in violence and likelihood of using violence if the candidate from the other party wins the presidency in a contested election	October 2020

Note: This table lists the outcome variables used in our study, with a short description of the item, the wave(s) in which the item was asked, and the chapter in which we present the relevant results.

[a] The perceptions of safety items were not asked in the April 2020 wave as much of the country was shut down (and hence most of these behaviors were not possible for most Americans).

[b] The likelihood of vaccination item was asked only in the April 2021 wave.

[c] The Biden item was not asked in the October 2020 wave.

[d] The members of Congress and state and local officials items were asked only in the April 2020 wave. The respondent's mayor item was asked only in the October 2020 and April 2021 waves.

[e] The FDA item was not asked in the April 2020 wave.

that were filed prior to each wave (again, full survey wordings are in appendix 3.3, which can be accessed online at the book's website).

POLICIES

We measured various policy positions in our April 2021 survey, which was the fourth and final one. One set of issues involved fully politicized policies with clear positions on both sides (e.g., the ACA, providing a pathway to citizenship for undocumented immigrants).[10] A second set included nonpoliticized issues on which the parties have not taken clear positions (e.g., a ban on government officials becoming lobbyists, negotiating lower drug prices for Medicare). Finally, we asked about policies where either the Democratic Party (supporting limiting assault rifles, supporting paid family leave) or the Republican Party (against the Green New Deal, against defunding police) had taken a clear position but the other party had not.

Given the lack of party signals on the nonpoliticized issues, we do not anticipate a relationship with animosity. In contrast, on the issues where at least one party offers a clear cue, we expect high-animus partisans to be more extreme in the direction of their party. This is especially the case when both parties offer those signals; when one party signals—as mentioned in chapter 2—we expect polarization, which should be most pronounced among those from the party whose signal is less clear (they follow an anti-cue).[11]

We also measured a range of COVID-19-related beliefs and behaviors in each of our waves that took place after the pandemic began (i.e., April 2020, October 2020, and April 2021 waves). We asked respondents what protective measures they were taking to avoid being infected (e.g., wearing a mask, working from home), what policies the government should adopt to halt the spread of the virus (e.g., stay-at-home orders, closing nonessential businesses), how safe they perceived various activities to be (e.g., socializing indoors, getting a haircut), and their intentions and behaviors concerning vaccination. These items reflect the country's fully politicized policies. As numerous studies have documented, party leaders took clear and contrasting positions on COVID-19 throughout the pandemic (P. Hart, Chin, and Soroka 2020; Adolph et al. 2022). From the beginning of the outbreak, Democratic politicians, relative to Republican ones, expressed greater concern about the virus, implored the public to take more precautions, supported more restrictive policies, and advocated for vaccine mandates (Lipsitz and Pop-Eleches 2020; Pink et al. 2021).[12] We thus expected to find a relationship between animosity and COVID-19 beliefs that track the elite positions.

That said, unlike the aforementioned policy issues, the issue of COVID-19 provides an opportunity to test our prediction that animosity effects decline or evaporate when the decisions are personally consequential, as accuracy motivations take hold. In an earlier paper, we analyzed the April 2020 data, operationalized the salience of the COVID-19 pandemic through county case counts, and found that animosity effects declined or disappeared in areas with a higher number of cases (Druckman et al. 2021a). Here, we extend that general logic to the October 2020 and April 2021 surveys. However, by the time of these waves, the virus had spread throughout the nation and nearly all counties had experienced significant numbers of cases and deaths, which muted the effects of this measure of salience.

We therefore turned to another strategy. While all counties had at least some COVID-19 cases and deaths, the virus threatened some Americans more than others. Put another way, the threat shifted from exposure via cases to concerns about severity. We therefore preregistered a different moderator for these later waves: the severity of respondents' actual or anticipated experiences with COVID-19 (see Constantino et al. 2022 for a similar approach).[13] We hypothesized that those who had experienced or who anticipated severe cases of COVID-19 would take the virus more seriously, and hence for these respondents, the partisan motivation would decline.

EVALUATIONS OF PUBLIC FIGURES

Our next outcome type focuses on evaluations of public figures. We primarily focused on evaluations of how public figures handled the COVID-19 pandemic, given its status as the most salient national issue during our period of data collection. With these items, we test our expectation that as animosity increases, partisans become more likely to evaluate politically ambiguous targets in a partisan fashion. As noted in chapter 2, we did this with an experiment in our April 2020 wave where respondents (randomly) evaluated either Trump's or the United States' response to COVID-19, with the expectation that high-animus voters would polarize in evaluating the United States, whereas low-animus voters would not politicize it and thus not polarize. We also expected that this would occur less regarding Trump, given that his political nature is unambiguous (see Druckman et al. 2021b).

Our other evaluation items assessed respondents' assessments of highly partisan figures (e.g., Biden, Trump, members of each party) in various contexts (e.g., handling COVID-19, vaccine distribution), political but not highly partisan figures (e.g., local elected officials), and ostensibly apolitical medical or scientific figures (e.g., Dr. Fauci, the FDA). We expected to find animosity effects for the more partisan figures relative to those who are less clearly partisan (Das et al. 2022). That said, as mentioned in chapter 2, animosity effects may be tempered for the most highly partisan figures (e.g., Biden, Trump) since all citizens, regardless of their levels of animosity, view them through a political lens.

The scientific figures serve as an important test since their politicization varied across time. For instance, at the start of the pandemic, Dr. Fauci was not highly politicized, but as time went on, he became extremely politicized due to repeated clashes with President Trump over how to address the pandemic. Since scientific advisers link directly to COVID-19 threat, we also anticipated that animosity effects—when they occur—would be moderated by perceptions of the threat's severity.[14]

POLITICAL COMPROMISE

Our next outcome type taps willingness to compromise with the other party, a crucial element for any democracy—especially a pluralistic one—to function (Gutmann and Thompson 2012). We did this with two experiments in our April 2021 survey, one abstract and one applied. The former asked participants about the importance of making compromises and having respect for opponents. In this set of questions, respondents were randomly assigned such that they answered in general, whether their party should or whether the other party should. The other experiment involved a *specific* compromise focused on people's willingness to move from their party's ideal spending point (drawn from Harbridge, Malhotra, and Harrison 2014). We predicted that partisans with high animosity would expect that the other party should bend and their party should not.

UNDEMOCRATIC PRACTICES, DEMOCRATIC NORMS, AND PARTISAN VIOLENCE

The final type of outcome we study concerns democratic attitudes. These include a heterogenous set of constructs, all of which may be construed as transgressions against democracy with widely varying degrees of threat (Ahmed 2023). We explore three types.

In our October 2020 survey, we included measures of undemocratic practices that gauged the extent to which respondents would support violations that favor their party in different settings, such as the Senate's confirmation power, gerrymandering, and whether candidates should contest a close election (Moore-Berg et al. 2020). These items capture the extent to which respondents privilege their party over procedures that are typically seen as democratic. We anticipated that increased animosity would lead to more support for undemocratic practices.

In both our initial April 2019 survey and our final April 2021 survey, we included a democratic norms battery. These measures capture more abstracted support for "rules of the game" such as constitutional protections related to limits on executive power. That we had the same items in the two surveys, one during Trump's presidency and the other two years later, during the Biden presidency, enabled us to conduct a crucial test. We expected that high-animus partisans would support norms only when the other party holds power, since when their party rules, they benefit from violating constitutional norms. Thus, we should see high-animus Democrats support the norms in July 2019 (with Trump in the White House), but not in April 2021 (when Biden is there); the reverse should be true of high-animus Republicans.[15]

Finally, in our October 2020 survey, we measured direct violations of the law, representing "the most egregious [type] of democratic transgression" (Ahmed 2023, 969). We specifically asked respondents how likely they would be to break the law without engaging in violence (e.g., defacing public property), as well as how likely to use violence should the other party's candidate win the upcoming presidential election. As we will discuss in chapter 8, here our expectation was less clear, as these actions involve extrasystemic steps that could dissolve the system and high-animus partisans have in fact, perhaps ironically, accepted the system via their presumed party attachment. We wanted to see whether this is a line that partisans, even those high in animosity, do not cross.

Testing the Impact of Partisan Animosity

Across all these different types of measures, we need an identification strategy that allows us to assess how they relate to animosity. Our expectation is that animosity will drive these outcomes, but only under two specific conditions: when the parties take clear stances on the issue (or the issue is politically ambiguous) and when the issue is not personally consequential. The effects of partisan animosity are conditional, both on the clarity of the party cues and on the personal relevance of the issue.

Testing these expectations proves exceedingly difficult due to the fundamental problem of causal inference (Holland 1986). How can we know that a Democrat with high animosity favors the Democratic Party's policy because of a high level of animus? Perhaps the opposite is true—could it be that the animosity grew *because* of a strong preference for the party's position or against the other party's position? How do we know that animosity drives a Republican to favor the Republican candidate so strongly? Is it not equally plausible that a strong preference for the Republican candidate or against the Democratic candidate might drive animosity? In essence, one can never identify a causal relationship with certainty since it requires simultaneously observing counterfactuals. For example, one needs to identify the relationship between animosity and an opinion for a given individual when they have a low level of animosity and a high level of animosity at the same exact time. This is, of course, impossible.

As these examples attest, if we were to find a correlation between animosity and beliefs, the relationship could stem from three possible scenarios: (1) animosity increases the tendency for partisans to follow party cues, as we predict, (2) partisans with more extreme ideological views (i.e., conservative Republicans and liberal Democrats) subsequently develop more animus (Fiorina 2017; Bougher 2017), or (3) political leaders influence the public to hold both more partisan views (Levendusky 2009) and more animosity (Rogowski and Sutherland 2016; Webster and Abramowitz 2017). As a result, it is difficult to determine how animosity connects to political beliefs.

For this reason, some scholars have turned to experiments that randomly vary respondents' levels of animus and then examine the downstream consequences (e.g., Broockman, Kalla, and Westwood 2023; Harteveld et al. 2022; Voelkel et al., "Interventions," 2023; Voelkel et al., "Megastudy," 2023). This is a valuable approach. However, as with any approach, it has drawbacks. In particular, the sorts of treatments used in those studies (asking, for example, someone to play a trust game with a member of the other party) estimate the local average treatment effect for the experimental compliers (i.e., those who alter their level of animus because of playing this game). Those individuals may not be the sort of people who actually change their level of animus in response to the types of real-world changes that are often of interest.[16] We view our work as providing a complementary strategy to the experimental approach and acknowledge that it too has limitations. At a minimum, the experimental paradigm is not the ne plus ultra for understanding this sort of phenomenon.

We take a different approach: having collected measures of animosity in a large sample of respondents in July 2019, we followed up with respondents in 2020 and 2021 to understand how animosity at time t affected behavior at time t+1 (see table 1.1 for more information on our survey timing). By surveying the same panelists over time, we can measure how their early animosity levels (recorded in July 2019) impacted their beliefs in later waves. This design allows us to rule out reverse causality, as we know that attitudes measured in 2020 or 2021 cannot *cause* levels of animosity that we measured in 2019. This over-time approach does not resolve all the challenges of causal inference—but it brings us closer to tracking the potential downstream consequences of animosity. We use different techniques throughout the book to try to reduce the risk of omitted variable bias though, of course, when using observational data one can never fully remove it.

Several examples of the strengths and weaknesses of our approach help to understand the scope conditions of our argument. First, consider the COVID-19 variables such as behaviors, safety, and policy support. Since the pandemic emerged *after* we measured animosity, we can rule out beliefs regarding COVID-19 or elite positions on COVID-19 as being a cause of animosity levels. This puts us in a uniquely strong inferential position, given the rarity of novel topics emerging onto the policy agenda. Thus, COVID-19 serves as a useful case since partisan elites took clear, distinct positions and we expected to find variation in accuracy motivation depending on context and health.

A second example involves studying beliefs on a topic on which the party signals changed after we measured animosity. This applies to the abstract democratic norms that were included in the July 2019 and the April 2021 waves. The flip in party control of government changes our predictions because partisans' views of the norms should change with the alteration of power in Washington, DC. Consequently, beliefs or elite polarization found in the April 2021 wave could not have altered our animosity measure. This design extends prior work on cue-taking that exploits cases of a sudden shift in party signals (Slothuus and Bisgaard 2021a) by also looking at animosity.[17]

A final scenario entails studying beliefs measured in the April 2020, October 2020, and April 2021 waves. Attitudes or elite polarization on the topics at the time of measurement could not have caused earlier animosity. However, we cannot definitively rule out that prior elite polarization or prior beliefs on the same topics shaped animosity at the July 2019 wave (and beliefs at the later waves), or that some other variable correlated with partisan animosity explains our results. We use this design in studying policy positions (chapter 4), evaluations of public figures (chapter 6), support for compromise (chapter 7), and some democratic attitudes (chapter 8). In such cases, we can only assess whether the evidence coheres with our expectations, rather than arriving at more definitive causal conclusions. In so doing, we emphasize the totality of the evidence we present over any particular test.

Generally, we recognize that pinpointing a relationship between animosity and any outcome (using any approach) is somewhat fraught, given the mapping of anxiety to similar concepts such as partisan social identity, partisan media consumption, and so on.[18] We revert to our theory where the relevant construct is animosity, and thus we test whether the data are consistent with our predictions (Druckman 2022). That said, even if the results we report are actually shaped by a related concept, they still have value as they reveal when "animus" or a close correlate shapes a wide range of opinions. In the end, differentiating whether this is animus or some other, similar concept is ultimately akin to scholasticism. The more important theoretical, empirical, and normative question is whether animus (or some related construct) has these effects. That is the task we set for ourselves in this book.

A final note concerns our presentational strategy. Throughout, we rely on graphical depictions of the relationship between animosity and the relevant outcome variable, placing statistical analyses largely in appendixes. We offer more information on our graphical approach when we present our first result in chapter 4 (figure 4.1). We direct readers there for further discussion.

Conclusion

The polarization of American society, and particularly the high levels of animosity, has attracted a remarkable amount of attention both within and beyond academia, as the examples with which we open the chapter attest. Politics seem different in contemporary society than in the past. Part of this may reflect the mid- to late twentieth century—bringing with it the onset of modern social science—as a uniquely less ideologically polarized time among elites (McCarty 2019). However, technological and demographic transformations have undoubtedly altered how government works. For most people, a consequence appears to be a more toxic environment, as substantiated by overtime partisan animosity data in the twenty-first century. Whether this affects our politics, however, is less clear than many analysts presume. In chapter 2 we offered a new theory that generated clear predictions about when animosity should shape political beliefs. Our goal in the next five chapters is to use the data described in this chapter to present an exhaustive evaluation of our hypotheses.

Our approach has downsides, most notably concerning precise causal inference, as we opted for a method that enables us to explore a wide range of outcomes over time. As with all scientific hypotheses, we cannot prove ours definitively but can only confirm consistent or inconsistent evidence. If we persuade readers that the data support the possibility that animosity has meaningful political consequences, it raises a host of questions—the ones with which we began the book, concerning the implications of animosity and polarization for a functioning pluralistic democracy. These are questions to which we will return later. For now, we will turn to our analyses and results with the questions of when and for whom animosity influences politics.

How Partisan Animosity Can Fuel Issue Polarization

Toward the end of the twentieth century, strong storms, floods, and wildfires began to affect the planet with alarming speed. Evidence supporting the harms of anthropogenic climate change continued to mount in the decades that followed, leading an international coalition of over two hundred medical journals to simultaneously publish an editorial that called climate change "the greatest threat to global public health" (Atwoli et al. 2021). Yet even in the face of this incontrovertible evidence, Americans today cannot agree on whether climate change is real, caused by human activity, or worth addressing. The disagreement does not stem from variations in education or scientific knowledge, but rather is largely due to politics (Bolsen, Druckman, and Cook 2015; Tyson, Kennedy, and Funk 2021). This was not always the case: survey data from 1997, for example, show that people on both sides of the political spectrum were equally likely to agree that climate change was human-made and to believe in climate change science (Tesler 2018).[1]

What changed? Climate change became partisan. As Democrats and Republicans in Washington diverged in their approach to climate change, the mass public followed suit (McCright and Dunlap 2011). In 2016 Donald Trump referred to climate change as a "hoax," claiming that it was "invented by the Chinese" to harm America (L. Jacobson 2016). He removed the United States from the Paris Climate Accord and rolled back many of the efforts that President Barack Obama had implemented to fight climate change. In contrast, many Democratic leaders—from Hillary Clinton to Alexandria Ocasio-Cortez to Joe Biden—took great pains to stress the realities of climate change and the need to address it. In turn, ordinary Americans' views on climate change have become driven by partisanship (Kahan 2010; Merkley and Stecula 2020).

Partisan cue-taking—rather than scientific evidence—shaped the public divide on this issue (Bayes and Druckman 2021).

One might dismiss climate change as atypical, a case where the consequences are long-term and the policies remote and technical, with an unclear mapping from policy change to outcome. But this same pattern of partisan cue-taking occurs even on issues with clear policy outcomes (Slothuus and Bisgaard 2021b); indeed, the strength of party cue-taking remains one of the most robust findings in political behavior (e.g., Zaller 1992; Lenz 2012; Bullock 2020). In this chapter, we explore *why* this occurs, and we show how partisan animosity affects it. When the parties divide on an issue, they send voters a clear signal about where party elites stand. These signals especially matter for those who hold the most disdain for out-party members. Voters are not simply embracing their own party's position. Just as importantly, they are turning *against* the other party. Voters who feel the highest levels of animosity toward the other party possess the most motivation to adopt the stances that the out-party opposes (i.e., the other party becomes an anti-cue; see, e.g., Nicholson 2012; Goren, Federico, and Kittilson 2009; Merkley and Stecula 2020).

To test our hypothesis about the relationship between animosity and policy opinions, in our April 2021 wave we asked respondents for their opinions on a range of policies. We found—consistent with our theoretical argument—that when elites polarize on an issue, those with high animosity polarize as well. But on issues where the parties do not divide—and hence do not provide a strong signal to voters—mass polarization does not follow, even among partisans with the highest levels of animus.

Why Partisan Animosity Drives Cue-Taking

Partisan cue-taking is one of the most studied topics in political behavior research, with several generations of work demonstrating that partisans tend to adopt their party's positions on issues of the day (e.g., Zaller 1992; Lenz 2012; Bullock 2020). These types of responses often reflect partisan directed motivated reasoning (Druckman, Peterson, and Slothuus 2013) where partisans adopt their party's position on an issue not so much because it constitutes the "best" position by some objective criteria, but rather because doing so allows them to reaffirm their partisan identity.[2] Adopting one's party's position on an issue signals allegiance with that party—and against the other party (Lenz 2012; Barber and Pope 2019).

When and why will voters be especially motivated to affirm their partisanship by following cues on issues? As we argued in chapter 2, partisan animosity serves as a proxy for partisan (directional) motivations: those with higher levels of animosity are more likely to follow their party's cues because they have a strong drive to be like their own party and different from the other party. Animus, in driving this differentiation between the parties, leads to cue-taking. This linkage, in turn, underscores the realization that past work has missed a key connection between ideological- and animosity-based polarization. Scholars have shown that ideological polarization heightens partisan animosity (Rogowksi and Sutherland 2016; Webster and Abramowitz 2017). Our argument suggests that the reverse also occurs—when partisan animosity drives party cue-taking, it leads to ideological or issue polarization. In turn, this reveals an endogeneity between ideological polarization and animosity (also see Levendusky 2023).

Our theory implies that positions taken by both parties should drive cue-taking. Same-party positions have an obvious connection to cue-taking, as scholars have long recognized (e.g., Zaller 1992). But out-party cues should matter as well; the logic of animosity is both about drawing closer to one's own party, as well as away from the disliked other party. Out-party cues therefore also will shape cue-taking by operating as an "anti-cue" demonstrating what *not* to do—in other words, if the Republicans support X, Democratic voters will support not-X (Nicholson 2012).

Further, as we argued in chapter 2, partisan animosity only drives cue-taking when party elites offer clear and divergent cues on the issue in question. For example, on low-salience issues where party cues are unclear—like, for instance, carbon nanotubes—animus should not drive cue-taking. Alternatively, if party elites agree on the issue (e.g., increasing spending on improving the nation's infrastructure), then even high-animus individuals from different parties will not differ in their views. In contrast, on high-profile issues with sharp elite divides—such as support for the ACA or whether the United States should provide a pathway to citizenship for undocumented immigrants—partisan animosity will drive cue-taking in both parties (i.e., as animus increases, Democrats and Republicans will increasingly diverge on the issue). The clarity of symmetric party cues (i.e., cases where both parties offer cues) leads to clear predictions about how animus maps onto party cue-taking.

The cases where the polarization is asymmetric—where only one party sends a signal of support or opposition and the other party does not (e.g., it divides on the issue)—are somewhat less clear.[3] On the one hand, the cues may be less apparent, which would decrease the incentive for voters to take a position themselves. On the other hand, those with high animus can draw on the signal from their own or the other party to take a position (the latter being an anti-cue). In this case, will an in-party cue or an out-party cue have a larger effect? While both will matter, given the centrality of out-party sentiment to partisan animosity, we expected out-party cues to matter more, as explained in chapter 2. So, for example, if Republicans took a clear position on an issue but Democrats did not, we would anticipate animus-driven polarization on both sides, but especially among Democrats.

Take, for example, the case of defunding the police. In the wake of George Floyd's murder by Minneapolis police officer Derek Chauvin, "Defund the police" became a rallying cry from many on the left, who argued that police funding should shift away from aggressive law enforcement tactics toward social safety spending (i.e., greater funding for mental health care, having social services work more closely with the police, more community policing programs, etc.). The slogan became a focal point among Republican elites, who used it to argue that Democrats would abolish police departments and allow crime and violence to run rampant in America. A prominent Trump advertisement from 2020 said, "Joe Biden's supporters are fighting to defund police departments. Violent crime has exploded. You won't be safe in Joe Biden's America" (Kessler 2020). In contrast, congressional Democrats divided on the issue. Some, especially those on the party's left wing, like representative Cori Bush of Missouri, embraced the position (CBS News 2020), but others—especially suburban Democrats, as well as President Biden—went to great lengths to disavow it (S. Murray 2021). There is an asymmetry in the strength of the cue that was provided: Republicans sent a consensus opposed signal, while the Democratic cue remained ambiguous. We therefore expected the animus effect would be relatively more pronounced among Democrats (following the anti-cue).

Testing Our Argument

To test our argument, we need a set of issues on which either both parties' elites, only one party's elite, or neither party's elites polarize(s); we did this with a battery of issue support measures in our April 2021 wave. Specifically, we identified issues by reviewing newspaper coverage of topics in American politics, as well as using ISideWith.com, a website that aggregates the parties' positions on a wide variety of issues and, thus, shows issues on which partisans agree, those on which they split, and those on which one side takes a clear position while the other does not. We use this cross-issue variation to test our theory's predictions about how the clarity of elite cues affects the relationship between animus and cue-taking.

We chose three long-standing highly divisive policies where both parties took clear positions (symmetric issues): raising the minimum wage to fifteen dollars an hour, supporting the ACA, and providing a pathway to citizen-ship for undocumented immigrants. All these were highly polarized issues. A higher minimum wage has long divided the parties, and the fifteen-dollar minimum wage became prominent in the wake of the "Fight for 15" cam-paign, as well as President Biden's endorsement of it (Alcorn 2021). Ever since its passage in 2010, the ACA has been an ongoing flashpoint in American politics as a defining legacy of the Obama administration (i.e., Democrats strongly support it while Republicans strongly oppose it). And similarly, pro-viding a pathway to citizenship for undocumented immigrants has gained substantial attention in recent years. While the idea had bipartisan backing a decade ago—it was part of the bipartisan "Gang of 8" proposal in the Senate in 2013 (Blake 2013)—since then, the politics of immigration have become de-cidedly more partisan, with the parties' positions diverging (i.e., with Demo-crats being supportive and Republicans opposed). On these three issues, we expect that as animus increases, partisans in each party will polarize.

Issues on which neither party takes a clear position are—almost by definition—lower in salience and less central to political debates. This serves as a plus, not a minus, from our perspective, because it allows us to test the prediction that on these issues, animus should be unrelated to cue-taking. We chose five issues with either no clear partisan position or robust bipartisan support for a position: a ban on government officials becoming lobbyists, an idea supported by both the Trump and Obama White Houses;[4] allowing cities to offer private companies tax incentives to relocate their offices (something supported by officials from both parties though not by economists; see Jensen 2017); allowing unions, private groups, and corporations to make unlimited donations to political parties and candidates (this is effectively the 2010 *Citi-zens United* decision but framed abstractly to avoid triggering partisanship); allowing Medicare to negotiate for lower drug prices, an idea with a long bi-partisan pedigree; and requiring immigrants to take a test on American his-tory and civics as part of the naturalization process (i.e., a status quo policy). On all these issues, the lack of a clear, differentiated policy signal was ex-pected to make animus effectively unrelated to party cue-taking.

Finally, we identified a set of issues on which one party offered a clear cue, while the other party sent a mixed signal (asymmetric issues). We opted for two issues with clear Democratic cues and two with clear Republican cues. On the Democratic side, we used paid family leave and support for an assault weapons ban, as the Democratic Party universally supports these issues and Republican positions remain ambiguous (e.g., Republican senators backed bipartisan gun control legislation in the wake of the May 2022 shooting in Uvalde, Texas, though they stopped short of an assault weapons ban, and a group of congressional Republicans proposed their own version of paid leave in 2019). On the converse side, we selected the Green New Deal and defunding the police, issues on which Republicans offer steadfast opposition and Democratic support varies across the ideological spectrum. How citizens respond to these issues is perhaps most interesting of all—we expected to find animosity effects that may be strongest for partisans from the party that does not offer a clear signal.

Does Animus Drive Cue-Taking?

First, we considered what happens on issues on which both parties send clear and unambiguous cues opposing one another: the ACA, a fifteen-dollar minimum wage, and a pathway to citizenship for undocumented immigrants. We expected that as animus increased, Democrats would increasingly support these three policies and Republicans would increasingly oppose them; put another way, we expected to observe that the distance between the parties widened as animosity increased. Figure 4.1 presents the results.

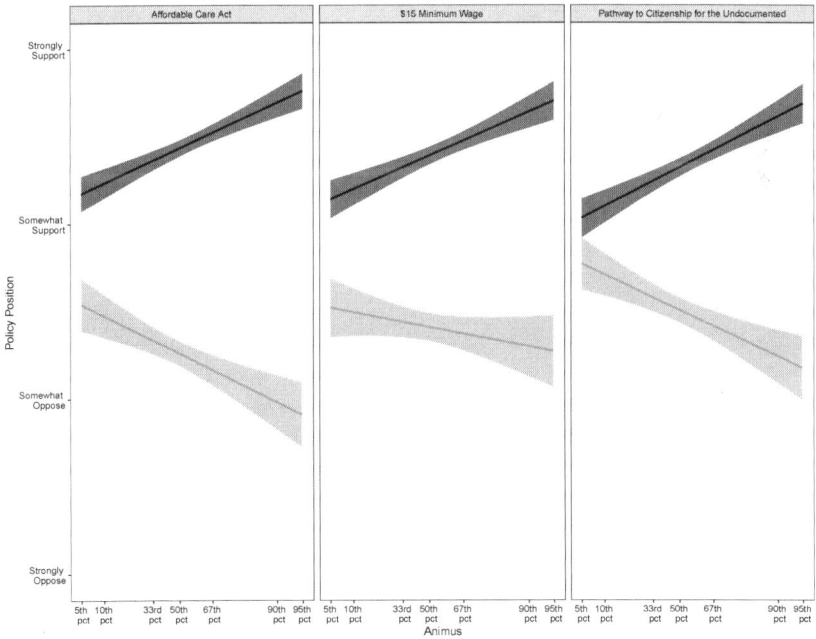

FIGURE 4.1. Cue-Taking When Both Parties Send Clear Cues
Note: The relationship between animosity and issue positions for Democrats is displayed in black; for Republicans, it is displayed in gray. The name of the specific issue in question is displayed at the top of each panel. Data are from the April 2021 wave of the study.

Since this is the first time we present a figure with substantive results, we discuss it in some detail, as we use analogous figures throughout the remaining chapters. Along the x-axis, we arranged respondents' levels of partisan animosity. As we did in chapter 3, we focused on percentiles of the distribution since animus has no natural scale. For example, it is not clear what it means to say that someone has an animus score of 0.54 on a [0,1] scale. Yet it makes sense to designate such a person as being at the 50th percentile (median) on the measure: it indicates that in comparison, half the respondents have more out-party animus and half have less. By focusing on percentiles, we can investigate how the effects shift as we move through the distribution. As we discussed in chapter 3 (and as is clear in the figure), we focus on those at the 5th through the 95th percentile of partisan animosity. Excluding those below the 5th percentile and above the 95th does not change any of our substantive conclusions; it simply focuses on the part of the distribution where we have the most data and precludes unwieldy interpolations (as discussed in chapter 3). On the y-axis, we have the level of support for the policy, and in the body of the graph, we present generalized additive model estimates of the relationship between animus and support for each issue, with Democrats plotted in black and Republicans plotted in gray. We present these results as an easy-to-understand visual summary, but we include regression models and associated sensitivity analyses in appendix 4.1. Readers can find statistical models corresponding to almost all our figures in the appendixes for each chapter at the end of the book.

By focusing on graphical displays throughout the book, we keep our findings straightforward, as the graphs make it obvious what occurs in most cases. That said, the downside concerns the lack of the statistical controls that some readers have surely come to expect, hence the analyses we have included in the appendixes for chapters 3–8.[5] This allows us to keep the body of the book accessible while still providing the necessary details.

Turning directly to figure 4.1, we see that the data strongly confirmed our expectations. Across the three issues, we observed the predicted pattern: as animus increased, Democrats and Republicans increasingly divided on the issue. In each case, low-animus voters were not particularly split on the issues. While Democrats exhibited more support of all three policies than Republicans in all cases, the gaps for low animus respondents remained modest. The gaps quickly increased along with animus, so that by about the 33rd percentile of animus the parties were deeply divided, and the higher the level of animus, the greater was the division. This strongly supports our argument that when the parties take clear and divergent cues on an issue, voters are driven by partisan animosity to follow suit.

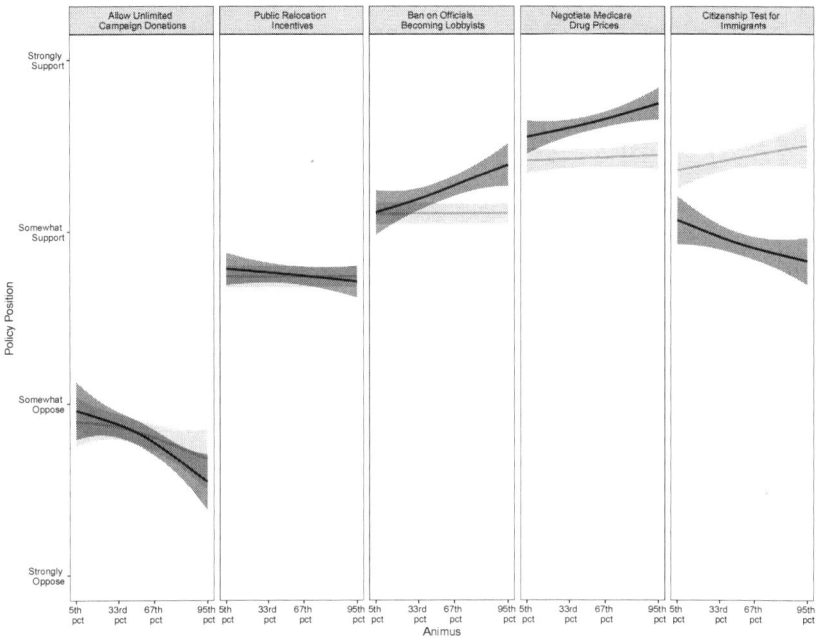

FIGURE 4.2. Cue-Taking When Neither Party Sends Clear Cues

Note: The relationship between animosity and issue positions for Democrats is displayed in black; for Republicans, it is displayed in gray. The name of the specific issue in question is displayed at the top of each panel. Data are from the April 2021 wave of the study.

What about the opposite case—when the parties do not take clear and divergent positions? We turn to our next set of issues, those where we expected to find little to no relationship between animus and issue positions. Figure 4.2 presents the results.

We again found support for our argument. For two of our items—allowing unlimited campaign donations and cities offering public money to relocate their businesses—there was functionally no relationship between attitudes and animus. Higher-animus members of both parties weakly supported banning donations, but there was no divergence at all. Similarly, we saw no relationship between animus and support for state and local governments offering relocation incentives to companies to lure them to their area; instead, there was a modest level of support among all respondents, regardless of party or animus. Positions on these issues were, effectively, uncorrelated with animosity.

For two of the issues, we found extremely slight polarization as animus increased. For the ban on officials becoming lobbyists, there was no effect of animus for Republicans, but for Democrats, as animus increased, so did their support for the proposal. As the graph makes clear, however, the effect of animus was extremely modest and all respondents supported the proposal. Having Medicare negotiate prescription drug prices was even more popular; indeed, it registered as the most popular issue in our survey, consistent with other polling showing strong bipartisan support. Once again, Republican support was independent of animus but support rose as animus increased for Democrats; the relationship for Democrats may stem from the centrality of this issue to well-known liberal senators such as Bernie Sanders of Vermont. But even for the most divided partisans, the differences remained very small, on the order of half a scale point on a 4-point Likert scale. This sharply contrasts with the 2- to 3-point gaps we observed in figure 4.1.

The same cannot be said, however, for our item about requiring immigrants to take a civics and history test (the last panel in the graph). As this policy is basically a description of the status quo, we thought respondents would see it as anodyne. But the inclusion of the word "immigrant" likely triggered sharp partisan motivated reasoning, drawing in the same considerations as the pathway to citizenship item above (though to a lesser degree). Notice that the partisan directions flipped relative to the pathway to citizenship for the undocumented item (see figure 4.1): on that item, animosity led to greater Democratic support and Republican opposition, while on the citizenship test item, the reverse pattern manifested. This makes sense since respondents presumably understand requiring a test as a restriction to immigration (i.e., the inverse of providing a pathway to citizenship).

This finding is an important reminder—which we will see echoed subsequently—that more so than carefully parsing each item, partisans respond to the parties' positions on the broader issue. Overall, however, these items support our hypothesis that without clear policy cues from the parties, animus does not drive issue polarization.

What about our third and final set of items, where only one party sent a clear cue on the issue while the other party's cue appeared muddled (asymmetric issues)? We anticipated that both parties will display animosity effects, with the larger effect when the opposing party offered the clear cue. In our case, that implies that Democrats, more so than Republicans, will have polarized on the Green New Deal and defunding the police items, while the reverse should be true on the assault weapons ban and paid family leave. Figure 4.3 presents these results.

We see a replication of figure 4.1, with both parties diverging as animus increased, on two of our issues: the assault weapons ban and the Green New Deal. No matter which party sent the clear cue, both sides reacted as if cue-taking were symmetric—counter to our prediction that one of the parties

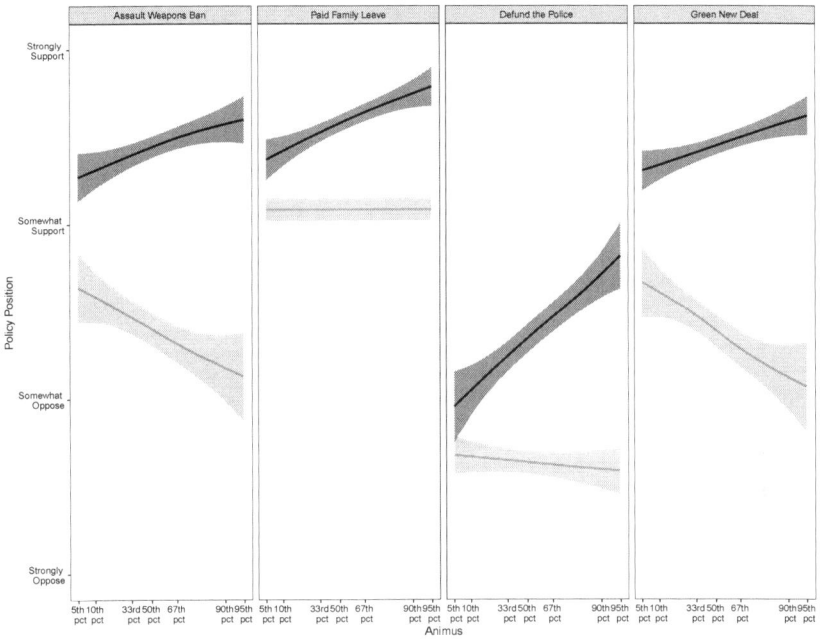

FIGURE 4.3. Cue-Taking When Only One Party Sends Clear Cues
Note: The relationship between animosity and issue positions for Democrats is displayed in black; for Republicans, it is displayed in gray. The name of the specific issue in question is displayed at the top of each panel. Data are from the April 2021 wave of the study.

should have polarized more. It may well be the case that these were not *perceived* as asymmetrically polarized issues. For instance, even if many Democratic politicians—including President Biden—have distanced themselves from the Green New Deal somewhat, in the eyes of many ordinary voters, it remained linked to the party. Indeed, gun policy and climate change have starkly divided the twenty-first-century parties, and voters may not have been attuned to the details of these specific policies. In an era of polarization, it appears difficult to communicate subtler policy distinctions. On the other two issues, we observed some asymmetry, with Democrats, but not Republicans, increasing their support as animus increased (paid family leave and defunding the police). This contradicts our expectation that Republicans, and not Democrats, should have responded to the paid family leave cue.

What does this mean theoretically? It is difficult to say; we do not find support for the asymmetric component of our theory, but animosity clearly mattered for cue-taking in these cases (just not exactly as we anticipated). The most obvious critique of our results is that, as intimated, we chose issues that were too "real world" and in so doing, asked respondents to recognize subtle distinctions between the parties' positions. After all, it would take a great deal of political knowledge to know the nuances of these issues and how they map onto contemporary divisions. Moreover, high-animosity voters tend to be more informed and hence know what issue positions they "should" report on a survey (Groenendyk, Kimbrough, and Pickup 2023). This aligns with our hypothesis (see chapter 2) that high-animus partisans politicize ambiguous targets; if a policy involves an issue area that often generates partisan conflict, these voters will focus on it, politicize the precise policy, and polarize (regardless of policy specifics). This also seemed to have occurred when animosity correlated with polarization on requiring immigrants to take a civics and history test (which we had thought was an issue without cues). In future studies of asymmetric cue-taking, it may be necessary to explicitly manipulate information about the homogeneity of each party's cue (e.g., Levendusky 2010) and/or exercise even more care in selecting issues that are clearly perceived to be asymmetric.

Nevertheless, although we do not see consistent asymmetric patterns, the results show that partisan cue-taking strongly relates to partisan animosity. When parties provide voters with clear signals, partisans who are highest in animosity divide the most sharply in their policy opinions.

Conclusion

In this chapter, we built on our theory in chapter 2 to argue that animus should be related to cue-taking. In cases where the parties provide voters with a clear signal about where they stand on the issues, as animus increases, so too does party cue-taking: voters high in animus both want to adopt their liked party's position and move away from the opposing party's disliked stance. However, when the elites do not send a clear signal about where they stand, animus does not map onto cue-taking. Partisan animosity acts as a mechanism underlying cue-taking in an era of elite polarization. Alternatively, the results in this chapter make clear that animosity matters when cues are clear but not likely to matter when they are not, as we theorized.

This has an important implication for the relationship between animosity and ideological polarization. Past studies show that ideological polarization begets animosity (Rogowski and Sutherland 2016; Webster and Abramowitz 2017). Our findings highlight that animosity drives cue-taking, which in turn, leads to ideological divides. This suggests ideological polarization and animosity (and, hence, affective polarization) are endogenous to one another (Levendusky 2023). Our patterns also underscore why sharp increases in animosity have not translated into large increases in mass ideological polarization.

Animosity drives ideological polarization through a nuanced cue-taking mechanism. As a result, it is not surprising that ideological divisions remain weak even while partisan animosity increases in the mass public.

One limitation of our analyses concerns our inability to disentangle party cue-taking from a party's general reputation on an issue. Even if most Democratic elites do not fully embrace policies like the Green New Deal or defunding the police, their reputation—as the more left-wing party—might lead voters to think that the party supports them. A better approach would be to use a totally novel issue so that the parties' past histories provide no information about how they would handle it. We do just that in the next chapter on the COVID-19 pandemic.

A Political Virus:
How Partisan Animosity Polarized Voters' Responses to the COVID-19 Pandemic

In December 2019, reports began to emerge online that there was a new type of respiratory infection circulating in Wuhan, China.[1] Scientists soon realized that this infection stemmed from a coronavirus and therefore named it coronavirus disease 2019, or COVID-19. At the time, few Americans noticed the story and even fewer thought it had implications for their lives. President Trump seemed to summarize the nation's thoughts on COVID-19 when asked, in late January 2020, whether he was worried about COVID-19. He stated, "No, not at all. We have it totally under control. It's one person coming in from China, and we have it under control. It's going to be just fine" (Belvedere 2020).

However, all was not fine and the country did not have COVID-19 under control. The United States had its first confirmed case on January 20 (though later documentation would show the virus was circulating in the country earlier than that; see Lewis 2021), and it spread rapidly, first in Seattle and California, and then, with the force of a tidal wave, in New York City. The nation watched in horror as New York City hospitals were flooded with cases; ambulance sirens replaced the normal din of the city that never sleeps. Fearing that New York City was prologue, President Trump declared COVID-19 to be a national emergency on March 13. Then, on March 19, California became the first state to issue a stay-at-home order, requiring citizens to remain in their homes unless they had to travel to obtain food, medicine, or other essential services. Only essential workers (e.g., doctors and other medical staff, police, firefighters) were allowed to go to work in person. In the subsequent weeks, forty-two states and territories followed suit, hoping to stop the spread of the virus and prevent the nation's health care system from becoming overwhelmed.

In these earliest days of the pandemic, partisan elites from both parties came together to fight the virus, but such unity was fleeting. While in many other nations, parties of all stripes worked together to combat the virus (L. Fowler, Kettler, and Witt 2020; Merkley et al. 2020), in the United States the issue soon polarized along partisan lines. As we discuss in the next section, Democratic and Republican elites divided over the pandemic, with Republicans—led by President Trump—taking the pandemic less seriously and, more generally, imposing fewer restrictions to combat the virus. This initial polarization only grew as the pandemic became a central issue in the 2020 campaign (Annenberg IOD Collaborative 2023). These divisions established the pandemic as a partisan issue, and therefore, animus became relevant to how citizens responded.

As we discussed in chapter 2, the COVID-19 pandemic allows us to test two of our hypotheses. First, as the elite signals on the pandemic became clearer, the effects of partisan animus should have become clearer as well (i.e., animosity requires the presence of cues). While at the outset, we expected that the gaps between high-animus Democrats and high-animus Republicans would be modest, we also expected that these gaps would grow in size over time as elites polarized (and as cues became clear). Further, over time, even lower-animus citizens should polarize in response to the clearer cues from elites. If we are right, this has a crucial implication for understanding the well-documented partisan divides over COVID-19 in the mass public (see, among many others, Gadarian, Goodman, and Pepinsky 2022). Democrats and Republicans did not simply take divergent positions on the pandemic, they did so because of partisan animosity.

Second, and perhaps even more importantly, the COVID-19 pandemic allows us to test our hypothesis about the role of personal consequences. In chapter 2, we argued that a personally consequential or salient issue interrupts the normal process of animus-driven cue-taking—accuracy goals displace partisan ones and individuals less reflexively follow party cues. Understanding when something is consequential to a given individual is difficult in most cases. However, the pandemic made it easy: those who had suffered from a severe case of the virus or knew someone who had (or anticipated such situations) presumably grasped the potential toll of COVID-19, and so would be expected to do more to seek out accurate information and work to avoid the virus regardless of partisanship (see Constantino et al. 2022). This search for accurate information will displace animus-driven partisan cue-taking, and as a result, the partisan gaps should be smaller when the chances of unwanted consequences increased.

Using our over-time panel data that we introduced in chapter 3, we found strong support for both these predictions. Because elites politicized the pandemic, directional partisan motivations guided how Americans responded to it. While there were partisan gaps between high-animus Democrats' and high-animus Republicans' attitudes toward the pandemic in our April 2020 wave (Druckman et al. 2021a), we show that those gaps grew over time as the parties clarified their cues on this issue. Further, over time, even low-animus voters moved apart as the partisan cues became harder to ignore. Additionally, we show that the severe COVID-19 experiences vitiated the animus-driven cue-taking. Partisan gaps were much smaller among those who were or had been infected with a severe case of COVID-19 or knew someone else in that position (or who anticipated such severe cases). When the virus became personally salient, accuracy motivations—the desire to avoid a deadly virus—replaced more partisan motivations, and the gap between the parties shrank (Constantino et al. 2022). Both these findings have significant implications for how we understand not just the nation's pandemic response but also for how citizens process information more generally.

How the Parties Clarified Their Cues about the Pandemic

In theory, partisanship should be an afterthought during a pandemic. Elected officials should coordinate with federal, state, and local health authorities to prevent the spread of the disease, with scientific advisers—not politicians—taking center stage (e.g., A. Flores et al. 2022). This is the policy that the nation's pandemic guidelines recommended. But as with many things during the Trump administration, the way things ought to have occurred does not match how they did occur.

Arguably, both the political and the public health apparatuses failed. The public health agencies failed to coordinate effectively across the federal, state, and local levels, and, as a result, did not move as swiftly as they could or should have (Lewis 2021). The political missteps were even more evident and more relevant to our story. Almost from the beginning, differences emerged in how the parties reacted to the disease. Democratic governors acted faster to enact stay-at-home orders, order nonessential business to close, require individuals to socially distance, and mandate that citizens wear face masks when in public (see L. Fowler, Kettler, and Witt 2020; Gusmano et al. 2020; Adolph et al. 2021, 2022). In their public communications, Democrats and Republicans talked about COVID-19 quite differently (J. Green et al. 2020). For example, relative to Republican officials, Democratic officials urged caution and encouraged individuals to engage in preventative behaviors like social distancing and mask wearing. These partisan differences were extensively covered by the media, making it easy for the public to notice them (P. Hart, Chinn, and Soroka 2020).

No figure exemplified this partisan division on the pandemic more than President Trump. It took very little time for him to politicize the disease. In a campaign rally on February 28, 2020, he called the Democrats' criticism of his handling of COVID-19 the "new hoax," saying that since they could not defeat him by talking about Russian collusion and election interference, or impeachment, so they had manufactured the hoax of COVID-19 to defeat him in November (Cook and Choi 2020). This contrasted with the concern that Democrats including Biden immediately put forth. Thus, even relatively early in the pandemic, high-animus voters received divergent cues from the parties about how to respond to the virus.

Once it became clear that COVID-19 was not a hoax, but instead was a genuine crisis, Trump downplayed the virus at every opportunity. He felt that attention to the virus would hurt his campaign, so he and his staff repeatedly interfered in the way the administration's scientific experts made their decisions (Diamond 2021; Leonnig and Rucker 2021). He minimized the severity of the virus, likening it to the sniffles (Panetta 2020) and repeatedly asserting that it would disappear on its own (Rieger 2020).[2] Once the CDC urged Americans to wear masks to prevent the spread of COVID-19 in April 2020, Trump undercut the advice, saying that he himself would not be wearing a mask. When asked why, he said, "I just don't want to be doing—I don't know, somehow sitting in the Oval Office behind that beautiful Resolute Desk, the great Resolute Desk. I think wearing a face mask as I greet presidents, prime ministers, dictators, kings, queens—I don't know, somehow I don't see it for myself. I just, I just don't" (Victor, Serviss, and Paybarah 2020). Indeed, Trump would almost never be photographed wearing a mask during the remainder of the pandemic.

The 2020 campaign made these partisan cues impossible to ignore, even for low-animus voters. The campaigns served as walking exemplars of the politicized pandemic. Over the summer, Trump resumed in-person campaign events, including large rallies, even though public health authorities, and his own aides, urged him not to do so (Karni 2020).[3] When people crowded near one another, Trump argued that masks were not required, saying that instead, people should "do what they want" (Swan 2020). For instance, Trump held an event for Supreme Court nominee Amy Coney Barrett at the White House where supporters gathered in close proximity, even indoors, without any sort of a mask mandate. At least eleven attendees subsequently contracted the virus (Yang and Deliso 2020). Further, after he contracted and recovered from COVID-19—a disease that allegedly very nearly killed him (Brewster 2021)—Trump continued to downplay the virus, saying, in a tweet, "Don't be afraid of Covid [*sic*]. Don't let it dominate your life. . . . I feel better than I did 20 years ago!" (Ben-Ghiat 2020). The message from the Trump camp remained consistent throughout the campaign: COVID-19 could largely be ignored, Americans should resume their prepandemic lives, and reopening the economy took precedence over stopping the spread of COVID-19.

Biden, by contrast, took pains at every turn to show that he was following public health guidance. Once COVID-19 emerged in the spring, Biden conducted a largely virtual campaign, appearing via video feed from his basement in Delaware. When in public, Biden always wore a mask and stood socially distanced from his aides. Instead of rallies, Biden had his supporters drive to parking lots, where they honked their car horns to show enthusiasm for his message. Biden argued that we needed to "end the politics and follow the science" (Edelman 2020). Biden also consistently criticized Trump over his handling of the pandemic; Trump's mismanagement of the pandemic became a central theme of Biden's campaign messaging (Annenberg IOD Collaborative 2023). In contrast to Trump, Biden argued life could not resume as normal, even considering the economic costs (Biden 2020). Where Trump zigged, Biden zagged, which made it clear where the parties stood on the virus. In the language of chapter 4, both parties sent the mass public clear (symmetric) cues.

The COVID-19 pandemic in the United States serves as an especially useful test case for our theory. Unlike the issues studied in chapter 4, COVID-19 was totally novel when it emerged early in 2020. Ex ante, citizens could not have known how they "should" respond based on party cues until elites began to politicize and divide on the issue. This also means that our measure of animosity—taken in our July 2019 wave—is truly exogenous to COVID-19 attitudes, since the disease had not yet emerged (see Druckman et al. 2021a). This allows us to track how partisan animosity drove responses to a new issue as elites divided in real time.

To study responses to the COVID-19 pandemic, we examine three broad categories of indicators:

- **Preventative measures taken**: In all three of our pandemic-era survey waves (April 2020, October 2020, and April 2021), we asked respondents about a set of preventative measures that they could take to stop the spread of the virus: wearing a face mask, social distancing from others, working from home, and so forth. Our expectation was that Democrats would engage in more of these behaviors than Republicans and that this would be especially pronounced among higher-animus individuals. In April 2021, we asked about vaccination status with the expectation that high-animus partisans would diverge there as well.

- **Perceived safety of various activities**: In the October 2020 and April 2021 waves, we asked respondents about how safe they felt when engaging in a wide variety of different indoor activities, including exercising in a gym, getting a haircut, traveling in an airplane, and so forth. Our expectation was that Democrats would, on balance, perceive indoor activities as less safe than would Republicans and that this difference would increase along with partisan animosity.
- **Policy support**: In all three of our pandemic-era survey waves, we asked respondents a set of items that measured support for various policies to stop the spread of the virus (i.e., continuing stay-at-home orders, requiring nonessential businesses to stay closed, etc.). Again, we expected to find the standard partisan gap, which should change along with degree of partisan animosity.

In addition to the novelty of the virus, the COVID-19 pandemic allowed us to test our prediction about the role of personal consequences. We expected that as a policy becomes more personally consequential, accuracy motivations should vitiate the directional motives that give rise to animus-fueled partisan divisions. Normally, measuring that sort of salience is a fraught exercise, but the pandemic made it easier to do. The virus mattered most to those who had experienced a severe case or knew someone who had (or anticipated such occurrences). We expected that when salience was high, the partisan gap would shrink: all respondents should take more preventative behaviors, deem various activities to be less safe, and support tougher policies to stop the spread. Given the partisan dynamics of the pandemic, this implies that Republicans (more so than Democrats) would change their behavior.

Did Animosity Drive Reactions to the Pandemic?

Consider what actions people were taking to prevent the virus from spreading. In every pandemic wave (our April 2020, October 2020, and April 2021 waves), we asked respondents to indicate which activities they were engaging in to prevent themselves and others from becoming infected: were they washing their hands more frequently? Were they practicing social distancing? Were they wearing a mask? Were they canceling nonessential travel? We presented respondents with a list of actions they could take and asked them to select all those they had taken. We show responses by wave, allowing readers to view the patterns over time.[4]

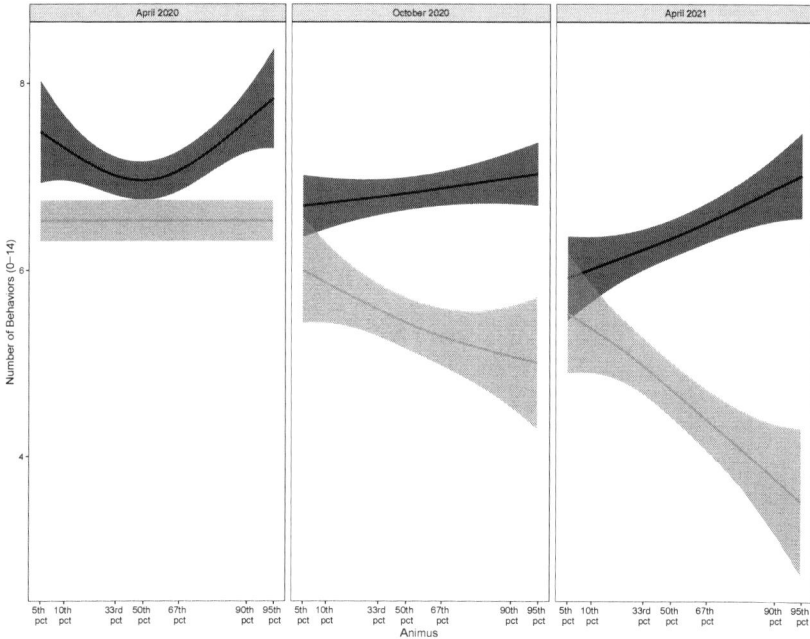

FIGURE 5.1. Animosity and COVID-19 Preventative Behaviors
Note: The relationship between animosity and the number of preventative behaviors undertaken to reduce the transmission of COVID-19 for Democrats is displayed in black; for Republicans, it is displayed in gray. Each panel presents the results from a different wave of the study.

Begin with responses in the April 2020 wave (the left-hand panel of figure 5.1). At that time, the partisan signals were present but were weaker than they would eventually become, so we would expect to see differences primarily among the highest-animus voters. This matches what we saw, with the differences driven more by Democrats than Republicans. The figure shows a curvilinear relationship for Democrats, with those who had moderate levels of animus engaging in the fewest preventative behaviors (though high-animus Democrats engaged in the most). Across levels of animosity, Democrats engaged in more preventative behaviors than Republicans did. As we demonstrated in Druckman et al. (2021a), Democrats were more worried about the pandemic than Republicans, and this greater worry likely translated into additional preventative actions (see also Annenberg IOD Collaborative 2023).

It is fascinating to see that among Republicans, animosity had no effect on the number of preventative activities undertaken (all Republicans, regardless of animosity, engaged in about 6.5 of the 14 activities from our list). Looking at the data activity by activity, all Republicans undertook the low-cost actions, like washing their hands more frequently, using hand sanitizer, and cooking at home more often, which was relatively easy to do in April 2020 as in-person dining was prohibited in most of the country. They avoided the higher-cost activities, such as canceling travel, as they likely felt that they had done enough.[5] In short, early in the pandemic, with only some partisan cue clarity, animus shaped behavior, but mostly for high-animus Democrats.

As the party leaders changed their messages, however, and strongly clarified their cues, voters should have followed suit. We expected to find that as the pandemic continued, (1) high-animus Democrats and high-animus Republicans polarized even more sharply, and that over time, (2) even lower-animus respondents became more divided. We found strong support for these predictions. The gap between the highest-animus respondents increased dramatically over time, from a difference of 1.3 activities in April 2020 to 2.05 activities in October 2020 and 3.56 activities in April 2021, a 173 percent increase over the course of our study. Further, this gap grew at all levels of animus over time, so that by the time of our later waves, even low- and moderate-animus respondents diverged. As the parties' signals about the pandemic crystallized, all voters—not just those who were highest in animus—engaged in the types of cue-taking predicted by our theory.

There is another striking aspect of figure 5.1 that supports our theory. Looking across the waves, it becomes clear that everyone engaged in fewer preventative behaviors over time. This was partially due to pandemic fatigue, but also to a better understanding of the virus itself (which rendered some activities, like wearing gloves, unnecessary), as well as to the vaccines (which reduced the importance of these behaviors). The falloff was smallest for the highest-animus Democrats and largest for the highest-animus Republicans, consistent with our cue-taking theory. Trump's abrogation of these measures, along with Biden's embrace of them, likely drove the behavior of our highest-animus respondents.

Of course, this sort of graphical display, while highly informative, does not fully utilize the panel nature of our data. To do that, we ran a series of panel regression models, analyzing how animus predicts changes in behavior over time. There, we show, consistent with our argument, that animus drove the changes in these behaviors. Throughout the work described in this and future chapters, whenever possible we ran panel data models to complement our graphical analyses of change over time. We have relegated them to the appendixes to avoid cluttering the main presentation of results in the text, but interested readers should consult the appendix for this more rigorous treatment of our data.

Animosity, Masking, and the Vaccine

We can see the predicted patterns in more detail when examining two of the most controversial, but effective, preventative behaviors of the pandemic: wearing face masks and receiving the COVID-19 vaccine. In theory, both should have been relatively uncontested public health recommendations, but because they became ensnarled in partisan politics, they were also likely to fall prey to the logic of animus-driven cue-taking (Pink et al. 2021). Take the case of masking; figure 5.2 presents the data.

In our April 2020 data, there was very little relationship between animosity and mask wearing. While a modest partisan gap existed, it was driven primarily by the behavior of the highest-animus Democrats, but still, only half of them were wearing masks at the time. While this might initially seem surprising, our April 2020 survey took place just a few weeks after the CDC reversed its initial guidance and suggested that everyone should wear a mask. The issue had not been fully politicized, as politicians, public health authorities,

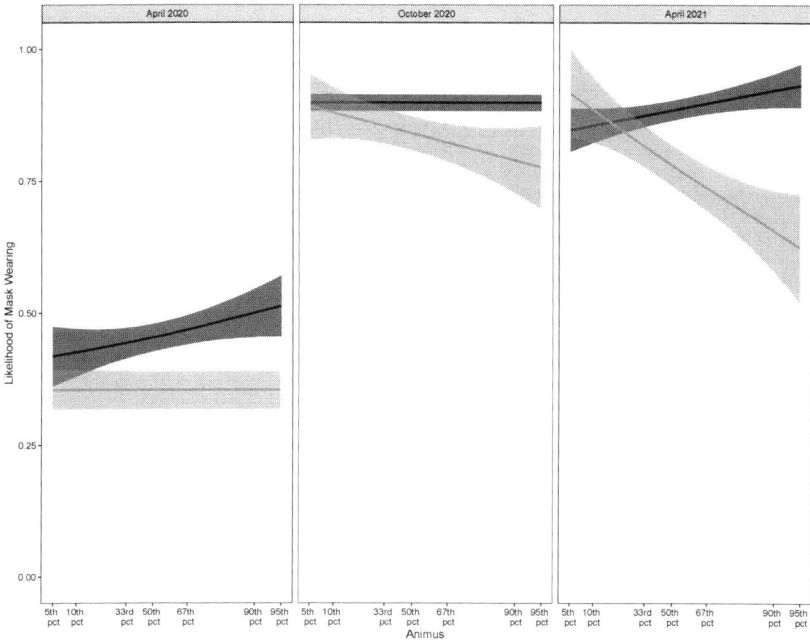

FIGURE 5.2. Animosity and Mask Wearing
Note: The relationship between animosity and wearing a face mask for Democrats is displayed in black; for Republicans, it is displayed in gray. Each panel presents the results from a different wave of the study.

and the public scrambled to figure out how to respond to the new guidance. The fact that higher-animus Democrats were more likely to wear a face mask likely reflected their greater worry about the virus (Druckman et al. 2021a).

We observed a different pattern in our later waves, in two respects. First, the polarization typical of the pandemic revealed itself. As animosity increased, Republicans became markedly less likely to wear a mask, especially by our April 2021 wave. Democrats exhibited some movement toward more mask wearing, but they also faced a ceiling effect (especially in our October 2020 wave). As masks became a political totem, partisans who were high in animosity divided on them sharply (Baxter-King et al. 2022). Over time, a gap also emerged among lower-animus voters, especially by the April 2021 wave, albeit to a much smaller extent. To be clear, that disparity remained modest, but it was apparent nevertheless. As the party leaders clarified their positions on masking and mask wearing became a political symbol, all but the lowest-animus voters followed their party's cues.

These partisan divisions obscure an another, equally important, aspect of the data: mask wearing became a social norm. In our April 2020 data, only 43 percent of our respondents reported wearing a face mask, but that jumped to 88 percent in our October 2020 data and 86 percent in our April 2021 data. Most Americans accepted the scientific consensus that face masks worked to slow the spread of the virus. The slight fall from October 2020 to April 2021 reflected the CDC guidance that fully vaccinated individuals no longer needed to wear a mask (though the agency would soon reverse itself as the Delta variant began to spread throughout the country). So, while we found differences in mask wearing between Democrats and Republicans, especially among those with the highest levels of animosity, it is also notable that most Americans adopted the behavior recommended by public health authorities.

This tension between division and consensus underlies an important point about how the mass media cover politics. Throughout the pandemic, the media ran a number of stories about the politicization of mask wearing (Walsh 2020). As our data show, a partisan divide existed, but focusing on that story ignores the broader effectiveness of the messaging strategy. Further, our data also underscore that the types of Republicans who were least likely to wear masks were the high-animus individuals, who were chronically overrepresented in media coverage of politics (Levendusky and Malhotra 2016). Most people wore masks (perhaps grudgingly), with only a narrow swath of the public refusing. By focusing on a particular subset of Republicans, media coverage distorted perceptions of what was actually occurring in the broader mass public. A small and unrepresentative group of Republicans became the stand-in for the entire party (Scoville et al. 2022) and, in so doing, fueled misperceptions and potentially deepened partisan animosity (Druckman et al. 2022).

What about perhaps the ultimate preventative behavior: receiving the COVID-19 vaccine? In our April 2021 wave, we asked respondents whether they had been vaccinated, and if not, how likely they were to receive the vaccine. The vaccine constitutes an interesting test for our partisan theory because, as we discuss in the next chapter, both Trump and Biden deserve some credit for the vaccine program and the efforts to distribute it to the public. This would seem to blunt its potential as a partisan signal. Yet because President Biden became symbolically attached to the vaccine—making vaccinating the public a goal of his administration and using it as a metric to evaluate his first 100 days in office—it came to be seen through a partisan lens.[6] On the flip side, Trump seemed to go out of his way to avoid endorsing the vaccine, much to the chagrin of his aides (Leonnig and Rucker 2021; Kenen and Mc-Graw 2021). Given this contrast, we expected to find animus-driven partisan polarization. Figure 5.3 presents the results. For the sake of simplicity, we fold those who had already been vaccinated—or had scheduled their appointment at the time of our survey—in with those who were "Extremely Likely" to receive the vaccine.

We found that partisanship colored the likelihood that individuals would receive the vaccine. Among Democrats, there was basically no relationship between animosity and vaccine uptake; at the time of the survey, Democratic respondents had either received the vaccine, were scheduled to receive it, or were extremely likely to receive it when they became eligible to do so.[7] For Republicans, we saw a sharp falloff in vaccine uptake at higher levels of animosity—high-animus Republicans were much less likely to say they would receive the vaccine.

This coheres with our partisan cue-taking mechanism. Democrats saw a whole set of partisan cues pushing them toward the vaccine, especially once President Biden and scientific advisers such as Dr. Fauci strongly advocated for it. For Republicans, in contrast, while Trump arguably deserved credit for the vaccine (due to its development through his Operation Warp Speed initiative), he did not publicly advocate strongly for the vaccine, and thus the cue ran in the opposite direction.[8] To be clear, at the time of our study, other factors also drove vaccine hesitancy (Covert 2021; Edwards-Levy 2021), but partisanship certainly was one of them. The consequences of these vaccine divides became apparent over the course of the pandemic, when large gaps in excess deaths based on partisanship emerged, linked largely to vaccine uptake (Wallace, Goldsmith-Pinkham, and Schwartz 2023). Partisan animus had clear real-world implications.

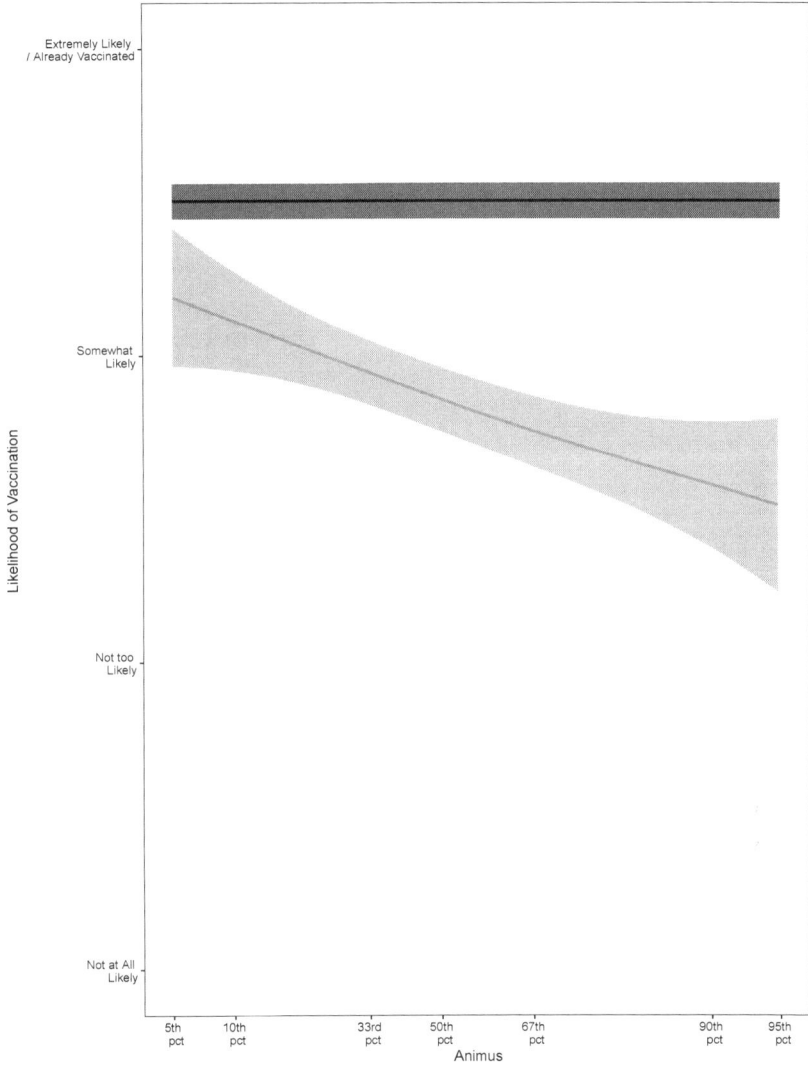

FIGURE 5.3. Animosity and Vaccination
Note: The relationship between animosity and likelihood of receiving the COVID-19 vaccine for Democrats is displayed in black; for Republicans, it is displayed in gray. Data are from the April 2021 wave.

Animus and Perceptions of Safety

The partisan cues throughout the pandemic changed the number of preventative behaviors Americans performed, especially among those who were high in partisan animus. Those same cues should also have changed their impressions of the safety of various indoor activities. Because the COVID-19

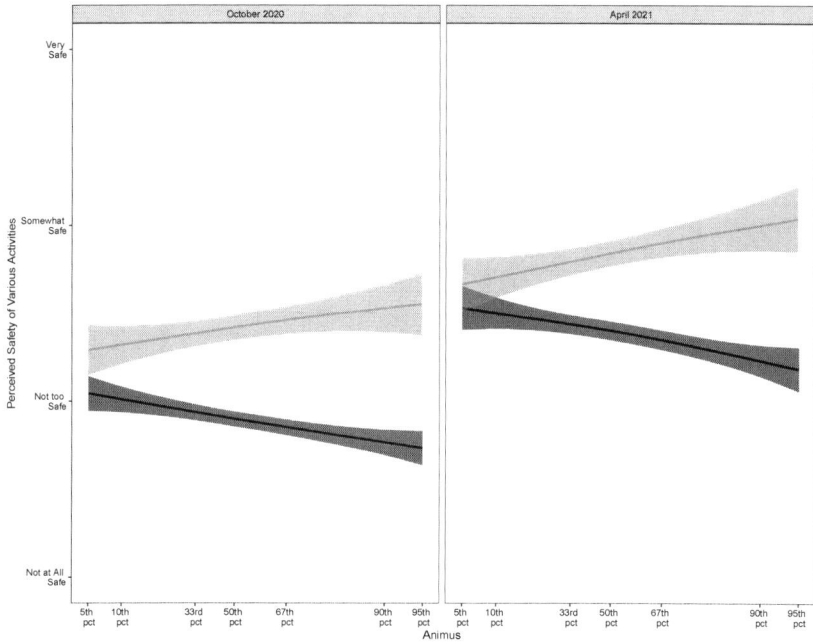

FIGURE 5.4. Animosity and the Safety of Indoor Activities
Note: The relationship between animosity and the average perceived safety of various indoor activities for Democrats is displayed in black; for Republicans, it is displayed in gray. Each panel presents the results from a different wave of the study.

virus spreads through the air, the scientific consensus was that while most outdoor activities were safe, except perhaps in large groups, indoor activities carried much more risk. Given the greater caution displayed by Democrats during the pandemic and the signals from Biden and other political elites, we expected to find animus-driven partisan gaps in the perceived safety of various indoor activities. In our October 2020 and April 2021 waves, we asked individuals to rate the safety of a number of indoor activities, ranging from getting a haircut to exercising in a gym to traveling in an airplane.[9] We predicted there would be gaps in the perceived safety of indoor activities as a function of animosity. Figure 5.4 presents our results.

We found strong support for the first part of our partisan cue-taking argument: the highest-animus Democrats and Republicans diverged, with high-animus Democrats perceiving these indoor activities to be less safe than their Republican counterparts. But contrary to our expectations, we did not find greater divergence over time: the animus-driven gaps in April 2021 look very similar to those in October 2020 (and indeed, in appendix 5.1, we show that this gap did not grow between waves). There is certainly an effect of animosity, but it did not increase over time in the same way as occurred for pandemic-related behaviors discussed earlier in the chapter.

The challenge with interpreting this result is that the safety of these indoor activities did, in fact, change over time once the vaccines became available. In April 2021, the CDC stated that all these indoor activities were safe for fully vaccinated individuals, so it might be that the respondents' referents had changed by our final wave. When we control for vaccination status, we find that those who had been vaccinated thought these activities were safer, but there is no interactive effect by animus, so, alas, it does not explain the over-time pattern.[10] In short, perceptions of safety only partially conformed to our predictions.

Animosity and Support for COVID-Related Policies

What about our final COVID-related outcome: did animus also drive support for various virus mitigation policies? In all three pandemic waves, we asked respondents whether they supported various policies designed to stop the spread of the pandemic. In our April 2020 wave, we asked about support for three policies: requiring essential businesses to close, keeping stay-at-home orders in place, and fining individuals who violated social distancing rules. In the October 2020 and April 2021 waves, because these issues were no longer under discussion, we asked respondents about a different set of more timely policies, including whether schools should be required to hold in-person classes, whether there should be limits on business capacity (i.e., limiting the number of people allowed in a store at a given time), and whether there should be fines for people who refused to wear face masks when required. We analyzed these items as a scale, with higher values indicating more support for the policy designed to reduce the spread of COVID-19 (e.g., support for stay-at-home orders and mask fines, but opposition to in-person classes). We analyzed the April 2020 wave items in Druckman et al. (2021a) and found strong support for our argument. Here, we turn our attention to the other two waves, which allows us to look at change over time.

In the October 2020 and April 2021 waves, we observed animus-driven polarization, as we can see in figure 5.5. In both these waves, the highest-animus respondents were the most divided by party, and in the April 2021 wave, we saw a sharper gap emerge by party. Pulling back across these different outcomes, we saw a consistent picture. Throughout the pandemic, the highest-animus Democrats and highest-animus Republicans polarized in their response to the pandemic. But over time, even lower-animus respondents followed the

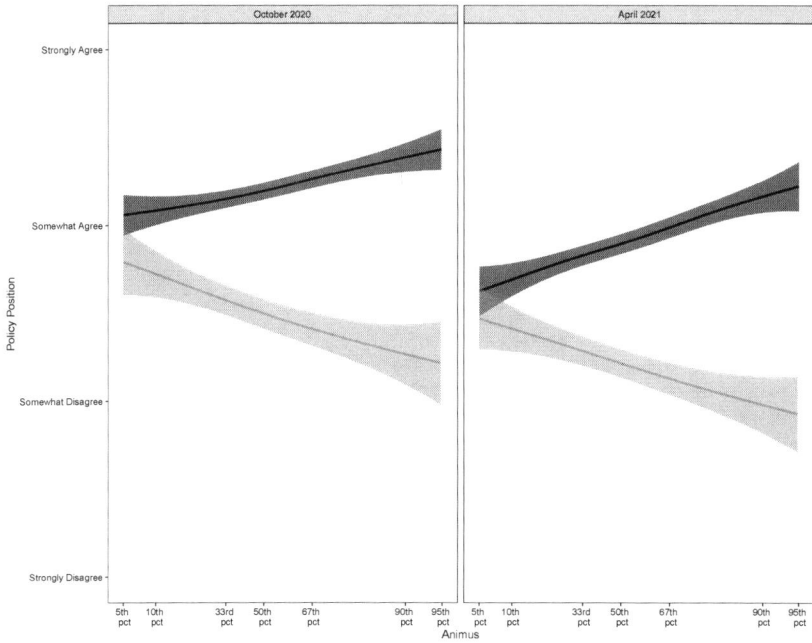

FIGURE 5.5. Animosity and Policy Support

Note: The relationship between animosity and support for policies designed to reduce the spread of COVID-19 for Democrats is displayed in black; for Republicans, it is displayed in gray. Each panel presents the results from a different wave of the study.

partisan cues sent by their parties, so that as the cues became clearer, even lower-animus respondents changed their behaviors. This, in turn, has an implication for how we understand the public opinion dynamics of the pandemic. Partisan gaps in pandemic responses have been well documented (see, e.g., Gadarian et al. 2022; Annenberg IOD Collaborative 2023). We have shown that it is animosity that drives these gaps (also see A. Flores et al. 2022). In the contemporary political milieu, animus drives how partisans interpret political cues.

Do Personal Consequences Vitiate Directional Motivations?

So far we have seen considerable evidence for our argument about cue-taking and partisan animus. Now we turn to testing another aspect of our argument. We hypothesized that animus-driven polarization would not always hold; when citizens perceive an issue to be personally consequential, the logic of cue-taking changes. Personally consequential issues heighten the effects of accuracy goals, thereby displacing partisan ones. Because COVID-19 is a highly contagious respiratory virus, individuals who view it as a severe threat will attend to its potentially lethal consequences. They thus will seek out the most accurate information possible about the virus—information from public health and medical officials. This should lead them to engage in more preventative behaviors, perceive various indoor activities as less safe, and be more supportive of policies to stop the spread of the virus.

There are multiple ways of measuring the salience of COVID-19. One could use contextual information: those living in an area where COVID-19 spread rapidly should perceive it to be more consequential. This was true early in the pandemic, when the virus was concentrated in a small number of areas in the United States. In Druckman et al. (2021a), we used this measure of salience (the number of cases in a respondent's county, averaged over the three days prior to their interview) and found strong moderating effects. This sort of contextual measure became less meaningful once the virus had spread throughout the country, however, as it had by our October 2020 wave. Not surprisingly, other analyses have found that the severity of COVID-19 in an area affected attitudes early in the pandemic but not later on (Bisbee and Lee 2022). In our subsequent waves, we thus used our respondents' personal experiences with COVID-19 (also see Constantino et al. 2022). If the respondent or someone whom they know had a severe experience with COVID-19 (or they anticipated such an experience), the disease should be more salient to the respondent.[11] We preregistered the change in our salience measure for the October 2020 and April 2021 waves.

We expected the effects of salience to manifest more for Republicans than for Democrats. For Republicans, heightening the consequences of the disease exposed the incongruity of their partisan directional motivations. If the disease was not salient, then Republicans would downplay it to signal their allegiance with their party. As it became more consequential, they realized that their directional goal may not have served them well and an accuracy motivation overtook it; in turn, they took the disease more seriously. This argument implies that when respondents experienced or knew people with severe cases of COVID-19, the partisan gap will shrink.

Did having or knowing someone who had a severe case of COVID-19 (or anticipating it) undo the impact of animosity on preventative behaviors, perceived safety, and support for COVID-19 mitigation policies? Since we split the data by severity, we pooled the October 2020 and April 2021 waves; if we analyzed them separately we would see the same patterns, but they would be much noisier because we would have half as much data. Our severity argument does not have a time-varying component, and thus, merging these two surveys should not bias our results. We present the results for preventative

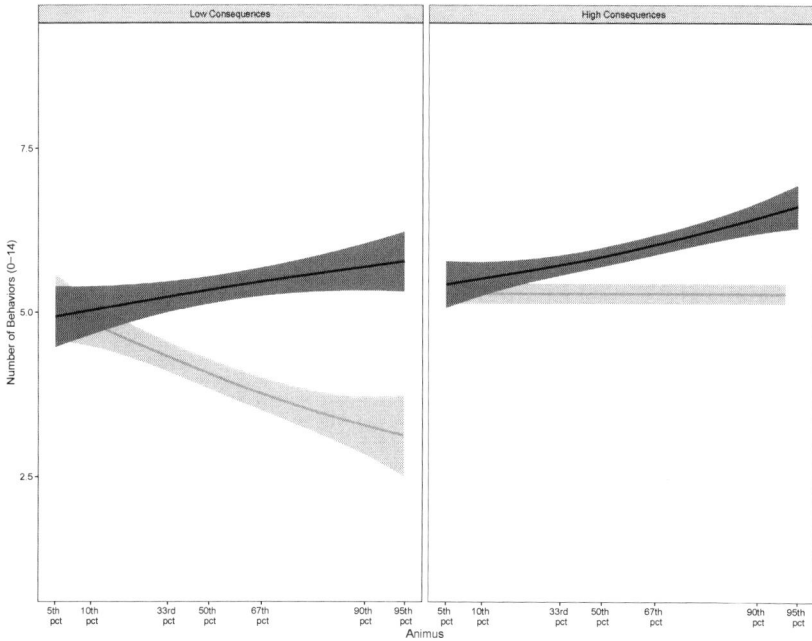

FIGURE 5.6. Animosity, Preventative Behaviors, and COVID-19 Consequences
Note: The relationship between animosity and the number of preventative behaviors undertaken to reduce the transmission of COVID-19 for Democrats is displayed in black; for Republicans, it is displayed in gray. The left-hand panel gives results for respondents for whom COVID-19 was not consequential, and the right-hand panel gives results for respondents for whom the virus was consequential.

behaviors in figure 5.6, perceived safety in figure 5.7, and policy support in figure 5.8.[12]

In all three plots, those for whom COVID-19 was personally consequential appear in the right-hand column, while those for whom it was not appear in the left-hand column.[13] Across all three figures, we found a consistent pattern of results. First, we observed a general "intercept shift"; those for whom the virus was highly consequential took more preventative behaviors, viewed activities as less safe, and more strongly supported policies to mitigate the virus. This provides evidence of strong construct validity for our salience measure.

Second, these results reinforce our theory. Among those for whom the virus was not consequential (the left-hand column), we see the expected pattern of sharp animus-driven polarization: as animus increased, so too did the partisan gap. But for those who saw the virus as consequential (the right-hand column), that gap appears markedly smaller. Third, that smaller gap primarily stemmed from changes in the behavior of Republicans. Among

Republicans, viewing the virus as consequential led them to alter their behavior and dislodged their partisan motivation (to downplay the virus). For Democrats, these motivations pointed in the same direction (to take the virus seriously), the effect appeared more modest. Personal consequence thus vitiated partisan motivated reasoning.

A further way we can test our argument exploits the panel nature of our data. Recall that we asked about personal experiences with the COVID-19 pandemic in both our October 2020 and April 2021 waves. Thus, some respondents will have experienced (or know someone who had experienced) a worse case of COVID-19 in April 2021 than they had in October 2020. Indeed, in our sample, 21 percent had experienced a worse case of COVID-19 by April than they had in October, consistent with the fact that the peak of the pandemic occurred that winter, before vaccines became widely available to the public. Having experienced a worse case of COVID-19, did they become more cautious about the disease? Did they take more preventative behaviors, did they think activities were less safe, and were they more supportive

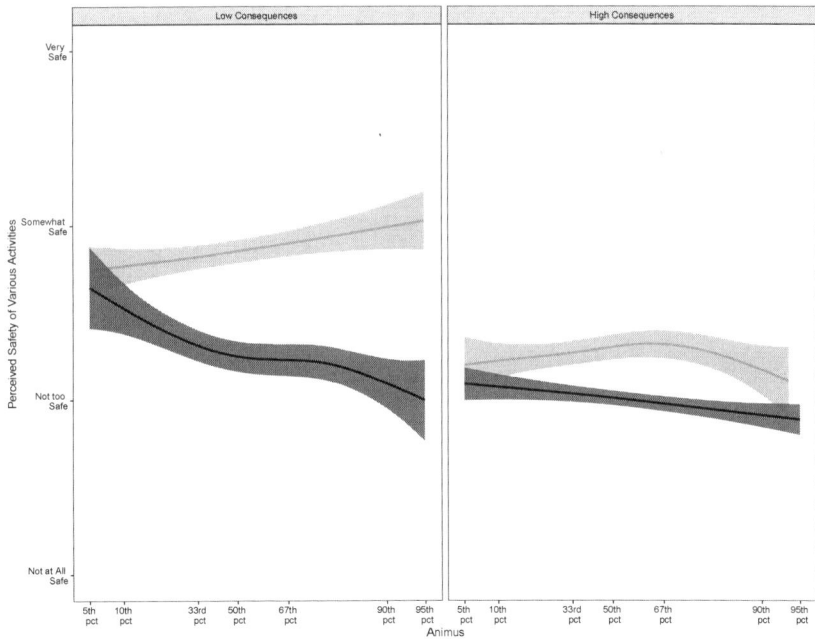

FIGURE 5.7. Animosity, Perceived Safety, and COVID-19 Consequences
Note: The relationship between animosity and the perceived safety of various indoor activities for Democrats is displayed in black; for Republicans, it is displayed in gray. The left-hand panel gives results for respondents for whom COVID-19 was not consequential, and the right-hand panel gives results for respondents for whom the virus was consequential.

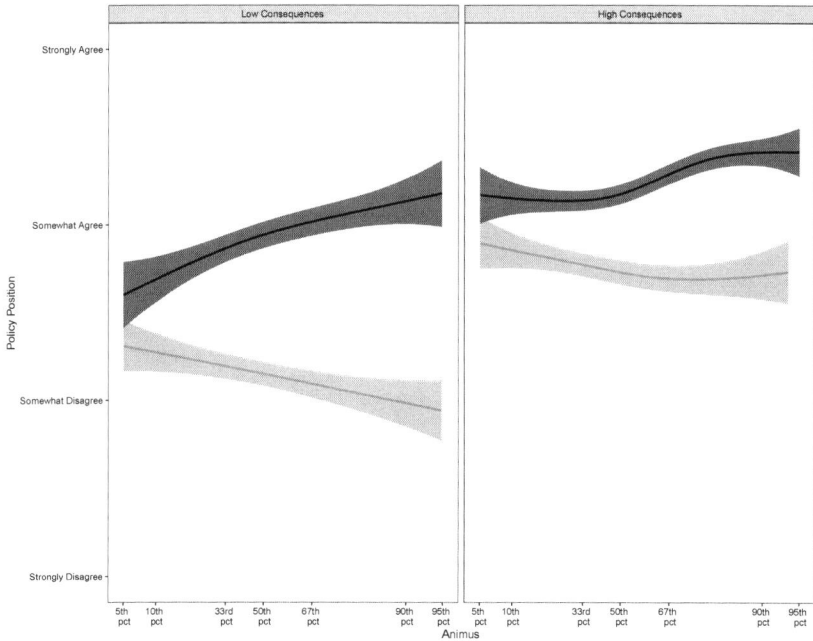

FIGURE 5.8. Animosity, Policy Support, and COVID-19 Consequences

Note: The relationship between animosity and support for policies designed to reduce the spread of COVID-19 for Democrats is displayed in black; for Republicans, it is displayed in gray. The left-hand panel gives results for respondents for whom COVID-19 was not consequential, and the right-hand panel gives results for respondents for whom the virus was consequential.

of policies to stop its spread, in April 2021 relative to October 2020? In essence, did people's attitudes shift in response to experiencing the effects of the pandemic?

We estimate the model $\Delta y_i = \beta_0 + \beta_1 \Delta cm_i + \varepsilon_i$, where $\Delta y_i = y_{i, April 21} - y_{i, Oct 20}$ (i.e., the change in respondent i's preventative behaviors, perceived safety, and policy support between our April 2021 and October 2020 waves), and $\Delta cm_i = cm_{i, April 21} - cm_{i, Oct 20}$ is the change in their most severe experience with COVID-19 between those same two waves. This is a standard two-period first-differences model, which removes any between-subjects heterogeneity and focuses on within-subject variation. This makes for a powerful test: does a given person change their behavior when they encounter worse cases of the virus? Table 5.1 presents the results for both the sample as a whole and Republicans only.

We found strong support for our argument. The intercept revealed what happened to those who had no change in their most severe experience of COVID-19 (or saw a less severe case as the worst-case scenario, likely reflect-

TABLE 5.1. Change in Personal COVID-19 Severity and Change in Attitudes, October 2020–April 2021

	Safety (all)	Behavior (all)	Policy (all)	Safety (Republicans only)	Behavior (Republicans only)	Policy (Republicans only)
Constant	0.427***	−0.466***	−0.277***	0.413***	−0.809***	−0.333***
	(0.018)	(0.068)	(0.017)	(0.033)	(0.121)	(0.032)
Change in	−0.079***	0.345***	0.069***	−0.100**	0.501***	0.104**
COVID-19	(0.019)	(0.072)	(0.018)	(0.035)	(0.128)	(0.034)
severity						
N	1,823	1,828	1,826	562	564	564
R^2	0.009	0.012	0.008	0.015	0.027	0.017

Note: Cell entries are OLS regression coefficients with associated standard errors in parentheses;
*$p < 0.1$; **$p < 0.05$; ***$p < 0.01$ for two-tailed tests.

ing their beliefs about the vaccine's efficacy). We can see that these individuals perceived activities to be safer, engaged in fewer preventative behaviors, and expressed less support for restrictive policies; this coheres with the data shown earlier in the chapter (i.e., on balance, people became less concerned with the pandemic over time). When respondents experienced (or anticipated) worse cases of COVID-19 over time, however, their behavior moved in the opposite direction—they perceived activities to be less safe, engaged in more preventative behaviors, and expressed more support for restrictive policies. We observed this pattern both among the sample as a whole (columns 1–3) and when examining only Republicans (columns 4–6). When personal experiences changed, so too did behaviors and attitudes.

Overall, we find a clear pattern: when the virus became personally consequential, partisan motivations faded and accuracy motivations took their place. Republicans consequently changed their behavior and emulated Democrats, and, more generally, the partisan gap dramatically shrunk.[14] The wedge between the parties induced by animosity diminished.

Conclusion

A public health pandemic might seem like an odd place to test a theory about politicization, but, sadly, given the contours of the COVID-19 pandemic in the United States, it proved to be fertile ground to assess our argument. In this chapter, we showed that as politicians politicized the pandemic and sent voters coherent signals about how pandemic behavior mapped onto political attitudes, polarization ensued. Throughout the pandemic, it was the highest-animus Democrats and Republicans who were the most affected by these cues, and hence the most polarized. As these cues clarified over time, even lower-animus Americans increasingly divided over the pandemic, though never to the same extent as those with the highest levels of animus. Overall, the partisan gaps widely noted by scholars and commentators were driven largely by animus.

However, this animus-driven polarization can be dampened. When the virus became personally consequential to people, their behavior changed as accuracy motives dislodged directional ones. And we showed that this is exactly what happened. For those for whom the virus was personally consequential, the partisan gap shrunk considerably as all respondents—regardless of partisanship—took the virus more seriously. This highlights the crucial role of politicization versus personalization. When a topic is highly politicized, cues become quickly available and animus shapes responses. Yet, when instead it becomes personally consequential, the role of animosity and partisanship can fade or disappear.

After we finished our data collection, we saw an example of the personal consequence argument. In summer 2021, the Delta variant became the dominant variant of COVID-19 spreading throughout the United States. In areas of the country with low vaccination rates, the virus spread like wildfire, and hospitals filled up largely with unvaccinated patients. Rochelle Walensky, the CDC director, said COVID-19 had become "a pandemic of the unvaccinated" (Anthes and Petri 2021). The wave of cases, hospitalizations, and deaths led some of those who had been vaccine hesitant to get vaccinated (Eunjung Cha, Hansen, and Dupree 2021). To be clear, vaccination remained strongly correlated with partisanship (Wallace, Goldsmith-Pinkham and Schwartz 2023), testifying to the power of animus and partisan signals. But, nevertheless, behavior did change, at least among some people.

Reading this chapter, one could reasonably ask about the inevitability of a polarized pandemic: no matter what Trump did or how Biden responded, in our contemporary political moment of extreme polarization, division over the pandemic was a given. But that is incorrect. Imagine, as a counterfactual scenario, that Mitt Romney had edged out Barack Obama in the 2012 election and that in January 2020, President Romney sat in the Oval Office (finishing a second term).[15] One could easily imagine him taking steps earlier to address the pandemic; coordinating the response of federal, state, and local actors; emphasizing the importance of wearing masks; and so forth. Had the president set a different course, then the pandemic would have played out differently. The vaccine serves as another case in point. Once it became clear that Biden had won the election and the vaccines had been proven to be safe and effective, Trump's aides begged him to stop talking about election fraud and instead focus on promoting the vaccine (Pink et al. 2021). Had Trump argued forcefully for the vaccine—and made it an in-group symbol among Republicans—the partisan dynamics would have played out quite differently (especially if President Biden had continued the push while giving credit to his predecessor). Indeed, Pink et al. (2021) found that hearing Trump endorse the vaccine substantially increases vaccine intentions among Republicans (also see Larsen et al. 2022). The polarization stemmed, in no small part, from President Trump's behavior. His polarizing actions led the country down this path.

In turn, we can see how polarizing a public health crisis can literally be the difference between life and death (Gollwitzer et al. 2020; Rodriguez et al. 2022). Achieving coordination between the various levels of the public health infrastructure—federal, state, and local—is difficult even at the best of times (Lewis 2021), which highlights the complexities of American federalism (Kettl 2020). Setting aside that issue, however, politicization crippled the U.S. response and led to the ensuing polarization. By making how to respond to the pandemic an issue of partisan politics, the country sidelined experts and avoided the steps needed to prevent excess deaths and countless untold cases of suffering.

The politicization of the pandemic also highlights a point about elite messaging. The case of mask wearing shows what happens when there is confusion in the initial messaging. Initially, public health officials believed that masks were effective at stopping the spread of COVID-19, but they worried that people would hoard masks and then health care workers would be left without them (Tufekci 2020). This undercut their credibility when they reversed course and recommended mask wearing several weeks later. This sort of mixed messaging, along with the uncertainty it promotes, made it easier for mask wearing to become politicized (Milosh et al. 2021). Had there been strong messaging on the key point—to wear a mask but save the N95 masks and respirators for health care professionals—it would have been harder to politicize this message. In short, clear communication and good administration are important bulwarks against politicization and polarization.

6

Partisan Animosity and Evaluations of Political Leaders

A few months into Biden's tenure as president, the political website FiveThirty
Eight.com noted that a striking pattern had emerged in American politics:
the classic presidential honeymoon had ceased to exist (Skelly 2021a). From
the start of Biden's administration, Republican voters did not simply disapprove of Biden—they *strongly* disapproved of him, even before he had any
legislative or administrative record to evaluate (Skelly 2021b). Indeed, their
disapproval was not of Biden per se, but rather that a Democrat was sitting
in the Oval Office—they were opposed to the president because of his partisanship, rather than his actions. While the trend was most pronounced for
Biden, the same finding had emerged in the Trump and Obama presidencies,
reflecting the fact that "citizens are increasingly substituting in partisanship
for approval" of the president and other leaders (Donovan et al. 2020, 1214).

This shift represents a threat to democratic accountability. Democracies
require that voters reward their representatives for successes and penalize
them for failures—and, in equal measure, that elected representatives anticipate such rewards and punishments. This induces leaders to push for "peace
and prosperity" (Hibbs 1989), as that ensures high approval and, in turn, legislative victories (J. Bond, Fleisher, and Wood 2003; Rivers and Rose 1985)
and reelection (J. Campbell 2016). But if approval has become a function of
partisanship—and not what leaders do—presidents lose a key incentive that
drives them to pursue good policies that benefit the nation (Hetherington and
Rudolph 2015). Has partisan animosity made it so that voters will never credit
elected officials from the other party, even when they enact good policy?

We examine how animus shapes evaluations of political leaders using the
framework developed in earlier chapters. Evaluations of partisan leaders inherently involve politics, and that triggers directional goals and a defense of

one's partisanship (Groenendyk and Krupnikov 2021). People who are higher in partisan animus respond more to party cues in general, and this likely translates to evaluations. Therefore, we expect that (1) those who are higher in animosity will politicize ostensibly neutral figures (in line with our hypothesis about ambiguous targets), (2) as animosity increases, so too will the partisan gap in (political) leader approval, and (3) as leaders become more closely linked to a political party, over time the partisan approval gap will increase, as even low-animus partisans divide in their evaluations of them. We use both variation between leaders and variation within individual leaders over time to test the expectations.

Moreover, as with the previous chapter, we use the COVID-19 pandemic to assess our prediction about personal consequences and their effect on the impact of animus. When an issue is personally consequential to someone, the normal process of animus-driven cue-taking short-circuits—accuracy goals displace partisan ones and individuals less reflexively follow their party's cues. We test this prediction by examining how our respondents evaluated scientific figures such as Dr. Fauci, the CDC, and the FDA. In theory, these are apolitical scientific advisers, but given the course of the pandemic and their public clashes with President Trump, they became partisan entities. Yet for those who experienced a severe case of COVID-19 or knew someone who did (or anticipated either), this effect should have been attenuated and the partisan gap should shrink considerably. Such individuals, regardless of partisanship, become motivated to access the highest-quality relevant science, and therefore to trust and approve of these leaders.

The data strongly confirm our hypotheses. In particular, this chapter reports four main findings. First, we show that people with higher levels of animosity politicize politically neutral, but potentially ambiguous, entities. In our April 2020 wave, we conducted an experiment in which we asked respondents to evaluate either President Trump's COVID-19 response or the United States' COVID-19 response. As we would expect, all voters polarized when asked about President Trump; even those with low levels of animosity viewed him through a partisan lens (although those with higher animus polarized more). On the other hand, we found that only among higher-animus partisans, the United States became a metaphorical stand-in for President Trump. As a result, only these participants polarized when asked about the nation. As partisan animosity increases, everything—even the nation itself—becomes linked to partisanship. Partisan animosity expands the scope of the political (see also Druckman et al. 2021b).

Second, we show that the more politicized a figure is, the more animosity drives responses to them. In our panel data, over time we tracked approval of several political figures at all levels of government from mayors, to state and local officials, to Presidents Trump and Biden. We show that for most voters, animus strongly predicted approval for highly politicized figures like President Trump or President Biden (although even partisans who are low in animus polarize somewhat in these cases). Approval of less politicized figures—such as state and local officials or mayors—depended much less on animus. While all elected officials are political they are not equally politicized, and this shapes public evaluations.

Third, we show that as figures politicized over time, the partisan approval gap grew. Over the course of our study, initially apolitical public health authorities—people like Dr. Fauci and institutions like the CDC—became figures of partisan controversy. As a result, animus had a larger effect on individuals' evaluations of them. Finally, we show that for respondents who viewed COVID-19 as personally consequential, the approval gap for scientific figures shrank, often quite markedly. Given the partisan dynamics of the pandemic, these effects primarily occurred among Republicans, with implications for understanding partisan dynamics over public health.

How Does Partisan Animosity Shape Leader Evaluations?

A voter's evaluation of an elected political leader invariably becomes political, given the partisan nature of elections. Directional goals, including a defense of the voter's partisanship, are therefore inherent in how voters assess political elites (Leeper and Slothuus 2014). Because directional goals have been implicated, individuals high in animosity have more motivation to differentiate themselves from the disliked out-group (and also draw themselves closer to the liked in-group).

This has several implications for how animus shapes evaluations. Those high in animosity will see more people and entities as political—even those that someone with less disdain for the out-party might not view as political at all.[1] This can play out in two related ways. First, those high in animosity will be more attentive to any partisan cues that exist, even weak ones given their motivation to find them. For example, early in the pandemic, when most Americans still viewed Dr. Anthony Fauci as an apolitical scientific adviser, that may not have been true for those with high animosity. Dr. Fauci publicly critiqued some of President Trump's statements about the pandemic, potentially leading those with higher levels of animosity (on both sides of the political spectrum) to perceive him as someone opposed to President Trump, for good or for ill. Our argument is not simply that those with high animus attend more to politics. Rather, these individuals also possess the motivation to act on partisan cues; it is that motivation that does the theoretical heavy lifting. Those who are interested in politics, but not high in animus, are unlikely to politicize to the same extent as their higher-animus peers.

Similarly, those high in animus politicize objects that lack clear partisan cues (but can be politicized). Since they view the world through partisan-colored glasses, they will see neutral but ambiguous objects as partisan. For example, Hetherington and Rudolph (2015) show that those high in partisan animosity trust government when their party holds power, but not when the opposing party does. Why? For them, the government is not an abstract entity in Washington, DC, composed of the three branches of the government, bureaucrats, and so forth. Instead, it is exemplified by the president. When Trump sat in the Oval Office, high-animus Republicans trusted the government because they trusted Trump. Once Biden took the oath of office, that trust evaporated; the converse was true for high-animus Democrats. In much the same way, those high in animus politicize other national symbols, such as the American flag (Nir 2021) or even the nation itself.[2] For voters high in animosity, few objects escape the pull of partisanship.

The centrality of partisanship also means that voters high in animosity more strongly approve of figures linked to their in-party, and more strongly disapprove of leaders linked to the out-party. This leads to divergent leader evaluations. Democrats and Republicans who have high levels of animosity will have more polarized evaluations of political figures than those with lower levels of animosity. This logic leads to a second implication of our theory for leader evaluations—the clearer the partisan cue about the leader in question, the larger the effect of animus. Clear cues emerge when a political figure epitomizes their party. In the present moment, the president constitutes such a figure. Indeed, the president functionally stands in for "the party" in the minds of voters (G. Jacobson 2019). Given this, even low-animosity voters will divide in how they perceive the president, though we would still expect that divide to grow as animosity increases. The same has become increasingly true of other federal office holders, such as Senators and members of the House of Representatives. While at one time these officials cultivated a personal vote that differentiated them from their party's brand (Cain, Ferejohn, and Fiorina 1987), today the personal vote has functionally disappeared, having been replaced by party (G. Jacobson 2015; Lapinski et al. 2016).[3] This can be seen in the shrinking number of "mismatched" members; that is, Democrats who represent districts carried by the Republican nominee for president (and the reverse), which were once common but are now increasingly rare. In the 118th Senate, for example, there were only five such senators: Sherrod Brown (Ohio), Joe Manchin (West Virginia), and John Tester (Montana) on the Democratic side of the aisle and Susan Collins (Maine) and Ron Johnson (Wisconsin) on the Republican side. One could even argue that the real number is four, not five, as it is debatable whether Johnson is truly mismatched in a state Biden carried in 2020 by 0.6 percent (just over 20,000 votes out of almost 3.3 million cast in the state).[4] For prominent national politicians, partisanship trumps nearly everything.

But for many other political leaders, this need not hold. For example, while partisanship plays an important role in how some governors brand themselves—think of Kristi Noem in South Dakota, Gavin Newsom in California, or Ron DeSantis in Florida—it does not do so for others. Indeed, some governors actively cultivate a brand that sets them apart from their national party. For example, Charlie Baker of Massachusetts, Larry Hogan of Maryland, and Phil Scott of Vermont all enjoyed high levels of approval during their time in office despite being Republicans representing states that overwhelmingly voted Democratic at the presidential level.[5] Former Montana governor Steve Bullock illustrates the difference in how voters see a governor versus a senator. As governor, distancing himself from his party's brand enabled Bullock to accentuate personal, rather than partisan, qualities and win two terms in the governor's mansion in a red state.[6] However, when he ran as a Senate candidate in 2020, he came to be seen as a vehicle to empower Bernie Sanders, Elizabeth Warren, and other Senate liberals, so voters saw him through a partisan lens (and hence he lost his race). Without an ability to project a separate brand, voters viewed Bullock as just another Democrat and hence divided along party lines.

This applies even more to officials at the local level. While the partisanship of some big-city mayors is obvious, for most local officials it remains opaque. Jin et al. (2023) asked 833 Americans from 724 towns across the country to report their mayor's partisanship and found that 27 percent could not even hazard a guess as to which party their mayor belonged. The three respondents from Atlanta, Georgia, all (correctly) identified their city's mayor, Keisha Lance Bottoms, as a Democrat. But the respondent from Darien, Georgia, did not know the party of their mayor, a man by the name of Bubba Hodge, and neither did the people from the four other towns across Georgia who participated in the nationwide study. A team of graduate students sought to find out these mayors' party affiliation and had no better luck than did the respondents. While an educated guess—based on endorsements or donations—is sometimes possible, it requires far more work than the average voter will invest. The limited salience of local officials' partisanship is reinforced by analyses of the language they use (Das et al. 2022), as well as their spending priorities (Ferreira and Gyourko 2009; Gerber and Hopkins 2011). Although partisans who are high in animosity may politicize seemingly neutral figures, they require *some* partisan cue to motivate them to do so; these types of even-minimal cues, however, often do not appear in local contexts. As a result, we expect that partisan animosity will have a smaller effect on evaluations of local politicians, especially when compared with evaluations of federal officials, and particularly the president.

What Do Voters See as Political?

We begin by testing our hypothesis that animus will be positively correlated with opinions (in the absence of clear party cues) if the target is politically ambiguous. All voters—even those with the lowest levels of animus—will view salient figures as political, and hence their partisanship will shape their evaluations. Those who are high in animosity will see much more as political, which falls under the umbrella of partisanship, and by extension, partisan animosity.

We assess this argument by examining how voters evaluated the nation's response to the COVID-19 pandemic. In our April 2020 wave, during the early days of the pandemic, we asked them to assess how the country was handling the ongoing COVID-19 outbreak. We randomly assigned participants to be asked either about President Trump's response or the United States' response (for more details on this experiment and full analyses of the data, see Druckman et al. 2021b). We expected that all respondents, even those with relatively low levels of animosity, would polarize when asked about President Trump's response, with Republicans much more likely to respond positively (given that Trump epitomizes the Republican Party). However, we anticipated that only those with higher levels of animosity would polarize when asked about the United States' response. For most voters, a "United States" frame would prime national identity, and the effects of partisanship would therefore abate (Levendusky 2018). But high-animus partisans would also politicize the United States, equating the country with the federal government, and hence President Trump.

To test this hypothesis, we estimated how approval of the COVID-19 response changed as a function of the respondent's level of partisan animus in both conditions (Trump and the United States), separately for Democrats and Republicans. Figure 6.1 presents the results.

In figure 6.1, in the left-hand panel shows how voters evaluated the United States' response, and the right-hand panel shows how they evaluated President Trump's response. Here we begin first with those asked to evaluate President Trump's response. We found a clear pattern of partisan polarization, where the average Republican approved of the president's response much

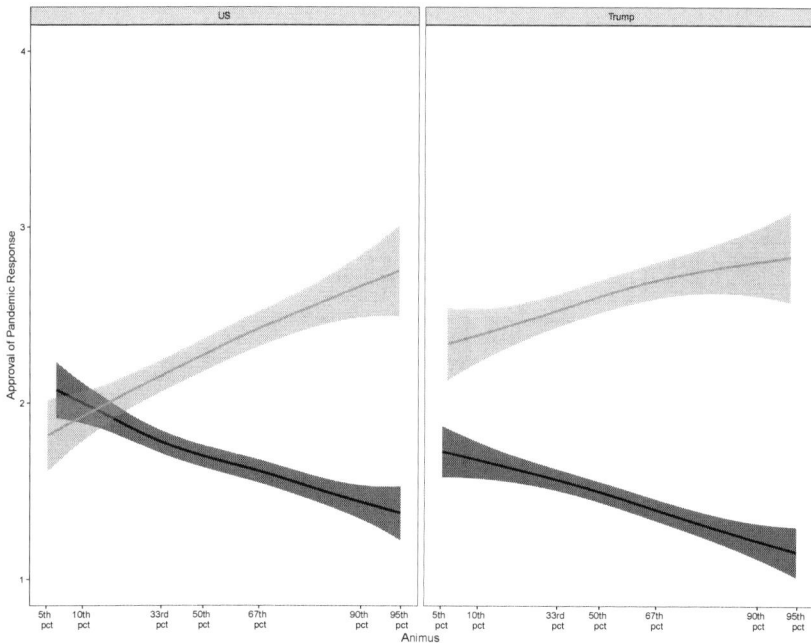

FIGURE 6.1. Animosity and Politicization of the Nation

Note: The relationship between animosity and approval of the pandemic response for Democrats is displayed in black; for Republicans, it is displayed in gray. The left-hand panel shows approval among those asked about the U.S.'s response, and the right-hand panel shows those asked about Trump's response.

more strongly than did the average Democrat, especially above about the 50th percentile of animus. Even among those with the lowest levels of animosity, however, there was a clear partisan divide.

This changes for those asked about the nation's response. At low levels of animus, Democrats—and not Republicans—exhibited more approval of the nation's response, and there was functionally no gap until around the 20th percentile of animosity. As animosity increased, however, that pattern reversed, and partisans increasingly saw the United States as synonymous with President Trump. Indeed, among the highest-animus Republicans, evaluations of the nation's pandemic response were effectively synonymous with their evaluations of President Trump's response. High-animus Democrats were similar, though perhaps not surprisingly, being even more critical of President Trump. Overall, as animosity increased, voters came to even see the nation itself through the lens of partisanship.

This logic explains why the scope of politics seems to have expanded so greatly. As Settle (2018), A. Lee (2021), Hiaeshutter-Rice, Neuner, and Soroka (2023), and others have noted, even seemingly apolitical symbols—where one chooses to eat lunch, the type of car one drives, one's leisure activities, and so forth—have become politically coded in the modern era. This likely reflects those with the most partisan animosity sending signals. For example, most people who eat at Chick-Fil-A do not think about the company's socially conservative politics, but for people who are high in animus, eating or not eating there has political implications. These individuals perceive a much larger part of the world as being "political," imputing politics to any ambiguous political target.

The Dynamics of Approval

The results in figure 6.1 demonstrate that high-animus individuals politicize seemingly apolitical concepts, but this does not tell us how those evaluations change over time or differ across other dimensions. Beginning in April 2020, we began to track voters' assessments of how various figures had responded to the COVID-19 pandemic. We asked about the pandemic not due to a desire to study the politics of COVID-19, but rather because it was the most salient issue at the time of our study, and hence it made the most sense to evaluate the public's evaluations of leaders in this area. As we will later detail, it also proves useful for again testing our hypothesis about personal consequences, paralleling the analyses we did in chapter 5.

We included figures that everyone should politicize and see in polarized terms—namely, President Trump and President Biden—as well as less politicized figures that only high-animus partisans (if anyone) should view in polarized terms. This latter group includes state and local officials and also members of Congress, considered as a collective. We predicted these groups would be seen by most, if not all, voters as less partisan and political than the president, and hence should escape politicization. While individual members of Congress would be seen in largely political terms, when we consider "members of Congress" as a whole, thinking about them collectively should cut against a partisan framing, especially given that, in April 2020, Democrats controlled the House of Representatives and Republicans controlled the Senate. We also looked more acutely at credit for vaccine development and distribution for Trump, Biden, and state governors to assess differences in national and state leader evaluations; we expected to find less polarization among governor evaluations as they are generally not as politicized.

Trump and Biden

We begin by considering voters' approval of President Trump's and President Biden's handling of the pandemic. We expected all respondents, even those low in animosity, to be relatively polarized in their response to the two presidents. In figure 6.2, we plot the over-time patterns of approval for President Trump, and in figure 6.3, for President Biden. As in earlier chapters, readers interested in regression analyses of these data are referred to appendix 6.1.

First we look at respondents' approval of President Trump's handling of the pandemic (figure 6.2). In every wave of the data, we saw a sharp division by party in approval of President Trump's handling of the pandemic, even for low-animus voters. For example, in our April 2020 data, at the 10th percentile of the animus scale there was a full-scale point gap in approval of President Trump (20 percent of the response scale), and it grew to approximately 2 full-scale points (40 percent of the scale) for those above the 70th percentile. The pattern replicated in the October 2020 and April 2021 data.

A fascinating finding was that even as partisans polarized across waves, they all also became more disapproving of Trump's handling of the pandemic. This was especially pronounced among low-animus Democrats, who gave President Trump the benefit of the doubt early in the pandemic but grew increasingly skeptical of his response over time. Republicans' ratings

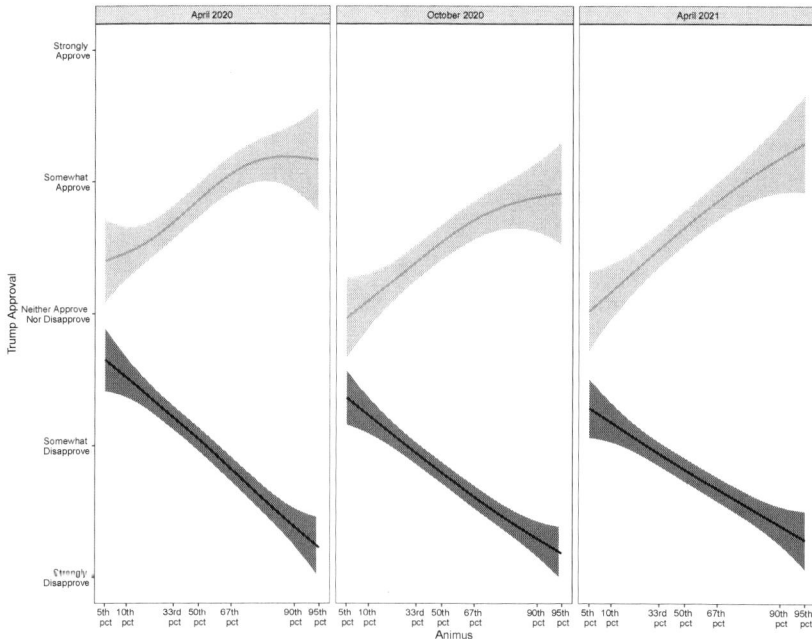

FIGURE 6.2. Animosity and Approval of President Trump

Note: The relationship between animosity and approval of Donald Trump's handling of the COVID-19 pandemic for Democrats is displayed in black; for Republicans, it is displayed in gray. Each panel presents results from a different survey wave.

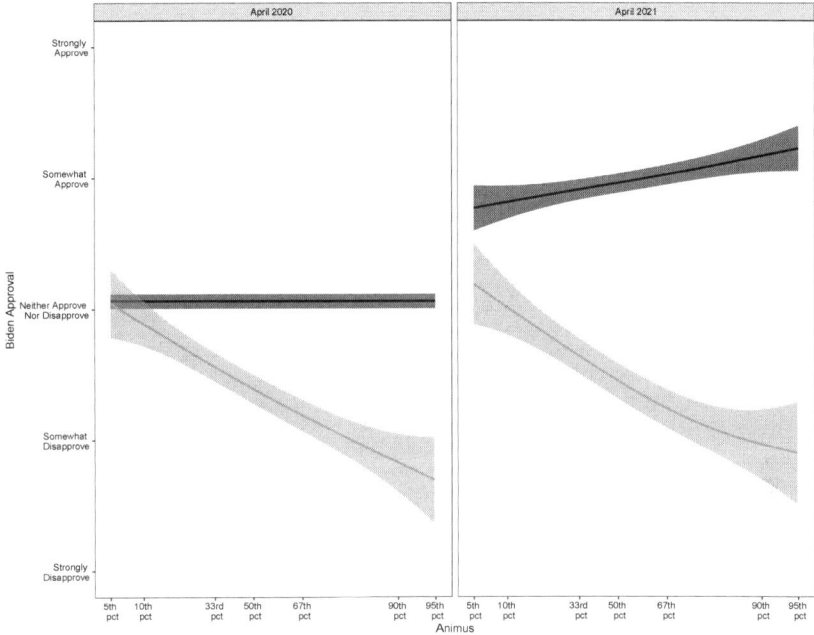

FIGURE 6.3. Animosity and Approval of President Biden

Note: The relationship between animosity and approval of President Biden's handling of the COVID-19 pandemic for Democrats is displayed in black; for Republicans, it is displayed in gray. Each panel presents results from a different survey wave. Note that the Biden item was omitted from our October 2020 survey.

of President Trump's handling of the pandemic also fell over the course of our survey waves, consistent with Annenberg IOD Collaborative (2023). The partisan cue matters for evaluations, but so does competence. Trump's mishandling of the pandemic, and not just animus, soured voters on his performance. This suggests, contrary to the emergent partisanship dominance over performance, that performance can matter in extreme scenarios.

We found a similar, though less stark, pattern for President Biden. We inadvertently left Biden off our October 2020 survey, so we present only results from the other two waves (April 2020 and April 2021).[7] We again found partisan divergence for all but very low-animus respondents, with the gap between the parties increasing rapidly as animus increases. In April 2020, when Biden was only a candidate for the presidency, evaluations diverged as animus increased, at least among Republicans. It is interesting that once Biden was in office, his partisan gap became smaller than the gap for Trump. And indeed, evaluations of Biden in April 2021 were higher than his April 2020 evaluations. We suspect this stems from how Biden handled the pandemic relative to Trump early in his presidency. Compared to his predecessor, Biden worked to tone down the degree of partisan rhetoric, listened to Dr. Fauci and other advisers, and did not involve himself as much in the headlines. For instance, in his inaugural address, only a bit over two months before our April 2021 survey, Biden called on Americans to "end this uncivil war that pits red against blue, rural versus urban, conservative versus liberal" (Biden 2021a), and he issued numerous calls to reach across the aisle and build bridges. This contrasts with Trump's "American Carnage" inaugural address from 2016 and his typical rhetoric while in office.

Further, while members of both parties responded to President Trump, President Biden drew a much stronger response from Republicans (i.e., an anti-cue). This underscores their distinctive styles. Trump's combative approach functioned as a clear cue to both sides of the aisle. In contrast, by toning down his approach and staying more in the background, Biden became a less salient cue for his own party's voters, and even for lower-animus Republicans. Only high-animus Republicans responded strongly to Biden's behavior. Different styles of leadership can generate different types of cues, with distinct relationships to animus. This insight complements other work showing that elites have become more partisan in their discourse (Gentzkow, Shapiro, and Taddy 2019) and that elite ideological divergence can generate animosity (Rogowski and Sutherland 2016; Webster and Abramowitz 2017). We add to this scholarship by showing that the nature of rhetoric affects the consequences of animosity.

State and Local Officials

While we expected to find partisan divides for highly polarizing figures like Trump and Biden, we did not expect this pattern to replicate for all governmental figures. In particular, we argued that for less politicized figures, partisan animosity would have a weaker relationship to approval. In our April 2020 survey wave, we asked respondents for their approval of their state and locally elected officials handling of the COVID-19 pandemic, and in our October 2020 and April 2021 waves, we asked them for their approval of mayor of their town's handling of the pandemic. We expected that both sets of actors would be seen in a less political light, and hence through a less partisan lens. This should be especially true of mayors. In figure 6.4, we present the trends in approval for state and local officials, and in figure 6.5, we present those for mayors.

In figure 6.4, we see that animus is weakly related to evaluations of state and local officials. The maximum partisan gap only reached 0.5 scale points on our 5-point scale, less than half of what it was for respondents at the 10th percentile of animus when assessing President Trump. Further, the approval of state and local leaders was quite high, never dipping below "Neither Approve nor Disapprove," which was the midpoint of our scale. High-animosity Republicans

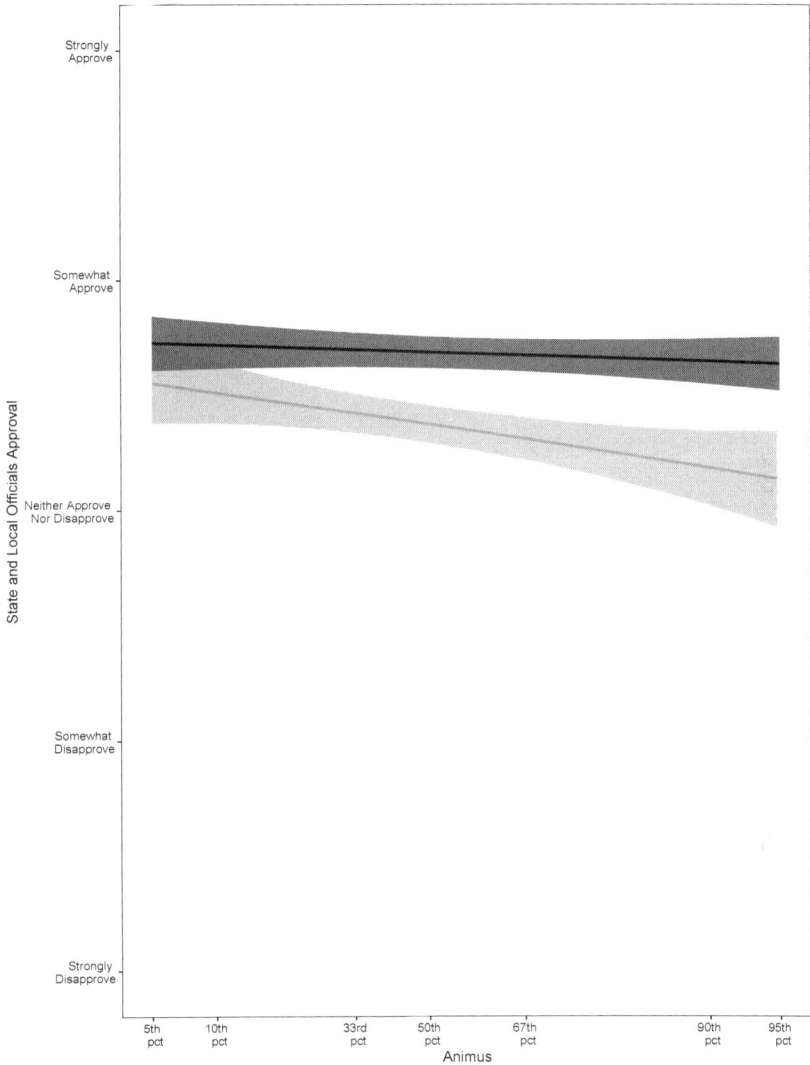

FIGURE 6.4. Animosity and Approval of State and Local Officials
Note: The relationship between animosity and approval of state and local officials' handling of the COVID-19 pandemic for Democrats is displayed in black; for Republicans, it is displayed in gray. Data are from the April 2020 wave.

probably exhibited lower levels of approval because they took COVID-19 less seriously and were less likely to view it as a threat in need of a response, and nearly all elected officials offered some kind of response to the pandemic. While the gap is small, the fact that there is a gap at all based on animosity reveals what occurs when local political issues become nationalized. High-animus

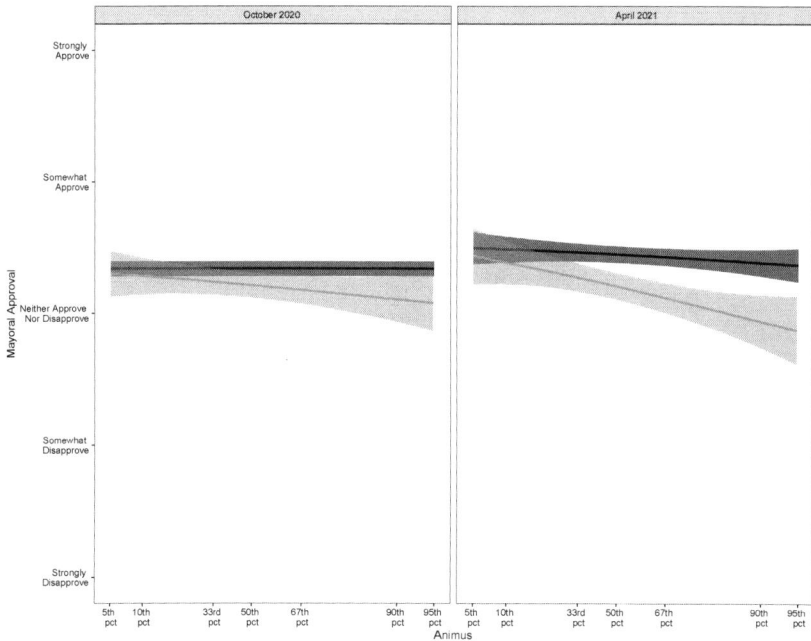

FIGURE 6.5. Animosity and Approval of Mayors

Note: The relationship between animosity and approval of the respondent's mayor's handling of the COVID-19 pandemic for Democrats is displayed in black; for Republicans, it is displayed in gray. Each panel presents results from a different survey wave.

Republicans ostensibly imputed some of the national debate about COVID-19 into evaluations of state and local officials (Abramowitz and Webster 2016).

We found a similar pattern for the evaluations of mayors, as shown in figure 6.5. While Democrats again expressed stronger approval than Republicans, the partisan gaps remained slim, most notably early in October 2020 when mayors were involved in tough choices about whether to reopen business and schools for in-person instruction. Even so, these subnational figures largely evaded politicization, indicating that animus mattered substantially less in how voters assessed them. To the (small) extent that animus did matter, it likely suggests spillover from national debates.[8]

Members of Congress

It is not only subnational figures who can escape the grip of politicization; national figures can as well if presented in a less partisan way. In our April 2020 data, we asked respondents to assess how "members of Congress" had handled the pandemic. Assessing Congress as a collective that contains members of both parties should cut against seeing it in a partisan lens. Further, the split control of Congress makes it more difficult to politicize, as Democrats controlled the House of Representatives while Republicans controlled the Senate. We expected these factors to vitiate the otherwise strong effect of partisanship. Figure 6.6 presents the results.

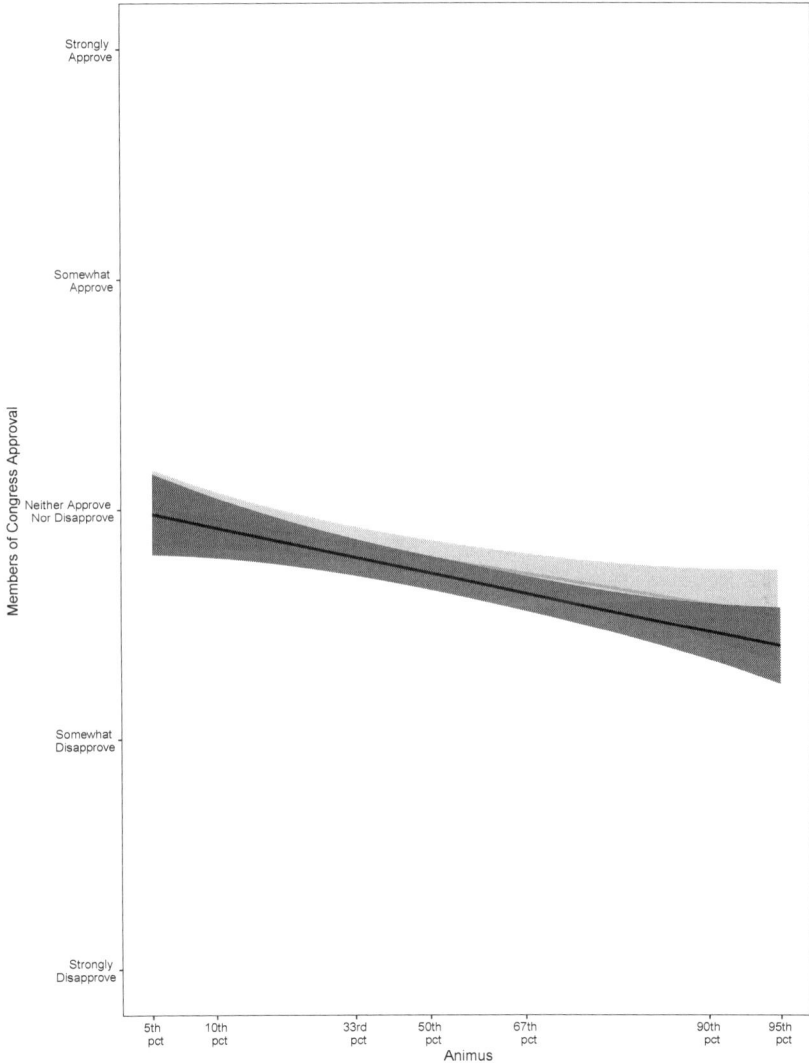

FIGURE 6.6. Animosity and Approval of Members of Congress
Note: The relationship between animosity and approval of the handling of the COVID-19 pandemic by members of Congress for Democrats is displayed in black; for Republicans, it is displayed in gray. Data are from the April 2020 wave.

We found that, as predicted, partisan animosity largely did not relate to levels of approval concerning Congress's overall pandemic response. In contrast to the state and local officials, high-animus *Democrats* exhibited less approval, though, again, the partisan gap was minuscule and the confidence intervals overlap. The fairer assessment would be to say that approval of members of Congress declines in both parties as animus increases but this relationship is very weak. Cueing Congress as a collective, rather than in its more usual partisan dimension, undercut the partisan cue, and hence the effect of animosity. Of course, had we asked about highly salient partisan leaders like Democratic House Speaker Nancy Pelosi of California or Senate Minority Leader Mitch McConnell of Kentucky, then the results likely would have paralleled the findings for Trump and Biden. But by cuing Congress as a collective and not providing a clear partisan signal, we can change evaluations.

Partisan Animosity and Vaccine Credit

If our argument is correct, it should not only be general approval that varies, but also credit for particular policy accomplishments. During this time, no policy accomplishment had greater significance than the development and distribution of the COVID-19 vaccines. The vaccines marked a monumental achievement, in terms of both the underlying science and governmental–private sector coordination. This is an ideal sort of public sector leadership, whereby the government worked alongside the private sector to develop life-saving medical advances and make them available to the public.

Will voters say that the out-party president deserves credit for vaccine development and distribution? At least in theory, they should, as both Trump and Biden played important roles in making the vaccine available to the public. Rapid vaccine development would not have been possible without President Trump's Operation Warp Speed. President Biden's mobilization of the Federal Emergency Management Agency (FEMA) and the National Guard ensured that the shots were actually administered to willing Americans. Yet the salience of the president's partisanship may lead voters to argue that their copartisan president deserves considerable credit and the opposing-party president deserves less, a gap that should increase with partisan animosity. Moreover, when we asked about this item in April 2021, President Biden had made vaccine distribution an extremely high priority, using it as one of the key benchmarks for his first one hundred days in office.[9] Given this, the partisan signal of the vaccine program vis-à-vis the president would be unmistakable even for low-animus voters.

Another set of actors who played a key role in the vaccine distribution program was the nation's governors, who oversaw coordination efforts that led to the opening of many of the vaccination clinics where Americans could receive their shots. While governors obviously have clear partisan identities, these identities are typically less salient than those of the president. Given this reduced saliency, the partisan gubernatorial gap should be smaller than the presidential one.

In our April 2021 survey, we asked respondents whether Trump, Biden, and their state's governor hurt or helped the development of the COVID-19 vaccines. We also asked (separately) whether these same figures hurt or helped in the distribution of the vaccines. For the analyses reported in this chapter, we combined these two distinct questions; the respective alphas for the out-party president, in-party president, and governor are 0.83, 0.78, and 0.88. Figure 6.7 presents how these evaluations differ across the levels of partisan animosity. The president figure differentiates in- and out-party evaluations (e.g., Trump is in-party for Republicans and out-party for Democrats), while the governor figure distinguishes whether the respondent is from the party of their state's governor. In both panels, we show same-party evaluations with a solid line and out-party evaluations with a dashed line.

With respect to presidential evaluations (the left-hand panel), we can see a sharp divide among all partisans, consistent with figures 6.1 and 6.2 earlier in the chapter. Even for low-animus partisans, we found a gap of a full-scale point for Trump versus Biden: voters thought that the out-party president "Neither Helped nor Hurt," while their copartisan president "Probably Helped." The difference for those with the most animosity is staggering—they think the out-party president almost "Definitely Hurt" the program. There is nearly a gap of 3 points on the 5-point scale between copartisan and out-partisan assessments. For those with the highest levels of animus, evaluations operate as an all-or-nothing proposition.[10]

Gubernatorial evaluations revealed a very different pattern (see the right-hand panel). For the bottom 50 percent of the partisan animosity distribution we found a modest partisan gap, and even for those with the highest animus, the gap was notably smaller than the presidential gap. Indeed, the gubernatorial gap for high-animosity respondents nearly matched the presidential gap among the lowest animosity respondents. The lower salience of the party cues muted the mapping of animus onto evaluations.

Pulling back, we see how the clarity of the partisan signal shapes how animus maps onto evaluations. When looking both at approval overall and at whether the leader helped or hurt during the pandemic, the clearer the partisan signal, the stronger are the effects of animus. Animus can, but does not

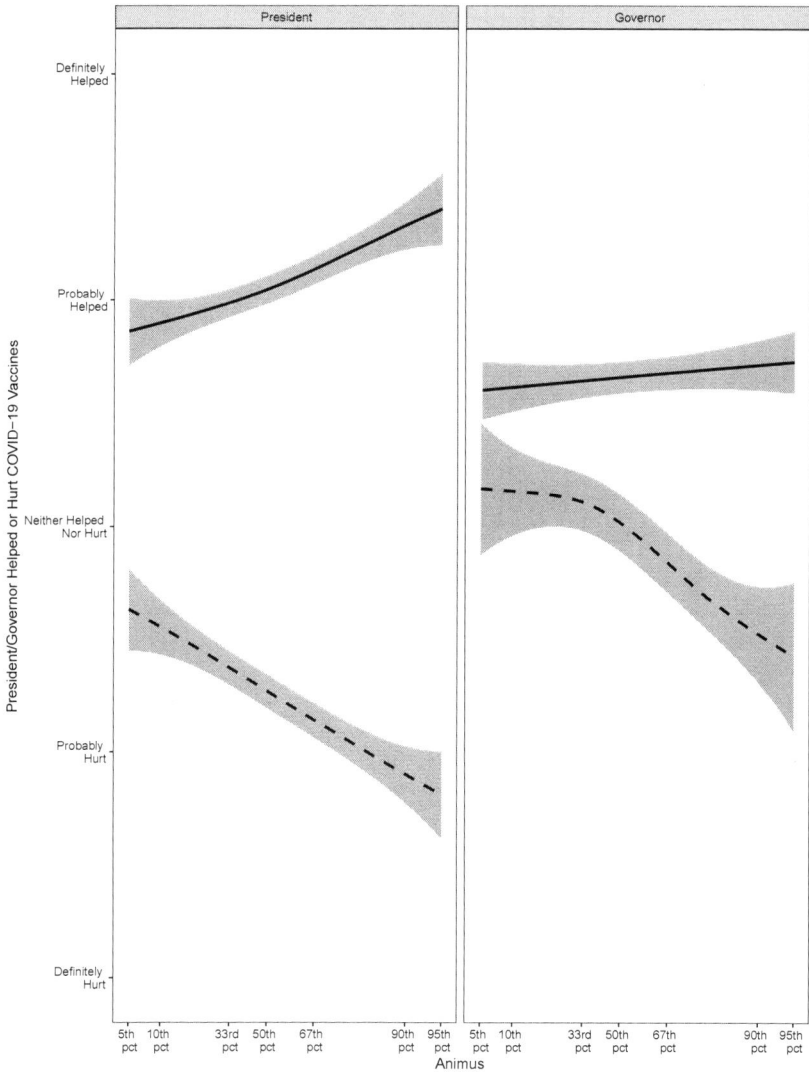

FIGURE 6.7. Animosity and Credit for the Vaccine Program

Note: The relationship between animosity and belief that leaders helped or hurt the development and distribution of the COVID-19 vaccine. The left-hand panel assesses respondents' evaluations of their state's governor, and the right-hand panel assesses their evaluations of Presidents Trump and Biden. In both panels, in-party leader evaluations are shown as the solid line and out-party leader evaluations are shown as the dashed line.

always, warp the credit or blame that people give for policy success or failure; when it does, however, it potentially distorts accountability.

The Increasing Partisan Clarity of Scientific Advisers during the Pandemic

So far, we have used between-leader differences in cue clarity to test our argument, contrasting more partisan leaders (like Biden and Trump) with less partisan ones (like mayors or state and local officials). But we can also test our cue hypothesis (i.e., that animus matters in the presence of clearer cues) by exploiting over-time data in which the signal connected to a figure evolves in a more partisan direction, which should enhance the role of animus. That is, we look at within-leader changes over time.

The pandemic, once again, provided a unique opportunity. At the outset, several scientific advisers received public attention due to their credentials, not their politics. Perhaps no figure better embodied this description than Dr. Anthony Fauci, head of the National Institute for Allergy and Infectious Diseases (NIAID) and a key pandemic adviser for both Presidents Trump and Biden. Prior to the pandemic, Dr. Fauci had not publicly affiliated with any political party; moreover, he had never publicly endorsed any political candidates, nor had he ever sought political office. Dr. Fauci served presidents of both parties, dating back to the Ronald Reagan administration. When asked to name one of his heroes in a 1988 debate, George H. W. Bush named Dr. Fauci, praising him for his pioneering work on AIDS (Dreier Roundtable 2020), and George W. Bush awarded him the nation's highest civilian honor— the Presidential Medal of Freedom—in 2008 in recognition of his years of service to the nation. Dr. Fauci should therefore be seen apolitically, without any obvious partisan cue to follow.

Yet for partisans with the highest levels of animosity, especially Republicans, Dr. Fauci had already become a partisan figure by April 2020. Initially, President Trump and Dr. Fauci had a positive relationship: President Trump even labeled him a "major television star," perhaps the highest praise the forty-fifth president could bestow on anyone, given his background in television and his ostensible persistent obsession with television ratings. Trump's relationship with Dr. Fauci soon soured as Fauci pushed back on the president's efforts to downplay the seriousness of the pandemic (Haberman 2020). Many people in the news media began to label him a "real-time fact checker" for the president during their briefings, which upset the commander in chief (Haslett 2020). When President Trump called the U.S. State Department the "deep state department" during a late March 2020 press conference, Dr. Fauci dropped his poker face and put his face in his hands, becoming a viral online meme.[11] This led many of the president's most ardent supporters—especially those reporting on conservative media outlets and online—to argue that Dr. Fauci was actively undermining the president (Alba and Frenkel 2020). That story remained relatively minor at the time, and hence most voters likely were unaware of this cue, except those with the highest levels of animus who pursued partisan information (see chapter 3).

Dr. Fauci's relationship with President Trump continued to spiral downward over the course of the pandemic. Trump's team argued that Fauci's arguments about wearing face masks, practicing social distancing, and so forth were tantamount to endorsing Biden; Trump's adviser Jason Miller, for example, argued that "he's [Fauci] out there campaigning against you" (Leonnig and Rucker 2021, 332). In a *60 Minutes* interview in October 2020, Dr. Fauci criticized the president for holding an in-person event for Supreme Court nominee Amy Coney Barrett at which few people wore masks, labeling it a "superspreader event." Days later, in a phone call with campaign staff, President Trump called Dr. Fauci "a disaster" and said that "every time he goes on television, there's always a bomb, but there's a bigger bomb if you fire him" (Shabad and Alba 2020). At President Trump's rallies, crowds began to chant "Fire Fauci!" When this occurred at a rally in Florida just days before the election, Trump replied, "Don't tell anybody, but let me wait until a little bit after the election, please" (Cummings and Subramanian 2020). Dr. Fauci explicitly contrasted the candidates in an interview with the *Washington Post* shortly before the election. As the *Post* noted, "Fauci said Biden's campaign 'is taking it seriously from a public health perspective.' Trump, Fauci said, is 'looking at it from a different perspective.' He said that perspective was 'the economy and reopening the country'" (Dawsey and Abutaleb 2020). For a public health figure who had previously been scrupulously nonpartisan, this came shockingly close to an explicit endorsement of Biden. Trump and Fauci's relationship further frayed after the election as Trump sought to blame Dr. Fauci for the pandemic (Din 2021) and Dr. Fauci reported he had said "Hallelujah" after President Biden was elected (Schneider 2021). Dr. Fauci—both through his own actions, and through the reactions of President Trump—became increasingly politicized across the course of our study.

We use voters' approval of Dr. Fauci's handling of the pandemic to track how partisan animus maps onto political evaluations as a figure becomes increasingly politicized. In April 2020, we expected that only voters with the highest levels of animosity would see Dr. Fauci through a partisan lens.[12] But over time, we expected that increasing numbers of voters should come to

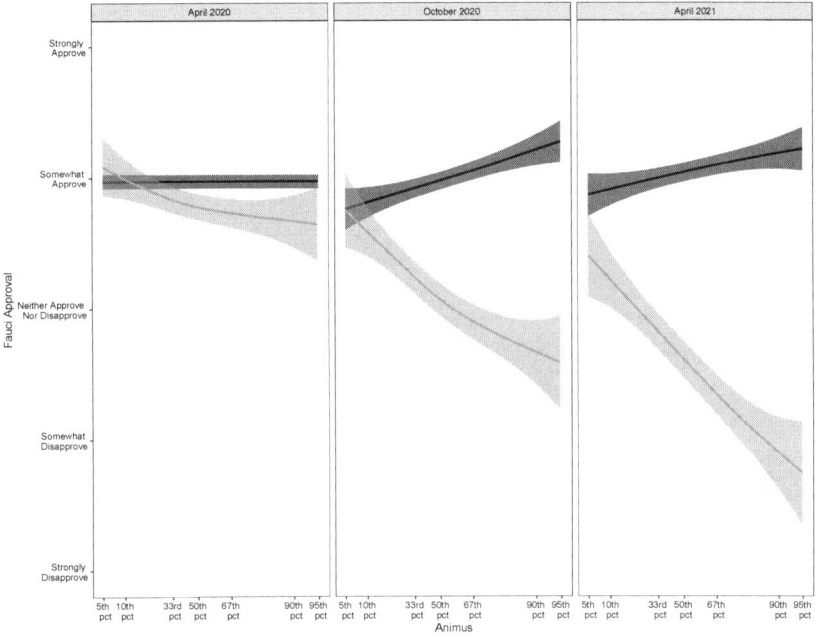

FIGURE 6.8. Animosity and Approval of Dr. Fauci

Note: The relationship between animosity and approval of Dr. Anthony Fauci's handling of the COVID-19 pandemic for Democrats is displayed in black; for Republicans, it is displayed in gray. Each panel presents results from a different survey wave.

see him as an explicitly political figure, and hence to support or oppose him based on their partisanship. Figure 6.8 presents the results.

Just as we expected, in April 2020, most voters viewed Dr. Fauci through a nonpartisan lens. There was functionally no relationship between Democrats approval and animus, and for Republicans, there was only a weak relationship. Even among the highest-animus respondents, the partisan gap was small, and everyone—Democrats and Republicans alike—was more likely to approve than disapprove of him.

This changed in our later waves. By October 2020, a clear partisan divide had emerged. Those who were at the 15th percentile of animus exhibited as much of a divide in October as those who were at the 95th percentile of animus in April. Further, while only high-animus Republicans responded in April 2020, by that October, both parties viewed Fauci through partisan lens, with Democrats embracing the adviser and Republicans increasing rejecting him. By April 2021, this polarization had only accelerated, with Republicans especially responding quite strongly against him. By the end of our study, for voters at the 67th percentile of animosity, we find an almost two-scale point gap in partisan approval on our 5-point scale. Looking at our most polarized respondents, the partisan gap in approval for Fauci increased more than seven-fold over the course of our study. As Dr. Fauci came to be seen through a partisan lens, partisan animosity increasingly drove approval of him. As partisan cues grew, so did polarized evaluations.

What about other scientific figures—do they show a similar pattern? We asked respondents whether they approved of the CDC's performance in every wave. In our October 2020 and April 2021 waves, we added the FDA, given the agency's role in approving the vaccine and other therapies to combat the virus. We expected respondents to see these organizations through an apolitical lens at the start of the pandemic as both were widely trusted public health agencies without partisan agendas. But over time, both agencies tangled publicly with President Trump. For example, in testimony to the U.S. Senate in September 2020, CDC director Dr. Robert Redfield said that a vaccine would not be available until summer or early fall 2021, contradicting President Trump's argument that it would be ready in 2020, and perhaps even before the election. Trump was furious over Redfield's statement and viewed it as a significant betrayal, which led him to critique the organization. Redfield went on to accentuate the importance of continued masking, another blow to President Trump, who had repeatedly downplayed the importance of masking during the pandemic (J. Flores, Rodriguez, and Shannon 2020).

Likewise, the FDA clashed with Trump over the drug hydroxychloroquine, which the president endorsed as an effective tool in fighting the disease. While the FDA initially gave emergency use authorization for the drug to treat COVID-19, it withdrew it shortly thereafter, when the data revealed that it was ineffective, and perhaps harmful, to patients (Beasley and Mishra 2020). When the FDA said it would issue stricter guidance for emergency use authorization for the COVID-19 vaccines (Weiland and LaFraniere 2020) and collect additional data on postvaccination health effects (which would take additional time, thereby slowing their decision), President Trump pushed back, saying this was a "political move" designed to hurt his reelection (Wise 2020; Leonnig and Rucker 2021). Indeed, when the Pfizer vaccine received emergency use authorization just days after the election, Trump tweeted that "the @US_FDA and the Democrats didn't want to have me get a Vaccine WIN [sic], prior to the election, so instead it came out five days later—As I've said all along!" (Leonnig and Rucker 2021, 369). While these agencies' clashes with President Trump were less dramatic than Dr. Fauci's, they were still expected to lead to animosity-driven polarization over time. Figures 6.9 and 6.10 present the data for the CDC and the FDA, respectively.

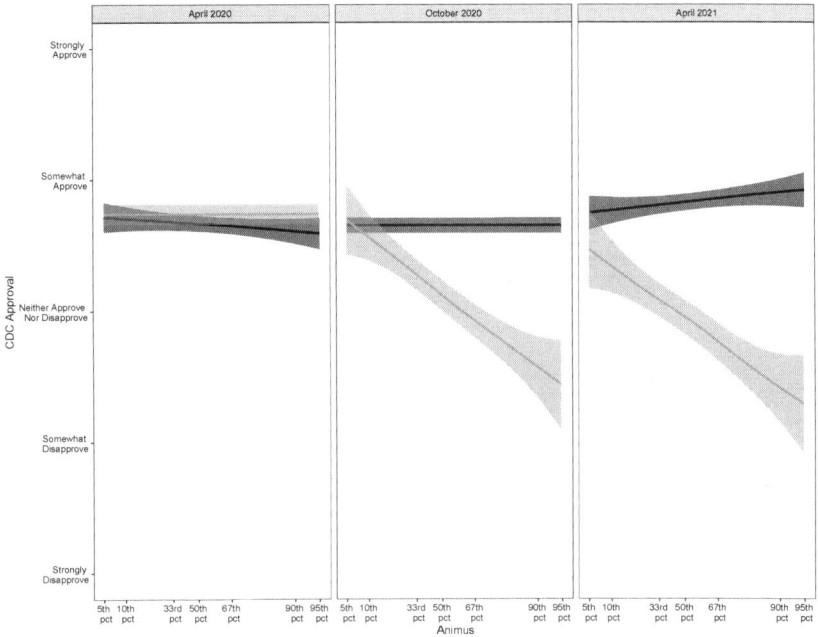

FIGURE 6.9. Animosity and Approval of the CDC

Note: The relationship between animosity and approval of the CDC's handling of the COVID-19 pandemic for Democrats is displayed in black; for Republicans, it is displayed in gray. Each panel presents results from a different survey wave.

As we expected, in our April 2020 data, almost all voters viewed the CDC as nonpartisan; there was very little divergence, even for those with the most partisan animus (see figure 6.9). By October 2020, a gap had emerged, and it grew larger by April 2021; the same pattern replicated itself for the FDA, though to a lesser degree (see figure 6.10). For both agencies, as party leaders' signals changed over time, so did the reactions of their voters, evidenced by the growing animosity-based polarization.

Looking across all three scientific figures, we additionally find a partisan difference, with more movement among Republicans than among Democrats. Trust in these institutions started at relatively high levels among all respondents; Democrats received consistent cues from their leaders that they should continue to trust these advisers. Given this, perhaps the lack of movement among Democrats reflects a ceiling effect. Alternatively, it could be that President Trump's clashes with these agencies simply garneted more attention from his copartisans.

Beyond our theory lies a darker aspect of these findings for American politics. These results underline how public health, and science more generally,

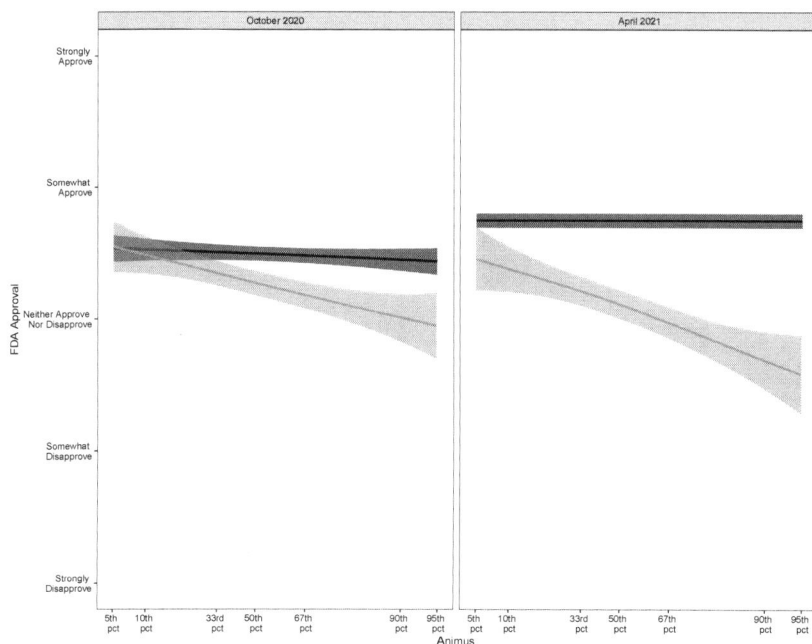

FIGURE 6.10. Animosity and Approval of the FDA

Note: The relationship between animosity and approval of the FDA's handling of the COVID-19 pandemic for Democrats is displayed in black; for Republicans, it is displayed in gray. Each panel presents results from a different survey wave.

has become politicized in American politics. This troubling development interferes with the ability of public health and scientific advisers to guide the public. If "trusting science" becomes just another partisan issue (H. Brady and Kent 2022), that has grave implications for the country's ability to respond to future pandemics. We have already seen signs of this, with a partisan differentiation in flu vaccine uptake in 2021 (Enten 2021). In the past, partisanship did not predict flu vaccine uptake, but in 2021, it did. All vaccines, not just the COVID-19 vaccine, became politicized. Given the centrality of vaccines to the nation's public health infrastructure, this constitutes a disturbing trend.

Personal Consequences and Scientific Evaluations

Much like in chapter 5, we use the COVID-19 pandemic to test the effects of personal consequences on animus. Recall that those who had experienced a severe case of COVID-19, or knew someone who had (or anticipated either) took more preventative behaviors, perceived various indoor activities to be less safe, and more strongly supported policies to mitigate the threat of the virus. The same logic should apply to their evaluations of scientific figures: the heightened salience of the virus for these respondents should trigger accuracy motivations that lead them to seek out the best information, regardless of their partisanship or animosity. That means the most accurate information on how to prevent infection, which would come from scientific advisers. As in chapter 5, while this should be true of both parties, given the partisan dynamics, the effect should be concentrated among Republicans. Accuracy motives should lead them to trust scientific individuals or organizations, regardless of animus, given that scientific figures constitute the best line of defense against the virus.[13] To test this hypothesis, in figure 6.11, we separately plot the approval for Dr. Fauci, the CDC, and the FDA for those with high COVID-19 severity versus those with low severity. As in chapter 5, we pool across the October 2020 and April 2021 waves; analyzing them separately would yield very similar, but nosier, results.

For all three entities, we see that the salience of COVID-19 makes a significant difference in evaluations. Those with more severe COVID-19-experiences

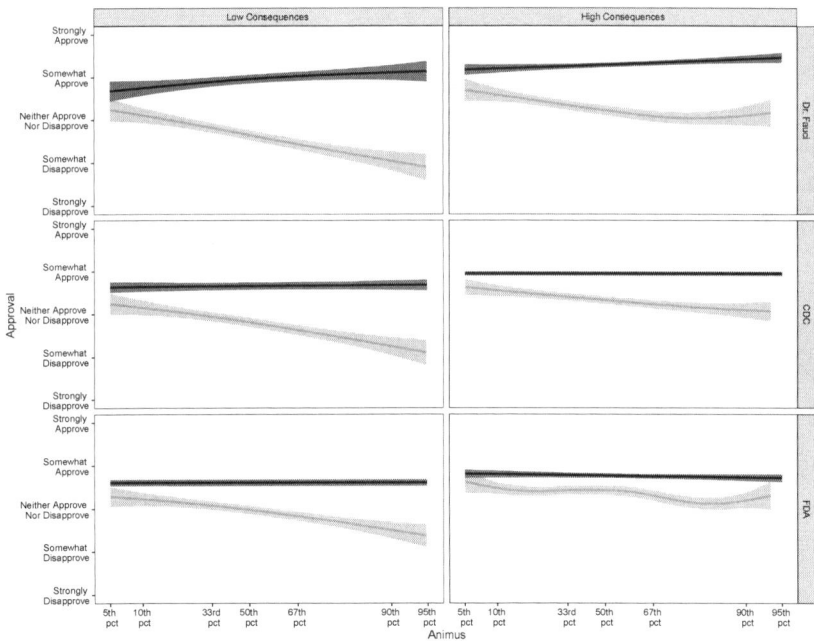

FIGURE 6.11. Animosity, Approval, and COVID-19 Consequences

Note: The relationship between animosity and approval of various scientific figures for Democrats is displayed in black; for Republicans, it is displayed in gray; each row gives the analysis for a different individual/agency. The left-hand column gives results for respondents for whom COVID-19 was not salient, the right-hand column gives results for respondents for whom the virus was salient.

were more likely to approve of Dr. Fauci, the CDC, and the FDA, regardless of their level of animus or their partisanship. As expected, given their higher levels of approval, the difference was quite modest for Democrats. But for Republicans—where the personal consequences of the disease undercut the partisan motivation—we found much larger effects. Two points stand out. First, these effects were most pronounced for Dr. Fauci and the CDC. Dr. Fauci was the most visible public scientific figure in the nation, and the CDC issued the government's official guidance during the pandemic. As such, those for whom the virus was consequential especially attuned to their advice and became more likely to approve of them. Second, the effects were especially strong for those at the highest levels of animus. The drop-off in approval we found for high-animus Republicans came primarily from those with little direct experience with COVID-19, who had the strongest incentives to engage in partisan motivated reasoning. As in chapter 5, personal consequences shaped the effects of animus on attitudes. It is those for whom an issue is not consequential where the effects of animus are strongest. When an issue hits home in a significant way, the animus effects attenuate considerably.[14]

Conclusion

How people evaluate their leaders is a fundamental component of democratic accountability. In theory, people should hold their leaders accountable for their actions, rewarding them for beneficial policies and punishing them for poor ones; this should be as true for copartisan leaders as it is for opposite-party ones. Partisan animosity, however, potentially undermines such accountability. If approval or disapproval depends only on the leader's party, rather than on the success or failure of their policies, this undercuts a leader's incentive to pursue good policy.

Our findings reveal that animus shapes evaluations of leaders, but only under some conditions. We showed that the centrality of partisanship for people who are high in animosity leads them to broaden the scope of what is seen as political. High-animus partisans grasp every minute political cue and therefore view ostensibly neutral actors as political. They imbue their evaluations with partisanship. Additionally, when partisan cues are clearer, animus matters a great deal. This occurs across different figures (comparing, say, the president with state and local officials), and for the same individuals over time (when the signals shift). When partisanship becomes central—as it is for people who have high levels of animus—people are less likely to reward and punish leaders for political outcomes; instead, they rely on partisan cues when evaluating leadership. However, when the consequences of making the wrong decision are significant, partisanship and animosity matter much less as people seek out the best possible advice. Animosity shapes evaluations, but its effects matter much more in some contexts than in others.

The animus-based polarization we find has substantial implications when considered in the context of the COVID-19 pandemic. More than partisan differences in the evaluations of partisan politicians, we find that animosity leads to a polarization in views of science and scientific figures. In other words, partisanship so defines those with high levels of animosity that it seeps into their perceptions of those who advise our nation's leaders about public health. Our findings on the trajectory over time show the importance of scientific figures remaining as politically neutral as possible (also see A. Flores et al. 2022). One overlooked dimension of this concerns the centrality of the public administration of health: politicians and experts working together behind the scenes to coordinate policy to avoid public flare-ups. One shortcoming of the Trump administration was a failure to coordinate effectively, so the president often clashed with his own advisers. When elected officials coordinate with their officials, and ensure everyone sings from the same hymnal, public confidence increases, because the public hears one message, and politicization diminishes. Put differently, politicians and experts both have duties to avoid politicizing public health crises. The stakes are simply too high to do otherwise.

Partisan Animosity and Political Compromise

On taking office, one of President Joe Biden's first legislative priorities was passing infrastructure legislation aimed at repairing America's roads, bridges, ports, and highways. On the surface, this seemed like an excellent choice. Experts argued that the nation's infrastructure desperately needed to be repaired (American Society of Civil Engineers 2021), voters of both parties recognized that need (Newport 2020), and infrastructure had historically received strong bipartisan support in Congress (e.g., Ferejohn 1974).

Biden insisted that any such legislation be bipartisan. According to some pundits, that was a death knell for the policy, as bipartisanship had vanished in the contemporary political environment. Many in the public shared this skepticism of bipartisanship. In a January 2021 survey, 24 percent of respondents had *no* confidence in Biden's ability to negotiate compromises between the parties (*Washington Post* / ABC News 2021). Indeed, the difficulty of this goal became evident almost immediately. Biden's initial proposal included an array of projects—not just funding for roads, bridges and so forth, but also broader initiatives, such as efforts to address climate change, paid family leave, and childcare. This latter policy group was referred to as human infrastructure, to differentiate it from the more traditional physical infrastructure. Republicans and some centrist Democrats argued that the proposal needed to be scaled back considerably or eliminated altogether.

On June 24, after weeks of discussion, Biden announced that a compromise on the infrastructure plan had, in fact, been reached: "We have a deal," he reported. This bipartisan deal would change the shape of Biden's original plan, narrowing it considerably. Many of the more expansive human infrastructure provisions were excised from the bill.[1] Likewise, at the behest of some Republicans and centrist Democrats, Biden and Democratic leaders dropped the provisions for increased IRS enforcement that were to pay for much of the new spending; instead, the bill was funded through increased deficit spending. In the end, the Senate passed the bill 69–30 in August, with 19 Republicans joining the Democrats in supporting the bill; in the House, the measure passed in early November by 228 to 206 votes, with 13 Republicans voting with the Democrats for the bill (6 liberal Democrats defected). President Biden signed the measure into law several days later, thus delivering on one of his key campaign promises.[2]

One might have expected a frustrated reaction from Biden given that the measure fell short of his ambitions. Yet he insisted that the need for everyone to sacrifice plays a key role in bipartisanship. "Let me be clear: Neither side got everything they wanted in this deal," Biden told the press, "and that's what it means to compromise" (Biden 2021b). Biden's definition of compromise accentuates that most compromises leave many people unsatisfied. Although they support bipartisanship in the abstract, and can recognize equitable compromise, partisans of all stripes likely perceive the type of compromise Biden touted as a policy loss (Harbridge, Malhotra, and Harrison 2014). Americans prefer compromises in which the *other* party loses more.

That people's partisan preferences affect support for compromise and bipartisanship is not surprising. More surprising is Wolak's (2020) optimistic perspective. She argues most partisans expect compromise not just from out-party elected officials but also from their own party leaders (Wolak 2020). This argument stands in contrast to broad, but largely untested, concerns that a polarized political climate undermines political compromise (Finkel et al. 2020). Politicians may *perceive* that their constituents do not want them to compromise, but on average, rank-and-file voters prefer it (Wolak 2020).

At the same time, politicians' perceptions may not be entirely unfounded. If they look to voters for cues, the voters most likely to be vocal may well oppose compromise (Krupnikov and Ryan 2022). In other words, even if the average voter prefers bipartisanship, a smaller but vocal group of voters may not, and it is these intense voters who grab politicians' attention (S. Anderson et al. 2020; Hill 2022). We suspect that voters with high levels of animosity offer the precise combination of not only being opposed to compromise but also being more likely to voice this opposition. This is a cause for concern since "governing in a democracy without compromise is impossible" (Gutmann and Thompson 2012, 1).

A central route to achieving such compromises involves respectful and civil dialogue between leaders (Gutmann and Thompson 2012). The effort to find common ground requires the recognition that the other side has a legitimate perspective and that neither side has a monopoly on truth. This entails, in no small part, demonstrating courtesy and civility to one another (Jamieson and Hardy 2012; Jamieson et al. 2017). Of course, civility is a broad and multifaceted concept (Keith and Danisch 2020); we focus here on a minimal definition whereby both sides (reciprocally) treat one another with respect.

Specifically, we considered the relationship between animosity and people's perceptions of, and support for, compromise, as well as the degree to which legislators should respect one another and treat each other civilly. We expected that all citizens would support compromise, at least in the abstract. But we anticipated that high-animus respondents would be distinctive in two ways. First, they should exhibit less support for compromise writ large. Unlike ordinary voters, these individuals should not want to find common ground, no matter the circumstances. Second, they should be especially opposed to efforts where *their* party sacrifices more. To be clear, we expected all respondents to oppose compromise whereby their side loses more (Harbridge, Malhotra, and Harrison 2014). We anticipated, however, that this tendency would be especially strong for partisans who are high in animus; for these individuals, compromise means the *other* party sacrifices more. In a parallel fashion, we expect that, at least in the abstract, all Americans will believe legislators should treat each other with respect, but this will be less true of high-animus individuals. Further, these individuals will be especially unlikely to attach importance to their own party's officials treating those from the opposing party with respect. Much like with compromise, we expect animus-driven differences.

And such animus-driven effects were just what we found. Animus heavily conditioned people's perceptions of the importance of compromise, as well as the process of compromise. We showed that high-animus partisans viewed compromise as less important overall, no matter the circumstances. This effect especially manifested when their *own* party did most of the compromising. In contrast, they perceived compromise as a much more important aspect of politics when the *other* side made concessions. The same pattern emerged when we consider respect for political leaders. High-animus partisans attached less importance to leaders treating one another with respect, particularly when it comes to their party treating the other party respectfully.

We studied these patterns, not only in the abstract but also within the context of a specific type of compromise, to see if this changed our results. In our April 2021 wave, we presented respondents with a scenario in which President Biden was negotiating with Republicans in Congress over funding for the National Aeronautics and Space Administration (NASA), based on a scenario taken from Harbridge, Malhotra, and Harrison (2014). We randomized the exact conditions of the compromise—sometimes the eventual outcome leaned toward the Democrats' original proposal, sometimes it fell closer to the Republicans' original proposal, and sometimes it landed exactly in the middle. We found that high-animus partisans expressed significantly more opposition to compromises in which their party sacrificed more, and significantly more support for compromises in which the other party lost out.

Jointly, our results point to the importance of partisanship in people's feelings about compromise, whether in the abstract or when faced with a specific negotiation scenario. On average, in our studies people perceive compromise through the lens of their party. However, not all partisans are alike, as animosity underlies the party effects. It is not simply partisanship that affects how people perceive compromise, but rather that high-animus partisans view compromise as a chance for their party to win.

What Is Compromise?

President Biden defined compromise as "neither side [getting] everything they wanted," which largely accords with how scholars define the term.[3] Gutmann and Thompson (2012, 10–11) explain that compromise has two key components: mutual sacrifice (both sides concede some of what they want to the other side), and willful opposition (what each side obtains depends on what the other side accepts). As they note, echoing Biden's remarks at the start of the chapter, most compromises "leave all parties unsatisfied" because everyone had to sacrifice some of their desires to make progress (13). Compromise ideally allows everyone to improve on the status quo in some way and avoids policy gridlock. While the definition implies some egalitarianism, a compromise need not mean that both sides make an equal number of policy concessions or equally important ones.

By definition, political compromise goes hand in hand with bipartisanship. Since the goal of seeking compromise entails earning the support of both parties, a successful compromise means that a policy has bipartisan support. Bipartisanship, however, does not necessarily mean compromise. A policy supported by members of both parties at the outset, for example, is a bipartisan policy (Paris 2017) even if no one compromised. In this chapter, we focus on compromise, and to the extent that we mention bipartisanship, it relates to the outcome of compromise rather than a process of its own.[4]

In the abstract, people support compromise (Harbridge, Malhotra, and Harrison 2014; Wolak 2020). A 2019 survey from the Pew Research Center reported that 65 percent of respondents believed it was "very important" for "elected officials to make compromises with their political opponents to solve important problems," and another 28 percent said it was somewhat important. Support spanned across the parties, with 92 percent of Republicans and 94 percent of Democrats endorsing the importance of compromise (Pew Research Center 2019a). These patterns cohere with the aforementioned arguments that Americans generally prefer bipartisanship and compromise to ideological bickering and gridlock (Fiorina with Abrams 2009; Robison and Mullinix 2016; Wolak 2020; Westwood 2022).

Yet, as Harbridge, Malhotra, and Harrison (2014) note, individuals differ in their beliefs about the *process* of legislation and their evaluations of the actual policies that are produced. In the abstract, people may report that it is "very important" for their party's politicians to compromise with the other party yet still balk at the actual policy outcome. Moreover, people often underestimate how much their own party's legislators toe the party line (Dancey and Sheagley 2018), which may cause them to overestimate their party's willingness and the other party's reticence to engage in compromise.[5] Ultimately, people like the idea of (or even the value of) compromise but dislike what compromise could mean for their party's policy plans—they may perceive it as a political loss. The reality is that some do not actually want a compromise. Instead, they just want to "win" and claim that they compromised.

Animosity and Perceptions of Compromise

Regardless of the eventual outcome, the legislative process—be it an ideological debate or a negotiation in the hopes of compromise—entails group conflict (Ramirez 2009). While the overtly conflictual aspects of policymaking may lead some partisans to perceive the entire legislative institution more negatively (Ramirez 2009), even the more benign types of partisan disagreement in Congress remind people that legislation comes from two teams jockeying for the primacy of their ideas: "In their roles as spectators of policymaking," write Harbridge, Malhotra, and Harrison (2014, 329), "citizens may be inclined to root for their team."

Rooting for one's political team is, of course, natural. When a party's legislators manage to shepherd their preferred policies through Congress, their party wins. We expect that animosity heightens responses to such wins or, conversely, losses. Partisans with high animus, we predict, should be especially attuned to a party's legislative loss, as it represents both a blow to their own political identity and a win for a political side they intensely dislike.

High-animus partisans seek to differentiate themselves from that other party and affirm their own partisan identity. As we demonstrated in chapter 6, these dual goals of differentiation and affirmation affect the way people evaluate political elites. As animosity increases, people offer more positive evaluations of politicians from their own party and more negative evaluations of those from the other side. Not only are partisans who are high in animus motivated to differentiate themselves from the other party, while affirming the connection to their own side, they also may have an easier time figuring out exactly *how* to achieve both those goals. They do this, in part, by perceiving nonpolitical objects through the perspective of partisanship. This tendency to politicize plays a pivotal role in perceptions of political compromise. Those with more animus will perceive compromise in terms of political wins and losses for their party. In turn, as animosity increases, any perceived losses loom larger.

The precise details of the compromise also matter. We expect that partisan animosity will decrease support for even equitable compromise, as a person who is high in animosity will react negatively to *any* loss for their party.[6] Animosity, however, will prove especially important in compromises where one party sacrifices more than the other. These types of "lopsided" compromises allow high-animus partisans to differentiate themselves from the other party and affirm their partisan identity. We expect that as animosity increases, we should see growing gaps in partisans' evaluations of compromises in which the other party sacrifices significantly more and those in which their own party does.[7]

How Much Importance Do Voters Attach to Compromise and Respect?

We begin by asking: do people believe in the importance of compromise and basic respect for political opponents? Of course, in the abstract, most people likely respond that compromise and respect should be important parts of the political process, as surveys suggest. Therefore, we also ask a different version of each of these questions to vary who, exactly, is doing the compromising and the respecting. In earlier chapters, we relied on over-time variation to test our hypotheses, but here, because of the difficulty of tracking compromise and respect over time, we turned to an experiment that randomly assigned individuals to one of three conditions. In one condition, we asked respondents how important it was that elected officials compromise with their political opponents and treat them with respect, without any mention of a party. This version serves as the control. In another (*in-party*) condition, we asked respondents how important it was that politicians from *their own* party (Democrat or Republican) compromise with and respect the opposing party (Republican or Democrat). In the final (*out-party*) condition, we asked respondents how important it was that politicians from the *other party* (Republican or Democrat) compromise with and respect politicians of the respondent's own party

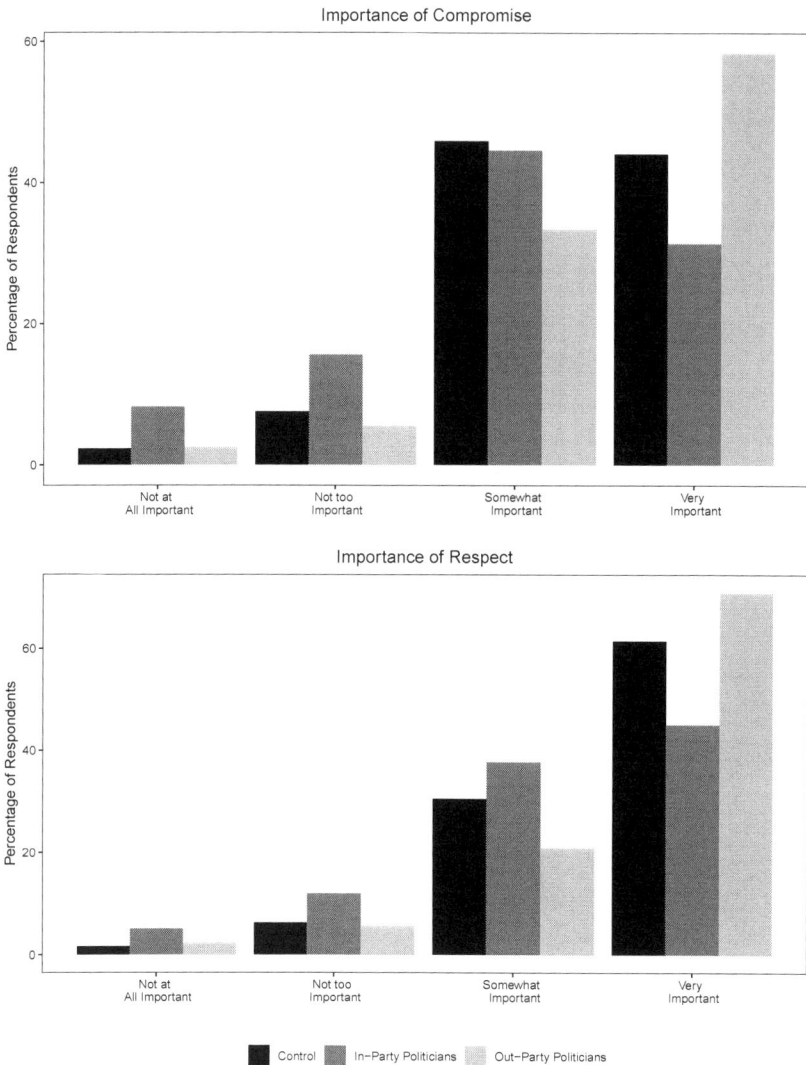

FIGURE 7.1. The Importance of Compromise and Respect

Note: This graph depicts the distribution of responses for the importance of compromise (top panel) and respect for political opponents (bottom panel). The colors of the bars correspond to experimental conditions. Data are from the April 2021 wave.

(Democrat or Republican). These different questions allow us to consider how the addition of partisanship affects perceptions of political compromise and respect. We asked these questions in the April 2021 wave of our study.[8] Figure 7.1 presents the distributions of these variables.

Across the entire sample of partisans, in the control conditions, participants generally believed in the importance of both compromise and respect. We present the compromise item in the top panel, and the respect item in the bottom panel. Approximately 90 percent of participants in the control condition reported that compromise was either somewhat or very important to them, and 92 percent of them thought that treating the other party with respect was either somewhat or very important. In short, as Harbridge, Malhotra, and Harrison (2014) suggest, in the abstract, people view compromise as a critical aspect of policymaking.

These distributions changed, as expected, when the questions specified which party did the compromising. When asked whether politicians from their party should compromise with the other side, 76 percent of respondents reported that it was either somewhat or very important—a drop of 14 percentage points from the control. In contrast, when the question asked about the other party compromising, the proportion of people who reported that compromise is either somewhat or very important matched the levels in the control: 91 percent. However, this similarity masked a difference within the importance categories. In the control, 44 percent believed compromise was "very important," while in the out-party condition, 58 percent selected the "very important" category. Even the descriptive data underscored how much people viewed the other party as central to compromise.

We found similar patterns with regard to respect. When asked whether their party should respect the opposition, 83 percent said it was either somewhat or very important—a 9 percentage point drop from the control. Notably, much of this drop occurred in the "very important" category, with 61 percent selecting that category in the control group, relative to 45 percent in the in-party condition. The importance of respect again grew in the out-party condition: 92 percent of respondents reported that respect is important; the bulk of them, 71 percent, selected the "very important" category.

What about the effects of animus? We expected that respondents' levels of partisan animosity would heavily condition how they responded to questions about compromise and respect. In figure 7.2 we see exactly this pattern (for regression analyses of these and the other experimental data from this chapter, see appendix 7.1). The columns correspond to our outcomes (with the importance of compromise and respect in the left-hand and right-hand columns, respectively), and the rows correspond to the experimental factors (whether subjects were assigned to the control, in-party politician, or out-party politician condition).

We obtained a fascinating set of results. There was functionally no relationship between animus and compromise or respect in the control condition, nor in the out-party condition. In both these cases, everyone—high- and

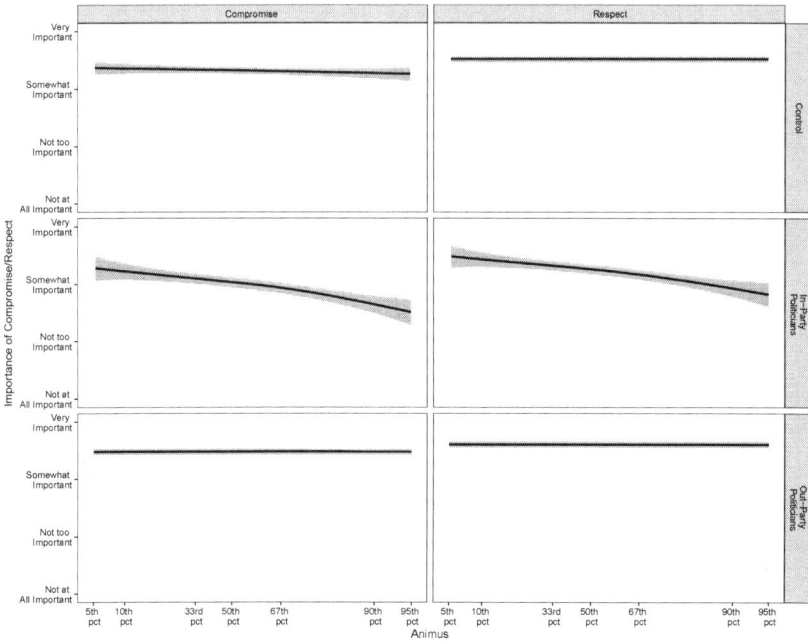

FIGURE 7.2. Animosity and Support for Compromise and Respect

Note: The relationship between animosity and the importance of compromise (left-hand column) and respect (right-hand column). Each row of the graph shows a different experimental condition.

low-animus respondents alike—thought it very important for politicians to compromise and respect one another. But there was a strikingly different pattern when respondents were asked about in-party politicians: as animus increased, respondents became much less likely to attach importance to compromise. Indeed, for the highest-animus respondents, while it was very important that the other side compromise, it was not particularly important that their own party do so; the same was true of respect. High-animus respondents valued compromise only when the *other* side made concessions, not the other way around. These individuals abandon Gutmann and Thompson's (2012) idea of mutual sacrifice—they do not ask both sides to compromise, only the opposition. They seemed untroubled by violating fundamental tenets of civility and compromise.

The fact that we have such strikingly parallel results in the control and out-party conditions underscores a critical dimension of how Americans perceive compromise and civility. When individuals bring the abstract ideas of compromise and respect to mind, they think about the other party: they should compromise so that our side can obtain more of what it wants. This is true for all respondents (see figure 7.1), but especially so for those who are highest in animosity.

Jointly, these results demonstrate that partisan animus shapes how people perceive compromise and respect, even in the abstract. High-animus respondents have a double standard such that they support respect and compromise in general (though less so than other Americans), but not reciprocally. Rather than endorsing a norm that depends on both sides sacrificing and being respectful, high-animus partisans believe the onus falls on the opposition.

Do Respondents See Specific Compromises Differently?

Our first study in this chapter suggests that as animus increases, people's views of compromise depend on *who* does the compromising. High-animus partisans politicize compromise and respect, assuming that only the other party must follow these norms. But perhaps this only occurs in the abstract and we would observe more symmetric patterns in a specific scenario. We address this possibility with an experiment that clarifies how much each side "lost" or "won" in the compromise.

We build on Harbridge, Malhotra, and Harrison (2014), who showed that individuals dislike compromise when it means their side sacrifices more; figure 7.3 presents the vignette shown to respondents in our April 2021 wave. We informed all individuals that President Biden and Republicans in Congress were negotiating funding for NASA. All participants learned that in 2020, NASA's budget was approximately $22.6 billion (the actual figure allocated to that agency in 2020) and that Biden and the Democrats proposed cutting $200 million for the 2021 budget, while the Republicans proposed cutting

---

President Biden and congressional Republicans are currently negotiating on how much spending to cut from NASA (the National Aeronautics and Space Administration) in 2021.

In 2020, NASA's budget was approximately $22.6 billion. President Biden and the Democrats propose cutting $200 million from NASA's 2021 budget. Congressional Republicans propose cutting $400 million from the budget.

Suppose that the outcome of the negotiations was that [**$225/$300/$375**] million in NASA spending was cut. *Recall the Democrats' proposal was to cut $200 million and the Republicans' was to cut $400 million.*

Would you say that you generally favor or oppose cutting [**$225/$300/$375**] million from NASA's 2021 budget?

FIGURE 7.3. An Experimental Test of Support for Compromise

Note: The vignette shown to respondents, with the experimentally randomized text shown in brackets.

$400 million. Next, we randomized participants to one of three conditions. In one condition, we told respondents that the outcome of the compromise was a $300 million cut to NASA's budget. This cut meant that Democrats and Republicans made equivalent concessions. In another condition, we told participants that the compromise was a $225 million cut, meaning that Republicans had made more concessions than Democrats. In the third condition, we told participants that the compromise was a $375 million cut—now, Democrats had made more concessions. We recoded these two partisan conditions to reflect whether the participant was assigned to a treatment in which their own party had lost more in the compromise (*favor out-party*) or a condition in which the other party had made the bulk of the concessions (*favor in-party*).

After reading the vignette, participants answered two questions. The first asked whether they supported cutting the proposed amount from NASA (where the amount of funds reflected the manipulated compromise proposal). The second asked participants what amount *they* thought a fair compromise between the Democrats and Republicans would be. In this question, the participants entered a number between $200 million (Democrats' proposal) and $400 million (Republicans' proposal) in a text box. To begin, we present the overall levels of approval, by condition, in figure 7.4.

Across the entire sample, we see that in the condition with equal concessions, the majority of respondents favored the compromise; 73 percent of the participants reported being either somewhat or strongly in favor of the proposal. The number was very similar in the *favor in-party* condition—67 percent supported the proposal (though more respondents strongly favor the proposal that favors their party). As expected, however, support dropped when the outcome favored the out-party: only 58 percent reported being in favor of the plan. This pattern replicates the findings of Harbridge, Malhotra, and Harrison (2014), who suggest that when people report support for compromise, they often perceive compromise as the other side sacrificing more than their own side.

We expected these effects to differ based on the respondents' level of animosity. It is interesting that figure 7.5 shows that for lower-animus respondents (the bottom 50 percent of the distribution or so), the most preferred outcome was the equal split: to them, the fairest outcome entailed the two sides meeting in the middle. For respondents with higher levels of animus, a very different picture emerged: as animus increased, the preferred outcome became the outcome that favored their party. Indeed, while everyone (even the lowest-animus respondents) was least supportive of the outcome favoring the out-party, that pattern was especially pronounced among high-animus

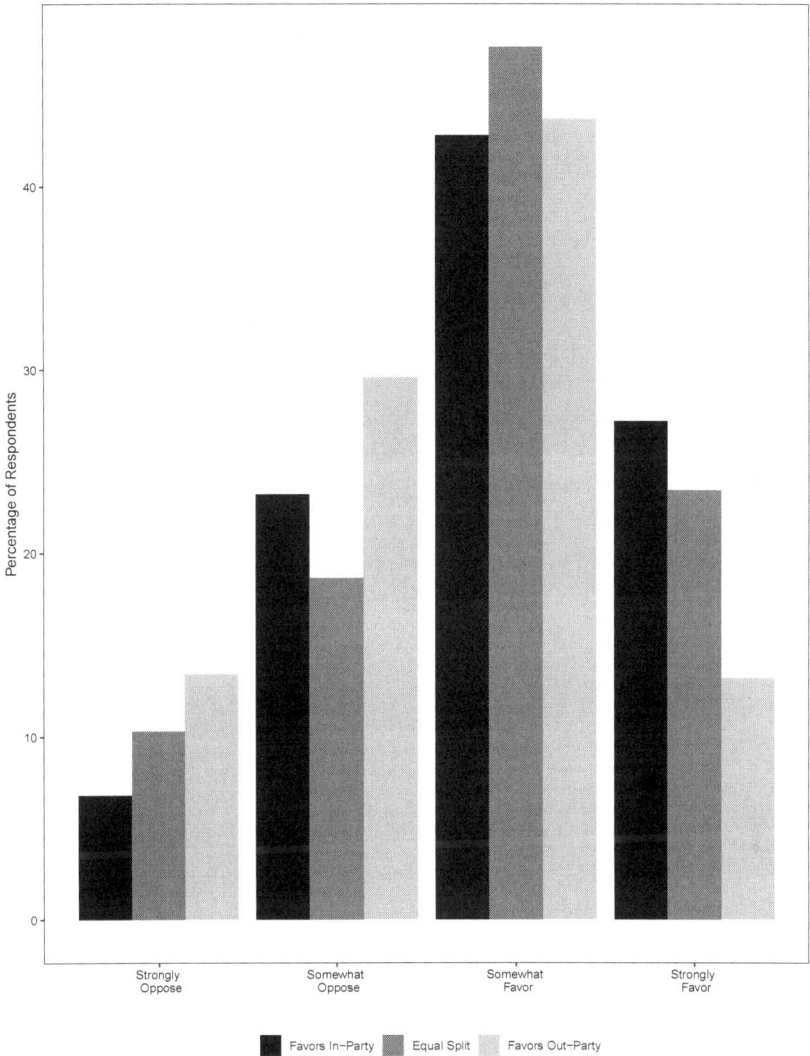

FIGURE 7.4. Distribution of Support for NASA Spending Cuts

Note: The distribution of responses to the vignette depicted in Figure 7.3, with the colors of the bars corresponding to the experimental conditions.

respondents. For these individuals, it was important that compromises should favor the in-party, not the out-party.

It is also quite interesting that the mapping from animus to support for the even split outcome was a flat line (i.e., there was no relationship to animosity). That underscores our argument that, in the absence of partisan cues, most people support compromise and concession as a give-and-take. But once those concessions include partisan asymmetries (and hence clear cues), animosity strongly shapes reactions.

There is an intriguing nonlinearity in how animus moderated our treatment effects. If we look only at respondents below the median of animus, there was only a very modest difference in the in-party and out-party conditions; further, they expressed the most support for the even split condition. For respondents between the 50th and 75th percentiles of animus, there was a modest difference in their attitudes in the in-party and out-party treatments. When we move to respondents between the 75th and 90th percentile of animus—that is, when we look at people who are high on animus as compared to the general public—the difference in the in-party and out-party treatments increased considerably. This gap stems from those with the most animosity loathing the idea of their side sacrificing more. They preferred their side "winning" more than people below the median, but the major difference was that those with the most animus could not tolerate losing while those simply above average on animus could, even if they did not prefer it.

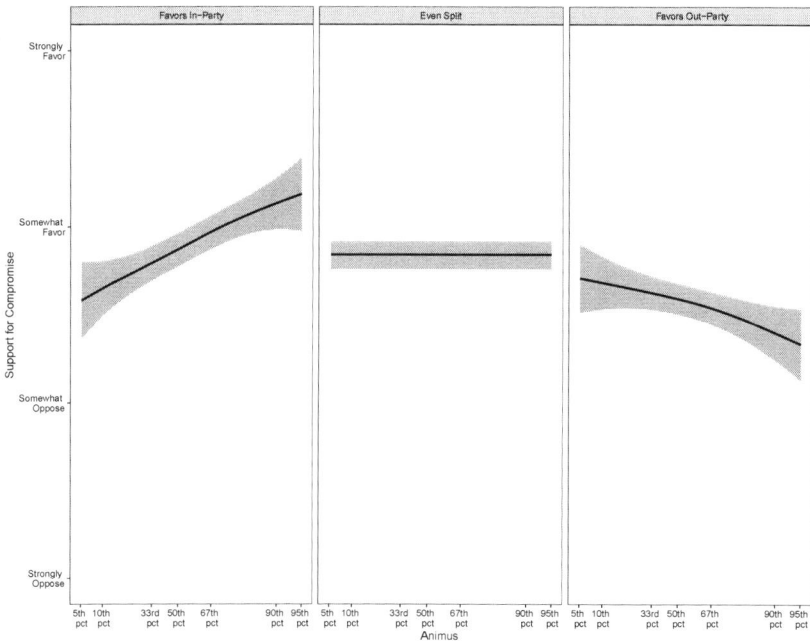

FIGURE 7.5. Animosity and Support for NASA Spending Cuts

Note: The relationship between animus and approval of the policy from the vignette depicted in Figure 7.3. Each panel shows responses from a different experimental condition.

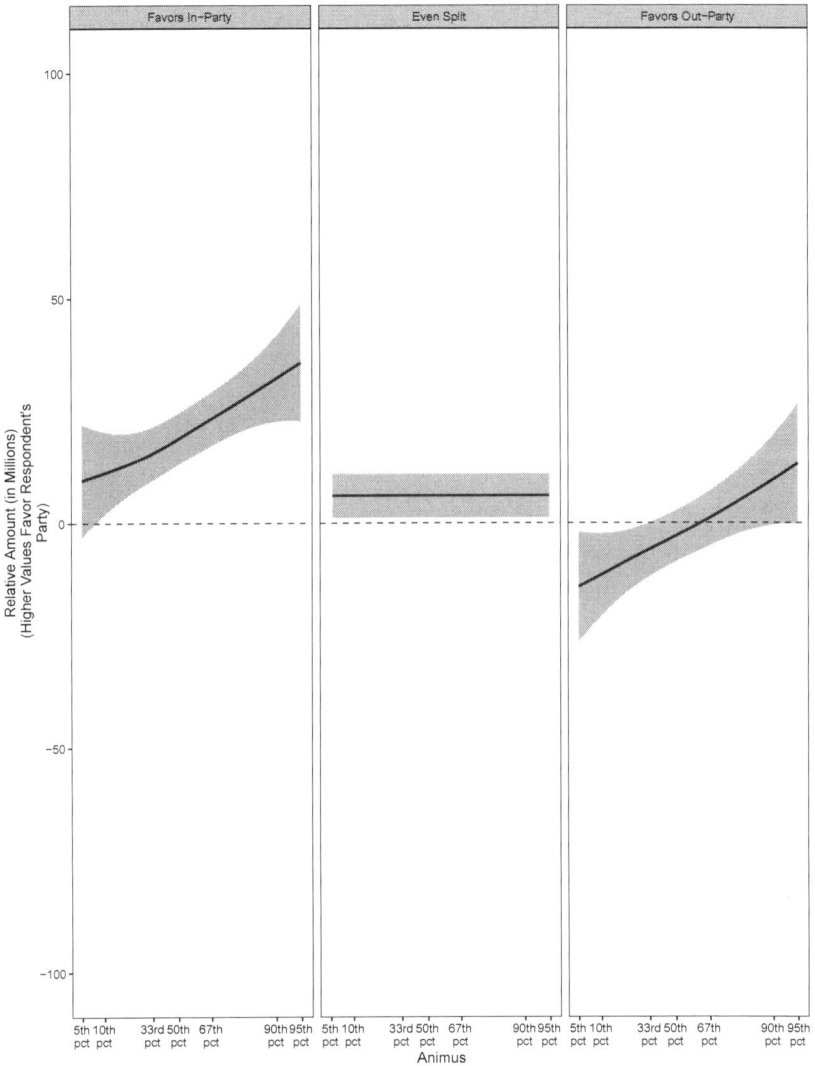

FIGURE 7.6. Animosity and Amount of NASA Spending Cuts

Note: The relationship between animus and the relative dollar amount (in millions) that respondents favor cutting from NASA's budget in response to the vignette depicted in Figure 7.3. Each panel shows responses from a different experimental condition.

The results from the second measure, which asked participants to report their own preferred funding compromise, echoed these patterns. In figure 7.6, we plot how a respondent's proposed level of funding varies with animus. The dependent variable is how much their proposal diverges from the equal split (cutting $300 million from the NASA budget), with higher values indicating greater movement toward the in-party proposal. For instance, an answer of $0 means taking the equal 50–50 split (of $300 million) while moving up (down) the scale to, say $50 million (-$50 million) means shifting by that much toward what their party (the other party) prefers by $50 million dollars.[9] We analyze Democrats and Republicans together because the effects are similar by party; we formally test this assumption of partisan similarity in appendix 7.1.

Replicating figure 7.5, we show that in the even split condition, there was functionally no relationship to animosity and everyone basically accepted the even split, adjusting it just slightly toward to their own party. Again, in the abstract—without any clear party signal—people saw compromise as a meeting in the middle (albeit with a slight bias to their side). Once the scenario gave a partisan cue, however, animus mattered. Note that there was some anchoring off the compromise, with everyone—even high-animus respondents—adjusting their amount based on the description. As a result, all respondents who saw the condition that favored the in-party gave a number closer to their party's ideal point; the converse was true for those who saw the out-party-favored condition (except for those with the highest levels of animosity). That said, in the two-party-cue conditions, we observed strong animus effects, as expected, with higher-animus respondents providing a figure closer to their party's ideal position. This reinforces what we saw earlier in the chapter: in the abstract, everyone likes compromise, but when it is clear which party will be doing the compromising, animus matters. For high-animus respondents, compromise means the *other* side makes the concessions.

Conclusion

That partisans support compromise more when the other party makes the bulk of the concessions is not surprising. Indeed, as Harbridge, Malhotra, and Harrison (2014) showed, what is unexpected is the asymmetry in views about compromise: partisans view it completely differently depending on which party compromises. We show that preferences for compromise not only depend on which party sacrifices more, but also on levels of animus. High-animus partisans politicize concepts and, consequently, view compromise, not as a vital part of governance, but rather as just another space in which to assert partisanship. Win-win scenarios do not exist, only a win-lose scenario, and the loss occurs when their side concedes anything to the disliked opposition. Put slightly differently, animus explains *why* some voters oppose compromises from their party.

Further, partisans with high levels of animosity do not treat all concessions equally. A concession by the opposing party and a concession by their own party do not produce parallel responses in opposing directions. High-animus partisans may be pleased with a compromise in which their party wins, but they are especially unhappy with a compromise in which their party loses. A policy win for the other party hurts to a greater degree than that to which a win for their own party feels good.

We also found that people with less animus support compromise more and shift their support based on partisan outcomes less. This coheres with Wolak's (2020) argument that, on average, Americans may be more supportive of compromise than politicians suspect. Legislators, she argues, mistakenly believe that their voters do not want to see them compromise with the other side (also see S. Anderson et al. 2020). That said, even if disdain for compromise concentrates among high-animus voters, the legislative (mis)belief makes sense (also see Harbridge and Malhotra 2011). High-animus partisans not only see partisanship in most political outcomes (i.e., they politicize more), but they care more about partisanship. Further, as we showed in chapter 3, they post more about politics on social media, talk more about politics, and so forth—they define what elites, and the public, think about politics. When elites think about who will contact them, it is exactly these sorts of individuals. Given that these voters react negatively to any outcome in which their party makes concessions, a legislator may come to prefer gridlock to many types of compromise. This reveals the potential power that high-animus partisans possess.

Our findings underscore why, even if most people like civility, politics can become highly uncivil (Skytte 2022). Most voters believe that politicians should treat one another with respect. Yet, high-animus voters do not value such respect. These voters make clear why incivility thrives, as they do not punish their side for it. Indeed, some of them probably like it. Regardless of whether many voters want civility and compromise, the preferences of voters with high animus make it difficult to obtain.

A Democratic Paradox:
Opposing the Practices and Norms That Uphold a Popular Democracy

WITH JON KINGZETTE

Speaking at a campaign event in Lancaster, Pennsylvania, in March 2008, Senator Barack Obama took aim at President George W. Bush: "I taught constitutional law for 10 years. I take the Constitution very seriously. The biggest problems that we're facing right now have to do with George Bush trying to bring more and more power into the executive branch and not go through Congress at all. And that is what I intend to reverse when I become president of the United States" (Karl 2014).

Given this stated commitment to the principle of limited executive power, one might have expected that, once elected, President Obama would have largely relied on the legislative process, eschewing the types of unilateral actions, such as executive orders, that he had critiqued so forcefully as a candidate. But that was not how Obama governed. According to the American Presidency Project, he issued 276 executive orders during his tenure in office, just 15 shy of the 291 issued by his Republican predecessor (American Presidency Project 2023). Obama used the agency rulemaking processes to achieve some of his most important policy goals, including those related to the environment and immigration. As a candidate, Obama may have stressed the importance of democratic norms that constrain the executive, but as president, he brushed aside these norms when they stood in the way of his broader policy goals.

Not surprisingly, many Republican members of Congress—who had scarcely voiced objections to President Bush's use of executive orders and other unilateral tools—argued that Obama had greatly overstepped his role. Responding to Obama's 2014 State of the Union address, Minnesota congresswoman Michele Bachmann said, "If he wants to move forward with this unilateral activity, he better be prepared for the lawsuit that the United States Congress will bring to him. . . . He may think he's king, he may declare he's a king, but that's not what he is under the constitution" (Mimms and *National Journal* 2014). Bachmann was not alone in her criticism; many other Republicans—from New Jersey governor Chris Christie to Speaker of the House Paul Ryan and the future president Donald Trump—decried Obama's use of these controversial tools (Blake 2018).

That Republican opposition, however, withered and died once President Trump was in the Oval Office. Even many of those who had jeered at President Obama's executive orders cheered the same actions from President Trump. Conservative radio host Mark Levin noted that Trump had no choice but to act unilaterally: "The president, and the American people, are sick and tired of [Speaker of the House Nancy] Pelosi, [Senate minority leader Charles] Schumer, and the media playing games with their lives and their families, and they are sick and tired of legislative blackmail by a wildly radical House speaker from San Francisco [Pelosi]. . . . Kudos to the President, the only person in Washington who actually wants to get things done on behalf of the people" (Levin 2020). In contrast, the Democrats now were the ones arguing that the president had overstepped his constitutional powers. When President Trump unilaterally declared a national emergency at the United States–Mexico border as a means of procuring more funding for a border wall, Pelosi and Schumer shot back in a joint statement that "the President's actions clearly violate the Congress's exclusive power of the purse, which our Founders enshrined in the Constitution" (Pelosi 2019).

Perhaps predictably, then, once President Biden took office, the parties' positions flip-flopped yet again. In a move that Biden himself described to reporters as "not likely to pass constitutional muster," the president unilaterally extended a nationwide moratorium on evictions as the COVID-19 pandemic persisted into fall 2021 (Biden 2021c). Biden's prediction proved prescient when the Supreme Court ruled 6–3 that Biden's move was, in fact, unconstitutional. Pelosi—who had emphatically critiqued Trump's actions—praised President Biden for this policy, referring to it as a moral imperative.

One might view these examples as little more than partisan hypocrisy; politicians and their supporters cheering their own side for taking actions for which they criticize the opposition (Simonovits, McCoy, and Littvay 2022). Yet this type of hypocrisy threatens democratic norms—"the 'fundamental values' or 'rules of the game' considered essential for constitutional government" (McClosky 1964, 362). Such norms—for example, limits on executive power stemming from checks and balances or support for a free press—play a crucial role in maintaining a healthy liberal democracy (Levitsky and Ziblatt 2018; Carey et al. 2019; Lieberman et al. 2019; Graham and Svolik 2020).

As we noted in chapter 1, what really matters is whether people support those norms when it cuts against their own short-term political interest: "Maintaining limits on the state requires that citizens oppose a violation even if they potentially benefit from it. In a society that has resolved its coordination dilemmas, citizens oppose violations for the same reason players of the prisoner's dilemma forgo defection: Although it is costly today, they benefit over the long run" (Weingast 1997, 261). If a norm benefits a citizen, then their support of it does not constitute a meaningful signal. It is when a norm harms a citizen's short-term interests that counts, because that requires understanding the necessity of short-term political sacrifice for long-term political stability. What the antidotes presented earlier reveal—support depending on political context—potentially opens the door to democratic backsliding. Understanding why citizens support norms is thus a crucial task.

In this chapter, we argue that support for democratic norms depends not just on political context, but also on partisan animosity. As animus increases, individuals become more willing to sacrifice norms that harm their party. We show that when President Trump was in the White House, high-animus Democrats advocated for strong checks on the executive's power, but once President Biden took office, this flipped and instead, high-animus Republicans rallied to defend those norms. Context matters, but so does partisan animosity.

While animus limits support for norms, we also find important limits to these effects. First, with one exception that we detail later, most of these results are quite modest, indicating that animus matters, but not dramatically so. While there are indeed effects, it is equally important not to overstate their size. In turn, this helps contextualize discussions about democratic backsliding. As we discuss in the conclusion to this chapter, there are valid concerns about democratic backsliding, but that is a story more about political leaders than the mass public. It is also vital to distinguish democratic dysfunction from backsliding directly—the former can certainly lead to the latter, but it does not definitively do so. Second, when we turn to the ultimate violation of a democratic norm, turning to extrasystemic actions (breaking the law, violence) instead of democratic procedures, we find no evidence of a relationship with animosity. Even the most hateful partisans do not advocate for breaking the law or violence as a way to resolve conflict and any such concern about extrasystemic actions like political violence should not presume the threat stems from the rise of partisan animosity.

What Are Democratic Principles?

What, exactly, are the "rules of the game" (to use McClosky's phrase) that underlie liberal democracy? As norms or principles are, by definition, somewhat amorphous, there is not a hard-and-fast list agreed on by all scholars. We mostly focus on norms related to support for the constitutional system of government, though we acknowledge that democratic norms overall include many other elements (see Kingzette et al. 2021).[1] Such constitutional norms play a crucial role in liberal democratic polities: if citizens do not support the system's basic framework, then the diffuse support critical for regime legitimacy collapses (Easton 1975). More specifically, we study limits to power, especially executive power. This entails support for checks and balances, the role of the media as an independent watchdog, a rejection of authoritarian techniques, and so forth. It is encompassed by Levitsky and Ziblatt's (2018) term forbearance: restraint when a leader has the legal right to do something but precedent suggests they should not. Forbearance acts, in effect, as a self-imposed limit on power, reflecting the fact that norms, unlike laws, depend on actors voluntarily agreeing to abide by them.[2]

One should not conflate American constitutional norms with pure democratic governance. The Constitution and the American system are profoundly countermajoritarian in many ways, with the malapportionment of the Senate and the Electoral College being the two most prominent examples. Nevertheless, we call these "democratic norms" because they reflect the "rules of the game" of the American system. While they may not qualify as democratic per se in the philosophical sense, they nevertheless undergird America's constitutional system.

As we discussed in chapter 2, animosity and context together should generally shape support for these norms. Elites in power—especially the president—will push against limits to their power precisely because they want to accomplish their policy aims. This coheres with the chapter's opening vignette: Obama critiqued Bush for his use of unilateral action while he was running for office, but then once he was in power, he used those same tools to achieve his policy goals. Pelosi critiqued Trump's executive orders but cheered President Biden's, even though constitutional experts cast doubt on the legitimacy of both. These examples can be generalized in that elites in power will almost always push against checks on their power as they seek to implement their agenda. Given this, voters receive clear cues from both parties' elites on support for these norms, and as we argued in chapter 2, those with higher animus will follow the cues most closely.[3] This implies that voters will be more supportive of forbearance norms when their party is out of power, and that such support will be highest for those with the most animosity.

In what follows, we first examine support for principles or norms in particular contexts—that is, situations in which one's party clearly benefits at the expense of the other party. We refer to these as undemocratic practices. We then move to support for abstract norms. Finally, we study the most worrisome outcome of all: support for extrasystemic actions, including violence. As we will explain, in these cases, counter to our forbearance hypothesis about animosity, we did not predict a relationship. Taken together, these investigations go to the heart of whether animosity poses a direct threat to the norms and values that support American democracy.

Partisan Animosity and Undemocratic Practices

Supreme Court Justice Anthony Scalia died in February 2016, nine months before the end of President Obama's second term in office. President Obama nominated judge Merrick Garland from the DC Circuit Court of Appeals to replace him. One might think that, given the historical precedent, Garland would have easily been confirmed, as every time a Supreme Court justice had died in an election year in the post–Civil War period, the Senate had approved his replacement (Wheeler 2020). But that was not to be. Republicans, led by Senate Majority Leader Mitch McConnell, argued that it would be inappropriate to even hold hearings on Judge Garland, let alone vote on his confirmation. On the floor of the Senate, McConnell said, "Let's let the American people decide. The Senate will appropriately revisit the matter when it considers the qualifications of the nominee the next president nominates, whoever that might be." McConnell argued that by even nominating someone, President Obama was "politiciz[ing] it [the nomination] for purposes of the election" (Kelly 2016).

McConnell's position seemed to suggest that no Supreme Court justice should be confirmed in an election year. One might expect, then, that had a Supreme Court justice died in 2020, McConnell would have argued that the winner of that year's election should appoint the new justice. That expectation, however, would have been incorrect. When Supreme Court Justice Ruth Bader Ginsburg passed away on September 18, 2020, there were less than four months remaining in Donald Trump's first term as president and only six weeks until Election Day. The Republican-led Senate seized the opportunity to replace the ideologically liberal Ginsburg with conservative jurist Amy Coney Barrett. When asked about his change of position in 2020 versus 2016,

McConnell responded that he had the right to do so, and the historical prece-dent supported his action, adding, "If our Democratic colleagues want to claim they are outraged, they can only be outraged at the plain facts of American history" (Levine 2020).

In light of this scenario, we asked our respondents about whether they supported senators blocking the president's nominees to the Supreme Court in our October 2020 wave.[4] We reminded our respondents that the Senate has the power to confirm or reject a president's nominee to the Court. We then asked them to consider whether, if the out-party candidate won the November 2020 election, their own party's senators should do "whatever they can" to block that president's nominees to the Supreme Court. In essence, we asked respondents if they supported their own party obstructing an out-party president's constitutional right to nominate a Supreme Court justice, making this an example of forbearance. Senators have the *right* to block a president's nominee, but the Constitution spells out their power as one of advice and consent, so it seems difficult to justify that they should block a candidate sim-ply because they were nominated by a president of the other party. Does animus shape support for this undemocratic practice?

We plot the effects in figure 8.1. As in earlier chapters, a respondent's level of partisan animosity appears on the x-axis, the y-axis displays the level of support for the undemocratic practice, and the body of the graph shows smoothed estimates of the relationship between animus and support.

The data clearly show that animus shaped support for this action. As animus increased in both parties, respondents became more likely to say that their party should block the opposing party's nominee. We found a notable partisan gap, with Democrats, relative to Republicans, being more willing to support blocking a future president's nominees. This likely reflects the temporal context: when we conducted our study in late October 2020, Justice Coney Barrett was in the process of being confirmed (and was confirmed before the completion of data collection). Hence, Democrats were still stinging from what they saw as McConnell's norm-violating behavior. In many ways, that makes this finding particularly illustrative. The context surely amplifies the effect of animus, and thus constitutes something of an upper bound. Nevertheless, respondents who are high in animus prioritized partisan gain over support for the norm.

To see if partisan animus shaped support for other undemocratic prac-tices, we included an additional item in the October 2020 wave that built on the work of Moore-Berg et al. (2020). We asked respondents about whether they would support a plan to gerrymander districts to provide their party with

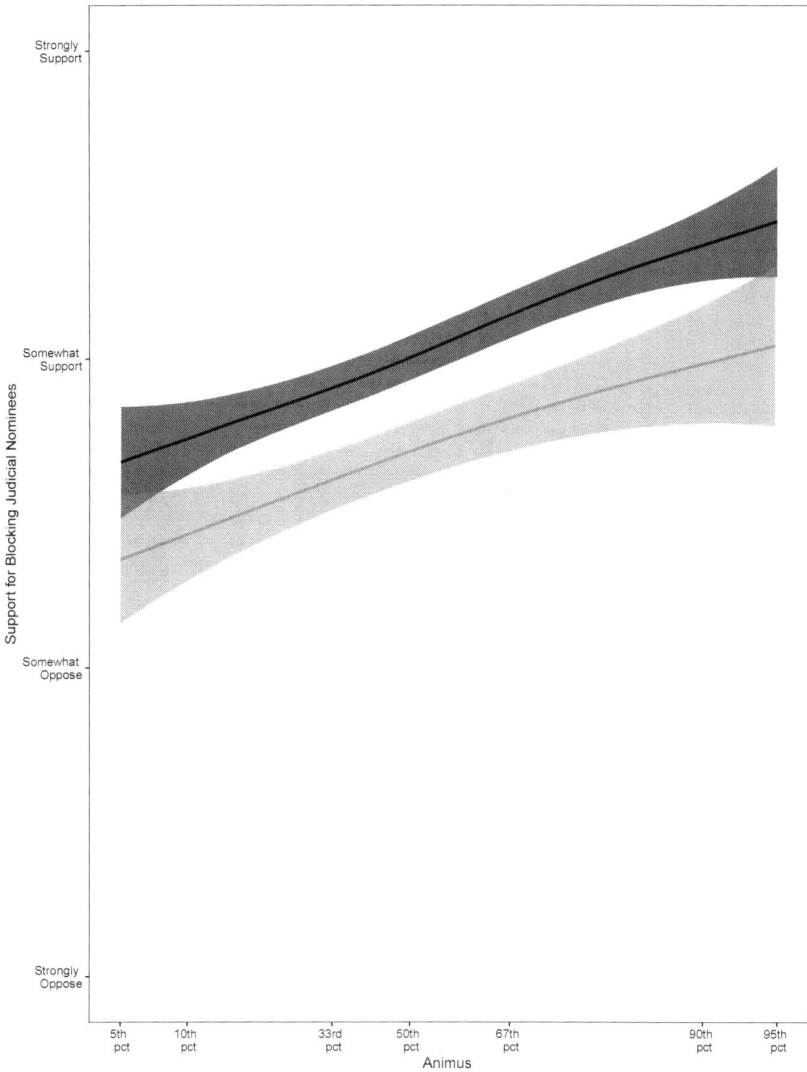

FIGURE 8.1. Animosity and Blocking Opposing-Party Court Nominees

Note: The relationship between animus and support for same-party senators blocking the U.S. Supreme Court nominees of an opposing-party president for Democrats is displayed in black; for Republicans, it is displayed in gray. Data are from the October 2020 wave.

an edge in elections. That is, would they support efforts to draw congressional districts that favored their party? This is another example of forbearance since it involves the spirit rather than the letter of the law. In principle, representative government implies a straightforward mapping from votes to seats: if a party wins, say, 50 percent of the votes in a state, they should control (roughly) 50 percent of the seats. But because of partisan gerrymandering, that often does not occur. For example, in the 2018 elections in Wisconsin, Democratic candidates for the state assembly received 53 percent of all votes cast but only won 36 percent of the chamber's seats. This same pattern repeats itself in many other states; scholars estimate that gerrymandering provides a modest but significant boost to Republicans in the contemporary United States (Peress and Zhao 2020).

In the abstract, voters strongly oppose partisan gerrymandering, viewing it as violating fundamental norms of fairness. In 2019, the Brennan Center for Justice, a nonpartisan think tank focusing on law and policy, reported that "Americans are united against partisan gerrymandering" (Brennan Center for Justice 2019). Referencing polling data from 2017 and 2019, the report showed that more than 70 percent of both Democrats and Republicans favor limits on the practice and that 59 percent of Republicans and 65 percent of Democrats view it as generally "unfavorable." This high-minded opposition, however, may evaporate when partisans realize that gerrymandering could help their party win sets in Congress. Would the public still be opposed if the gerrymandering helped their party?

In our survey, we asked respondents to consider a gerrymander done by their own party, and we specified that it would benefit their party's electoral fortunes. Under these circumstances, we expected animosity to predict support for the plan and that those with higher levels of animus should be more inclined to favor their party's efforts to gerrymander the legislature. Figure 8.2 shows the results.

There are some partisan differences, in that Democrats showed almost no relationship, while Republicans exhibited a positive one, so that Republican partisans with higher animosity were more supportive of the proposed gerrymander. At the same time, support overall remained relatively low: even those with the highest levels of animosity opposed more than supported the proposal. This was not an action that most voters thought politicians should take, regardless of their party or level of animosity. Animus and context matter, but they also have limits when shaping support for democratic norms. Both the Court and gerrymander scenarios are examples of what Moore-Berg et al. (2020) term "out-group spite." That is, they are policies that benefit the in-party at the expense of the out-party, even if this means harming the collective good. Moore-Berg et al. found that out-group spite can be predicted by how much individuals believe that members of the opposing party dehumanize people from their own party. To this, we add animosity toward the other party as a factor that, at least somewhat, contributes to such spite.

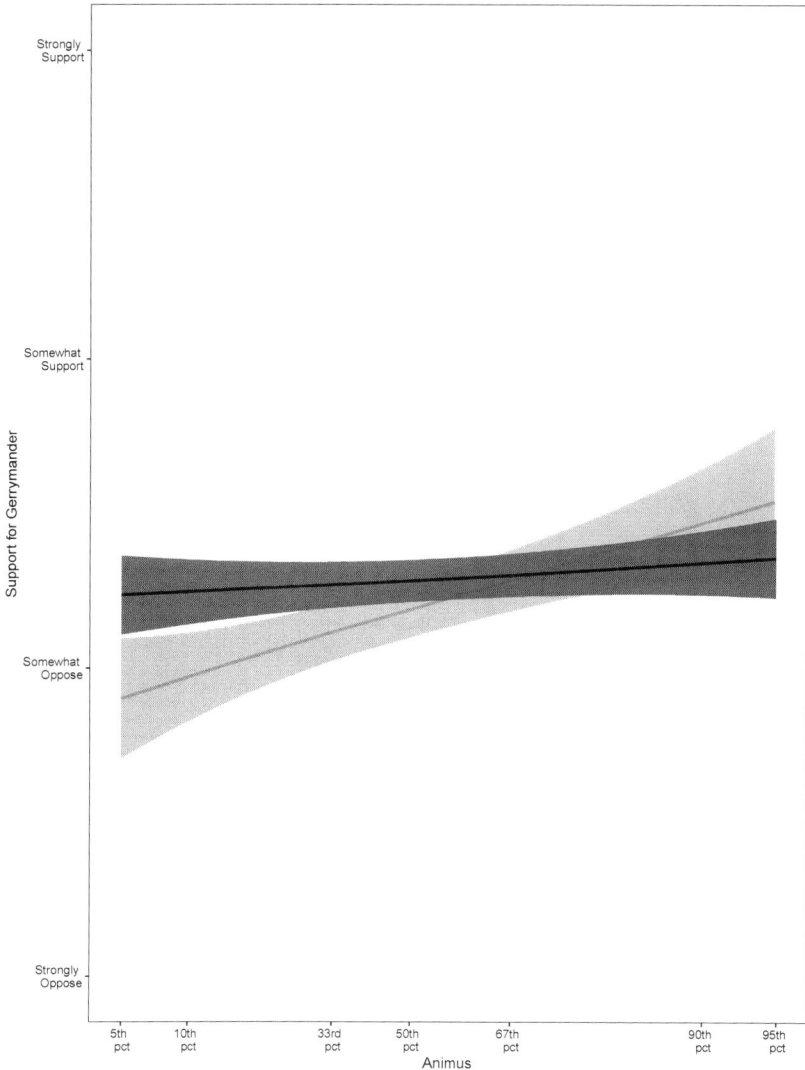

FIGURE 8.2. Animosity and Support for Same-Party Gerrymandering
Note: The relationship between animus and support for redistricting plan gerrymandered to benefit the respondent's party for Democrats is displayed in black; for Republicans, it is displayed in gray. Data are from the October 2020 wave.

The 2020 Presidential Election

Donald Trump's refusal to accept that Joe Biden was the legitimate winner of the November 2020 election is perhaps the most shocking and consequential norm violation in recent decades of American political history. His mendacity in spreading this lie originated even before the election, when he claimed that Democrats would use mail-in voting to steal the election from him. After it was clear that Trump had lost and more than sixty courts had ruled against his lawsuits (often issuing strident rebukes of his position), he continued to promulgate this falsehood, as did others in the Republican Party (Annenberg IOD Collaborative 2023). Indeed, Republicans removed representative Liz Cheney as the party's conference chair over her criticism of President Trump's claims of election fraud and formally censured her and representative Adam Kinzinger for agreeing to serve on the House Select Committee to Investigate the January 6th Attack on the United States Capitol.

Perhaps not surprisingly, ordinary Republican voters likewise viewed Biden's victory with skepticism. In March 2021, the polling company Ipsos asked whether survey respondents agreed or disagreed that "the 2020 Election was stolen from Donald Trump." It found that 60 percent of Republicans agreed the election had been stolen, relative to 13 percent of Democrats; and data from 2022 showed very similar results.[5] Support for the claim of election fraud, no matter how many times it has been debunked, has become a shibboleth in the Republican Party.

This belief in a thoroughly discredited falsehood threatens the lynchpin democratic norm. There is no more sacred and central idea in democracy than the tenet that elections determine who holds the reins of power. As Przeworski (1991, 10) puts it, democracy is "a system in which parties lose elections," and without electorally determined power holding, a country is not really a democracy. This premise, in turn, depends on losing candidates accepting the electoral outcome and on their supporters' belief in the fairness of the electoral process (C. Anderson et al. 2005; Danillier and Mutz 2019). What occurred in the aftermath of the 2020 presidential election likely reflects polarization in a highly politicized climate. Does one's level of partisan animosity shape beliefs about election legitimacy?

To answer this question, in our October 2020 survey we asked the respondents to consider an electoral outcome in which their candidate lost (i.e., Democrats were asked to consider a Biden loss and Republicans were asked to consider a Trump loss). We then randomly varied the magnitude of the loss. One-third of the respondents received a scenario in which their candidate loses a key swing state by 100,000 votes; another third considered their candidate losing that state by 10,000 votes; and a final third were told of an outcome where their candidate loses it by just 1,000 votes.[6] We varied the magnitudes to signal the closeness of the race, and therefore the potential for irregularities or a recount to change the outcome. While only the largest irregularities could reverse a 10,000-vote gap, let alone a gap of 100,000 votes, a 1,000-vote margin could be reversed due to factors such as challenges to

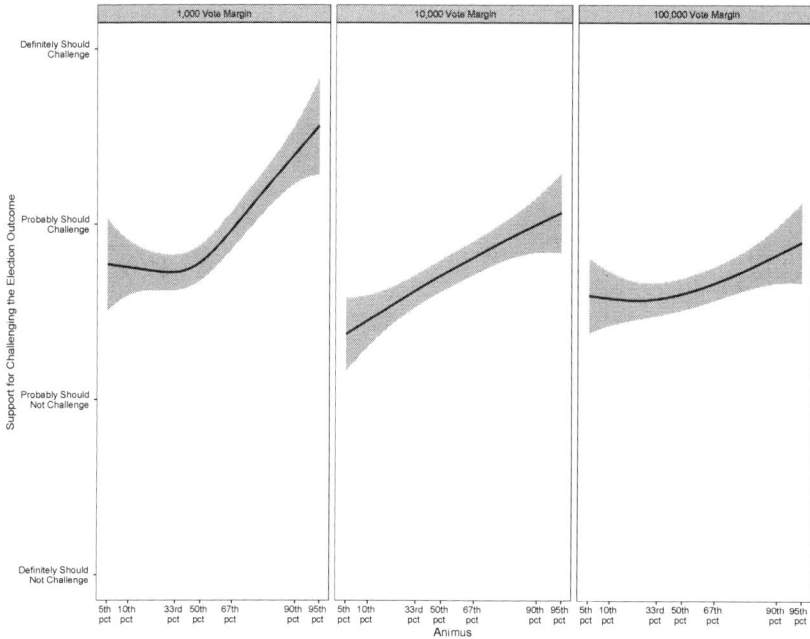

FIGURE 8.3. Animosity and Support for an Election Challenge
Note: The relationship between animus and support for the same-party presidential nominee challenging the results of the election in court (both parties are pooled together because they provided very similar responses). Each panel gives the results for a different margin of defeat.

provisional ballots. We asked all respondents the same question: in that scenario, should their candidate challenge the electoral outcome in court? Figure 8.3 presents the results. We pooled Democrats and Republicans together because the two parties' responses paralleled one another nearly perfectly.

When we conducted the survey, we did not know how prescient this question would be. First, we found that the vote margin matters—as it narrows, respondents became (slightly) more likely to believe the candidate should pursue a court challenge. What is fascinating, however, is that most voters did not believe the candidate should challenge the election results in court. For those in the bottom half of the animus distribution, a 1,000-vote margin—a tiny number, one in which the outcome could easily change based on provisional votes, recounts, and so forth—would not suffice to push a challenge forward (i.e., not until the 67th percentile of animus would a respondent say the candidate "probably should" challenge the results in court). For the 10,000- and 100,000-vote margins, only those with the highest levels of animus said their candidate "probably should" challenge the results in court. For most voters, support for these sorts of electoral challenges remained quite modest. Higher-animus voters were more likely to endorse this potentially undemocratic practice, but even they were not highly (e.g., "definitely") supportive. The support was modest rather than massive. And even when a respondent voiced support, it appeared reasonable—for instance, a legal challenge to an extremely close election does not constitute a serious flouting of democratic norms.

Looking back across figures 8.1–8.3, we can see some important commonalities. First, we found a consistent mapping between partisan animosity and undemocratic practices, but the relationship appears much weaker than one might expect from some of the rhetoric surrounding the issue. Overall, support for challenging democratic practices was modest in most cases. The one exception appeared in figure 8.1, regarding support for blocking opposing-party Supreme Court nominees. The timing of our survey, with Republicans having had just added Amy Coney Barrett to the bench to replace Ruth Bader Ginsberg, complicates the interpretation of this item. Our Democratic respondents—especially those who were high in animus—likely saw this as a tit-for-tat: Republicans had bent the rules to ensure a Republican president could appoint a Supreme Court nominee, so they should do the same when given the opportunity, regardless of electoral timing. And not to be outdone, Republican respondents probably assumed that Democrats would do the same, hence the parallel results.

This underscores an important point about mass public support for these sorts of norm violations. It is not simply that they lay bare when one party gains and the other party loses, but also a sense that one party has escalated so the other party should respond in kind. This highlights the significance of elites adopting what Pozen (2018) calls anti-hardball tactics—tactics whereby the parties strengthen norms (and even laws) that safeguard constitutional guardrails. This also accentuates a fundamental point we return to in the concluding chapter: voters and animus matter to the story of backsliding, as our results show. More importantly, though, elites play the most vital role as their behavior ultimately shapes support for these democratic norms (Stouffer 1955).

Does a Change in Political Context Predict a Change in Support for Abstract Democratic Norms?

It is easy to support limits on executive power when the opposition leads the executive branch; it is more challenging when a copartisan holds power. We suspect partisans who are high in animosity will support weakening norms on executive power when their party controls the executive. This would enable their party to accomplish its goals more easily. In an earlier paper, we showed support for this argument using data from our July 2019 data (King-zette et al. 2021). But what would happen post-2020, when control of the presidency shifted from Trump to Biden? Did high-animus Democrats—rather than Republicans—come to oppose these norms once they obtained power, as our theory would predict?

This was, in many ways, the most direct test of our core hypothesis about animus and support for norms. Analyzing the same items at two different points in time—with a different party in control of the presidency—allows us to use the panel nature of our data to explore whether the same respondents change their support for norms when the party in power differs.

We tested this with our July 2019 and April 2021 waves, in which respondents answered the same battery each time. In both waves we asked respondents whether they agreed or disagreed (using a 5-point Likert scale) with four different items, with a shorthand for each norm provided after it in parentheses:

- I do not mind a politician's methods if he or she manages to get the right things done. (Gets Things Done) (Reverse Scaled)
- The executive, legislative, and judicial branches of government should keep one another from having too much power. (Checks and Balances)
- When the country is in great danger, it is often necessary for political leaders to act boldly, even if this means overstepping the usual processes of government decision-making. (Executive Power) (Reverse Scaled)
- It is important that the government treats other institutions with respect, such as news organizations, religious communities, scientific groups, or business associations. (Respect for Institutions)

The items that say "Reverse Scaled" are such that disagreement with the item indicates support for the norm. The precise items come from Kingzette (2021). They were derived with the intent of capturing forbearance or constraints on power, with a focus on executive power. They encompass more abstract concepts than those presented earlier in the chapter, and hence allow us to test whether animus also predicts support for norms in a less direct context that does not explicitly invoke partisan gain and loss.

We expected to find a clear relationship between animus and support for these norms. Respondents should support the norms when the opposing party holds power (as they constrain the party in power) but not when their own party controls the executive. These effects should strengthen as animus increases (i.e., higher-animus respondents react more strongly to the cue). Thus, high-animus Democrats should support the norms in July 2019 (with

Trump as president) but oppose them in April 2021 (with Biden as president), while high-animus Republicans should do the reverse.

We evaluated our expectation by exploiting the panel nature of our data, comparing responses of the same individuals to the same items in July 2019 and April 2021. We specifically plotted the relationship between animus and support for the norm for each item by party and wave. We also ran a panel regression model (shown in appendix 8.1) and found results very similar to those reported here. Figure 8.4 shows the results.

The results from the July 2019 survey are in the left-hand column of figure 8.4, while those from the April 2021 survey are in the right-hand column. We used the original scales, so for "Reverse Scaled" items displayed in the first two rows (i.e., Executive Power and Gets Things Done), greater support for the underlying norm means *disagreeing* with the item for these two measures. Overall, figure 8.4 somewhat supports our prediction but with some interesting variation across norms. We saw the clearest pattern of support for the Executive Power item ("When the country is in great danger, it is often necessary for political leaders to act boldly, even if this means overstepping the usual processes of government decision-making"), but the position of the parties flipped over time. High-animus Democrats were more opposed to the violation of this norm in July 2019, but it was high-animus Republicans who had stronger opposition to violations in April 2021 (recall that this item is reverse-coded, so higher values indicate greater norm violation and lower values indicate greater norm support). Those in the opposition fear a president of the other party overstepping presidential bounds. Likewise, we saw support in the checks and balances item ("The executive, legislative, and judicial branches of government should keep one another from having too much power"). When Trump held power, high-animus Democrats strongly supported this item, but that support flipped to high-animus Republicans once Biden took the oath of office. The drop among the highest-animus Democrats stands out, suggesting a particular responsiveness to this norm.

We saw a similar, albeit weaker, pattern for the other items. The Respect for Institutions item ("It is important that the government treats other institutions with respect, such as news organizations, religious communities, scientific groups, or business associations") shows some differences for Republicans. Moderately high-animus Republicans were less supportive of this norm in July 2019, perhaps responding to the "news organizations" in the item and thinking of President Trump's sparring with the media, but there is less of a mapping in 2021. The only item for which we found no political context effect at all is the Gets Things Done item ("I do not mind a politician's methods if he or she manages to get the right things done"). While a partisan division

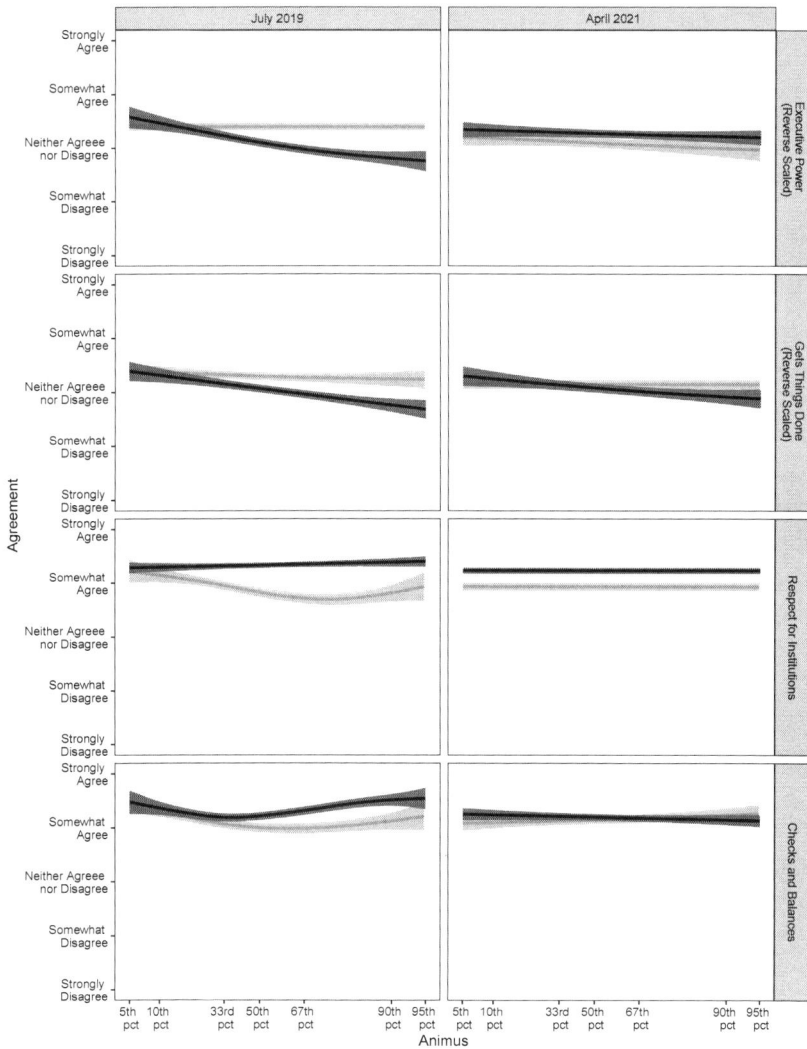

FIGURE 8.4. Animosity and Support for Democratic Norms

Note: The relationship between animus and support for democratic norms related to forbearance for Democrats is displayed in black; for Republicans it is displayed in gray. Each row gives support for a different norm. The left-hand column gives responses from the July 2019 wave, and the right-hand column gives responses from the April 2021 wave.

appeared and it increased with animus, there was no change over time. As animus increased, Democrats always expressed more opposition, even with Biden in the White House, whereas for Republicans, animus had a lesser effect on support over time.

Most importantly, all these differences are vanishingly small. In appendix 8.1, we show statistically significant effects in panel regressions, confirming that animus and context interact to shape support. The overall message, however, is that context has a small effect on how most Americans view these norms. Most Americans do *not* perceive the abstract principles through a substantial lens of partisanship. This suggests that high levels of animosity do not lead partisans to quickly abandon the democratic system.[7] More generally, the abstract norm violations that receive even modest overall support involve executive power and getting things done (recall, for these two, more agreement indicates violations). This likely reflects frustration with gridlock, but even here, the averages never reach "somewhat agree" with the violations. We next turn to an even more direct test by exploring whether animosity relates to support for extrasystemic actions, most notably partisan violence.

Animosity and Extrasystemic Partisan Actions

While concern about partisans supporting or engaging in extrasystemic actions, including violence against those from the other side, is not new (e.g., Kalmoe 2020), its possibility has recently garnered substantial attention. A 2019 poll showed that the average American thought the United States was approaching "the edge of civil war" (Georgetown University Institute of Politics and Public Service 2019; also see B. Walter 2022). These data cohere with scholarship suggesting support for partisan violence (Kalmoe and Mason 2022; although see Westwood et al. 2022), and with violent events such as those in Charlottesville, Virginia; Portland, Oregon; and, most notably, at the U.S. Capitol on January 6, 2021. Avoiding political violence (or other types of lawbreaking) can be thought of as a democratic norm insofar as violence (in particular) constitutes a substitution for politics: rather than settling differences through the electoral and policymaking processes, actors resort to combat. As the philosopher Charles Sanders Peirce (1877) describes it, "When complete agreement could not otherwise be reached, a general massacre of all who have not thought in a certain way has proved a very effective means of settling opinion in a country." In short, violence and similar types of partisan motivated lawbreaking involve a rejection of the political system as a means of solving disputes, and hence a dismissal of the norms that underlie a liberal democratic system.[8]

In our October 2020 survey, we asked respondents what they would do if the candidate from the opposing party (i.e., Trump for Democrats and Biden for Republicans) won the presidency in a contested election. Respondents reported how likely they would be, on a 4-point scale ranging from "Not at

All Likely" to "Very Likely," to break the law but do so without engaging in violence (e.g., deface public property), and then, separately, how likely they would be to use violence. We investigate the (former) lawbreaking item since, as suggested, it involves extrasystemic actions (violating the rule of law) but is not as extreme as engaging in violence.[9]

What would our theory predict here? Key leaders of both parties have denounced violence in strong terms. Joe Biden has, again and again, denounced violence, and indeed, his reaction to the violence in Charlottesville inspired him to seek the 2020 nomination (see the discussion in Annenberg IOD Collaborative 2023, chapter 1). While one could claim that President Trump inspired the violence on January 6th, even on that day he only called for his supporters to make their voices known peacefully, and only fringe voices in the party have more vocally endorsed violence. Given this, there is no clear party cue leading people to break the law or engage in violence.

Further, people typically endorse extrasystemic actions such as violence to advance or protect ideologies. Webber et al. (2020, 108) explained that "to promote violence, an ideology must portray (or preference) violence as a means through which a political goal is likely to be achieved."[10] As articulated at the start of the book, animosity stems more from identity considerations than ideological ones (N. Dias and Lelkes 2022). One can intensely dislike the opposition without holding extreme views, as the title of Mason's (2018) book—*Uncivil Agreement*—suggests. And while these individuals likely talk about politics and post about then on social media (see chapter 3), they probably resemble Hersh's (2020) hobbyists—that is, people who talk about politics more than who do politics. Consequently, we should not see partisans with high animosity to be any more likely to take actions to challenge the system than those with low animosity.[11]

Figure 8.5 presents our results, estimated separately by party to check for any partisan differences. There was a small partisan difference for nonviolent lawbreaking, with Democrats being very slightly more likely to engage in it than Republicans were.[12] But this small difference obscures the bigger picture, and it does so in two ways. First, there was absolutely no relationship with animus, and second, there was almost no support for nonviolent lawbreaking at all. Seventy-one percent of our respondents said they were "Not at All" likely to engage in this activity, and only 11 percent said they were "Somewhat Likely" or "Very Likely" to engage in it. For engaging in violence, the results were even more lopsided. There was no partisan difference, no relationship with animus, and basically no support at all for this action. This confirms our expectation as well as other studies that show scant or a negative relationship between animosity and political violence (see, e.g., Kalmoe and

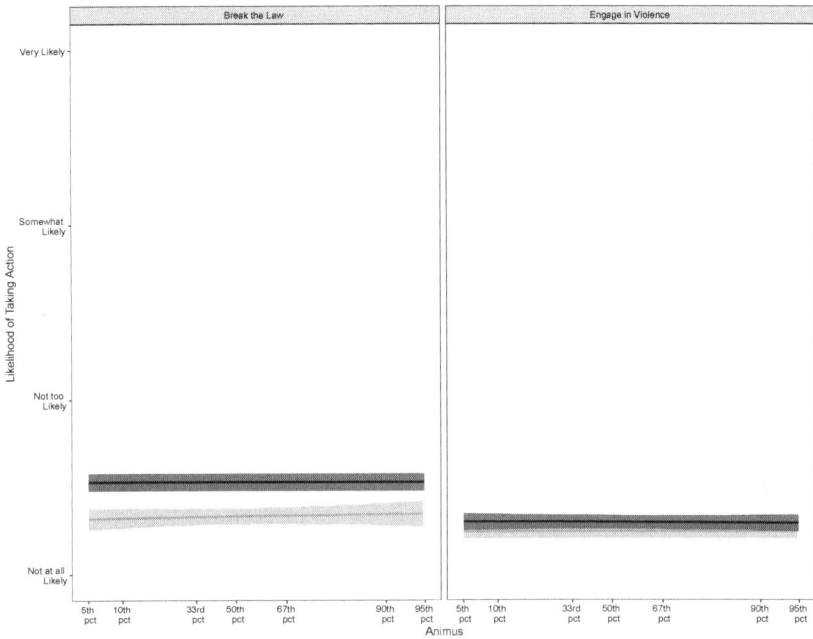

FIGURE 8.5. Animosity and Support for Extralegal Action

Note: The relationship between animus and support for nonviolently breaking the law is shown in the left-hand panel, and the relationship for engaging in violence is shown in the right-hand panel. In both panels, Democrats are shown in black, and Republicans are shown in gray.

Mason 2020; Mernyk et al. 2022). Second, as suggested, support for violence was incredibly low: 81 percent of our sample was "Not at All Likely" to engage in violence, and only 2.3 percent of our sample was "Very Likely" to engage in violence (and of course even some of this may be expressive responding rather than a sincere intention). To be sure, even low levels of support for violence deserve careful investigation. Yet these findings show that animus does not fuel partisan violence.

Conclusion

The results in this chapter are the most nuanced in the book. We have shown that animus, combined with political context, shapes support for undemocratic practices and democratic norms. Specifically, relative to their low-animus counterparts, high-animus partisans support undemocratic practices including blocking Supreme Court nominees from the other party, gerrymandering congressional districts to its advantage, and challenging an extremely close election outcome in court. While these actions certainly make democratic functioning more difficult—such as delaying or tying up judicial processes—they do not necessarily lead to backsliding. Moreover, overall, support for undemocratic practices was not high.

We also find that support for abstract political norms changes along with levels of animus, with high-animus partisans opposing norms about limiting executive power when their party controls the presidency. But such effects are extremely modest, and in many cases, most Americans largely remain committed to these core values with the partial exceptions of moderately accepting politicians and leaders who overstep to accomplish their goals.[13] This can hamper functioning as partisans support the exploitation of executive authority to pursue a partisan agenda, which is then overturned when the other party gains power. But it need not undermine the system unless elites exploit it, as we will shortly discuss. Additionally, we find no evidence that animosity correlates with support for extrasystemic actions including partisan violence. Taken together, then, these findings indicate that scholars and pundits need to be careful not to exaggerate the effects of animosity on democratic backsliding. The outcomes under study matter a great deal when it comes to animosity.

But with all this said, we do not mean to minimize the seriousness of our findings—animosity does shape support for fundamental norms, after all, and even modest effects on norms matter. Easton (1975) makes a classic distinction between diffuse and specific support. Citizens may have limited specific support for particular politicians or policies, but they will have high levels of diffuse support for the system as a whole that helps to ensure the government's legitimacy and stability. Norms play a critical role in diffuse support—they ensure that the system is fair. That is why, as Weingast (1997) points out, abiding by norms when they harm your side is so crucial; doing so makes the system self-enforcing. When norms become politicized, the distinction between diffuse and specific collapses and citizens view everything through the lens of whether their party holds power. That sets the stage for a worrying situation, whereby partisans only trust their party to govern (Hetherington and Rudolph 2015). That can undercut the legitimacy of the system in a troubling way since partisans believe only their party rightfully holds power. In a system designed around alternating power, that could be problematic should elites exploit it for their own ends.

Put another way, the question is whether the modest but real leeway that voters provide to elites to dismiss norms enables those elites to seek despotic power. This could occur even if voters are unaware that they are providing leeway—for instance, they may not connect blocking court nominees or gerrymandering to democratic backsliding even if elites use these maneuvers to consolidate power (Ahmed 2023) or they may rationalize such attitudes as being democratic if they are the beneficiaries (Krishnarajan 2023). Further, mounting evidence suggests that political elites undermine norms to stack the deck in their favor (Grumbach 2022, 2023). In his study of European democracies, Bartels (2023) finds that democracy erodes, not from public opinion, but rather from elites' actions (also see Beremo 2016, Druckman et al. 2023). It may be these actions that contribute more to why three major rating institutions—the *Economist* Intelligence Unit, V-DEM, and the Center for Systemic Peace (creators of the Polity scores)—recently downgraded the quality of American democracy, noting debates over voting rights and growing polarization, as well as threats to checks and balances and freedom of the press. Unlike most citizens, some political elites will not feel constrained at all by norms, as has been thoroughly documented over time. Even when voters show high support for norms, if selected elites undermine them, the norms will continue to erode and democracy will backslide.

The Challenges of Partisan Hostility
for American Democracy

We began this book by describing the fraught 2000 presidential election, which effectively ended with the Supreme Court's December 12, 2000, decision in favor of President Bush. Bush claimed the presidency by five Electoral College votes while garnering roughly 500,000 *fewer* popular votes than his rival, the vice president, Al Gore. In 2000, once the Court ruled for Bush, Gore stated, "Partisan rancor must now be put aside. . . . I accept the finality of the outcome, which will be ratified next Monday in the Electoral College. . . . And tonight, for the sake of our unity as a people and the strength of our democracy, I offer my concession." Bush then stated that the "nation must rise above a house divided. . . . I was not elected to serve one party, but to serve one nation" (History.com 2009).

Twenty years later, virtually to the day (December 11, 2020), the Supreme Court dismissed a suit filed by the Texas attorney general to invalidate the 2020 presidential election results in Georgia, Michigan, Pennsylvania, and Wisconsin. The suit's goal was not subtle: to shift the election result to President Trump, despite the fact that he lost to Biden by seventy-four Electoral College votes and more than 7 million popular votes. Trump's 2020 reaction could not more starkly contrast with Gore's 2000 response. Once Biden was declared the winner, Trump stated, with no credible evidence, "It remains shocking that the Biden campaign . . . wants ballots counted even if they are fraudulent, manufactured, or cast by ineligible or deceased voters. Only a party engaged in wrongdoing would unlawfully keep observers out of the count room—and then fight in court to block their access. So what is Biden hiding? I will not rest until the American People have the honest vote count they deserve and that Democracy demands" (*Al Jazeera* 2020). Trump and his legal team filed more than sixty lawsuits alleging fraud or other improprieties. In nearly all those lawsuits, their claims were dismissed for lack of evidence, often featuring stinging rebukes by Democratic and Republican judges alike. Nevertheless, he persisted, spreading what the House select committee on the January 6th insurrection would call "the big lie" (the false claim that the election had been stolen from him due to voter fraud). He further pledged to pardon the January 6th insurrectionists if he were to win the presidency in 2024 (Reuters 2022) and said that if he assumed the presidency again, he would have the power to even suspend the Constitution in order to prevent voter fraud (Gans 2022).

This radical shift in behavior two decades into the twenty-first century reflects the altered state of American democracy, in which some people believe partisan considerations dwarf democratic ones and hostility is often painted as the culprit (e.g., Finkel et al. 2020; Boese et al. 2022). Our book has sought to specify the relationship between partisan hostility (i.e., partisan animosity) and American democracy. We produced substantial evidence that partisan animosity matters in politics: it shapes attitudes and behaviors, but only under certain specific conditions. These conditions do not always hold, and the existence of high levels of animosity do not invariably indicate democratic backsliding or collapse. But partisan animosity does shape American politics and could contribute to democratic erosion.

We begin our concluding reflections by returning to the four key points that we introduced in chapter 1. These points identify the scope conditions for the effects that we found throughout the book.

- **Democratic Functioning versus Democratic Collapse**. We find broad-ranging effects of animosity on policy attitudes (chapter 4), COVID-19 pandemic responses (chapter 5), evaluations of public figures (chapter 6), political compromise (chapter 7), and undemocratic practices (e.g., gerrymandering, challenging close elections; chapter 8). In each of these cases, animosity divides individuals in ways that can hamper democratic functioning. Animosity has some effect when it comes to evaluating fundamental norms, but they are extremely small; it has no impact on promoting illegal activities or violence (chapter 8). The implication is that animosity exacerbates the challenges of democratic functioning but is not a direct, proximate threat leading to collapse.

- **Availability of Party Cues**. For animosity to matter, citizens must know where to stand on a given topic or impute such a stance. That means that animosity matters when parties send clear signals or a target is sufficiently ambiguous to facilitate its politicization by high-animus partisans. If those conditions do not exist, animus does not matter. While public attention often focuses on politicized, polarizing topics, there are many issues that receive less attention on which even those with the most animus toward the other party do not differ (chapter 4).

- **Personalization versus Politicization**. Partisans' motivations are central to the impact of animosity. When a decision has clear personal consequences, animosity effects decrease or disappear, given the desire to arrive at the most accurate outcome. During the COVID-19 pandemic, people who experienced or anticipated severe consequences for themselves (or those in their network) ostensibly put partisan considerations aside in evaluating policies and scientific advisers and in making behavioral choices (chapters 5 and 6). For instance, high-animus Republicans, who otherwise flouted scientific advice, followed the science. On the flip side, when a topic becomes politicized, animus increases in relevance, as was made clear by the evolution of mask-wearing decisions (chapter 5) and evaluations of Dr. Fauci and other key scientific agencies (chapters 6).

- **Hateful partisans**. High-animus partisans appear quite different than low-animus partisans on a variety of measures. They have relatively stronger political identities and are more politically engaged (chapter 3), hold different attitudes and engage in different behaviors (chapters 4 and 5), evaluate public figures through a more partisan lens and view more topics as political (chapter 6), exhibit less support for political compromise (chapter 7), and have greater toleration for undemocratic practices when conducted by their own party (chapter 8). These hateful partisans pose the most notable threat to democratic functioning.

Each of these points has significant implications for understanding the consequences of animosity for American democracy, and they also raise several questions that we believe can guide future inquiries. In the remainder of this concluding chapter, we delve into each of the four points, in reverse order, with the goal of clarifying the book's contributions and what they imply for the country's politics.

Identifying and Studying Hateful Partisans

As we emphasized throughout, many of our findings reveal that partisan gaps become particularly notable at higher levels of animus. It is the most hostile or hateful partisans who present the greatest challenge to democratic functioning. This finding has implications for (1) the study of affective polarization and its measurement, (2) the conceptualization of types of polarization, and (3) the understanding of power in American democracy.

First, regarding measurement, we discussed in chapter 3 that our inferential approach of using observational over-time panel data contrasts with recent experimental studies of the effects of animosity. For example, Broockman, Kalla, and Westwood (2023) had subjects participate in a partisan trust game where someone from the other party either acts in an untrustworthy or trustworthy fashion toward them, which in turn leads to notable changes in animosity. They then examined the effects of the treatment(s) on accountability (e.g., learning about issue positions of their representatives), adopting their party's position (cue-taking), supporting bipartisanship, endorsing democratic norms (e.g., having state legislators decide election results), and perceptions of objective conditions (e.g., the unemployment rate under Trump). The authors found that the animosity manipulation (i.e., trust game) had no effect on any of these outcomes. They (826) concluded that for "interpersonal topics[,] . . . affective polarization [animosity] may be more likely to have an impact. . . . However, when it comes to political judgments, our argument suggests greater skepticism." Similarly, Voelkel et al. ("Interventions," 2023) changed levels of partisan animosity using an alternative approach—namely, interventions that decrease animosity by correcting partisan misperceptions about the other side, asking partisans to think about interpartisan friendships, or showing an interpersonal friendship between elite partisans. They found that shifts in animosity had no effect on support for undemocratic practices (e.g., sacrificing good outcomes for the sake of one's party), undemocratic candidates (e.g., supporting a partisan even if they violate democratic norms), or partisan violence.

These studies have the clear advantage of making precise causal inferences about manipulated animosity levels on outcomes. They also suggest that animosity interventions may have no downstream political consequences. We cannot fully reconcile their largely null findings with our results, given a host of differences including differences revolving around measurement. Instead, we offer two points for consideration. First, the experimental papers make the point that observational work cannot rule out the possibility of omitted variables such as changes in media over time or various sorting phenomena. We acknowledged this possibility in chapter 3, while emphasizing the totality of our evidence. In the end, it is possible that our measure of animosity is confounded with over-time socializing factors that contribute to a given animosity level—indeed, individuals seem to acquire animosity at an early age, shaped by their parents (Tyler and Iyengar 2023). Ideally, one would identify the precise construct at work; however, it also is the case that if the measure of animosity we used is a proxy for a related construct, we do not view that as a fundamental indictment of our findings. It means instead that animosity is a symptom of some other political feature in need of identification. Second, we value the experimental approaches but also point out a potential downside (as discussed in chapter 3), that voters who are high in animus prior to the experimental treatment may resist manipulations of partisan animosity. They have less room for movement if the manipulation is meant to increase animosity (a ceiling effect) and they hold more tightly to their stronger identities and so may be less likely to move regardless of the direction of treatment (Howe and Krosnick 2017). If this is true, then experimental results depend on movement in animus among people with low or moderate levels, not those with the highest levels. Consequently, the experiments might inadvertently miss effects that are present among or driven by those with the most animus (since their treatment does not influence them).[1] Experiments play a crucial role in the study of animosity, but they also have limitations. In the end, researchers in this area benefit from relying on both experimental and observational evidence, thus identifying points of overlap and questions involving differences. We are not suggesting that our results invalidate the experimental finding or are superior per se; rather, we believe there should be more dialogue between those employing distinct approaches.

A second implication of our results concerning high-animus (hateful) partisans involves types of polarization. As explained in the first chapter, initial studies of mass political polarization focused on ideological or issue-based divergence, which was characterized by Fiorina with Abrams (2008) as moving toward the extremes and away from the center with respect to issues, ideology, or both (also see McCarty 2019). While elite ideological discord is far from the only, or even a primary, cause of partisan animosity, there is a connection between the two (Iyengar et al. 2019). For example, Webster and Abramowitz (2017) showed that ideological differences strongly predict out-party animosity concerning attitudes about social welfare policy and, to a lesser extent, abortion and gay rights, thus shaping negative feelings about the opposing party (also see Rogowski and Sutherland 2016; Enders and Lupton 2021; N. Dias and Lelkes 2022). We find that the converse also holds. That is, animosity shapes the policy positions that people, especially the people highest in animus (hateful partisans), adopt. As animus increases, individuals become more likely to adopt their party leaders' positions on the issues when the leaders send clear signals. As we have mentioned throughout the book, this implies a profound reciprocal linkage between ideological and affective polarization (also see Levendusky 2023).

The finding additionally provides clarity on why the monotonic rise in animosity and the emergence of so many hateful partisans have *not* resulted in a clear concomitant increase in mass ideological polarization (Fiorina 2017). Specifically, animosity leads to issue polarization only in the presence of clear party signals sans personal salience (i.e., clear personal consequences). Only the partisans with the most animosity have the motivation to engage with these cues, and they may well already be polarized for other reasons. Consequently, the impact of issue and ideological polarization on affective polarization and animosity dwarfs the reverse.

A final implication of our results is that they accentuate the need to study high-animus (hateful) partisans as a distinct political class. In chapter 3, we showed that, relative to people who are low in animus, those who are high in animus also have stronger political identities (e.g., hold stronger partisan identities and are ideologically sorted) and are more engaged (e.g., discuss politics and post on social media about politics). The subsequent chapters show that these individuals also exhibit relatively higher levels of policy polarization, a tendency to politicize public officials and even the country itself, an aversion to compromise, and antidemocratic attitudes. Their high levels of political activity make them more visible to journalists, on social media, and to other citizens. This surely leads to citizens' well-documented misperceptions of the parties as much more hostile, engaged, and extreme (particularly on contentious issues) than they actually are (Wilson, Parker, and Feinberg 2020; Druckman et al. 2022).

On the one hand, these misperceptions could have negative consequences (e.g., an aversion to interaction), as we discuss later in this chapter. On the other hand, one could raise the question of just how much these are misperceptions. That is, it may be true that the modal or average partisan is less engaged, and more moderate, than these high-animus partisans. But what if these high-animus partisans exert more influence in the system? For instance, these same individuals may act as opinion leaders or influencers who shape the views of others (e.g., Katz 1957). Druckman, Levendusky, and McLain (2018) show that opinion leaders who are exposed to partisan media can spread the views expressed in the media to those who are not exposed—thereby amplifying its influence. Carlson (2019, 2024) finds that in passing along messages, individuals inject their own biases and the message changes over time. Consequently, if people who are high in animus act as conduits from elites to less engaged citizens, they may pass along not only their own, more ideologically polarized views, but also revise information that originated with others to match those views. Along these lines, Osmundsen et al. (2021) have offered evidence that partisan animosity correlates with sharing fake news stories that disparage the other side (also see Jenke 2023). If high-animus partisans are social referents in networks (i.e., individuals who have outsized influence), they can substantially shape what others believe (e.g., Paluck, Shepherd, and Aronow 2016).[2]

Apart from influence on other citizens, hateful partisans also may exert unequal influence on government officials. A sizable literature reveals representational biases based on various demographics, such as income (e.g., Bartels 2008; Gilens 2012) and race (Butler 2014), as well as political engagement, such as donations (Kalla and Broockman 2016). Hill (2022) finds that representation is driven by voters with intense issue positions (regardless of what the majority prefers), who may very well be those with high animus. Whether those individuals with more animus disproportionally shape elite behavior is an open question. If they do, however, it may explain why elite divides ostensibly outpace those found among citizens, and it would also suggest that even if citizens generally overestimate the extent of the animosity, extremity, and engagement of those from the other party, this assessment may reflect the disproportionate power of those individuals.

Personalization versus Politicization: Local Information and the American States

Another of our main findings concerns voters' motivations. When an issue or actor becomes politicized, animosity is much more likely to be associated with beliefs. In this case, animosity will be more easily linked to the topic at hand. Imagine if the scientific community had been subject to less politicization during the COVID-19 pandemic; it could have saved many lives (e.g., A. Flores et al. 2022). Alternatively, when one recognizes clear and significant personal consequences, animosity effects dwindle or disappear and citizens ostensibly engage in more deliberative decision-making. This raises the question of what triggers politicization versus personalization. Elites' reactions are crucial as they choose whether to take sides on a topic and whether to politicize an event. They also have the incentive to portray the other side in negative terms, which can generate misperceptions and increase animosity and politicization. Indeed, it typically is elites who polarize and politicize issues, with the public following suit (Lenz 2012). In the United States, no issue exemplifies this more than the environment and climate change. Partisan differences on environmental issues among political elites go back to at least the 1970s (Lindaman and Haider-Markel 2002). By the early 1990s, a sizable gap was evident in congressional voting patterns. Citizens lagged elites, only becoming polarized starting around the mid-1990s. As one set of authors put it, "Over the course of a little more than 20 years, the environment was transformed from the least to the most polarized issue" (Egan and Mullin 2017, 219). This issue is particularly telling as well given that for some of those who directly experience the consequences (e.g., extreme climate events), climate change can be personalized. This is particularly true at the local level. For instance, Wiest, Raymond, and Clawson (2015) showed that localized information (relative to global information) about climate change increases perceptions of severity and the desire for state-level policy action, even among Republicans, who tend to express climate skepticism.

Climate change and COVID-19 are examples of issues with which citizens may have direct experiences; other examples include gun violence, access to reproductive health care, parental control in education, local crime, unemployment, inflation, and health insurance coverage. In these cases, experiences can naturally counter politicization and animosity effects (as we showed in chapters 5 and 6). Yet, many other topics and/or people are more distant, and the personal connection may be much more obtuse, meaning that citizens must rely on information from others. Here, changes in politics and the information ecosystem may limit personalization and hence exacerbate animosity effects. The nationalization of politics (Abramowitz and Webster 2016; Hopkins 2018; Pierson and Schickler 2020) and the decline of local news (Moskowitz 2021) may decrease personalization and facilitate the politicization of topics (B. Lee and Bearman 2020). Moskowitz (2021) showed that access to local television news coverage led to increased political knowledge and split-ticket voting (which could reflect more accuracy processing). One report estimates that more than a fifth of the nation's citizens live in (or is at risk to live in) news desserts, with very limited access to local news (Abernathy 2022).

The possibility of reduced access to localized information that connects people's lives to government comes at an inauspicious time—local information may be declining just as the power of local, and particularly state, governments has increased. This has occurred due to legal decisions, most notably the Supreme Court's *Dobbs* ruling, which delegates the regulation of abortion to the states. Moreover, state governments have taken various actions deemed undemocratic in recent years: instead of being laboratories for democracy as traditionally depicted, states may be becoming laboratories for backsliding (Grofman 2022; Grumbach 2022, 2023). Rocco (2022) explains that "The constitution makes the states into the *infrastructure* of democracy: state laws shape the exercise of rights and liberties, structure national elections and legislative districts, and affect the development of civil-society institutions in ways that have national reach. Indeed, episodes of democratic collapse at the state level have had profound reverberations for national politics" (301; italics in the original). This same trend can be seen in particular public policy areas, as accentuated by the COVID-19 experience. For instance, as Woolf (2022, 1331–1332) points out, "Disparities in health across the 50 states are growing, a trend that began in the 1990s. . . . Although the divergence in state health trajectories might reflect changes in demographic and socioeconomic characteristics, a more likely potential explanation is the growing polarization of public policies across states . . . medical and public health professionals and the public [should] shift their focus from the political standoffs in Washington, DC, to the escalating activity in state capitols." How these contrasting trends of declining local information, at least in terms of nonpartisan professional outlets, and increasing salience of state and local government shape personalization and politicization—and consequently animosity's impact—remains to be seen.

A related question revolves around factors that explain democratic outcomes and public policy at the state level and the relevance, if any, of animosity. Grumbach (2022, 2023) showed that state-level electoral democracy backsliding stems from Republican control of state government; he also reported scant influence of party competition, and ideological polarization. He attributes the Republican effect to the incentives of groups that comprise the Republican Party (e.g., wealthy elites, voters who feel threatened by historically marginalized groups) that prefer limiting electoral expansion. It is interesting that the lack of a consistent effect of competitiveness contrasts with Gamm and Kousser's (2021) finding that from 1880 to 2010, party competition (and not party control) has shaped state-level spending on education, health, and other areas of human capital, which, in turn, affect well-being (e.g., means to achieve a longer life expectancy or higher income).

These conflicting findings, which may stem from exploring distinct time periods and outcomes, accentuate a key topic for future work on animosity. Extant work, including our own, focuses on feelings toward the other party or parties. However, a distinct question concerns the extent to which voters dislike certain factions *within* the two parties. For instance, the contemporary Republican Party is divided between a Trump contingent and a more traditionally ideological conservative faction. The 2022 midterms saw a number of primary battles—in both safe Republican districts and competitive districts—that pitted members of the factions against each other. Undoubtedly, voters supporting one of these factions felt some animosity toward the other, suggesting a need to study intraparty (factional) affective polarization. While not as prevalent in 2022, the Democrats also factionalize into progressive and moderate wings. In choosing between primary contenders in a safe seat, when do some voters support a candidate who endorses antidemocratic tactics to achieve particular policy victories (e.g., flouting federal gun policy or even state-level policies such as on reproductive rights), and which voters will do so?

In short, the discussion makes clear that going forward, more attention must be paid to intraparty animosity and what happens within party primaries when prioritizing policy or other goals against democratic practices (see Gidengil, Stolle, and Bergeron-Boutin 2021). In these cases, high levels of intraparty animosity could lead to deleterious outcomes at the state level and, consequently, the national level. Alternatively, personalization on topics on which individuals have strong positions could lead them to endorse antidemocratic candidates or tactics, not because of partisan preferences, but rather due to policy preferences (as they view the consequences on the topic as more salient than the democratic system). Here accuracy leads voters to prioritize their policy positions at the expense of democracy, making clear that "good" motivations do not always lead to salubrious collective outcomes. This highlights a thorny theoretical question of how to treat democratically made collective decisions that undo democracy (e.g., Wollheim 2016). An example occurred in the 2022 elections when the Republican Party chose 202 election deniers to run, thereby seeking power via the very democratic electoral process that they claim does not work (Kamarck and Eisen 2022). What is the role of intraparty animosity and when does personalization either improve or undermine democratic outcomes? Overall, motivation matters when it comes to the impact of animosity on American politics. Motivation, in turn, depends on whether topics are personalized or politicized, and how that will occur in the future likely will reflect developments in state-level competition and information.

Party Cues and Democratic Safeguards

We argued that animosity matters when partisans receive cues of where their party stands on a particular topic. Partisan signals serve as a guide for animosity effects. This basic dynamic reveals why the founders worried about parties. In his farewell address more than 225 years ago, Washington captured the concerns in arguing that a faction—akin to a proto-party—"agitates the community with ill-founded jealousies and false alarms, kindles the animosity of one part against another, foments occasionally riot and insurrection. It opens the door to foreign influence and corruption, which finds a facilitated access to the government itself through the channels of party passions" (G. Washington 1796). These ills—animosity, insurrection, and foreign influence—echo many descriptions of the 2016 and 2020 elections, which saw Russian interference and the January 6th insurrection.[3] In this view, parties can be damaging, and this stems in part from animosity. Of course, as political scientists have long noted, parties also serve crucial roles, including the provision of collective responsibility (Fiorina 1980). Further, as argued in the *Federalist Papers*, the country should be protected from the tyranny of factions or parties via two safeguards: pluralism and institutional checks and balances (Hamilton, Madison, and Jay [1787–1788] 1961).

In the first chapter, we discussed the importance of pluralism in American democracy. The theory, which may be Madison's central insight in the *Federalist Papers*, holds that a large and heterogeneous country makes democracy more effective, not less, because it introduces a wide variety of interests and ideologies that compete with one another. Cleavages become cross-cutting, and this prevents any one group from becoming the dominant one in society, thereby promoting stability, as he famously argued in *Federalist* 51: "In the extended republic of the United States, and among the great variety of interests, parties, and sects which it embraces, a coalition of a majority of the whole society could seldom take place on any other principles than those of justice and the general good" (Hamilton, Madison, and Jay [1787–1788] 1961, 325). There is much to unpack in this statement, but for us, the most notable aspect concerns the word "seldom." Alas, "seldom" is not the same as never, and the worry for many now is that the two parties have evolved into entities that have near electoral majorities on principles distinct from "justice and the general good." Indeed, an underlining assumption of pluralism posits that groups agree to the pursuit of a common good or shared value, which lends stability to the overall system. Partisan animosity epitomizes these concerns such that partisan disdain for the other side overshadows concern for a common good.

Some of our results give credence to this perspective. That animosity strongly connects to policy polarization, collective inaction in response to a crisis (COVID-19), the politicization of evaluations and attributions, and inflexibility in political compromising certainly means that it contributes to democratic dysfunction. Representatives who dutifully follow their party's constituencies will not only fail to accomplish much but also fail to ensure the provision of crucial public goods. COVID-19 made clear that the consequences of blind party cue-following can be horribly fatal.

Yet, at the same time, we find clear limits: partisans act in their own interests, regardless of their party, when the stakes are high, and they also hesitate to condone rampant violations of democratic norms. These latter findings suggest the continued existence of a pluralistic nation—more so than one might have imagined. Along these lines, a robust set of studies show that partisans hold vast misperceptions of the other side. For instance, Ahler and

Sood (2018) asked respondents to estimate the proportion of Democrats or Republicans that have certain demographic characteristics and found that respondents overestimated the prevalence of "prototypical" characteristics by large margins. For instance, respondents estimated that 31.7 percent of Democrats are lesbian, gay, or bisexual, when the true figure in the sample was 6.3 percent. Individuals also overestimated the proportion of Republicans who were evangelicals by 20 percentage points (also see Rothschild et al. 2019). Partisans, more generally, tend to view the other party as more extreme (Westfall et al. 2015; Van Boven, Ehret, and Sherman 2018), more prejudiced (Moore-Berg et al. 2020), more obstructionist (Lees and Cikara 2020), and less committed to democratic norms (Pasek et al. 2022).[4]

Building on this work, in the October 2020 wave of our survey, when we asked whether respondents would be likely to break the law or engage in violence should the candidate from the opposing party win a contested election, we also asked them to estimate how likely it would be for those from the *other* party to do so if their party's candidate lost. As presented in chapter 8, there was no meaningful relationship between a respondent's animus and their likelihood of breaking the law or engaging in violence. However, we found a strong relationship between animus and thinking that those from the other party will engage in violence. The effect on perceptions of those from the other party engaging in violence was especially noteworthy—individuals with the highest levels of animus thought, on average, that those from the other party were "Somewhat Likely" to engage in violence (where the choices were "Not at All Likely," "Not Too Likely," "Somewhat Likely," and "Very Likely"). Yet that is almost the exact opposite of the truth: more than eight in ten partisans said they were "Not at All Likely" to engage in violence. These misperceptions are staggeringly large, on the order of 200 percent (also see Mernyk et al. 2022). Animus thus may not drive highly deleterious behaviors, but it does lead people to think the other side engages in them.

In other parts of our work, we found that partisans dramatically overestimated the ideological extremity of out-partisans, believing that 69 percent of out-partisans were ideologically sorted (i.e., are liberal Democrats or conservative Republicans) when only 38 percent actually are. They did the same with their political engagement as well, responding that 64 percent of out-partisans frequently talked about politics when the reality came closer to 27 percent (Druckman et al. 2022). When combining the categories, partisans overestimated the frequency of out-party ideologues who frequently discussed politics by a factor of 3.5. This means that they also were vastly underestimating the number of moderates who only sometimes or rarely discuss politics.[5] These beliefs, in turn, lead partisans to hold more animus toward the other party: when considering their assessments, they imagine engaged ideologues prone to violence, whom they like much less than the "real" typical member, who is a less engaged—and more peaceful—moderate.

This ties back to our findings in chapter 3, where we showed that partisans with higher animosity are more ideologically extreme and sorted, and that they also discuss politics and post about politics on social media more frequently than those with lower animus. These individuals make their presence better known and thus become the types of partisans seen on social media, in social contexts, and on the news (see Levendusky 2013; Levendusky and Malhotra 2016; Settle 2018; Cohn and Quealy 2019; Hughes 2019; McGregor 2019; Peterson and Kagalwala 2021). In short, citizens assume that the images they see on mass media and on social media reflect reality, and thus that the other party consists of extremists who are deeply committed to politics and who may even be violent (i.e., they are subject to the out-group homogeneity effect; see Quattrone and Jones 1980).[6]

This suggests that people perceive the other party in ways that could be problematic to pluralism—as partisans pursuing extremely distinct belief systems with no common ground to be had. Fiorina (2017, 61) captures this logic in noting that when Democrats imagine a Republican, they think of "an evolution-denying homophobe," and likewise, that Republicans thinking of a Democrat envision "an American-hating atheist," though neither is accurate.

Hence, the ironic implications for pluralism: if the reality was what partisans perceive, it would be a substantial threat to democracy, given that it would mean the other side is ideologically extreme and engaged—and, as mentioned, also obstructionist, prejudiced, not committed to democratic norms, and violent. Yet the actual state of the country is nowhere nearly as grim, and most partisans remain moderate, less-engaged citizens, not fervent ideologues who are violent. Pluralism sustains the democratic system and, as shown in chapter 8, common ground can generally be found: there is a commitment to democratic norms (even if there remain slight relationships with animosity) and no tolerance for violence. This is all good news. But, alas, the bad news is that many partisans fail to realize this due to their misperceptions. And these misperceptions provide a concerning opening for political elites to exploit; as Wilson, Parker, and Feinberg (2020, 224) note, "Political elites with the weakest policy positions (policies unlikely to gain popular appeal on their own merit) will be most tempted to amplify polarization to ensure the loyalty of their base." People perceive those on the other side to be dangerously different themselves (i.e., violent), and while they may not have the passion or interest to act, they accept and vote for others who may do so. And such misperceptions become easy to maintain given the contemporary vitriol and the extreme events that have occurred (e.g., the January 6th attack on the Capitol).[7]

Of course, the misperceptions may be more accurate once we adjust for the particular citizen's political power. Being a high-animus partisan is unusual even in modern America, but this minority may be the driving force in American politics because of increased engagement and greater influence among other citizens and office holders. Regardless, another supposed democratic safeguard is the power of the democratic institutions that structure how government works. We see in chapter 8 that even though animus has some effect, citizens generally support these institutions. That said, institutions themselves are endogenous to political actors (Riker 1980); the stability of democratic institutions stems from coordination whereby each side anticipates the other side upholding those rules and norms (Weingast 1997). The worry is that nefarious lawmakers take steps toward undoing democratic institutions for their own gains. Grumbach (2022, 2023) showed that Republican state legislators have been willing to do this, stemming, in part, from the demographic sorting of parties whereby minority voters staunchly support Democrats, which incentivizes Republicans to restrict their voting rights (Helmke, Kroeger, and Paine 2021). The unraveling could continue if Democrat elites, in turn, take steps to disenfranchise Republicans or otherwise alter democratic institutions to expand their own power. Partisans move away from coordinating on an equilibrium of shared democratic norms and backsliding follows (Weingast 1997). Moreover, what is undemocratic to one partisan is not undemocratic to another. Krishnarajan (2023) shows that partisans rationalize what is and is not undemocratic such that they view typical policies with which they disagree (e.g., proposing to increase everyone's taxes to spend more on unemployment benefits) as more undemocratic than objective democratic transgressions where they agree with the policy (e.g., reduce everyone's taxes, spend less on unemployment benefits, and prohibit all labor union leaders from running for Congress for ten years). This finding suggests that conditions are ripe for backsliding. Moreover, one might expect this to occur among those who are higher in animus and who engage in more directional reasoning such that they rationalize decisions or, as Krishnarajan (2023, 476) puts it, "ignore the democracy dimensions of a given behavior and instead transmit their policy approval/disapproval into their democratic perceptions."

A counterpoint is that a critical mass of elites may hold values and not prioritize their own power over procedures (Virgin 2023). The problem with that argument, though, is that even a small number of elites with a small amount of leeway could cause a significant amount of damage. And, the (relatively low) incentives to run for office in contemporary America contributes to the election of more extreme partisans (Hall 2019), some of whom may not hold democratic values. Grillo and Prato (2023) show that if an extreme politician with antidemocratic inclinations wins office but then does not act as undemocratically as citizens expected, prodemocracy voters will offer support, ironically, because the incumbent is ostensibly more democratic than they had anticipated (as long as there is some uncertainty about the incumbent's ideology). The politician will win office and can take an undemocratic action to some extent, but not enough that it will lead to a loss. With this strategy they can win and act more democratically and then the process will continue, with erosion occurring gradually.

Grillo and Prato (2023) suggest that in some circumstances, mass polarization (presumably focusing on ideological polarization), lowers the likelihood of backsliding since it weakens reactions to an incumbent's shifting of the reference point (i.e., the incumbent will not win polarized voters from the other side). However, they add that polarization still can contribute to more severe backsliding since it provides broader leeway. One point, however, is that if an incumbent shifts the reference point, it could establish new criteria for evaluation of all politicians and erosion across sides. Put another way, it may not be a single incumbent who generates erosion by shifting the reference point, maintaining power, and acting undemocratically. Instead, incumbents can change understandings of what is democratically acceptable over time, thereby fueling backsliding. In essence, their work reveals that politicians can slowly shift the idea of what is "democratic," while high-animus voters cling to their partisan evaluations (e.g., see chapter 6) and fail to view the potential personal consequences of undemocratic behavior as clearly (according to our theory) after being given a new general reference point.[8] Partisans tolerate the undemocratic behavior of a few elites and then, over time, the system gradually erodes.

For American democracy, the question then becomes whether protections—particularly pluralism and institutional checks—can control the potentially harmful features of parties in an age of high animosity. Our results (described in chapter 8) make clear that while animosity may contribute to some acceptance of antidemocratic actions, animosity itself is not a direct threat to democracy. The story is more subtle, though. The rise in animosity stems partially from the ostensible decline of cross-cutting cleavages. Concomitantly, partisans hold exaggerated misperceptions of the other side, which heightens animosity and thereby contributes to further misperceptions. This opens the door for elites to exploit animosity and maintain partisan support since the other side is viewed so poorly. Institutional checks can clearly limit backsliding—for example, when the courts rejected Trump's efforts to overturn the 2020 election. Yet elites can alter institutions (see Druckman 2023b). This can occur slowly in the following sequence of: high-animus partisans evaluate their partisan elites positively regardless of their actions, these elites gain office by not revealing any undemocratic intent, once in office, these elites alter institutions in an undemocratic direction, those from their party do not perceive it as such and support them, those from the other party rally against it but then view commensurate undemocratic actions as acceptable given the changed status quo, and so on. In this process, animosity is not a direct mechanism of erosion, but it plays a crucial role since it leads voters to support fellow partisans regardless of their behavior and likely facilitates the rationalization of antidemocratic actions. In this story, animosity is a threat to democracy via elites. This does not mean the end result will be authoritarianism or civil war, as some have suggested. The process just described is neither inevitable nor without limits, as citizens may, at some point, recognize the personal consequences of this erosion and opt for more democratic candidates, thus restoring a democratic focal point. With this possibility in mind, we now turn to our final central point concerning the state of democracy.

Animosity and Democracy: Connecting Public Opinion to System Outcomes

In Figure 1.1 (in chapter 1), we provided a graphical depiction of the growth of animosity over time, which revealed a steady, monotonic rise since the turn of the century. The time period aligns with a worldwide decline in democratic governments. The Varieties of Democracies project asserts that "democracies peaked in 2012 with 42 countries and are now [2021] down to the lowest levels in over 25 years—34 nations home to only 13% of the world population." The report downgraded American democracy significantly, dropping it out of the top 10 percent in terms of its liberal democracy score. It further explained that over this same time period, "toxic polarization, respect for counterarguments and associated aspects of the deliberative component of democracy got worse in more than 32 countries" (Boese et al. 2022, 6). These trends of animosity and democratic backsliding have led many scholars to link the two (e.g., Drutman 2020; Finkel et al. 2020). Others, however, have questioned that linkage (e.g., Broockman, Kalla, and Westwood 2023; Voelkel et al., "Interventions," 2023; Voelkel et al., "Megastudy," 2023). We have offered evidence relevant to this discussion that accentuates two crucial points.

First, one must step back and ask: what exactly does it mean to be democratic or to democratically backslide or even collapse? Obviously there is no agreement on this, with answers ranging from the mere occurrence of an election to the existence of a fully enfranchised deliberative public, and many more in between. While enough consensus ostensibly exists to conclude that the United States had become less democratic in the twenty-first century, that does not mean that democracy will cease to exist or these trends cannot be reversed. What our results make clear is that one needs to distinguish factors that make democratic functioning more difficult from those that directly lead to democratic collapse. Our findings suggest that animosity contributes to the former much more than the latter. For instance, relative to those with less animosity, high-animus partisans hold more polarized issue positions, see more things as political, and express weaker support for political compromise. The challenge for analysts is to isolate the extent to which public beliefs substantially undermine functioning, given that such functioning depends on elites' actions. Moreover, there is the question of when decreased functioning provides an opportunity for autocrats to gain power and erode democracy, however one defines it.

The second dimension of discussions about democratic backsliding involves the level of analysis (Druckman 2023b). Systems backslide or collapse, not individuals. Much scholarship, including this book, focuses on citizens' opinions with an implicit presumption that they relate to the health of democracy. Yet most proximately, elites are the ones who shape how the system performs, including whether democratic rules are kept in place. Bartels (2023) makes a compelling case that democracies erode from the top (also see Beremo 2016, Hopkins 2023). This does not, however, mean that citizens' opinions are irrelevant. Instead, it raises the question of how these micro-level preferences link to macro-level outcomes. Ahmed (2023, 972) explains, "This micro-level analysis is in many ways incommensurable with the nature of backsliding, which often consists of acts that are on their face democratic." Citizens may not recognize that the attitudes they hold or the decisions they make contribute to backsliding—not only due to their motivated reasoning but also because they do not link particular attitudes to macro-level outcomes. This is a tricky question. On the one hand, any intolerant stance, antiparticipatory view, or antisocial action could be construed as leading to backsliding as it provides state actors with opportunities to dissemble democratic liberal institutions (Sullivan and Transue 1999). On the other hand, more proximate antidemocratic attitudes entail citizens accepting and/or supporting elites who undermine democratic processes. At the bluntest level, this would mean voting for an antidemocratic candidate who shares one's partisanship or views— something that has, in fact, been linked to increased animosity (Voelkel et al., "Megastudy," 2023). More generally, though, attitudes that make democratic functioning more difficult by leading to gridlock, policy polarization, or politicized evaluations open the door to elites. As explained, this makes it easier for a nefarious elite to make the case for taking antidemocratic actions to "get things done." Along these lines, our results shown in chapter 8 showed that a main norm that voters seemed willing to violate was allowing a politician to use any method if they manage to get things done. This exemplifies how animosity can set off backsliding.

That said, the translation even from this preference to backsliding or collapse is complex (Druckman 2023b). In between the micro-level opinions of citizens and macro-level outcomes driven by elites are meso-level processes. Advocacy groups and social networks play a crucial mobilizing force. Long ago, Truman (1951) in fact suggested that democracy survives because a latent group of voters awaits mobilization on the event that democracy is threatened. It subsequently became evident that such collective action is far from a given (Olson 1965), and thus a crucial question for democratic stability is exactly how meso-level factors work to mobilize citizens to connect public policy to their own opinions (and thus move away from partisan biases), and ultimately to recognize and act against threats to democracy (Disch 2021). In politics, no societal institution that operates at least somewhat on the meso level matters more than parties; we therefore conclude by addressing the challenge facing parties in contemporary America.

Reforming Parties

An underlying question in this book has been: are political parties a force for good or for ill in U.S. politics? The founders saw parties as factions that would undermine the embryonic nation, and worked to limit them, though ironically, many of the founders, including Madison and Jefferson, would then become staunch partisans. Later generations of scholars argued that parties were essential and democratic governance could not function without them, which led to calls to strengthen them. But when those stronger parties developed, scholars lamented them, claiming that parties were now a threat to democracy, as Americans put party over principle, just as George Washington had feared. How should we think of parties, as currently constituted? Are they fundamental to democratic governance or are they now a threat to the stability of American democracy?

We agree with the classic Schattschneiderian (1942, 1960) line that democracy cannot work without political parties.[9] Yet we have also argued that partisan animosity can produce dangerous consequences for democracy. Partisanship is too important, and too central, to democracy to simply do away with it; we thus need to tame its worst effects. The problem of animus is that it encourages an unproductive and unhelpful form of political engagement. This sort of fervor "sends partisans into action for the wrong reasons" and gives them "a desire for victory that exceeds their desire for the greater good" (Mason 2018, 6). It promotes an irresponsible partisanship, one focused on defeating the other side rather than solving problems, one that highlights the partisan gain over governing, just as the founders had feared (also see Gutmann and Thompson 2012).

This abrogates what partisanship ideally provides. Parties are essential to democratic governance because they structure the choices in a polity and highlight the stakes in a given conflict (Rosenblum 2008); they also link citizens to government and policy outcomes, providing a mechanism for accountability (Fiorina 1980). When partisanship reveals the values at stake and how choices map onto fundamental understandings of how the world works, it constitutes what Muirhead (2014) calls "high partisanship." This describes what might be, rather than what exists. But hopefully, highlighting this disjunction makes it clear what we might strive for and what a more constructive type of political engagement would look like.

Our work underscores that partisan animus matters the most when the issues matter least to voters. On highly salient topics, accuracy motives displace partisan ones, as we highlighted with our results about the COVID-19 pandemic. We studied the pandemic because it provided a clear metric of salience, but the logic applies more broadly. A way of dampening the effects of animosity, then, is to make politics more directly relevant to people's lives. One could argue, however, that many political issues will always be remote for most voters, and there is some truth to that. That also highlights why parties play such a crucial role, especially in this era of declining local media. At their best, parties help voters make those connections and see how these issues map back to their lives. And this has the effect of making politics more meaningful. Rather than simply engaging politics as hobbyism (e.g., Hersh 2020), voters can engage in it in meaningful ways that may actually make their lives better. This is not to say that we encourage voters to become engaged ideologues; rather, that voters must recognize that particular political issues connect to their lives.

Recognizing this connection also accentuates the challenges facing parties. The competitiveness of contemporary politics leads elite parties to eschew problem solving in favor of finding issues and messages that strategically mobilize their voters (F. Lee 2016). Typically, this means politicizing issues and sending voters cues about them for the sole purpose of political gain. Ironically, the exact opposite facilitates the passage of actual meaningful policy reforms (Bazelon and Ygelias 2021). The danger in the current environment involves the former entirely displacing the latter.

The COVID-19 pandemic provides a clear example of this danger, even if some partisan effects were tempered by salience. It is not just that the pandemic became politicized, it is that over time, that politicization spread to broader trust in science, experts, and public health more generally. Over time, partisanship has become a dividing line in terms of trust in scientists. We see this playing out with figures like Dr. Anthony Fauci, who had Republican political candidates actively running on platforms opposing him (Stolberg 2022), and Senator Rand Paul—himself a doctor—working to abolish Fauci's position and calling him the "dictator-in-chief" (Paul 2022). Of course, one can critique Dr. Fauci's actions and public officials and bureaucrats certainly should be held to account (Bendor and Bullock 2021). There is certainly plenty of blame to go around in the public health community about how the nation responded to the pandemic (Lewis 2021). But the danger arises when public health politicizes, and we see differences in flu shot uptake and other public health measures (Enten 2021). If disagreement about how to respond to the pandemic evolves into a broader politicization of public health authorities, in which ignoring life-saving advice becomes a political symbol, it constitutes a dangerous path to head down (Patashnik, Gerber, and Dowling 2017).

We also see this in foreign policy more broadly. While once politics stopped at the water's edge, today it does not, as debates over Russia and Ukraine highlight. Given the linkages between President Trump and the Russian president, Vladimir Putin—and the role Ukraine played in Trump's first impeachment—it was perhaps no surprise that during the Trump years, many Republicans' views became much more favorable toward Russia. Indeed, even on the eve of Russia's 2022 invasion of Ukraine, Tucker Carlson and other conservative commentators attempted to argue that Putin did not deserve American enmity (Bella 2022). One can (of course) reasonably disagree about the correct course of American foreign policy, but when national security issues become "just another partisan squabble" (Hounshell and Askarinam 2022), all Americans suffer. When Republicans would "Rather Be a Russian Than a Democrat" (Beauchamp 2018), all Americans suffer. The danger from elites entails broadening the scope of conflict so dramatically that they politicize too much. Not politicizing some issues is just as important as politicizing others.

There is no easy answer to this problem, as it is a structural issue without any clear resolution. It highlights the challenge to American democracy—when everything becomes politicized, then animus becomes more relevant and its danger increases. The solution, to the extent one exists, means being in a position to embrace what Gutmann and Thompson (2012) refer to as the "spirit of compromise," which entails the recognition that both parties need to work together to solve problems rather than simply trying to score political points. Of course, one could point out that they face few incentives to do that. We can only agree, and sadly, can offer no remedy to that apart from hope that the second quarter-century is more democratic than the last.

Acknowledgments

This book reflects the role of serendipity in the research process, as well as the state of American politics over the past several years. The project began in 2018 when Samara made a passing comment to Jamie during a break at a board meeting for the American National Election Studies. Subsequent discussion and correspondence led us to realize that our respective "research teams"—Jamie and Matt, and Samara, Yanna, and John—had overlapping interests. Jamie and Matt were working on the measurement of partisan animosity while Samara, Yanna, and John were working on the differences between unengaged and engaged partisans. The five of us decided to work on what we thought would be just one paper. We collected data that measured animosity among a large sample of respondents in summer 2019, and we eventually published it as Druckman et al. (2022).

Then in March 2020, as the COVID-19 lockdown froze the nation, Yanna realized that the data we had collected might allow us to offer novel insights about the pandemic response. We thus reinterviewed our initial respondents and reported the results in Druckman et al. (2021a, 2021b). The pandemic continued, the country ostensibly polarized even further, the country's largest protests ever occurred in response to the murder of George Floyd, and the 2020 presidential election became increasingly contentious. Matt, and then the rest of us, realized that it made sense to continue surveying our respondents, and we thus conducted another survey wave before Election Day. The subsequent claims of election fraud, the January 6th Capitol insurrection, a second impeachment of President Trump, President Biden's inauguration, and the availability of COVID-19 vaccines to the mass public led us to collect data for a fourth and final wave. All of these data enabled us to isolate how animosity (i.e., hostility) influenced American politics during one of the most eventual and difficult periods in contemporary times. What began with a brief informal conversation turned into a large panel data set that, as John initially recognized, required a book length treatment. The process highlights how a collaboration can take one into truly unexpected and interesting places.

We first want to thank Jon Kingzette, who developed the democratic norm index used in chapter 8 and then collaborated with us on Kingzette et al. (2021) and chapter 8. The inclusion of these items on our initial 2019 survey was a fortuitous event that came about because Jon and Jamie happened to sit next to one another at a conference dinner where Jon explained his interests and Jamie mentioned the planned data collection. Without Jon's help, we would not have developed that part of our argument.

Along the way, we have discussed the project with many colleagues and seminar audiences. We thank Delia Baldassarri, Adam Berinsky, Levi Boxell, David Broockman, James Chu, Mina Cikara, Elizabeth Connors, Jacob Conway, Nic Dias, Elias Dinas, Eli Finkel, Morris Fiorina, Matthew Gentzkow, Don Green, Eric Groenendyk, Matt Hall, Liesbet Hooghe, Elisabeth Iversflaten, Shanto Iyengar, John Jost, Josh Kalla, Jeff Lees, Yph Lelkes, Jeremy Levy, Joe Mernyk, Samantha Moore-Berg, Sophia Pink, Dave Rand, Jake Rothschild, Rune Slothuus, Nick Stagnaro, Dietlind Stolle, Dan Stone, Leaf Van Boven, Jan Voelkel, Robb Willer, and seminar audiences at the American Political Science Association conference; the Association for Psychological Science conference; Columbia University; Cornell University; the European University Institute; the Florida Health Policy Leadership Academy; the Hot Politics Lab; Indiana University; the National Academies of Sciences, Engineering, and Medicine; Northwestern University; the Society for Personality and Social Psychology conference; Stanford University; the University of Michigan; the University of Notre Dame; and the University of Pittsburgh for many helpful comments.

Special thanks are due to Greg Huber, Cindy Kam, Stuart Soroka, and Sean Westwood, who participated in a manuscript workshop in summer 2021. Their detailed and profound feedback made the book substantially stronger than it otherwise would have been. Sean deserves special praise for suggestions on how to redo the graphs in a way that makes them much easier to understand. There surely have been many others who offered insights along the way, and we thank them and apologize for not explicitly recognizing them here; blame this oversight on the quality of our postpandemic collective memories rather than on the quality of their comments.

We also thank Adam Berinsky and Sara Doskow from the University of Chicago Press for their superb advice and sage guidance. We further recognize Greg Bovitz and Rick Konopka for their help with data collection (and extraordinary patience with our many requests); Talbot Andrews, Ben Hempker, Jennifer Lin, Caroline Pippert, Natalie Sands, Anna Wang, and Jinwen Wu for excellent research assistance; and Northwestern University, Stony Brook University, the Annenberg Public Policy Center, and the University of Arizona for financial support.

All books require thanking one's friends and family, but that is doubly true for any project that took shape during the COVID-19 pandemic. We are grateful to those who provided childcare and support for our kids, who kept our campuses running, and who supported us at work and in our homes as we persistently pursued this project. We especially thank our friends, family, and children for tolerating us and allowing us to work as much as we did.

Appendixes

We collected our data on Bovitz Inc's Forthright Panel (http://bovitzinc.com
/index.php). As with most internet survey panels, respondents participate in
multiple surveys over time and receive compensation for their participation.
The sample size and retention rate by wave are as follows: wave 1: (N = 3,345;
2,860 partisans), wave 2: (N = 2,484; 74 percent retention rate; 2,118 partisans),
wave 3: (N = 2,220; 66 percent; 1,882 partisans), wave 4: (N = 2,039; 61 percent; 1,743 partisans).[1] The dates of the waves are provided in table 1.1 (see the
subsequent discussion for more details on wave 1, which occurred over three
cycles). We preregistered our predictions for each wave. The preregistrations
refer to data and hypotheses beyond what is presented in the book, some of
which are presented in other published works (e.g., Druckman 2021a). The
wave 2 preregistrations are at: https://aspredicted.org/tp99f.pdf, and https://as
predicted.org/7pd2i.pdf. The wave 3 preregistration is at https://aspredicted
.org/46s3z.pdf. The wave 4 preregistrations are at https://aspredicted.org/8gj
9k.pdf and https://aspredicted.org/zq7vv.pdf.

The July 2019 survey included other measures, some of which we display
in table A3.1, which provides a demographic portrait of each wave of our sample as compared to 2018 benchmarks from the U.S. Census Bureau, via the
American Community Survey (unless otherwise noted). We focus on respondents who answered the animosity questions since those form the basis for
our analyses throughout the book. However, in the table, we include pure Independents and some other respondents excluded from our analyses, as we describe later (to ensure clear comparisons to the benchmarks).

We found general stability in the demographics over waves. The most notable changes include: a small decline in the proportion of younger respondents

meaning a commensurate proportional increase in the older respondents, a slight decline in female respondents, and a slight increase in college graduates.

In terms of representativeness, the sample largely mirrors census benchmarks, with a few exceptions. First, it underrepresents younger and (especially) older people, and overrepresents middle aged people (particularly thirty-five- to fifty-year-olds). Second, it underrepresents people who are less educated and overrepresents those with some college or a college degree. Third, it underrepresents those from the higher income brackets and also the lowest bracket. These issues are well-known limitations of any survey sampling procedure, not just our own—the age and education skews are linked in that those populations are not online, and those with high incomes are also typically underrepresented across all survey modes. We also see an underrepresentation of strong Republicans and an overrepresentation of strong Democrats, which is a consistent recent development in political surveys (Pew Research Center 2021). Finally, there is a slight underrepresentation of respondents from "other" racial/ethnic groups and an underrepresentation of Hispanics or Latinos. This latter statistic is misleading, however, since our measure included "Hispanic/Latino" as a choice in a single race/ethnicity question while the census item asks about it separately from the race/ethnicity question, which includes other categories. There also appears to be substantial underrepresentation of Protestants, but that likely reflects that our religion question offered only "Protestant" as a category whereas the benchmark offers subcategories including "Evangelical," "Mainline," and "historically Black." For us, it may be that some who are within those Protestant subcategories chose "other" (which our sample overrepresented). We also slightly overrepresented "not religious" versus the benchmark.

We more formally explored attrition over waves. One concern with any panel data is that respondents will drop out of the sample in a way that is correlated with the topic: so, for example, perhaps only the highest-animus partisans remain for four waves. To be clear, as in all opt-in panels, we experienced churn across the four waves. However, this was not strongly related to animosity (e.g., the mean animus score for those who did not participate in the last wave is 0.55, which is the same mean animus scores for those who did). If anything, it is actually those in the *middle* of the animosity scale who were most likely to drop out of the sample. The strongest predictors of attrition were knowledge and age: younger and less informed respondents were less likely to remain in the panel over time. Overall, these are relatively modest effects, and while people dropped out of the panel, this was not strongly related to our key predictor variables.

TABLE A3.1. Sample Demographics

	July 2019 (wave 1)	April 2020 (wave 2)	October 2020 (wave 3)	April 2021 (wave 4)	Population benchmark
Age					
18–24 (%)	9.42	8.29	7.88	6.62	12.08
25–34 (%)	19.61	18.40	18.02	16.97	17.87
35–50 (%)	35.04	35.39	35.32	35.26	24.54
51–65 (%)	24.96	26.61	27.66	29.08	24.88
Over 65 (%)	10.97	11.31	11.13	12.06	20.65
N	3,345	2,484	2,220	2,039	
Gender identity					
Male (%)	50.82	51.03	51.37	52.06	49.2
Female (%)	48.19	48.09	47.68	46.96	50.8
Transgender (%)	0.72	0.64	0.81	0.79	—[a]
None of the categories offered (%)	0.27	0.24	0.14	0.20	—[a]
N	3,343	2,483	2,219	2,038	
Primary racial/ethnic group					
White (%)	69.66	70.73	70.81	71.11	72.2
Black (%)	14.47	13.81	13.56	13.19	12.7
Asian American (%)	4.13	3.99	4.19	4.32	5.6
Hispanic or Latino (%)	9.36	9.02	9.01	8.93	18.3
Native American (%)	0.87	0.85	0.77	0.74	<1
Other (%)	1.52	1.61	1.67	1.72	5
N	3,345	2,484	2,220	2,039	
Annual family income before taxes					
<$30,000 (%)	27.28	26.83	26.88	26.45	29.4
$30,000–$69,999 (%)	38.14	38.11	38.48	37.56	30.3
$70,000–$99,999 (%)	16.86	17.37	16.78	17.31	12.5
$100,000–$200,000 (%)	15.51	15.27	15.38	16.27	20.9
>$200,000 (%)	2.22	2.42	2.48	2.41	6.9
N	3,340	2,482	2,217	2,034	
Education level					
Less than high school (%)	2.12	2.01	2.16	1.81	12.0
High school graduate (%)	20.84	20.41	20.63	19.62	27.1
Some college (%)	26.79	26.57	25.90	25.70	28.9[b]
Associate's degree/2-year degree (%)	15.19	14.61	14.68	14.86	—[b]
Bachelor's/4-year degree (%)	25.80	26.69	26.80	28.00	19.7
Advanced degree (%)	9.27	9.70	9.82	10.00	12.3
N	3,345	2,484	2,220	2,039	

(continues)

TABLE A3.1. (*continued*)

	July 2019 (wave 1)	April 2020 (wave 2)	October 2020 (wave 3)	April 2021 (wave 4)	Population benchmark
Religion[c]					
Protestant (%)	23.15	23.48	23.16	24.44	43
Catholic (%)	21.00	20.50	20.50	20.36	20
Jewish (%)	3.32	3.75	3.92	4.32	2
Muslim (%)	0.81	0.85	0.81	0.98	1
Hindu (%)	0.57	0.64	0.68	0.69	1
Other (%)	20.52	19.29	19.33	18.25	8
Not religious (%)	30.63	31.49	31.59	30.96	26
N	3,343	2,483	2,219	2,038	
Partisanship[d]					
Strong Democrat (%)	27.65	28.06	28.69	29.18	21
Democrat (%)	15.78	15.46	15.59	15.35	14
Leaning Democrat (%)	11.93	11.92	11.58	10.69	11
Independent (%)	14.50	14.73	15.23	14.52	15
Leaning Republican (%)	9.96	10.27	10.14	10.69	11
Republican (%)	9.84	9.86	9.46	9.61	12
Strong Republican (%)	10.34	9.70	9.32	9.96	16
N	3,345	2,484	2,020	2,039	

[a] The U.S. Census Bureau does not currently ask about transgender identity, so there is no government-provided benchmark for that quantity. A report from the Williams Institute at UCLA estimated that fewer than 1 percent of Americans identify as transgender, consistent with our estimates here; for more details, see UCLA School of Law, Williams Institute, "How Many Adults and Youth Identify as Transgender in the United States?," June 2022, https://williamsinstitute.law.ucla.edu/publications/trans-adults-united-states/.

[b] "Some college" and "Associate's degree/2-year degree" are combined in the data.

[c] Population data are from the Pew Research Center, accessed January 25, 2022, https://www.pewforum.org/wp-content/uploads/sites/7/2019/10/Detailed-Tables-v1-FOR-WEB.pdf. Their "Not religious" category is labeled "Nothing in particular/Atheist/Agnostic."

[d] Population data are from the 2016 American National Election Studies, "The ANES Guide to Public Opinion and Electoral Behavior," accessed January 25, 2022, https://electionstudies.org/resources/anes-guide/top-tables/?id=21.

Wave 1 Cycles

Our wave 1, July 2019, data collection occurred in three cycles. All participants who completed the first cycle were invited to participate in the other two cycles (i.e., they could participate in the third cycle even if they skipped the second cycle). In the first cycle—from July 9, 2019, to July 17, 2019—we asked participants about their demographic and political characteristics. The second cycle—occurring July 16, 2019, to July 25, 2019—contained our animosity measures. It also included an experiment regarding the animosity measures (see Druckman et al. 2022; also see appendix 3.2). The third cycle, from July 26,

2019, to August 2, 2019, included questions about the way people perceived the political parties, as used in Druckman et al. (2022). Respondents were only invited to participate in a subsequent cycle when at least six days had passed from their completion of the prior cycle.

Exclusion Criteria in Our Analyses

In our analyses throughout the book, we excluded four sets of individuals, though as noted, we include them in the demographics presented in table A3.1. (They are not, however, included in the analyses in chapter 3.) First, we excluded those who were not asked to complete the measure of partisan animosity in our July 2019 wave (we used these randomly chosen respondents for another part of the study described in Druckman et al. 2022). Because they lacked the baseline measure of partisan animosity, we could not include them in our main analyses.

Second, we excluded pure Independents (i.e., those who do not lean toward one party or the other), consistent with earlier work on partisan animosity (e.g., Druckman and Levendusky 2019). Specifically, we excluded those who identify as a pure Independent across waves (approximately 5 percent of our total sample). A larger share of our sample identified as pure Independents in one wave of the study but adopted partisan identities in another wave. Many of these moves were from Independent leaner to pure Independent and back again, so excluding them is an overly restrictive rule that affects the bottom of the animus scale (because many of these individuals have low levels of animosity toward the other party). Given this problem, we only excluded those who consistently adopted a pure Independent identity, as these individuals do not clearly have an in-party and out-party (since they do not identify with either major party), and hence animus is not defined for them.

Third, we excluded those who change their partisan identity across waves. Many individuals changed the strength of their partisanship across waves (e.g., moving from a weak to a strong Democrat), but far fewer changed their partisan identity and moved from Democrat to Republican or vice versa over time. Consistent with other studies about the stability of partisan identity (i.e., D. Green, Palmquist, and Schickler 2002), this is approximately 6 percent of the total sample. For these individuals, our measure of partisan animosity is less well defined over time. Take, for example, someone who identifies as a Democrat in July 2019 but a Republican in April 2021. In July 2019, when we measured out-party animus, we would have asked them about their attitudes toward Republicans (the other party). But once they changed their identification to become a Republican, this was no longer a measure of out-party animus. Indeed, this out-party animosity might have led to this change in partisanship. Given this, we excluded these individuals from our analyses.

Finally, we exclude respondents in the top and bottom 5 percent of the animus scale. The bottom 5 percent of our animus measure are individuals who feel extremely positively toward the other party, and as shown in figures 3.2 and 3.3, any models we run on our data must do a large amount of interpolation. These individuals bounce around on our measures, leading us to suspect they are likely low-quality responses (i.e., survey trolls or people paying little to no attention as they complete our study). Their inclusion induces some odd nonlinearities into the graphical displays used throughout the book. Including them does not change the underlying patterns of results, it simply introduces noise into our data, so we excluded them from the analyses.

Our primary animosity measure—which underlies nearly every analysis in the book—was captured following an experimental treatment designed to change respondents' answers to the questions that comprise the measure. Specifically, we (experimentally) randomly varied two factors in describing the partisans being rated: (1) their ideological profiles (i.e., no profile, a moderate, an extremist) and (2) their political engagement (i.e., no profile, rarely discuss politics, occasionally discuss politics, frequently discuss politics). Thus, for example respondents may have rated "Democrats" or "Republicans" as in the conventional animosity items used in previous studies. Or they may have been asked, for example, about "Conservative Republicans who frequently talk about politics," "Liberal Democrats who frequently talk about politics," and so forth, as in the aforementioned 3 (Ideology) × 4 (Engagement) design. The details of the experiment are available in Druckman et al. (2022).

It is reasonable for a reader to wonder whether this is a problem. After all, there is much concern about bias in estimates from regression models that include posttreatment variables as control variables (Acharya, Blackwell, and Sen 2016). Experiments allow for estimates of causal effects because random assignment means the various treatment groups are alike in every way (on average) with the exception of the treatment to which they were assigned. If the treatment affects something that the researcher wants to use as a mediating or moderating variable, then the groups could be different in ways beyond the treatment (Montgomery, Nyhan, and Torres 2018).

Klar, Leeper, and Robison (2020) argue that measuring certain variables posttreatment is not a concern because the demographic variables that researchers often care about are fairly stable and not affected by the treatment.[1] As a result, the responses would be the same regardless of when the questions were asked. In our case, however, the measure we were using is definitely different posttreatment—that is the entire point of the experiment. What we were doing, however, is also different from how people think about posttreatment bias. We were not attempting to determine how some covariate that is measured posttreatment conditions the effect of the treatment on the dependent variable. We are using the dependent variable (from the experiment) as an independent variable in a separate model.

We do not believe this is a problem because of an assumption that we make about our treatment effects. Essentially, we assume that our treatment is randomly adding a constant (with some noise) to values of the out-party animus measure that we would have captured if everyone had been in the control group. Consider the following two equations:

(1) $Y = \alpha + \beta X$

(2) $Y = \alpha + \beta(X + c)$

People who work in applied statistics understand that the estimated β in both equations would be exactly the same even if they have never thought about why that is the case.[2] It is why, for example, they are not concerned if a seven-point partisanship measure is coded 0 to 6, 1 to 7, or −3 to 3. The β is the effect of a one unit change in the independent variable on the dependent variable. Since adding a constant does not change the meaning of "one unit change" in the independent variable, then the β does not change either.

Of course, the idea that all our experiment is doing is adding a constant (with some noise) to values of out-party animosity is an important assumption that we need to justify. When we say that the treatments are "adding a constant," this implies that treatment effects in the initial experiment are homogeneous across groups. Given the strong association between strength of partisanship and animosity (Klar, Krupnikov, and Ryan 2018), we might expect that strong partisans responded differently to the treatments than weak or leaning partisans. Strong partisans' dislike for the out-party might be so great that they see no difference between a moderate out-partisan who rarely talks about politics and an extreme out-partisan who does so frequently. It is possible that leaners and weak partisans make distinctions between different types of out-partisans but strong partisans do not. If this were true, then strength of partisanship would condition our treatment effects.

The first model presented in table A3.2 demonstrates that this is not the case, however. The OLS regression model has out-partisan animosity as the dependent variable and the experimental treatments as the key independent variables. All the treatments are interacted with a dummy variable coded 1 if

TABLE A3.2. Effects of Experimental Conditions and Partisan Strength on Affect

	Out-party affect (animus)	In-party affect
Constant	0.557***	0.654***
	(0.009)	(0.007)
Strong partisan	0.060***	0.099***
	(0.013)	(0.010)
Discussion conditions		
Rarely	−0.110***	−0.004
	(0.012)	(0.010)
Occasionally	−0.032***	−0.035***
	(0.012)	(0.010)
Frequently	0.029***	−0.045***
	(0.012)	(0.009)
Strong partisan × rarely	0.021	−0.043***
	(0.018)	(0.014)
Strong partisan × occasionally	0.024	0.015
	(0.018)	(0.014)
Strong partisan × frequently	−0.007	0.001
	(0.018)	(0.014)
Ideology conditions		
Moderate	−0.030***	0.022***
	(0.011)	(0.008)
Extreme	0.009	0.000
	(0.011)	(0.009)
Strong partisan × moderate	0.001	−0.039***
	(0.016)	(0.012)
Strong partisan × extreme	0.000	−0.008
	(0.016)	(0.012)
N	2,887	2,896
R^2	0.11	0.10

Note: Cell entries are OLS regression coefficients with associated standard errors in parentheses; *$p < 0.1$; **$p < 0.05$; ***$p < 0.01$ for two-tailed tests.

the respondent is a strong partisan and 0 if the respondent is a weak or leaning partisan. For each treatment, the confidence intervals on the estimated treatment effect (i.e., the interactions) for strong partisans and weak/leaning partisans overlap, indicating that the treatment has the same effect on respondents regardless of strength of partisanship. Since the treatment has the same average effect on all respondents, we can act as if the treatments were simply adding a constant to values of the animosity variable.

This assumption does not hold for our in-party measures. The second model in table A3.2 presents the same independent variables as before, but this time in-party evaluations are the dependent variable. We saw two main differences in how strong partisans responded to the treatments compared to weak/leaning partisans. First, the "rarely" talks about politics treatment has no statistically significant effect on weak or leaning partisans, while strong partisans like in-partisans who rarely talk about politics *less* than partisans in the control group. Second, and more starkly, weak and leaning partisans give higher ratings to in-partisans in the moderate condition than in the control group, while strong partisans give lower ratings in the moderate condition.

Theoretically, this difference between how the treatments affect in-party and out-party ratings is understandable. When asked to rate out-partisans, all respondents preferred that the out-partisans refrain from talking about politics either because they wanted to avoid disagreement or because they did not want to pay attention to beliefs they find objectionable. They also all preferred moderate out-partisans because everyone dislikes the extreme version of the out-party more. But with in-partisans, the thinking changes. While people generally disliked talking about politics, some of the strong partisans enjoyed it and would like to associate with others who are like them both in party preference and in involvement in politics (Krupnikov and Ryan 2022). Strong partisans might also see more extreme members of the in-party as providing ballast for a system that would tip toward the extremists in the out-party without these in-party extremists.

In sum, we can use the out-party ratings as a key explanatory variable in our analyses (but not the in-party ratings). This means that we cannot conclusively study textbook "affective polarization"—which includes both increased dislike for the out-party and increased positive feelings toward the in-party (Iyengar and Westwood 2015). This is not too much of concern, however, since we theoretically believe that the out-party animosity is the key driving factor of the effects of polarization on our current political system.

Appendix 3.3: Question Wording

Question wording for all items is available on this book's page at the University of Chicago Press website (www.press.uchicago.edu).

Appendix 3.4: Animosity Description by Party

Figures A3.1, A3.2, and A3.3 provide descriptive portraits for political identity (A3.1), issue extremity (A3.2) and engagement (A3.3), estimated separately by party. While we found some differences in levels across parties, the trends are

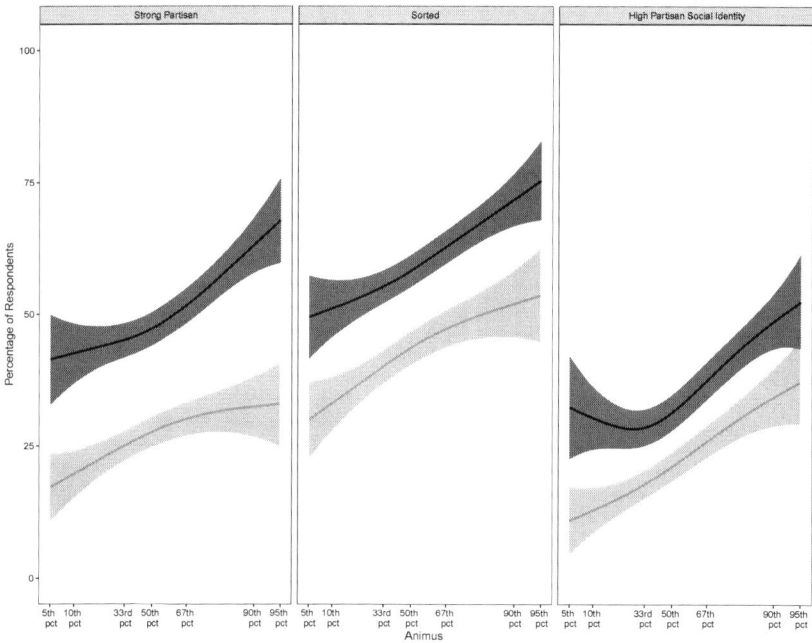

FIGURE A3.1. Political Identity and Animosity by Party

Note: The figure panels depict the relationship between animosity and partisan strength (left-hand panel), partisan sorting (middle panel), and partisan social identity (right-hand panel). Democrats are displayed in black, and Republicans are displayed in gray.

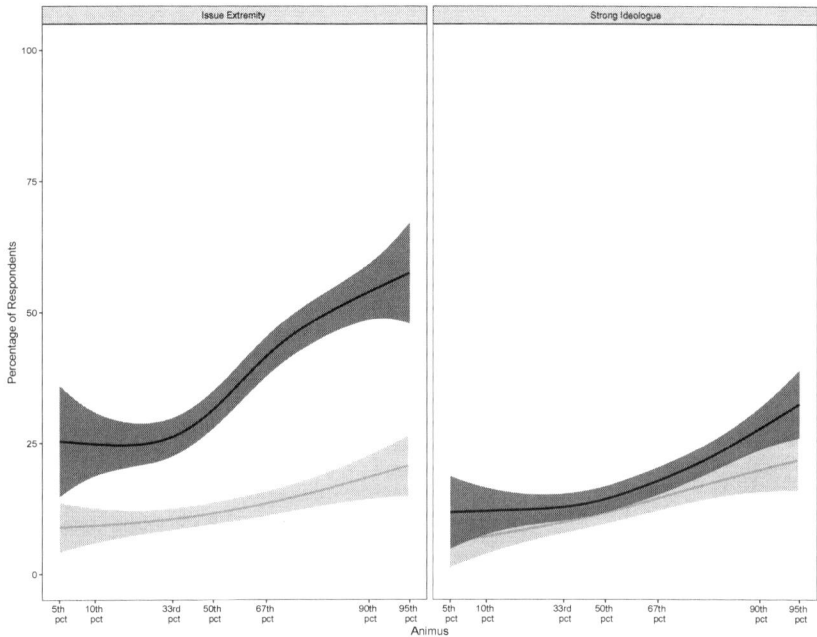

FIGURE A3.2. Issue Extremity and Animosity by Party

Note: The figure panels depict the relationship between animosity and issue position extremity (left-hand panel) and strength of liberal-conservative self-identification (right-hand panel). Democrats are displayed in black, and Republicans are displayed in gray.

the same with the exception that the political engagement measures show a monotonical increase for Republicans while being more parabolic for Democrats (but still increased to the highest levels mostly at the higher animosity percentiles).

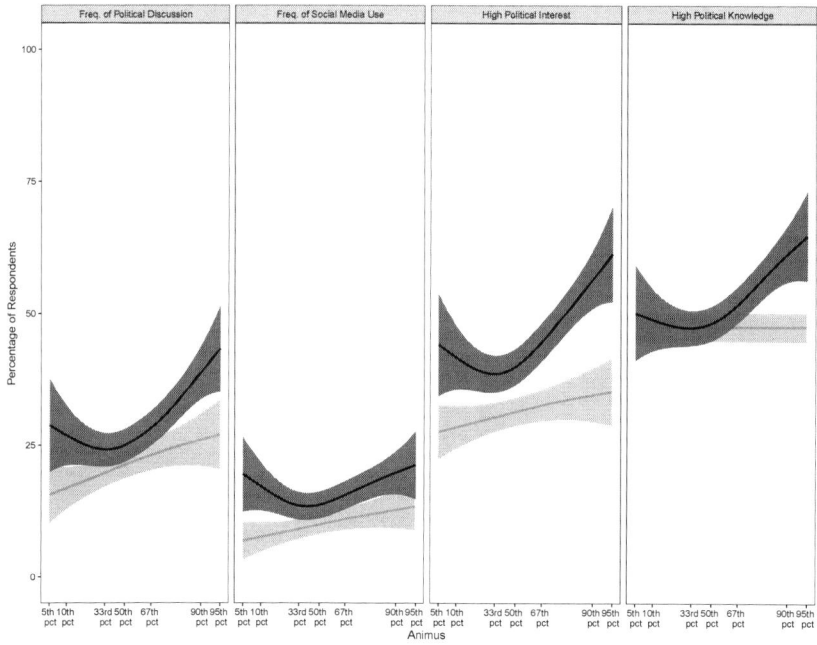

FIGURE A3.3. Political Engagement, Knowledge, and Animosity by Party

Note: The figure panels depict the relationship between animosity and the frequency of political discussion (left-most panel), frequency of social media usage, political interest, and political knowledge (right-most panel). Democrats are displayed in black, and Republicans are displayed in gray.

Appendix 4.1: Regression Models

As mentioned in the chapter, we have relied primarily on simple graphs to present our results throughout the book, as this best allows us to convey our findings. Readers might, correctly, want to know what happens in a multiple regression model: do we still find the relationship between animus and cue-taking in a more complete regression model? We tested that question with our data, using the set of control variables we included in our earlier published work with these data (Kingzette et al. 2021), except for two small changes. First, we also controlled for age, consumption of the Fox News Channel, and partisan social identity (Huddy, Mason, and Aarøe 2015), given the importance of these variables in predicting attitudes on many topics. Second, Kingzette et al. (2021) used a measure of political conservativism taken from issue positions on health care, social services, and so forth that would be inappropriate here given that we are predicting some of the same issues. Instead, we substituted liberal-conservative self-identification. In tables A4.1, A4.2, and A4.3, we present the results for polarized elite cues, nonpolarized elite cues, and asymmetrically polarized cues, corresponding to figures 4.1–4.3.

In all three tables, we show that, even controlling for a host of other important predictors, the effects discussed in the body of the chapter are apparent. We also tested for interactions with education and political knowledge, but we found no consistent pattern of results there (though we may be underpowered to detect any such effects).

One concern with this sort of analysis is that our findings could still suffer from omitted variable bias. Because people who are high in animus differ from those who are low in animus in many ways, we undoubtedly missed some control variables. To examine the sensitivity of our estimates to such omitted variable bias, we turned to the work of Cinelli and Hazlett (2020), who

TABLE A4.1. Cue-Taking on Symmetrically Polarized Issues

	Minimum wage	Obamacare	Pathway to citizenship
Constant	3.582***	3.192***	2.863***
	(0.182)	(0.168)	(0.175)
Partisan animosity	0.730***	0.696***	0.554**
	(0.176)	(0.162)	(0.169)
Republican	0.270	0.420**	0.432*
	(0.177)	(0.163)	(0.170)
Political knowledge	−0.051**	−0.001	0.060***
	(0.016)	(0.015)	(0.015)
Liberal-conservative self ID	−0.187***	−0.180***	−0.142***
	(0.017)	(0.016)	(0.016)
Education	−0.044**	−0.012	0.008
	(0.016)	(0.015)	(0.016)
Non-Hispanic White	−0.113*	−0.100*	−0.077
	(0.051)	(0.047)	(0.049)
Female	0.120**	0.007	0.067
	(0.044)	(0.041)	(0.043)
Protestant	−0.273***	−0.129*	0.062
	(0.067)	(0.062)	(0.064)
Catholic	−0.195**	−0.121⁺	−0.001
	(0.068)	(0.063)	(0.065)
Jewish	0.004	−0.023	0.032
	(0.118)	(0.109)	(0.113)
No religion/atheist	−0.128*	−0.144*	0.042
	(0.063)	(0.058)	(0.061)
Age	0.003	0.012	−0.085***
	(0.022)	(0.020)	(0.021)
Fox News viewer	0.026	0.094*	0.267***
	(0.047)	(0.043)	(0.045)
Partisan social identity	0.108***	0.098***	0.064**
	(0.023)	(0.021)	(0.022)
Partisan animosity*Republican	−1.713***	−2.369***	−1.787***
	(0.325)	(0.300)	(0.312)
N	1,826	1,824	1,824
R^2	0.333	0.401	0.276

Note: Cell entries are OLS regression coefficients with associated standard errors in parentheses; $^{+}p < 0.10$; $^{*}p < 0.05$; $^{**}p < 0.01$; $^{***}p < 0.001$ for two-tailed tests.

provide a set of sensitivity analysis tools. Their tools allow researchers to estimate how much unobserved confounding (i.e., omitted variable bias) would need to occur for significant effects to become insignificant. We did not use this tool in subsequent chapters since in those chapters we were able instead to exploit the panel nature of our data to address omitted variable bias.

Take, as a case in point, the model for the minimum wage (models for other issues look very similar). For our key estimates to go to 0 (e.g., for the

TABLE A4.2. Cue-Taking on Nonpolarized Issues

	Lobbyist ban	Campaign donations	Relocation incentives	Drug negotiation	Immigration test
Constant	2.013***	3.319***	2.739***	2.962***	2.677***
	(0.167)	(0.169)	(0.169)	(0.134)	(0.176)
Partisan animosity	0.266	−0.422**	−0.095	0.245⁺	−0.387*
	(0.162)	(0.164)	(0.163)	(0.130)	(0.170)
Republican	0.070	0.216	0.230	−0.017	−0.205
	(0.163)	(0.165)	(0.164)	(0.130)	(0.171)
Political knowledge	0.097***	−0.197***	−0.022	0.062***	−0.040**
	(0.015)	(0.015)	(0.015)	(0.012)	(0.015)
Liberal-conservative self ID	−0.031*	0.020	0.005	−0.063***	0.092***
	(0.016)	(0.016)	(0.016)	(0.013)	(0.016)
Education	0.032*	−0.033*	0.010	−0.009	−0.017
	(0.015)	(0.015)	(0.015)	(0.012)	(0.016)
Non-Hispanic White	0.054	−0.222***	−0.065	0.080*	0.007
	(0.047)	(0.047)	(0.047)	(0.037)	(0.049)
Female	−0.118**	−0.063	−0.090*	0.059⁺	0.010
	(0.041)	(0.041)	(0.041)	(0.033)	(0.043)
Protestant	−0.012	−0.035	0.066	−0.009	−0.025
	(0.062)	(0.062)	(0.062)	(0.049)	(0.065)
Catholic	0.104⁺	0.019	0.058	0.015	0.027
	(0.062)	(0.063)	(0.063)	(0.050)	(0.066)
Jewish	−0.031	0.123	−0.017	−0.107	−0.048
	(0.109)	(0.110)	(0.110)	(0.087)	(0.114)
No religion/atheist	0.104⁺	−0.082	−0.082	0.009	−0.097
	(0.058)	(0.059)	(0.059)	(0.047)	(0.061)
Age	0.091***	−0.103***	−0.012	0.086***	0.117***
	(0.020)	(0.020)	(0.020)	(0.016)	(0.021)
Fox News viewer	0.100*	−0.161***	0.006	−0.002	−0.081⁺
	(0.043)	(0.044)	(0.043)	(0.035)	(0.045)
Partisan social identity	0.040⁺	0.103***	0.058**	0.029⁺	0.037⁺
	(0.021)	(0.021)	(0.021)	(0.017)	(0.022)
Partisan animosity*Republican	−0.162	−0.260	−0.268	−0.120	0.926**
	(0.299)	(0.302)	(0.301)	(0.240)	(0.314)
N	1,824	1,825	1,825	1,825	1,825
R^2	0.094	0.201	0.020	0.089	0.126

Note: Cell entries are OLS regression coefficients with associated standard errors in parentheses; ⁺$p < 0.10$; *$p < 0.05$; **$p < 0.01$; ***$p < 0.001$ for two-tailed tests.

interaction term between Republican and animus to go to 0), we would need to have one or more unmeasured confounders—which are orthogonal to our included covariates—that would explain more than 11 percent of the residual variance of both the treatment and the outcome.[1] Given the number of controls included, something that strongly relates to both the treatment and the

TABLE A4.3. Cue-Taking on Asymmetrically Polarized Issues

	Assault weapons ban	Family leave	Green New Deal	Defund the police
Constant	2.535***	3.316***	3.634***	2.943***
	(0.203)	(0.152)	(0.170)	(0.183)
Partisan animosity	0.326⁺	0.519***	0.306⁺	1.021***
	(0.196)	(0.147)	(0.164)	(0.178)
Republican	0.265	0.171	0.268	0.542**
	(0.197)	(0.148)	(0.165)	(0.178)
Political knowledge	−0.001	0.011	−0.050***	−0.040*
	(0.018)	(0.013)	(0.015)	(0.016)
Liberal-conservative self ID	−0.184***	−0.076***	−0.191***	−0.142***
	(0.019)	(0.014)	(0.016)	(0.017)
Education	0.008	−0.017	0.005	−0.001
	(0.018)	(0.014)	(0.015)	(0.016)
Non-Hispanic White	0.033	−0.018	−0.061	−0.270***
	(0.056)	(0.042)	(0.047)	(0.051)
Female	0.130**	0.216***	0.026	−0.047
	(0.049)	(0.037)	(0.041)	(0.045)
Protestant	0.041	−0.093⁺	−0.141*	−0.171*
	(0.075)	(0.056)	(0.063)	(0.068)
Catholic	0.130⁺	−0.090	−0.093	−0.252***
	(0.076)	(0.057)	(0.063)	(0.068)
Jewish	0.330*	−0.118	0.028	0.060
	(0.132)	(0.099)	(0.110)	(0.119)
No religion/atheist	−0.007	−0.013	−0.082	0.161*
	(0.070)	(0.053)	(0.059)	(0.064)
Age	0.112***	−0.071***	−0.018	−0.162***
	(0.024)	(0.018)	(0.020)	(0.022)
Fox News viewer	0.233***	0.150***	0.178***	0.019
	(0.052)	(0.039)	(0.044)	(0.047)
Partisan social identity	0.043⁺	0.066***	0.053*	0.073**
	(0.025)	(0.019)	(0.021)	(0.023)
Partisan animosity*Republican	−1.581***	−0.951***	−1.837***	−1.634***
	(0.362)	(0.272)	(0.304)	(0.328)
N	1,824	1,826	1,825	1,825
R^2	0.249	0.182	0.368	0.281

Note: Cell entries are OLS regression coefficients with associated standard errors in parentheses; ⁺$p < 0.10$; *$p < 0.05$; **$p < 0.01$; ***$p < 0.001$ for two-tailed tests.

outcome seems unlikely. Cinelli and Hazlett (2020) also provide a useful approach for using a benchmark in terms of other covariates. We employed liberal-conservative self-identification (i.e., ideology) as a benchmark, as that is a sensible, and important, predictor of policy attitudes. We were asking how much stronger of an effect would the unobserved confounders need to have, relative to ideology, for our effects to become either insignificant or go to 0?

We found that for our effects to become insignificant, the effect would need to be twice as strong as the effect of liberal-conservative self-identification. This highlights that our results are quite robust to omitted variable bias. Omitted predictors would need to be extremely important to erase our results. Of course, a single cross-sectional analysis like this will always be subject to critiques. In later chapters, therefore, we moved to more robust methods of testing our hypotheses, relying on the panel nature of our data and experiments.

Appendix 5.1: Panel Data Regression Models

In the body of the chapter, using the same procedures as in other chapters, we graphed the effects of animus on COVID-19–related outcomes. In Druckman et al. (2021a), we analyzed our April 2020 data, showing results when controlling for a wide variety of variables and model specifications. As with any such analyses, one concern is omitted variable bias: perhaps there is some variable that is correlated with animus (but not animus itself) that drives support for these outcomes. To be clear, we can never fully eliminate this possibility, but we can use the panel nature of our data to estimate regression models to verify that our findings are not simply spurious.

We estimate the following model: $outcome_{i,t} = \beta_0 AP_i * wave_t + \beta_1 wave_t * Rep_i + \beta_2 AP_i * Rep_i * wave_t + \gamma_i + \eta_t + \epsilon_{it}$, where $outcome_{it}$ gives respondent i's value on each of our outcome measures (preventative behaviors, mask wearing, perceived safety, and policy support; we can only include items that were asked repeatedly over time so we cannot include vaccination) at time t. The variable AP_i indicates the respondent's level of animus (measured in July 2019), Rep_i is an indicator for whether the respondent is a Republican (versus a Democrat), $wave_t$ indicates in which wave the response was given (April 2020, October 2020, or April 2021), γ_i and η_t are individual and time-fixed effects, and ϵ_{it} is a stochastic disturbance term.[1] The variable β_0 tells us how the effect of animus changed over time for Democrats, β_1 tells us how Republican support changed over time, and then β_2 tells us how the animus-driven partisan gap changed over time. Table A5.1 presents the results.

We found evidence supporting the findings presented throughout the chapter for the behavior outcome. There, over time, we found that the partisan gap grew as animus increased (i.e., β_2 is statistically significant). Consistent with the analyses in the chapter, Democrats engaged in more COVID-19-mitigation

TABLE A5.1. Effects of Animus and Party on COVID-19-Related Attitudes

	Behavior	Face mask	Safety	Policy
Republican*wave	0.500	0.138*	−0.226	0.104
	(0.308)	(0.056)	(0.162)	(0.140)
Animosity*wave	0.322	0.037	−0.201	0.429**
	(0.314)	(0.057)	(0.162)	(0.141)
Animosity*Republican*wave	−1.992***	−0.219*	0.289	−0.233
	(0.544)	(0.098)	(0.287)	(0.249)
N	2,918	4,434	2,920	4,434
R^2	0.746	0.586	0.822	0.881

Note: Cell entries are OLS regression coefficients with respondent and time fixed effects, with associated standard errors in parentheses; $*p < 0.05$; $**p < 0.01$; $***p < 0.001$ for two-tailed tests.

activities while Republicans engaged in fewer of them. We found the same pattern for mask wearing.

For policy support, as in the body of the chapter, we only examined the data from the October 2020 and April 2021 waves (recall that in the April 2020 wave we asked a different set of policy items). Here, we found that the interaction term was correctly signed but fell short of conventional levels of statistical significance, and the same was true for the safety item. Looking at figures 5.4 and 5.5, we can see why: there was little growth in the animosity-driven partisan gap, and instead, a large gap more or less persisted across waves. The effects of animosity, therefore, are driving the parties apart, but it does not significantly accelerate that difference over time.

One concern is that perhaps animus is simply serving as a proxy for some other factor that is correlated with it. As we explained in chapter 3, this is unlikely theoretically, but we can also evaluate this empirically. Two of the most plausible suspects would be strength of partisan identity (i.e., whether you are a strong or weak Democrat/Republican) and partisan social identity (i.e., the degree to which you perceive yourself to be a member of a partisan in-group). We can interact these variables with wave, paralleling the model just described, and see if this changes our results. If our argument is correct, the effect of these models should simply parallel those of the models in table A5.1. Table A5.2 presents the results with the respective controls added.

We found that these results directly parallel the findings in the previous table, suggesting that animus is not simply serving as a proxy for these related variables. At some level, there is a problem of infinite regress: there are many variables (including unobserved variables) correlated with animus, and we cannot rule out all of them. But finding that our results hold in these sorts of specifications, when controlling for the theoretically most relevant variables, is reassuring.

TABLE A5.2. Effects of Animus, Partisan Strength, and Partisan Social Identity on COVID-19-Related Attitudes

	Behavior		Masking		Safety		Policy	
	Model 1	Model 2	Model 1	Model 2	Model 1	Model 2	Model 1	Model 2
Republican*wave	0.579	0.560	0.204**	0.176**	-0.149	-0.140	0.128	0.100
	(0.362)	(0.378)	(0.065)	(0.068)	(0.191)	(0.199)	(0.165)	(0.172)
Animosity*wave	0.330	0.332	0.047	0.065	-0.205	-0.190	0.443**	0.455**
	(0.315)	(0.317)	(0.057)	(0.057)	(0.163)	(0.164)	(0.141)	(0.142)
Strength*wave	-0.016	0.007	-0.020'	0.009	0.011	0.033	-0.030	-0.007
	(0.063)	(0.079)	(0.011)	(0.014)	(0.032)	(0.041)	(0.028)	(0.035)
Social identity*wave		-0.033		-0.036**		-0.028		-0.030
		(0.061)		(0.011)		(0.032)		(0.028)
Strength*Republican*wave	-0.048	-0.055	-0.042*	-0.065**	-0.042	-0.041	-0.020	-0.040
	(0.100)	(0.122)	(0.018)	(0.022)	(0.053)	(0.065)	(0.046)	(0.056)
Social identity*Republican*wave		0.006		0.027		-0.012		0.024
		(0.105)		(0.019)		(0.056)		(0.048)
Animosity*Republican*wave	-1.964***	-1.933***	-0.195*	-0.202*	0.310	0.351	-0.220	-0.225
	(0.547)	(0.558)	(0.098)	(0.100)	(0.288)	(0.296)	(0.250)	(0.256)
N	2,918	2,916	4,434	4,431	2,920	2,918	4,434	4,431
R^2	0.746	0.746	0.589	0.591	0.822	0.822	0.881	0.881

Note: Cell entries are OLS regression coefficients with respondent and time fixed effects, with associated standard errors in parentheses; $p < 0.10$; $^*p < 0.05$; $^{**}p < 0.01$; $^{***}p < 0.001$ for two-tailed tests.

Appendix 6.1: Panel Data Regression Models

As with chapter 5, we used the panel nature of our data to estimate regression models that verify that our findings are not spurious. We estimate the following model: $eval_{i,t} = \beta_o AP_i * wave_t + \beta_1 wave_t * Rep_i + \beta_2 AP_i * Rep_i * wave_t + \gamma_i + \eta_t + \epsilon_{it}$, where $eval_{it}$ gives respondent i's evaluation of a given leader or institution at time t, AP_i gives the respondent's level of animus (measured in July 2019), Rep_i is an indicator for whether the respondent is a Republican (versus a Democrat), $wave_t$ indicates which wave the response was given in (April 2020, October 2020, or April 2021), γ_i and η_t are individual and time-fixed effects, and ϵ_{it} is a stochastic disturbance term. The variable β_o tells us how animus mapped onto support for our outcomes for Democrats in our April 2020 wave (or the first wave in which the item was asked), β_1 tells us how Republican support changed over time, and then β_2 tells us how the partisan gap changed as animus increased. Table A6.1 presents the results.

For evaluations of Trump and Biden, we found partisan differences, but those gaps do not increase over time. For Trump, the effect of animus grew larger over time, but not the partisan gap. This is consistent with both the findings in figures 6.2 and 6.3 and our theory: because Biden and Trump were highly salient political figures, even low-animus respondents polarized in their evaluations of them. Likewise, the results show that mayoral approval was basically unrelated to our variables, consistent with our claim that mayoral partisanship is functionally invisible outside major cities.

In contrast, we observed strong over-time polarization effects for two of our three scientific figures: Dr. Fauci and the CDC; however, the effect for the FDA fell short of conventional levels of statistical significance. This is consistent with the strong polarization we presented in figures 6.8–6.10 in the body of the chapter.

TABLE A6.1. Effects of Animus on Evaluations

	Trump	Biden	Mayor	Fauci	CDC	FDA
Animosity*Republican	0.129	−0.343**	−0.254	−0.161	0.038	−0.300
	(0.108)	(0.131)	(0.218)	(0.120)	(0.121)	(0.224)
Animosity*wave	0.392***	0.139	−0.414⁺	0.121	0.216⁺	0.099
	(0.109)	(0.131)	(0.219)	(0.122)	(0.123)	(0.225)
Animosity*Republican *wave	−0.208	−0.194	0.241	−1.027***	−1.128***	−0.446
	(0.190)	(0.231)	(0.387)	(0.212)	(0.213)	(0.398)
N	4,432	2,994	2,920	4,432	4,431	2,920
R²	0.874	0.825	0.816	0.748	0.697	0.781

Note: Cell entries are OLS regression coefficients with respondent and time fixed effects, with associated standard errors in parentheses; $^{+}p < 0.10$; $^{*}p < 0.05$; $^{**}p < 0.01$; $^{***}p < 0.001$ for two-tailed tests.

As in chapter 5, we can look at the change in COVID-19 severity between the October 2020 and April 2021 waves and examine whether that changed attitudes toward the scientific and /medical actors: Dr. Fauci, the CDC, and the FDA. We expected to find that individuals who experienced a more severe case of COVID-19 (i.e., those for whom the virus becomes more salient) rated these agencies more positively. Table A6.2 tests this expectation, using the same empirical strategy as table 5.1.

As in chapter 5, we found strong support for our argument: approval for all three actors increased among respondents who experienced a severe case of COVID. Here, when we reestimated our model with only Republican respondents (a more stringent test), we found a significant result for the CDC, and a marginally significant result for Dr. Fauci ($p = 0.15$, two-tailed), and no effect for the FDA. That is consistent with what we observed earlier: because Dr. Fauci became "exhibit A" for pandemic overreach among many Republicans, the effect is somewhat weaker, even when personally relevant. And consistent with table A6.1 and figure 6.10, the FDA was simply less politicized than the other two entities. But overall, as severity changed and COVID-19 became more salient, the partisan response was undercut and the accuracy motivation took over.

TABLE A6.2. Change in Personal COVID-19 Severity and Change in Scientific Figure Evaluations, October 2020–April 2021

	Dr. Fauci (All)	CDC (All)	FDA (All)	Dr. Fauci (Republicans only)	CDC (Republicans only)	FDA (Republicans only)
Constant	−0.120***	0.045'	0.115***	−0.578***	−0.244***	−0.215***
	(0.027)	(0.025)	(0.026)	(0.053)	(0.049)	(0.049)
Change in COVID-19 severity	0.076**	0.064*	0.091***	0.080	0.112*	0.058
	(0.029)	(0.027)	(0.027)	(0.056)	(0.052)	(0.052)
N	1,826	1,825	1,826	564	563	564
R^2	0.004	0.003	0.006	0.004	0.008	0.002

Note: Cell entries are OLS regression coefficients with associated standard errors in parentheses; '$p < 0.10$; *$p < 0.05$; **$p < 0.01$; ***$p < 0.001$ for two-tailed tests.

Appendix 7.1: Regression Models for the Experimental Data

We analyzed our data using regressions as a check on the graphical presentations in the body of the chapter. We began with an analysis of the compromise and respect experiment that we presented in figures 7.1 and 7.2. Table A7.1 presents the results.

Consistent with the results presented in the chapter, we found that everyone likes compromise and respect: the intercepts are 3.5–3.6 on a 1–4 scale, so at baseline, everyone attaches a great deal of importance to them both. However, we found differences across our experimental conditions. Most notably, we found the largest effects of animosity in the in-party condition: as animus increases, individuals attach much less importance to politicians of their own party compromising with, and being respectful of, other politicians. The effects of animus in the other conditions were much weaker, consistent with an argument that everyone likes respect and compromise overall. In columns 2 and 4 we show that controlling for partisan strength does not eliminate the effect of animosity. Instead, even here, we found the same substantive story. These regression results reinforce what we reported in the chapter: for high-animus individuals, compromise and respect are a one-way exchange that only the other side needs to practice.

We present the results of the NASA compromise experiment in table A7.2. Our findings again parallel those presented in the chapter. The lowest-animus respondents preferred the 50–50 split, likely reflecting their belief that compromise means everyone sacrificing (i.e., the negative main effects of the in-party condition). But for higher-animus respondents, that was not the case. These individuals preferred the split that favored their party and opposed the one favoring the other party. In column 2, we test for heterogeneous effects by party, which shows that the results were largely symmetric, though higher-

TABLE A7.1. Importance of Compromise and Respect

	Compromise		Respect	
	Model 1	Model 2	Model 1	Model 2
Constant	3.492***	3.457***	3.545***	3.445***
	(0.124)	(0.131)	(0.119)	(0.126)
Partisan animosity	−0.313	−0.332	−0.048	−0.102
	(0.217)	(0.219)	(0.210)	(0.210)
Partisan strength		0.024		0.068*
		(0.029)		(0.028)
In-party condition	0.171	0.266	0.282⁺	0.397*
	(0.170)	(0.180)	(0.164)	(0.174)
Out-party condition	−0.106	−0.143	0.014	0.017
	(0.171)	(0.182)	(0.165)	(0.175)
In-party*animosity	−0.914**	−0.859**	−1.047***	−0.983***
	(0.300)	(0.301)	(0.289)	(0.291)
Out-party*animosity	0.480	0.449	0.133	0.121
	(0.301)	(0.303)	(0.290)	(0.292)
In-party*partisan strength		−0.065		−0.079*
		(0.041)		(0.039)
Out-party*partisan strength		0.026		−0.001
		(0.042)		(0.041)
N	1,828	1,828	1,826	1,826
R^2	0.082	0.085	0.060	0.066

Note: Cell entries are OLS regression coefficients with associated standard errors in parentheses;
$^+p < 0.10$; $^*p < 0.05$; $^{**}p < 0.01$; $^{***}p < 0.001$ for two-tailed tests.

animus Republicans especially favored the in-party condition. Column 3 shows that even when controlling for partisan strength, we still found the same mapping (i.e., animus is not simply a proxy for partisan strength), though we only found a significant effect for the out-party condition.

What about the amount that was to be cut? In column 4, we analyze the deviations from $300 million (the even split outcome). Recall that this outcome is scaled so that higher values mean individuals move toward their own party, so for Republicans this means cutting more and for Democrats, cutting less. We find that everyone concedes a bit in the out-party condition: those at the lowest level of animus concede roughly $31 million to the other party, likely reflecting a sense that compromise means conceding some of what your side wants. As animus increases, however, everyone moves toward their party in the in-party and out-party conditions. Column 5 tests the hypothesis that there are differential effects by party and shows few substantively meaningful differences. In column 6, we test for differential effects by partisan strength, and while the effects are in the right direction, they are no longer statistically significant.

TABLE A7.2. Support for Compromise, NASA Experiment

	Support			Amount		
	Model 1	Model 2	Model 3	Model 1	Model 2	Model 3
Constant	2.945***	2.835***	2.776***	0.792	13.709	-4.230
	(0.142)	(0.169)	(0.177)	(9.772)	(11.184)	(11.499)
Partisan animosity	-0.176	0.106	0.076	9.677	7.827	-0.838
	(0.252)	(0.299)	(0.299)	(17.368)	(19.754)	(19.351)
Partisan strength			0.040			11.971***
			(0.037)			(2.423)
In-party split	-0.702***	-0.507*	-0.624*	-8.823	-4.592	-4.689
	(0.195)	(0.234)	(0.243)	(13.409)	(15.489)	(15.772)
Out-party split	0.067	0.161	0.259	-31.108*	-21.007	-15.377
	(0.199)	(0.241)	(0.250)	(13.746)	(15.985)	(16.245)
In-party*animosity	1.237***	0.771'	0.607	41.463'	32.301	20.764
	(0.342)	(0.405)	(0.407)	(23.562)	(26.829)	(26.405)
Out-party*animosity	-0.578	-0.872*	-0.791'	41.966'	23.491	14.765
	(0.353)	(0.422)	(0.425)	(24.343)	(27.977)	(27.624)
Republican		0.415	0.560		-34.642'	1.417
		(0.310)	(0.344)		(20.614)	(22.314)

In-party*Republican	-0.758⁺	-0.791		5.108	4.032
	(0.425)	(0.481)		(28.189)	(31.185)
Out-party*Republican	-0.400	-0.623		-18.113	-49.525
	(0.430)	(0.475)		(28.566)	(30.883)
In-party*partisan strength		0.113*			3.758
		(0.052)			(3.373)
Out-party*partisan strength		-0.075			-0.449
		(0.054)			(3.531)
In-party*animosity*Republican	1.795*	1.932*		-4.931	0.829
	(0.763)	(0.763)		(50.530)	(49.508)
Out-party*animosity*Republican	1.144	1.024		35.305	35.410
	(0.771)	(0.773)		(51.331)	(50.435)
In-party*partisan strength*Republican		-0.034			-1.450
		(0.123)			(7.962)
Out-party*partisan strength*Republican		0.147			15.331⁺
		(0.125)			(8.087)
N	1,826	1,826	1,803	1,803	1,803
R^2	0.032	0.048	0.033	0.111	0.156

Note: Cell entries are OLS regression coefficients with associated standard errors in parentheses; ⁺$p < 0.10$; *$p < 0.05$; **$p < 0.01$; ***$p < 0.001$ for two-tailed tests.

Appendix 8.1: Panel Model of the Norms Data

As with chapters 5 and 6, we used the panel nature of our data to estimate regression models to verify that our findings are not simply spurious. We can estimate the following model: $norm_{i,t} = \beta_o AP_i * wave_t + \beta_1 Rep_i * wave_t + \beta_2 AP_i * Rep_i * wave_t + \gamma_i + \eta_t + \epsilon_{it}$, where $norm_{it}$ gives respondent i's support for some norm at time t. The variable AP_i indicates the respondent's level of animus (measured in July 2019), Rep_i is an indicator for whether the respondent is a Republican (versus a Democrat), $wave_t$ indicates whether the response comes from the July 2019 wave or the April 2021 wave, γ_i and η_t are individual and time-fixed effects, and ϵ_{it} is a stochastic disturbance term. The variable β_o shows how animus mapped onto support for our outcomes for Democrats in our April 2021 wave, β_1 shows how Republican support changed over time, and then β_2 shows how the partisan gap changed as animus increased. Here we coded all the norms so that higher scores indicated upholding them (and thus there is no reverse coding, as there is in the figures). Table A8.1 presents the results.

It is apparent that the results directly parallel those presented in figure 8.4. We found that for all these norms save the "Respect for Institutions" item, higher-animus Democrats are more opposed in the April 2021 wave (i.e., β_o is negative and significant), but high-animus Republicans are more supportive (i.e., β_2 is positive and significant) (other than for "Get Things Done"). Much as we saw in the chapter, context and animus shape support for the norm. We also tested for heterogeneous effects by education and political information and found none (though again, we were almost certainly underpowered to detect them).

TABLE A8.1. Support for Democratic Norms, July 2019–April 2021

	Executive power	Gets things done	Respect for institutions	Checks and balances
Animus*April 2021 wave	−1.223***	−0.524⁺	−0.161	−0.652**
	(0.297)	(0.277)	(0.228)	(0.214)
Republican*April 2021 wave	−0.187	0.171	−0.402⁺	−0.640**
	(0.297)	(0.277)	(0.227)	(0.213)
Animus*Republican*April 2021 wave	1.592**	0.234	1.090**	1.555***
	(0.524)	(0.489)	(0.401)	(0.377)
N	3,300	3,301	3,299	3,301
R^2	0.700	0.736	0.737	0.745

Note: Cell entries are OLS regression coefficients with respondent and wave fixed effects; associated standard errors are presented in parentheses; $^+p < 0.10$; $^*p < 0.05$; $^{**}p < 0.01$; $^{***}p < 0.001$ for two-tailed tests.

Notes

Chapter One

1. Baldassarri and Park (2020) offer an alternative viewpoint, that the entire electorate has become more liberal over time on social issues but this change occurred more quickly among self-identified liberals compared with self-identified conservatives, leading to temporary gaps. Of course, that can only explain attitudinal changes on those issues and not the pattern on other topics, such as race or economic views, which suggests the occurrence of a broader dynamic. See Jost (2021) for a discussion of ideology more generally.

2. We focus on over-time changes, which differs from the alternative approach of looking at the state of polarization at a given time (see Lelkes 2016; Jost, Baldassari, and Druckman 2022).

3. It is impossible to pinpoint the exact cause of the mode differences. They likely stem both from sample selection effects (i.e., a different set of people respond online versus face-to-face; see Malhotra and Krosnick 2007) and also from differences in how respondents answer questions online versus face-to-face (Homola, Jackson, and Gill 2016).

4. The in-party trend could mask some shifts among those within the party (e.g., comparing strong partisans to weak partisans; see, e.g., Klar, Krupnikov, and Ryan 2022).

5. Further, sorting magnifies the effects of animus among more sophisticated voters, who can detect such policy differences (Lelkes 2018).

6. Other ostensible causes for the rise in partisan animosity include a changed media environment, especially the rise of the internet (e.g., Lelkes, Sood, and Iyengar 2017; cf. Boxell, Gentzkow, and Shapiro 2017; Shmargad and Klar 2020), the lack of exposure to cross-cutting information (Levy 2021; cf. Bail 2021), elite ideological polarization (Rogowski and Sutherland 2016; Webster and Abramowitz 2017), charged elite rhetoric (Lau et al. 2017; Gentzkow, Shapiro, and Taddy 2019), the nationalization of U.S. elections and the media (Abramowitz and Webster 2016; Moskowitz 2021; Pierson and Schickler 2020), economic inequality (Gidron, Adams, and Horne 2020), and majoritarian institutions (Gidron, Adams, and Horne 2020). Individual-level variables include high levels of empathy (Simas, Clifford, and Kirkland 2020), authoritarianism (Luttig 2017), and misperceptions (Ahler and Sood 2018). We do not discuss these or other factors in detail here, as they are somewhat orthogonal to our purposes.

7. There is evidence that policy beliefs play a role in driving levels of partisan animosity. However, in the most direct test of this hypothesis, N. Dias and Lelkes (2022) found that policy has a role, but it is dwarfed by identity (cf. Orr, Fowler, and Huber 2023).

8. At time of our April fielding, Biden had not formally secured enough delegates to become the Democratic Party's nominee; however, he became the presumptive nominee when Senator Bernie Sanders—his last opponent for the nomination—suspended his campaign on April 9.

9. Throughout the fall, Trump claimed the election was being stolen from him using mail-in ballots. He even remarked, perhaps most famously, during the first presidential debate with Joe Biden: "As you know, today there was a big problem. In Philadelphia, they [my supporters] went in to watch. They're called poll watchers, a very safe, very nice thing. They were thrown out. They weren't allowed to watch. You know why? Because bad things happen in Philadelphia" (Commission on Presidential Debates 2020). While this was perhaps his most egregious example, it fit into a larger pattern of trying to delegitimize the election (Annenberg IOD Collaborative 2023).

10. In October 2020, the Centers for Disease Control released a report, highlighting that "at least one indicator used to monitor COVID-19 activity [was] increasing in each of the ten HHS [Health and Human Services] regions, and many regions [were] reporting increases in multiple indicators" (Centers for Disease Control and Prevention 2020).

11. As we explain in chapter 2, our theory treats partisan identification and a given level of animosity as (individually) exogenous and addresses the question of when animosity will influence opinions.

Chapter Two

1. While all these authors argue that there is a social group basis for partisanship, there are differences between their arguments. Notably, Green, Palmquist, and Schickler (2002) distinguished themselves from earlier work on partisanship (e.g., A. Campbell et al. 1960), suggesting that partisans can and do update assessments of national conditions and party capabilities.

2. These are referred to respectively as the confirmation bias, prior attitude effect, and disconfirmation bias.

3. For most Americans, partisanship and politics are not front and center in how they present themselves. For example, R. Bond and Messing (2015) found that 6.2 million Americans liked at least two political pages on Facebook. Yet according to the Pew Research Center (2014), a few years after the years in the Bond and Messing data, approximately 60 percent of American adults used Facebook, so only about 5 percent of U.S. adult Facebook users met even this very low threshold of partisan expression. Likewise, Bakshy, Messing, and Adamic (2015) reported that only about 7–8 percent of Facebook users self-identified themselves politically on the platform. Of course, because those who put partisan considerations at the center of their lives are the most active online, people often misperceive how central partisanship is to others (Settle 2018).

4. We focus on the effects of animus, rather than the nature of party identification per se. A. Lee et al. (2022) showed that for most Americans, partisans attach to their party for both positive and negative reasons, and often the positive ones are no less important than the negative ones. In that sense, partisanship is not primarily negative. We do not view our focus on animosity as being at odds with this conceptualization since we do not seek to explain the nature of partisan attachments, but rather the impact of affective reactions. Additionally, Guay and Johnston (2022) found little evidence that centrality of political identity promotes directional motivated

reasoning. They operationalize identity using partisanship as a social identity (Huddy, Mason, and Aarøe 2015). This also differs from our focus on animosity. Further, Guay and Johnston (2022) looked at situations without the direct availability of partisan cues, which is distinct from our approach.

5. An implication is that, as with party identification, it is possible that animosity reflects some instrumental considerations (e.g., Orr and Huber 2020). However, our perspective is that people with high animus act on it in a way that coheres more with the expressive view of partisanship.

6. In some sense, our expectation here expands our definition of "party cue" to include, not just explicit endorsements, but also internal assessments of where the parties stand (i.e., a reasoning heuristic; Druckman et al. 2010), with the point being that those who are high in animus will apply this heuristic more readily. This hypothesis also makes clear that animosity can matter even if party leaders equivocate, which they often do (e.g., Tomz and Van Houweling 2009). We recognize our vagueness in defining what constitutes an ambiguous target; this is a limitation of the theory, but in our empirical test, we used fairly straightforward examples.

7. Other work shows that elite ideological polarization affects citizens' opinions (e.g., Hetherington 2001; Levendusky 2010; Druckman et al. 2013). We differ from this scholarship by focusing on elites' influence, regardless of their levels of polarization, among those who hold distinct levels of animosity.

8. As stated, we recognize the possibility of distinct nondirectional goals and also of hybrid directional and nondirectional motivations, but we put these aside for our purposes.

9. The sorting trends, discussed in chapter 1, have made partisanship an increasingly useful proxy for other identities (i.e., social sorting; see Mason 2018; Westwood and Peterson 2022) and values (ideological sorting; see Levendusky 2009). Moreover, people may be apt to rely on partisanship over other social categorizations (e.g., gender, race) when making decisions since there are fewer social norms against doing so (Iyengar and Westwood 2015).

10. There is one counterargument. Specifically, increased out-party animosity could increase the likability of one's own party, making it more persuasive—or at least a better source of accurate information. Yet likability on its own, particularly among people who are motivated by accuracy, is unlikely to be sufficient. Lupia and McCubbins (1998, 198) explain that likability may correlate with factors that drive persuasion, but ultimately, it is perceptions of shared interest and knowledge (credibility) that affect persuasion. They go so far as to state that "feeling thermometers are a *terrible* measure of what it is about a speaker that induces a principal to follow or ignore his advice. Feeling thermometers do not allow for such factors as a speaker's perceived knowledge or interests" (italics in the original). Further, the role of likability—as even a heuristic for credibility—becomes weaker with regard to topics of high personal consequence, which, as we next discuss, are those that trigger accuracy motivations (Kang and Herr 2006; O'Keefe 2016, 199). Thus, when conditions prompt accuracy processing, we are unlikely to see a relationship between animosity and political opinions.

11. Groenendyk and Krupnikov (2021) point out that the baseline for directional reasoning stems, not from a default per se, but rather from the contemporary conception of politics as conflictual.

12. Mullinix's (2016) results accentuate the differences between the importance of one's prior opinion and the importance of the issue for one's welfare (also see Holbrook et al. 2005; Visser, Bizer, and Krosnick 2006). Accuracy processes occur more often when the outcomes of

decisions are consequential (not when a standing attitude is important; see Amit et al. 2021 for a general discussion on types of thinking).

13. This is similar to work showing that people are more likely to display accurate knowledge when incentivized to do so (Bullock et al. 2015; Prior, Sood, and Khanna 2015). Other work has shown that another way to stimulate nondirectional processing is through a prompt encouraging people to be a good citizen (Kam 2007; Groenendyk 2013).

14. Other examples of personal threat seemingly leading individuals to pivot away from partisan or ideological motivations have been documented regarding climate change (Scannell and Gifford 2013; Milfont et al. 2014; Ripberger et al. 2017; Boudet et al. 2020; Constantino et al. 2022), gun control (Garcia-Montoya, Arjona, and Lacombe 2022), and gender equity policies (E. Washington 2008; Druckman and Sharrow 2023). In each of these cases, personal experiences and expectations shape preferences regardless of partisan or ideological leanings.

15. People must perceive personal consequences for them to matter. Long, Chen, and Rohla (2020) found a notable partisan split in hurricane evaluations, with Republicans ignoring warnings. They attribute this split to more right-leaning news outlets casting doubt on the warning systems, which led partisans to ignore them.

16. Constantino et al. (2022) offered evidence consistent with our hypothesis, showing that partisan gaps in concern, policy support, and behavioral intentions narrow as people report more adverse experiences with COVID-19. They offer similar evidence for climate change opinions. They do not, however, explore the role of partisan animosity. In contrast, Rodriguez et al. (2022) drew on terror management theory to suggest that existential threat (e.g., death) leads individuals to rely on their predispositions, including their partisan identifications, rather than assessing information and updating their beliefs. This is counter to our theory insofar as we argue that personal relevance envelopes such threats. Rodriguez et al. tested their theory with regard to COVID-19 and found limited evidence for it.

17. We recognize that we do not theorize about heterogeneities in the impact of animosity on opinions, based on constructs such as the need for affect (Arceneaux and Vander Wielen 2013, 2017). We leave such questions for future work. We also do not theorize about partisan asymmetries. Generally, polarization could stem from ego-, group-, or system-justifying motivations (Jost et al. 2022). We focus on group-justifying motivations (i.e., partisan identity). Asymmetries are most evident with regard to system-justifying motivations. That said, they can exist with group-justifying motivations; for example, Republicans may be less willing to update an opinion when faced with uncongenial information (e.g., Morisi et al. 2019). We do not explore that possibility due, in part, to statistical power considerations. Also, the most relevant context (for us) in which to assess it is with COVID-19, and, for reasons that we note in chapter 5, it may not be possible given the dynamics of COVID-19.

18. While we explored a sizable range of outcomes, there also are options that we did not study. Of particular note is that we did not study how animosity shapes social and economic relationships (e.g., Druckman and Levy 2022), which could, in turn, affect political opinions (e.g., Sinclair 2012).

19. It may require some attentiveness among high-animus individuals to realize the possibility of politicizing a target; however, it is their animosity that motivates people to do so. Those who are high in interest and attentiveness but low in animus lack the motivation to politicize the target. This also interacts with our previous point: not only are people who are high in animus more attentive to cues that exist, they are also more likely to go looking for them, even when they do not really apply.

20. As Levitsky and Ziblatt (2018) made clear, in earlier eras in American politics, party was a less clear dividing line, and so this argument with regard to norms may not travel back in time. Our argument is designed to apply to the current era of highly polarized national (elite) politics.

21. As we will explain in chapter 8, these cues have been relatively clear during recent administrations. For example, many have noted that President Trump, during his term, "act[ed] as if [institutions] are bona fide only to the extent that they deliver results consistent with his needs, an assumption that makes him the arbiter of institutional legitimacy" (Jamieson and Taussig 2017, 635–636; also see Cottrell, Herron, and Westwood 2018). The cues from the Democratic Party have not been as explicit, but we would expect Democrats with high animosity to observe Trump and other Republicans and do the opposite (Nicholson 2012). Conversely, during President Obama's term, Republicans argued that his administration, and the Democratic Party more broadly, violated these norms by criticizing the Supreme Court during the State of the Union address, eliminating the filibuster for judicial appointments, and using executive action to reform immigration.

22. We do not test the psychological mechanisms directly—that is, we do not isolate the relationship between animosity and directional reasoning. We instead focus on the implications of our argument for political outcomes, leaving precise psychological inquiries to future work.

Chapter Three

1. This figure was calculated using a Google Scholar search performed on August 17, 2023.

2. The marriage item uses a scale which asked about how upset they would be on a scale from "Not at All Upset" to "Extremely Upset." It was then reverse coded.

3. In appendix 3.2, we discuss an experiment that was embedded in our animosity items (described in more detail in Druckman et al. 2022) and explain why it did not influence the results we present.

4. For example, the Pew Research Center (2014) suggested the opposite pattern—Republicans have greater animus.

5. We prefer these generalized additive models over LOESS because in cases with small numbers of respondents, as sometimes occurs in our results, a LOESS can be too sensitive, effectively overfitting the data. This often obscures more than it clarifies because the model is responding to very small numbers of respondents rather than a general trend in the underlying data.

6. See Iyengar and Tyler (2022) on the reliability of partisan feeling thermometers.

7. Out-party feeling thermometer ratings also correlate highly across waves. The correlations between the July 2019 feeling thermometer ratings and the subsequent waves from April 2020, October 2020, and April 2021 are 0.73, 0.62, and 0.68, respectively. The most notable change is that in the October 2020 wave, we found respondents reporting slightly more animus toward the out-party (and slightly more favorability toward their own party). This is sensible given that the presidential campaign likely strengthened party sentiments. These shifts, however, are quite modest, on average 2–3 degrees, and sentiments largely returned to earlier levels in our April 2021 wave (after the intensity of the election subsided).

8. For political discussion and social media posting, figure 3.7 reports the percentage who responded they "frequently" do each.

9. For versions of figures 3.5–3.7 separated by party, see appendix 3.4. These figures show that while the levels of these factors differed by party, the overall patterns were the same; hence, we present the pooled figures.

10. We identified partisan positions (or lack thereof) using the website ISideWith.com as well as Google searches for elite positions.

11. While there likely exist constituencies on some of these issues for whom direct consequences are clear (e.g., the ACA, paid family leave), we did not design our survey to measure such subgroups and thus cannot test our accuracy prediction in this context.

12. President Trump—with his dismissal of the virus, demands to reopen the economy, and refusal to wear a mask—was the apotheosis of this trend (Annenberg IOD Collaborative 2023). However, he was far from the only example. The partisan divide also emerged among governors and other elected officials (L. Fowler, Kettler, and Witt 2020), as well as within the media (P. Hart, Chinn, and Soroka 2020).

13. Specifically, in our October 2020 and April 2021 waves, we asked (separately) whether the respondent, anyone in the respondent's household, or someone else the respondent knew had contracted COVID-19. If so, we asked about the severity. If not, we asked the respondent to project how severe they thought COVID-19 would be personally, in the household, and/or for someone the respondent knew. We took the maximum severity score from these questions as a measure of personal threat.

14. As we will note in chapter 6, we did not preregister these moderated predictions, so readers may wish to treat them as more exploratory than our other analyses.

15. During our July 2019 survey, Republicans held the Senate majority and the presidency (though Democrats controlled the House of Representatives); during our April 2021 survey, Biden had won the presidency and Democrats had unified control of the government. Because the norms focus mostly on limits on executive power, the control of the presidency is the crucial shift.

16. The following analogy might be helpful: imagine that we allowed respondents to look up the answer to a set of political knowledge items. They would "know" the information, but that is not the same as actually learning it and absorbing it into long-term memory. We thank Cindy Kam for this example. Further, to be clear, this is also a criticism one could make of some of the authors' own work (see, e.g., Voelkel et al., "Interventions," 2023; Voelkel et al., "Megastudy," 2023; Levendusky 2023).

17. It is possible that prior elite polarization or general attitudes concerning norms contributed to partisan animus; however, this could not be true in this precise application—after the flip—since elite positions and presumably attitudes shifted after we measured wave 1 animosity.

18. Our substantive conclusions remain virtually identical when we control for these other variables (see the various chapter appendixes). Of course, no dispositive proof is possible here, but this increases the plausibility of our argument.

Chapter Four

1. Tesler (2018), however, looked at divides by ideology rather than partisanship.

2. An earlier generation of work on cue-taking argued that cues were effectively a heuristic: individuals use cues as a short-cut (e.g., Kam 2007). Later studies, however, showed that cue-taking appears to be more consistent with the effortful processing driving motivated reasoning (Bang Petersen et al. 2013; Bolsen, Druckman, and Cook 2014).

3. We employ the terms *symmetric* and *asymmetric* to refer to the provision of cues as being, respectively, from both parties or from one party. This differs from work on symmetric or

asymmetric reasoning in which partisans employ distinct information processing strategies or perspectives (e.g., Jost 2021; Guay and Johnston 2022; Jost, Baldassarri, and Druckman 2022).

4. Just days before leaving office, Trump rescinded his earlier ban (Solender 2021). But given that it took place amid the ongoing investigation of the January 6th insurrection at the Capitol and plans for his second impeachment trial, it drew almost no media attention.

5. In particular, beginning in chapter 5, we exploited the panel nature of our data to run a series of fixed effects models that allow us to more credibly assess how animus maps onto our outcomes of interest (in this chapter, because we only included policy positions in one wave of our study, we cannot do that, but we did include an appendix with statistical controls).

Chapter Five

1. For a timeline of events related to the pandemic, see *AJMC* Staff (2021).

2. While this is what Trump said in public, his private conversations with reporter Bob Woodward suggest he knew the virus was dangerous and airborne early in the year but chose not to act (see Trump and Woodward 2020).

3. As Leonnig and Rucker (2021, 177–180) discuss, Trump viewed the restrictions as a ploy by public health officials to restrict his rallies and deny him a second term.

4. As noted in figure 5.1, the number of possible behaviors was fourteen, although in the April 2021 wave it was fifteen.

5. There is ambiguity in this measure: an individual who had never made travel plans to begin with could not have canceled them as the pandemic began.

6. This sort of pattern is not without precedent: as Krupenkin (2021) showed, other vaccines have followed similar patterns of partisan uptake depending on the party of the president in power.

7. As we reported in chapter 3, the April 2021 wave was fielded between April 9 and April 23, 2021. By the time our survey started, thirty-eight states had already implemented universal eligibility for the vaccine for any person older than age sixteen. The remaining states declared universal eligibility as our study was in the field.

8. It is interesting to speculate what would have happened had the vaccine become available during Trump's time in office. In this case, we might well have seen more muted gaps in uptake, given that Trump likely would have done more to trumpet its success.

9. In our October 2020 wave, we also asked about a few outdoor activities (such as socializing with friends outside or exercising outside), but these were functionally unrelated to animus and were perceived to be quite safe by everyone, consistent with the guidance from the CDC and other public health agencies.

10. We also included an experiment in the April 2021 wave of our data collection asking people whether activities would be safer once the public was fully vaccinated, but we found null results in this experiment.

11. As explained, we asked people (separately) whether they themselves, someone in their household, or someone they knew personally had had COVID-19. If they had, we asked them how severe that infection had been. If not, we asked them to imagine how severe it would be if they or someone close to them were infected. We used the most serious infection, as it should dominate perceptions of disease risk. We acknowledge the potential endogeneity of such a measure, but when using self-reported survey data, this is an unavoidable issue.

12. As mentioned, the April 2021 wave included fifteen (not fourteen) possible behaviors.

13. We use a 4-point scale of COVID-19 infection severity, from "Not at All Severe" to "Very Severe." For simplicity of presentation, we split the scale in half, though other operationalizations of these data provide substantively similar results.

14. As previously noted, our results do not directly speak to debates about partisan asymmetries in information processing. Some researchers have asserted that Republicans are less willing to update when faced with uncongenial information (e.g., Morisi, Jost, and Singh 2019; although see Guay and Johnston 2022). In the context of COVID-19, this would lead to the expectation that Republicans would reject new information that runs against their standing beliefs. We cannot, however, offer a strong test of this expectation for three reasons. First, prior beliefs on COVID-19 were not well formed. Second, Republicans received cues consistent with rejecting information about COVID-19, which led to a situation of observational equivalence. Third, while we found that Republicans updated their opinions in high-severity situations (and also came around to wearing masks), we also acknowledge that these were extreme circumstances and we have no relative comparison since Democrats were not faced with noncongenial information.

15. An interesting follow-on question is whether as president, Hillary Clinton could have prevented this sort of polarization. While she arguably would have managed the crisis better— Trump's malfeasance is uniquely his own (Kapucu and Moynihan 2021)—in all likelihood, she would have spurred a Republican response against her actions.

Chapter Six

1. This directly parallels how Krupnikov and Ryan (2022) talk about the "deeply involved," referring to partisans who put politics at the center of their lives. While this is a separate concept from partisan animosity, many of the deeply involved have high levels of partisan animus (see chapter 3).

2. We also see this in highly polarized responses to various political and social institutions that are linked to the parties (i.e., scientific figures, the media, the police, etc.; see Brenan 2021).

3. For particularly striking examples of this pattern, see Klein's (2020) description of Senator Ben Nelson's "cornhusker kickback" and the ACA vote in 2010 (208–214), as well as the primary loss suffered by longtime West Virginia Congressman David McKinley in 2022 (Hohmann 2022). McKinley lost to another representative, Alex Mooney, who labeled him as insufficiently Republican because he voted for the bipartisan infrastructure bill. Mooney also secured President Trump's endorsement, which undoubtedly signaled his Republican bona fides.

4. According to the Wisconsin Electoral Commission, in the 2020 presidential election, there were 3,298,041 total votes cast for president in the state, of which Joe Biden won 1,630,866 and Donald Trump won 1,610,184. This made Biden's margin of victory 20,682 votes, or 0.63 percent. See https://elections.wi.gov/sites/default/files/legacy/County%2520by%2520County%2520 Report%2520-%2520President%2520of%2520the%2520United%2520States%2520post%2520 recount.pdf.

5. We obtained gubernatorial approval ratings from the Morning Consult, at the following link: https://morningconsult.com/governor-rankings/. For example, in April 2023, all but five governors enjoyed approval ratings of 50 percent or greater (and even the five rated below 50 percent were not far off, ranging from 42 percent to 49 percent) (Yokley 2023). This reflects the fact that governors address state-level issues, rather than becoming ensnarled in national-level partisan politics.

6. A recent Cook Partisan Voting Index puts Montana at R+11, meaning that on balance, Republican presidential candidates have performed 11 points better in Montana than they have in the country as a whole (A. Walter 2021).

7. Even though Biden did not yet hold office in April 2020, he was the presumptive nominee (for most of our April 2020 fielding period), and voters could express approval or disapproval for his platform concerning the pandemic.

8. There also may have been issue-based affective polarization on contested issues such as school closures within partisan-homogeneous areas (on such issue-based affective polarization, see Hobolt, Leeper, and Tilley 2021).

9. Biden pledged to administer 200 million doses of the vaccine within one hundred days of assuming office. He achieved that target on April 21, shortly before the end of our survey. The importance of this goal was widely covered in the media (see, e.g., Murphy 2021).

10. There is an interesting contrast here with our results in chapter 5. There, we showed that high-animus Republicans were less likely to report that they had been or would be vaccinated. Yet here, they also said that Trump helped with the vaccine. How can we square that circle? We suspect the rationale is that in both cases they were signaling their partisanship: they recognized the partisan signal that Biden is provaccine, so they said they did not want it. Yet if there is any credit to be awarded for this program, it belongs to President Trump, not President Biden.

11. The "deep state" refers to a conspiracy theory positing that the real power lies in the federal bureaucracy. The idea was especially popular during the Trump administration, when the president argued that many federal bureaucrats were undermining his agenda (Ingber 2017).

12. Dr. Fauci was seemingly widely known by the start of April; for instance, an April 1 *Washington Post* article labeled him the "face of U.S. Coronavirus response" (Stanley-Becker, Abutaleb, and Barrett 2020). A study conducted from April 30th to May 1st reported that only 3.5 percent of respondents did *not* know of Dr. Fauci (V. Johnson et al. 2022).

13. As noted in chapter 3, this prediction is one of the few in the book that was not preregistered, as it only occurred to us while working on the manuscript. As such, readers may wish to view it as more exploratory than many of our other analyses.

14. As in chapter 5, we can use within-respondent change in COVID-19 severity as a further test of our argument. We did so in the appendix to this chapter and found strong support for our argument.

Chapter Seven

1. While these policies were slated to be considered as a separate stand-alone bill, they never were, and they were not enacted into law during the 117th Congress.

2. One might quibble about whether the bill was really bipartisan, given that Democratic rebels almost sank it (because they wanted to pass the more expansive human infrastructure bill at the same time). This is actually the typical pattern: it is within-party, rather than between-party, dissensus that foils many efforts at lawmaking (Curry and Lee 2020).

3. Although, in theory, an outcome in which one party sacrifices and the other party does not could be considered a form of compromise.

4. It is also possible for compromise to occur when the bill is not seen as bipartisan. For example, if the party in the Senate majority puts forth a bill that differs from their true preference and, in exchange, the Senate minority agrees not to filibuster the bill. The final passage could be completely split down party lines, but a compromise has occurred.

5. Westwood (2022) shows that legislators use the language of bipartisanship, even when the policy is not *actually* bipartisan.

6. Relatedly, high-animus partisans likely view unintended consequences of their sides' policies as unavoidable but view similar trade-offs from the other party as harmful (Goya-Tocchetto et al. 2022).

7. Doherty and Wolak (2012) showed people are most likely to engage in directional reasoning when the policy process appears ambiguous; when the policy process is transparently fair, people are more likely to engage in accuracy processing when evaluating the resulting policy. As Harbridge et al. (2014) argued, a legislative process is likely to be ambiguous—indeed, it is unlikely to have the transparency that Doherty and Wolak (2012) included in their experimental treatments leading to accuracy processing. Their line of reasoning, however, would suggest that under certain procedural conditions, even partisans with more animosity would be supportive of a compromise. Given our expectations about the primacy of party, it is difficult to specify the precise procedural conditions necessary for such accuracy motivations to dominate.

8. Within these conditions, the order of the two questions always remained the same: all participants first answered the compromise question and then answered the respect question.

9. For Democrats, higher values indicate cutting less, and for Republicans they indicate cutting more.

Chapter Eight

1. In Kingzette et al. (2021), we also considered norms about equal political participation, but we found that they only weakly and inconsistently related to animus, theoretically and empirically. We therefore omitted a discussion of them here, although understanding how other dimensions of norms map back onto animus is an important topic for future work (see Bankert 2023).

2. This also relates to Beremo's (2016) concept of executive aggrandizement, whereby the executive removes limits on their power (aggrandizement is a type of backsliding, so this is its opposite as ensuring that limits on power remain in place is a defense of norms). Much like Levitsky and Ziblatt's (2018) forbearance, the key lies in political actors respecting the limits on executive power. Of course, one might be concerned with other aspects of a constitutional system and other checks on power (such as limits to the judiciary). While we focus on executive power, given its focus in the literature, future work can and should investigate these other dimensions of constitutional norms.

3. Voters also underestimate the other party's commitment to democratic norms (Pasek et al. 2022).

4. Barrett had been nominated on September 26 prior to the start of our October 2020 data collection, which took place from October 20 until November 3. She was confirmed during data collection on October 26.

5. For the 2021 data, see Reuters / Ipsos (2021). For 2022 data, see M. Murray (2022).

6. We also varied whether the swing state was Pennsylvania or Florida; we did not expect, nor did we find, that the choice of state had an effect on responses.

7. That there were generally stronger animus effects (and slightly less democratic support) on the applied undemocratic practices items than the abstract items echoes the abstract-applied distinction (with more consistent and stable support in the abstract) found in the literature on political tolerance (e.g., Sullivan and Transue 1999).

8. Indeed, Braley et al. (2023) included an item asking about using violence to block laws from the other party in their measure of democratic subversion.

9. We included analogous items in the April 2021 survey and obtained virtually identical results.

10. Other corelates of support for partisan violence include antiestablishment beliefs (i.e., attitudes that question the legitimacy of the existing system; see Uscinski et al. 2021); trait aggression (Kalmoe and Mason 2022); strong partisan identity, which is distinct from animosity (Kalmoe and Mason 2022); perceptions that members of the other party are likely to engage in violence (Mernyk et al. 2022); conspiratorial beliefs among those suffering from depression (Baum et al. 2023); and dehumanization of members of the other party (Saguy and Reifen-Tagar 2022).

11. In fact, in our preregistration, we purposefully did not predict a relationship between animosity and breaking the law or engaging in violence (see appendix 3.1).

12. One possible explanation of this may be that Democrats conjured up civil disobedience when they imagined nonviolent lawbreaking, which made them more likely to endorse it (i.e., protestors occupying the offices of members of Congress and being arrested to protest various social ills).

13. The general support we found aligns with other data showing that 95 percent of Americans believe checks and balances are important ways of maintaining American democracy and 83 percent believe it is important for the media to criticize national figures (*Economist* / YouGov 2021).

Chapter Nine

1. In essence, the experiments may have noncompliance among those with high animus, and thus the estimates are of a local average treatment effect rather than a sample or population average treatment effect (see D. Campbell 1986; Mutz 2011; Druckman 2022).

2. To be clear, we are unaware of evidence directly showing that high-animus partisans are more likely to be opinion leaders, but their higher levels of engagement make them strong candidates.

3. Research suggests that Russian interference via social media in the 2016 election did not seem to have meaningful effects on individual political behavior (Eady et al. 2023).

4. Fernbach and Van Boven (2022) provide a cognitive model of misperceptions that points to categorical thinking, oversimplification, and emotional amplification.

5. It is interesting that, relative to parties in other countries the ideological divide between Republicans and Democrats is small—Garcia-Rada and Norton (2020, 1) explain that "when viewed in the full distribution, polarization between Democrats and Republicans appears relatively small, even on divisive issues such as abortion, sexual preference, and freedom of religious speech."

6. Even politically disengaged individuals cannot escape caricatured images of partisans, thanks to the preponderance of media coverage of political conflict (Robison and Mullinix 2016) and discussions with more politically engaged friends and family members (Druckman, Levendusky, and McLain 2018).

7. One solution involves correcting misperceptions, which several studies have shown to be possible with relatively simple nudges (e.g., Ahler and Sood 2018; Lees and Cikara 2020; Ruggeri 2021; Mernyk et al. 2022; Braley et al. 2023). Yet whether these corrections endure over long periods of time and can sustain competition from strategic elites remains unclear (Druckman 2023a).

8. Aside from animosity, some voters also will support antidemocratic candidates because they share their extreme ideological positions (Graham and Svolik 2020), group antipathies (Bartels 2020), or antiestablishment views (Uscinski et al. 2021).

9. Madison (1792) wrote, in the *National Gazette*, that parties are "natural to most political societies [and are] likely to be of some duration in ours."

Appendix 3.1

1. The *N*s refer to all respondents who answered the animosity items.

Appendix 3.2

1. For Klar, Leeper, and Robison (2020), the greater concern in these cases is that asking about a variable pretreatment could prime an experimental effect.

2. In our particular situation, we needed to control for experimental treatment because we were not assigning the same constant to all cases. Including that control made the βs in the two equations the same.

Appendix 4.1

1. In Cinelli and Hazlett's (2020) notation, this is the robustness value.

Appendix 5.1

1. In many ways, this is very similar to the model we estimated in table 5.1. The difference is that we are pooling all three of the COVID-era waves and running a broader fixed effects analysis (rather than just looking at changes based on the salience of the virus).

References

Abernathy, Penny. 2022. "The State of Local News: The 2022 Report." Northwestern University Local News Initiative, June 29. https://localnewsinitiative.northwestern.edu/research/state-of-local-news/report/.

Abramowitz, Alan I. 2010. "Transformation and Polarization: The 2008 Presidential Election and the New American Electorate." *Electoral Studies* 29 (4): 594–603.

Abramowitz, Alan I., and Kyle Saunders. 2008. "Is Polarization a Myth?" *Journal of Politics* 70 (2): 542–555.

Abramowitz, Alan I., and Steven W. Webster. 2016. "The Rise of Negative Partisanship and the Nationalization of U.S. Elections in the 21st Century." *Electoral Studies* 41 (March):12–22.

———. 2018. "Negative Partisanship: Why Americans Dislike Parties But Behave Like Rabid Partisans." *Advances in Political Psychology* 39 (S1): 119–135.

Acharya, Avidit, Matthew Blackwell, and Maya Sen. 2016. "Explaining Causal Findings Without Bias: Detecting and Assessing Direct Effects." *American Political Science Review* 110 (3): 512–529.

Adolph, Christopher, Kenya Amano, Bree Bang-Jensen, Nancy Fullman, Beatrice Magistro, Grace Reinke, and John Wilkerson. 2022. "Governor Partisanship Explains the Adoption of Statewide Mask Mandates in Response to COVID-19." *State Politics and Policy Quarterly* 21(1): 24–49.

Adolph, Christopher, Kenya Amano, Bree Bang-Jensen, Nancy Fullman, and John Wilkerson. 2021. "Pandemic Politics: Timing State-Level Social Distancing Responses to COVID-19." *Journal of Health Politics, Policy and Law* 46 (2): 211–233.

Ahler, Douglas J., and Gaurav Sood. 2018. "The Parties in Our Heads: Misperceptions about Party Composition and Their Consequences." *Journal of Politics* 80 (3): 964–981.

Ahmed, Amel. 2023. "Is the American Public Really Turning Away from Democracy? Backsliding and the Conceptual Challenges of Understanding Public Attitudes." *Perspectives on Politics* 21 (3): 967–978.

AJMC Staff. 2021. "A Timeline of COVID-19 Developments in 2020." *American Journal of Managed Care (AJMC)*. January 1. https://www.ajmc.com/view/a-timeline-of-covid19-developments-in-2020.

Alba, Davey, and Sheera Frenkel. 2020. "Medical Expert Who Corrects Trump Is Now a Target of the Far Right." *New York Times*, March 28.

Albarracín, Dolores. 2002. "Cognition in Persuasion: An Analysis of Information Processing in Response to Persuasive Communications." *Advances in Experimental Social Psychology* 34:61–130.

Alcorn, Chauncey. 2021. "Fight for $15 Minimum Wage Heats Up after Biden Endorsement." CNN, May 8. https://www.cnn.com/2021/05/08/business/minimum-wage-biden-walmart/index.html.

Al Jazeera. 2020. "Donald Trump's Statement in Full after Joe Biden Declared Winner." November 7. https://www.aljazeera.com/news/2020/11/7/trump-biden-rushing-to-falsely-pose-as-the-winner.

Allcott, Hunt, Levi Boxell, Jacob Conway, Matthew Gentzkow, Michael Thaler, and David Yang. 2020. "Polarization and Public Health: Partisan Differences in Social Distancing during the Coronavirus Pandemic." *Journal of Public Economics* 191:104254.

Alwin, Duane. 1997. "Feeling Thermometers versus 7-Point Scales: Which Are Better?" *Sociological Methods & Research* 25 (3): 318–340.

American Presidency Project. 2023. "Executive Orders." https://www.presidency.ucsb.edu/statistics/data/executive-orders.

American Society of Civil Engineers. 2021. "Report Card for America's Infrastructure." Press release. https://infrastructurereportcard.org/wp-content/uploads/2020/12/National_IRC_2021-report.pdf.

Amit, Adi, Sari Mentser, Sharon Arieli, and Niva Porzycki. 2021. "Distinguishing Deliberate from Systematic Thinking." *Journal of Personality and Social Psychology* 120 (3): 765–788.

Anderson, Christopher, André Blais, Shaun Bowler, Todd Donovan, and Ola Listhaug. 2005. *Loser's Consent: Elections and Democratic Legitimacy*. New York: Oxford University Press.

Anderson, Sarah, Daniel Butler, and Laurel Harbridge-Yong. 2020. *Rejecting Compromise: Legislators' Fear of Primary Voters*. New York: Cambridge University Press.

Annenberg IOD Collaborative. 2023. *Democracy amid Crises: Polarization, Pandemic, Protests, and Persuasion*. New York: Oxford University Press.

Anthes, Emily, and Alexandra E. Petri. 2021. "CDC Director Warns of a Pandemic of the Unvaccinated." *New York Times*, July 16. https://www.nytimes.com/2021/07/16/health/covid-delta-cdc-walensky.html.

Arceneaux, Kevin, and Ryan J. Vander Wielen. 2013. "The Effects of Need for Cognition and Need for Affect on Partisan Evaluations." *Political Psychology* 34 (1): 23–42.

———. 2017. *Taming Intuition: How Reflection Minimizes Partisan Reasoning and Promotes Democratic Accountability*. Cambridge: Cambridge University Press.

Armaly, Miles T., and Adam M. Enders. 2021. "The Role of Affective Orientations in Promoting Perceived Polarization." *Political Science Research and Methods* 9 (3): 615–626.

Atwoli, Lukoye, Abdullah Baqui, Thomas Benfield, Raffaella Bosurgi, Fiona Godlee, Stephen Hancocks, Richard Horton, Laurie Laybourn-Langton, Carlos Augusto Monteiro, Ian Norman, Kirsten Patrick, Nigel Praities, Marcel G. M. Olde Rikkert, Eric J. Rubin, Peush Sahni, Richard Smith, Nick Talley, Sue Turale, and Damián Vázquez. 2021. "Call for Emergency Action to Limit Global Temperature Increases, Restore Biodiversity, and Protect Health." *Lancet* 398 (10304): P939–941.

Bail, Chris. 2021. *Breaking the Social Media Prism*. Princeton, NJ: Princeton University Press.

Bakker, Bert N., Yphtach Lelkes, and Ariel Malka. 2020. "Understanding Partisan Cue Receptivity: Tests of Predictions from the Bounded Rationality and Expressive Utility Perspectives." *Journal of Politics* 82 (3): 1061–1077.

Bakshy, Eytan, Solomon Messing, and Lada A. Adamic. 2015. "Exposure to Ideologically Diverse News and Opinion on Facebook." *Science* 348 (6239): 1130–1132.

Baldassarri, Delia, and Barum Park. 2020. "Was There a Culture War? Partisan Polarization and Secular Trends in American Public Opinion." *Journal of Politics* 82 (3): 809–827.

Bang Petersen, Michael, Martin Skov, Søren Serritzlew, and Thomas Ramsey. 2013. "Motivated Reasoning and Political Parties: Evidence for Increased Processing in the Face of Party Cues." *Political Behavior* 35 (4): 831–854.

Bankert, Alexa. 2021. "Negative and Positive Partisanship in the 2016 U.S. Presidential Elections." *Political Behavior* 43: 1467–1485.

———. 2023. *When Politics Becomes Personal: The Effect of Partisan Identity on Democratic Behavior.* New York: Cambridge University Press.

Barber, Michael, and Jeremy C. Pope. 2019. "Does Party Trump Ideology? Disentangling Party and Ideology in America." *American Political Science Review* 113 (1): 38–54.

Bargh, John A., Wendy J. Lombardi, and E. Tory Higgins. 1988. "Automaticity of Chronically Accessible Constructs in Person × Situation Effects on Perception: It's Just a Matter of Time." *Journal of Personality and Social Psychology* 55 (4): 599–605.

Baron, Jonathan, and John T. Jost. 2019. "False Equivalence: Are Liberals and Conservatives in the United States Equally Biased?" *Perspectives on Psychological Science* 14 (2): 292–303.

Bartels, Larry M. 2008. *Unequal Democracy: The Political Economy of the New Gilded Age.* Princeton, NJ: Princeton University Press.

———. 2020. "Ethnic Antagonism Erodes Republicans' Commitment to Democracy" *Proceedings of the National Academy of Sciences* 117 (37): 22752–22759.

———. 2023. *Democracy Erodes from the Top: Leaders, Citizens, and the Challenge of Populism in Europe.* Princeton, NJ: Princeton University Press.

Bassan-Nygate, Lotem, and Chagai M. Weiss. 2022. "Party Competition and Cooperation Shape Affective Polarization: Evidence from Natural and Survey Experiments in Israel." *Comparative Political Studies* 55 (2): 287–318.

Baum, Matthew A., James N. Druckman, Matthew Simonson, Jennifer Lin, and Roy H. Perlis. 2023. "The Political Consequences of Depression: How Conspiracy Beliefs, Participatory Inclinations, and Depression Relate to Support for Political Violence." *American Journal of Political Science.* https://doi.org/10.1111/ajps.12827.

Baumeister, Roy F., and Mark R. Leary. 1995. "The Need to Belong: Desire for Interpersonal Attachments as a Fundamental Human Motivation." *Psychological Bulletin* 117 (3): 497–529.

Baxter-King, Ryan, Jacob R. Brown, Ryan D. Enos, Arash Naeim, and Lynn Vavreck. 2022. "How Local Partisan Context Conditions Prosocial Behaviors: Mask Wearing during COVID-19." *Proceedings of the National Academy of Sciences* 119 (21): e2116311119.

Bayes, Robin, and James N. Druckman. 2021. "Motivated Reasoning and Climate Change." *Current Opinion in Behavioral Sciences* 42 (December): 27–35.

Bayes, Robin, James N. Druckman, Avery Goods, and Daniel C. Molden. 2020. "When and How Different Motives Can Drive Motivated Political Reasoning." *Political Psychology* 41 (5): 1031–1052.

Bazelon, Simon, and Matthew Ygelsias. 2021. "The Rise and Fall of Secret Congress." *Slow Boring*. https://www.slowboring.com/p/the-rise-and-importance-of-secret.

Beam, Michael, Myiah Hutchens, and Jay Hmielowski. 2018. "Facebook News and (De)polarization: Reinforcing Spirals in the 2016 U.S. Election." *Information, Communication & Society* 21 (7): 940–958

Beasley, Deena, and Manas Mishra. 2020. "Trump Critical of FDA Decision to Revoke Emergency Use of Drug He Has Promoted for COVID-19." Reuters, June 15. https://www.reuters.com/article/us-health-coronavirus-hydroxychloroquine-idUSKBN23M283.

Beauchamp, Zach. 2018. "Trump's Republican Party, Explained in One Photo." *Vox*, August 6. https://www.vox.com/policy-and-politics/2018/8/6/17656996/trump-republican-party-russia-rather-democrat-ohio.

Beck, Nathaniel, and Simon Jackman. 1998. "Beyond Linearity by Default: Generalized Additive Models." *American Journal of Political Science* 42 (2): 596–627.

Bella, Timothy. 2022. "Tucker Carlson, Downplaying Russia-Ukraine Conflict, Urges Americans to Ask, 'Why Do I Hate Putin?'" *Washington Post*, February 23.

Belvedere, Matthew J. 2020. "Trump Says He Trusts China's Xi on Coronavirus and the U.S. Has It 'Totally under Control.'" CNBC, January 22. https://www.cnbc.com/2020/01/22/trump-on-coronavirus-from-china-we-have-it-totally-under-control.html.

Ben-Ghiat, Ruth. 2020. "Trump, the Coronavirus, and What Happens When Strongmen Fall Ill." *New Yorker*, October 13. https://www.newyorker.com/culture/cultural-comment/trump-the-coronavirus-and-what-happens-when-strongmen-fall-ill.

Bendor, Jonathan, and John G. Bullock. 2021. "Lethal Incompetence: Leaders, Organizations, and the U.S. Response to COVID-19." *Forum* 19 (2): 317–337.

Beremo, Nancy. 2016. "On Democratic Backsliding." *Journal of Democracy* 27 (1): 5–19.

Biden, Joseph R. 2020. "My Plan to Safely Reopen America." *New York Times*, April 12.

———. 2021a. "Inaugural Address by President Joseph R. Biden, Jr." Press release. *White House*, January 21. https://www.whitehouse.gov/briefing-room/speeches-remarks/2021/01/20/inaugural-address-by-president-joseph-r-biden-jr/.

———. 2021b. "Remarks by President Biden on the Bipartisan Infrastructure Deal." Press release. *White House*, June 24. https://www.whitehouse.gov/briefing-room/speeches-remarks/2021/06/24/remarks-by-president-biden-on-the-bipartisan-infrastructure-deal/.

———. 2021c. "Remarks by President Biden on Fighting the COVID-19 Pandemic." Press release. *White House*, August 3. https://www.whitehouse.gov/briefing-room/speeches-remarks/2021/08/03/remarks-by-president-biden-on-fighting-the-covid-19-pandemic/.

Bisbee, Joshua, and Diana Da In Lee. 2022. "Objective Facts and Elite Cues: Partisan Responses to COVID-19." *Journal of Politics* 84 (3): 1278–1291.

Blake, Aaron. 2013. "Gang of Eight Pledges Tough Enforcement, Difficult Path to Citizenship." *Washington Post*, April 18.

———. 2018. "The GOP Decried 'King Obama.' Now It's Mostly Quiet on Trump's Effort to Revise the Constitution by Himself." *Washington Post*, October 31.

Boese, Vanessa A., Nazifa Alizada, Martin Lundstedt, Kelly Morrison, Natalia Natsika, Yuko Sato, Hugo Tai, and Staffan I. Lindberg. 2022. *Autocratization Changing Nature? Democracy Report 2022*. Gothenburg, Sweden: Varieties of Democracy Institute.

Bogardus, Emory. 1959. *Social Distance*. Los Angeles: University of Southern California Press.

Bolsen, Toby, James N. Druckman, and Fay Lomax Cook. 2014. "The Influence of Partisan Motivated Reasoning on Public Opinion." *Political Behavior* 36 (2): 235–262.

———. 2015. "Citizens,' Scientists,' and Policy Advisors' Beliefs about Global Warming." *Annals of the American Academy of Political and Social Science* 658 (March): 271–295.

Bond, Jon, Richard Fleisher, and B. Dan Wood. 2003. "The Marginal and Time-Varying Effect of Public Approval of Presidential Success in Congress." *Journal of Politics* 65 (1): 92–110.

Bond, Robert, and Solomon Messing. 2015. "Quantifying Social Media's Political Space: Estimating Ideology from Publicly Revealed Preferences on Facebook." *American Political Science Review* 109 (1): 62–78.

Boudet, Hilary, Leanne Giordono, Chad Zanocco, Hannah Satein, and Hannah Whitley. 2020. "Event Attribution and Partisanship Shape Local Discussion of Climate Change after Extreme Weather." *Nature Climate Change* 10 (1): 69–76.

Boudreau, Cheryl, and Scott A. MacKenzie. 2014. "Informing the Electorate?: How Party Cues and Policy Information Affect Public Opinion about Initiatives." *American Journal of Political Science* 58 (1): 48–62.

Bougher, Lori. 2017. "The Correlates of Discord: Identity, Issue Alignment, and Political Hostility in Polarized America." *Political Behavior* 39 (3): 731–762.

Boxell, Levi, Jacob Conway, James N. Druckman, and Matthew Gentzkow. 2022. "Affective Polarization Did Not Increase during the COVID-19 Pandemic." *Quarterly Journal of Political Science* 17 (4): 491–512.

Boxell, Levi, Matthew Gentzkow, and Jesse M. Shapiro. 2017. "Greater Internet Use Is Not Associated with Faster Growth in Political Polarization among U.S. Demographic Groups." *Proceedings of the National Academy of Sciences* 114 (40): 10612–10617.

Brady, Henry E., and Thomas B. Kent. 2022. "Fifty Years of Declining Confidence & Increasing Polarization in Trust in American Institutions." *Daedalus* 151 (4): 43–66.

Brady, William J., Molly J. Crockett, and Jay J. Van Bavel. 2020. "The MAD Model of Moral Contagion: The Role of Motivation, Attention, and Design in the Spread of Moralized Content Online." *Perspectives on Psychological Science* 15 (4): 978–1010.

Brady, William J., Julian A. Wills, John T. Jost, and Jay J. Van Bavel. 2017. "Emotion Shapes the Diffusion of Moralized Content in Social Networks." *Proceedings of the National Academy of Sciences* 114 (28): 7313–7318.

Braley, Alia, Gabriel S. Lenz, Dhaval Adjodah, Hossein Rahnama, and Alex Pentland. 2023. "Why Voters Who Value Democracy Participate in Democratic Backsliding." *Nature Human Behaviour* 7: 1282–1293.

Braman, Eileen, and Thomas E. Nelson. 2007. "Mechanism of Motivated Reasoning? Analogical Perception in Discrimination Disputes." *American Journal of Political Science* 51 (4): 940–956.

Brenan, Meghan. 2021. "American's Confidence in Major Institutions Dips." Press release. Gallup. https://news.gallup.com/poll/352316/americans-confidence-major-institutions-dips.aspx.

Brennan Center for Justice. 2019. "Americans Are United against Partisan Gerrymandering." Brennan Center. https://www.brennancenter.org/our-work/research-reports/americans-are-united-against-partisan-gerrymandering.

———. 2021. "Voting Laws Roundup: March 2021." Brennan Center. https://www.brennancenter.org/our-work/research-reports/voting-laws-roundup-march-2021.

Brewster, Jack. 2021. "Trump's Chief of Staff Feared President Was Going to Die When He Had Covid, New Book Alleges." *Forbes*, June 24. https://www.forbes.com/sites/jackbrewster/2021/06/24/trumps-chief-of-staff-feared-president-was-going-to-die-when-he-had-covid-new-book-alleges/?sh=2fb8321d616d.

Broockman, David, Joshua Kalla, and Sean Westwood. 2023. "Does Affective Polarization Undermine Democratic Norms or Accountability? Maybe Not." *American Journal of Political Science* 67 (3): 808–828.

Brooks, David. 2021. "The Case for Biden Optimism." *New York Times*, January 21.

Bullock, John G. 2011. "Elite Influence on Public Opinion in an Informed Electorate." *American Political Science Review* 105 (3): 496–515.

———. 2020. "Party Cues." In *The Oxford Handbook of Electoral Persuasion*, edited by Elizabeth Suhay, Bernard Grofman, and Alexander H. Trechsel, 129–151. New York: Oxford University Press.

Bullock, John G., Alan S. Gerber, Seth J. Hill, and Gregory A. Huber. 2015. "Partisan Bias in Factual Beliefs about Politics." *Quarterly Journal of Political Science* 10:519–578.

Butler, Daniel M. 2014. *Representing the Advantaged: How Politicians Reinforce Inequality*. New York: Cambridge University Press.

Cain, Bruce, John Ferejohn, and Morris Fiorina. 1987. *The Personal Vote: Constituency Service and Electoral Independence*. Cambridge, MA: Harvard University Press.

Campbell, Angus, Phillip E. Converse, Warren E. Miller, and Donald E. Stokes. 1960. *The American Voter*. New York: Wiley.

Campbell, David, Geoffrey Layman, and John Green. 2020. *Secular Surge: A New Fault Line in American Politics*. New York: Cambridge University Press.

Campbell, Donald T. 1986. "Relabeling Internal and External Validity for Applied Social Scientists." Special issue, *New Directions for Program Evaluation*, no. 31 (Fall): 67–77.

Campbell, James. 2016. "The Trial-Heat and Seats-in-Trouble Forecasts of the 2016 Presidential and Congressional Elections." *PS: Political Science and Politics* 49 (4): 664–668.

Carey, John M., Gretchen Helmke, Brendan Nyhan, Mitchell Sanders, and Susan Stokes. 2019. "Searching for Bright Lines in the Trump Presidency." *Perspectives on Politics* 17 (3): 699–718.

Carlson, Taylor N. 2019. "Through the Grapevine: Informational Consequences of Interpersonal Political Communication." *American Political Science Review* 113 (2): 325–339.

———. 2024. *Through the Grapevine: Socially Transmitted Information and Distorted Democracy*. Chicago: University of Chicago Press.

Carpenter, Christopher J. 2019. "Cognitive Dissonance, Ego-Involvement, and Motivated Reasoning." *Annals of the International Communication Association* 43 (1): 1–23.

CBS News. 2020. "Cori Bush Explains Her Position on 'Defund the Police' while Paying for Private Security." August 6. https://www.cbsnews.com/news/cori-bush-defund-the-police-private-security-response/.

Centers for Disease Control and Prevention. 2020. "COVIDView Summary Ending October 31, 2020." November 6. https://covid.cdc.gov/COVID-data-tracker/.

Chen, M. Keith, and Ryne Rohla. 2018. "The Effect of Partisanship and Political Advertising on Close Family Ties." *Science* 360 (6392): 1020–1024.

Chua, Amy. 2018. *Political Tribes: Group Identity and the Fate of Nations*. New York: Penguin Random House.

Chudy, Jennifer, and Hakeem Jefferson. 2021. "Support for Black Lives Matter Surged Last Year. Did It Last?" *New York Times*, May 22.

Cinelli, Carlos, and Chad Hazlett. 2020. "Making Sense of Sensitivity: Extending Omitted Variable Bias." *Journal of the Royal Statistical Society: Statistical Methodology, Series B* 82 (1): 39–67.

Clifford, Scott, Thomas J. Leeper, and Carlisle Rainey. 2023. "Generalizing Survey Experiments Using Topic Sampling: An Application to Party Cues." *Political Behavior*. https://doi.org/10.1007/s11109-023-09870-1.

Clinton, Joshua, John Cohen, John Lapinski, and Marc Trussler. 2021. "Partisan Pandemic: How Partisanship and Public Health Concerns Affect Individuals' Social Mobility during COVID-19." *Science Advances* 7 (2): abd7204.

Cohn, Nate, and Kevin Quealy. 2019. "The Democratic Electorate on Twitter Is Not the Actual Democratic Electorate." *New York Times*, April 9.

Commission on Presidential Debates. 2020. "September 29, 2020 Debate Transcript." https://www .debates.org/voter-education/debate-transcripts/september-29-2020-debate-transcript/.

Constantino, Sara, Alicia Cooperman, Robert O. Keohane, and Elke U. Weber. 2022. "Personal Hardship Narrows the Partisan Gap in COVID-19 and Climate Change Responses." *Proceedings of the National Academy of Sciences* 119 (46): e2120653119.

Cook, Nancy, and Matthew Choi. 2020. "Trump Rallies His Base to Treat Coronavirus as a 'Hoax.'" Politico, February 28. https://www.politico.com/news/2020/02/28/trump-south-carol ina-rally-coronavirus-118269.

Coppock, Alexander. 2023. *Persuasion in Parallel: How Information Changes Minds about Politics*. Chicago: University of Chicago Press.

Cottrell, David, Michael C. Herron, and Sean J. Westwood. 2018. "An Exploration of Donald Trump's Allegations of Massive Voter Fraud in the 2016 General Election." *Electoral Studies* 51 (February): 123–142.

Covert, Bryce. 2021. "No, the Unvaccinated Aren't All Just Being Difficult." *New York Times*, August 6.

Crockett, Molly J. 2017. "Moral Outrage in the Digital Age." *Nature Human Behaviour* 1 (11): 769–771.

Cummings, William, and Courtney Subramanian. 2020. "'I Appreciate the Advice': Trump Tells Crowd Chanting 'Fire Fauci!' to Wait Until after the Election." *USA Today*, November 2.

Curry, James, and Frances Lee. 2020. *The Limits of Party: Congress and Lawmaking in a Polarized Era*. Chicago: University of Chicago Press.

Dahl, Robert. 1971. *Polyarchy: Participation and Opposition*. New Haven, CT: Yale University Press.

Dancey, Logan, and Geoffrey Sheagley. 2018. "Partisanship and Perceptions of Party-Line Voting in Congress." *Political Research Quarterly* 71 (1): 32–45.

Danillier, Andrew, and Diana Mutz. 2019. "The Dynamics of Electoral Integrity: A Three-Election Panel Study." *Public Opinion Quarterly* 83 (1): 46–67.

Das, Sanmay, Betsy Sinclair, Steven Webster, and Hao Yan. 2022. "All (Mayoral) Politics Is Local." *Journal of Politics* 84 (2): 1021–1034.

Dawsey, Josh, and Yasmeen Abutaleb. 2020. "'A Whole Lot of Hurt:' Fauci Warns of COVID-19 Surge, Offers Blunt Assessment of Trump's Response." *Washington Post*, October 31.

DellaPosta, Daniel. 2020. "Pluralistic Collapse: The 'Oil Spill' Model of Mass Opinion Polarization." *American Sociological Review* 85 (3): 507–536.

Diamond, Dan. 2021. "Messonnier, Birx Detail Political Interference in Last Year's Coronavirus Response." *Washington Post*, November 12.

Dias, Elizabeth. 2020. "Biden and Trump Say They're Fighting for America's 'Soul.' What Does That Mean?" *New York Times*, October 17.

Dias, Nicholas, and Yphtach Lelkes. 2022. "The Nature of Affective Polarization: Disentangling Policy Disagreement from Partisan Identity." *American Journal of Political Science* 66 (3): 535–790.

Din, Benjamin. 2021. "Trump Lashes Out at Fauci and Birx after CNN Documentary." *Politico*, March 29. https://www.politico.com/news/2021/03/29/trump-fauci-birx-cnn-documentary -478422.

Disch, Lisa Jane. 2021. *Making Constituencies: Representation as Mobilization in Mass Democracy*. Chicago: University of Chicago Press.

Doherty, Carroll. 2014. "7 Things to Know about Polarization in America." Pew Research Center, June 12. https://www.pewresearch.org/fact-tank/2014/06/12/7-things-to-know-about-polarization-in-america/.

Doherty, David, and Jennifer Wolak. 2012. "When Do the Ends Justify the Means? Evaluating Procedural Fairness." *Political Behavior* 34 (2): 301–323.

Donovan, Kathleen, Paul Kellstedt, Ellen Key, and Matthew Lebo. 2020. "Motivated Reasoning, Public Opinion, and Presidential Approval." *Political Behavior* 42 (4): 1201–1222.

Downs, Anthony. 1957. *An Economic Theory of Democracy*. New York: Harper.

Dreier Roundtable at Claremont McKenna College. 2020. "George H. W. Bush Praised Fauci in 1988." https://drt.cmc.edu/2020/03/23/george-h-w-bush-praised-dr-fauci-in-1988/.

Druckman, James N. 2022. *Experimental Thinking: A Primer on Social Science Experiments*. New York: Cambridge University Press.

———. 2023a. "Correcting Misperceptions of the Other Political Party Does Not Robustly Reduce Support for Undemocratic Practices or Partisan Violence." *Proceedings of the National Academy of Sciences of the United States of America* 120 (37): e2308938120.

———. 2023b. "How to Study Democratic Backsliding." *Advances in Political Psychology*. https://doi.org/10.1111/pops.12942.

Druckman, James N., Cari Lynn Hennessy, Kristi St. Charles, and Jonathan Weber. 2010. "Competing Rhetoric over Time: Frames versus Cues." *Journal of Politics* 72 (1):136–148.

Druckman, James N., Suji Kang, James Chu, Michael N. Stagnaro, Jan G. Voelkel, Joseph S. Mernyk, Sophia L. Pink, Chrystal Redekopp, David G. Rand, and Robb Willer. 2023. "Correcting Misperceptions of Out-partisans Decreases American Legislators' Support for Undemocratic Practices." *Proceedings of the National Academy of Sciences of the United States of America* 120(23): e2301836120.

Druckman, James, Samara Klar, Yanna Krupnikov, Matthew Levendusky, and John Barry Ryan. 2021a. "Affective Polarization, Local Contexts and Public Opinion in America." *Nature Human Behaviour* 5 (1): 28–38.

———. 2021b. "How Affective Polarization Shapes Americans' Political Beliefs: A Study of Responses to the COVID-19 Pandemic." *Journal of Experimental Political Science* 8 (3): 223–234.

———. 2022. "(Mis)Estimating Affective Polarization." *Journal of Politics* 84 (2): 1106–1117.

Druckman, James N., and Thomas J. Leeper. 2012. "Is Public Opinion Stable?: Resolving the Micro/Macro Disconnect in Studies of Public Opinion." *Daedalus* 141 (Fall): 50–68.

Druckman, James N., and Matthew S. Levendusky. 2019. "What Do We Measure When We Measure Affective Polarization?" *Public Opinion Quarterly* 83 (1): 114–122.

Druckman, James N., Matthew S. Levendusky, and Audrey McLain. 2018. "No Need to Watch: How the Effects of Partisan Media Can Spread via Interpersonal Discussions." *American Journal of Political Science* 62 (1): 99–112.

Druckman, James N , and Jeremy Levy. 2022. "Affective Polarization in the American Public." In *Handbook of Politics and Public Opinion*, edited by Thomas J. Rudolph, 257–271. Cheltenham, UK: Edward Elgar Publishing.

Druckman, James N., and Mary C. McGrath. 2019. "The Evidence for Motivated Reasoning in Climate Change Preference Formation." *Nature Climate Change* 9 (2): 111–119.

Druckman, James N., Erik Peterson, and Rune Slothuus. 2013. "How Elite Partisan Polarization Affects Public Opinion Formation." *American Political Science Review* 107 (1): 57–79.

Druckman, James N., and Elizabeth A. Sharrow. 2023. *Equality Unfulfilled: How Title IX's Policy Design Undermines Change to College Sports.* New York: Cambridge University Press.

Drutman, Lee. 2020. *Breaking the Two-Party Doom Loop: The Case for Multiparty Democracy in America.* New York: Oxford University Press.

Dunning, David. 2015. "Motivated Cognition in Self and Social Thought." In *APA Handbook of Personality and Social Psychology, Volume 1,* edited by Mario Mikulincer and Phillip R. Shaver; vol. 1, *Attitudes and Social Cognition,* edited by Mario Mikulincer, Phillip R. Shaver, Eugene Borgida, and John A. Bargh, 777–803. Washington, DC: American Psychological Association.

Eady, Gregory, Tom Paskhalis, Jan Zilinsky, Richard Bonneau, Jonathan Nagler, and Joshua A. Tucker. 2023. "Exposure to the Russian Internet Research Agency Foreign Influence Campaign on Twitter in the 2016 US Election and Its Relationship to Attitudes and Voting Behavior." *Nature Communication* 14 (62). https://doi.org/10.1038/s41467-022-35576-9.

Eagly, Alice H., and Shelly Chaiken. 1993. *The Psychology of Attitudes.* Fort Worth, TX: Harcourt Brace Jovanovich College Publishers.

Easton, David. 1975. "A Re-Assessment of the Concept of Political Support." *British Journal of Political Science* 5 (4): 435–457.

Economist / YouGov. 2021. "June 13–15, 2021—1500 U.S. Adult Citizens." Poll. https://docs.cdn .yougov.com/uagnfc262c/econTabReport.pdf#page=98&zoom=100,48,140.

Edelman, Adam. 2020. "Biden Slams Politicization of Covid Pandemic: 'It's a Virus, Not a Political Weapon.'" NBC News, October 6. https://www.nbcnews.com/politics/2020-election /biden-slams-politicization-covid-pandemic-it-s-virus-not-political-n1242350.

Edwards-Levy, Ariel. 2021. "A New Poll Shows Why Some Vaccine-Hesitant Americans Decided to Get the Covid-19 Shot." CNN online, July 13. https://www.cnn.com/2021/07/13/politics /poll-covid-19-vaccine-decision/index.html.

Egan, Patrick J., and Megan Mullin. 2017. "Climate Change: US Public Opinion." *Annual Review of Political Science* 20 (1): 209–227.

Enders, Adam, and Robert Lupton. 2021. "Value Extremity Contributes to Affective Polarization in the U.S." *Political Science Research and Methods* 9 (4): 857–866.

Enten, Harry. 2021. "Flu Shot Uptake Is Now Partisan. It Didn't Used to Be." CNN, November 14. https://edition.cnn.com/2021/11/14/politics/flu-partisan-divide-analysis/index.html.

Erikson, Robert. 1979. "The SRC Panel Data and Mass Political Attitudes." *British Journal of Political Science* 9 (1): 89–114.

Eunjung Cha, Ariana, Rose Hansen, and Jacqueline Dupree. 2021. "A Rush to Get Shots." *Washington Post,* July 30.

Fazio, Russell H. 1990. "Multiple Processes by Which Attitudes Guide Behavior: The Mode Model as an Integrative Framework." *Advances in Experimental Social Psychology* 23:75–109.

———. 2007. "Attitudes as Object-Evaluation Associations of Varying Strength." *Social Cognition* 25 (5): 603–637.

Feinberg, Matthew, and Robb Willer. 2013. "The Moral Roots of Environmental Attitudes." *Psychological Science* 24 (1): 56–62.

———. 2019. "Moral Reframing: A Technique for Effective and Persuasive Communication across Political Divides." *Social and Personality Psychology Compass* 13 (12): e12501.

Ferejohn, John. 1974. *Pork Barrel Politics: Rivers and Harbors Legislation, 1947–1968.* Redwood City, CA: Stanford University Press.

Fernbach, Philip M., and Leaf Van Boven. 2022. "False Polarization: Cognitive Mechanisms and Potential Solutions." *Current Opinion in Psychology* 43 (February): 1–6. https://doi.org/10.1016/j.copsyc.2021.06.005

Ferreira, Fernando, and Joseph Gyourko. 2009. "Do Political Parties Matter?: Evidence from Cities." *Quarterly Journal of Economics* 124 (1): 399–422.

Finkel, Eli J., Christopher A. Bail, Mina Cikara, Peter H, Ditto, Shanto Iyengar, Samara Klar, Lilliana Mason, Mary C. McGrath, Brendan Nyhan, David G. Rand, Linda J. Skitka, Joshua A. Tucker, Jay J. Van Bavel, Cynthia S. Wang, and James N. Druckman. 2020. "Political Sectarianism in America." *Science* 370 (6516): 533–536.

Fiorina, Morris P. 1980. "The Decline of Collective Responsibility in American Politics." *Daedalus* 109 (3): 25–45.

———. 1981. *Retrospective Voting in American National Elections*. New Haven, CT: Yale University Press.

———. 2017. *Unstable Majorities: Polarization, Party Sorting and Political Stalemate*. Stanford, CA: Hoover Institution Press.

Fiorina, Morris P., with Samuel J. Abrams. 2009. *Disconnect: The Breakdown of Representation in American Politics*. Norman: University of Oklahoma Press.

Fiorina, Morris P., with Samuel J. Abrams, and Jeremy C. Pope. 2005. *Culture War? The Myth of a Polarized America*. New York: Pearson Longman Press.

Fishbach, Ayelet, and Melissa J. Ferguson. 2007. "The Goal Construct in Social Psychology." In *Social Psychology: Handbook of Basic Principles*, edited by Arie W. Kruglanski, and E. Tory Higgins, 490–515. New York: Guilford Press.

Flores, Alexandra, Jennifer C. Cole, Stephan Dickert, Kimin Eom, Gabriela M. Jiga-Boy, Tehila Kogut, Riley Loria, Marcus Mayorga, Eric J. Pedersen, Beatriz Pereira, Enrico Rubaltelli. David K. Sherman, Paul Slovic, Daniel Västfjäll, and Leaf Van Boven. 2022. "Politicians Polarize and Experts Depolarize Public Support For COVID-19 Management Policies Across Countries." *Proceedings of the National Academy of Sciences* 119 (3): e2117543119.

Flores, Jessica, Adrianna Rodriguez, and Joel Shannon. 2020. "Coronavirus Updates: CDC's Robert Redfield Likens Masks to Vaccine, Sparking Clash with Donald Trump; 2-month-old Dies in Michigan." *USA Today*, September 16.

Fowler, Anthony. 2020. "Partisan Intoxication or Policy Voting?" *Quarterly Journal of Political Science* 15(2): 141–179.

Fowler, Luke, Jaclyn Kettler, and Stephanie Witt. 2020. "Democratic Governors Are Quicker in Responding to the Coronavirus than Republicans." *Conversation*, April 6. https://theconversation.com/democratic-governors-are-quicker-in-responding-to-the-coronavirus-than-republicans-135599.

French, David. 2020. *Divided We Fall: America's Secession Threat and How to Restore Our Nation*. New York: MacMillan Publishers.

Freund, Tallie, Arie W. Kruglanski, and Avivit Shpitzajzen. 1985. "The Freezing and Unfreezing of Impressional Primacy: Effects of the Need for Structure and the Fear of Invalidity." *Personality and Social Psychology Bulletin* 11 (4): 479–487.

Gadarian, Shana Kushner, Sara Wallace Goodman, and Thomas B. Pepinsky. 2022. *Pandemic Politics: The Deadly Toll of Partisanship in the Age of COVID*. Princeton NJ: Princeton University Press.

Gamm, Gerald, and Thad Kousser. 2021. "Life, Literacy, and the Pursuit of Prosperity: Party Competition and Policy Outcomes in 50 States." *American Political Science Review* 115 (4): 1442–1463.

Gans, Jared. 2022. "Trump Calls for 'Termination' of Election Rules in Constitution to Overturn 2020 Election." *The Hill*, December 3. https://thehill.com/blogs/blog-briefing-room/news/37 60916-trump-calls-for-termination-of-election-rules-in-constitution-to-overturn-2020-election/.

García-Montoya, Laura, Ana Arjona, and Matthew Lacombe. 2022. "Violence and Voting in the United States: How School Shootings Affect Elections." *American Political Science Review* 116 (3): 807–826.

Garcia-Rada, Ximena, and Michael I. Norton. 2020. "Putting Within-Country Political Differences in (Global) Perspective." *PLOS ONE* 15 (4): e0231794.

Garrett, R. Kelly, Shira Gvirsman, Benjamin Johnson, Yariv Tsfati, Rachel Neo, and Aysenur Dal. 2014. "Implications of Pro- and Counter-attitudinal Information Exposure for Affective Polarization." *Human Communication Research* 40 (3): 309–332.

Gentzkow, Matthew, Jesse M. Shapiro, and Matt Taddy. 2019. "Measuring Group Differences in High-Dimensional Choices: Method and Application to Congressional Speech." *Econometrica*, 87 (4): 1307–1340.

Georgetown Institute of Politics and Public Service. 2019. "New Poll: Voters Find Political Divisions So Bad, Believe U.S. Is Two-Thirds of the Way to 'Edge of a Civil War.'" *Georgetown University McCourt School of Public Policy*, October 23. https://politics.georgetown.edu/2019 /10/23/new-poll-voters-find-political-divisions-so-bad-believe-u-s-is-two-thirds-of-the-way -to-edge-of-a-civil-war/.

Gerber, Elisabeth, and Daniel Hopkins. 2011. "When Mayors Matter: Estimating the Impact of Mayoral Partisanship on City Policy." *American Journal of Political Science* 55 (2): 326–339.

Gerring, John. 2001. *Social Science Methodology: A Criterial Framework*. Cambridge: Cambridge University Press.

Gidengil, Elisabeth, Dietlind Stolle, and Oliver Bergeron-Boutin. 2021. "The Partisan Nature of Support for Democratic Backsliding: A Comparative Perspective." *European Journal of Political Research* 61 (4): 901–929.

Gidron, Noam, James Adams, and Will Horne. 2020. *American Affective Polarization in Comparative Perspective*. New York: Cambridge University Press.

Gilens, Martin. 2012. *Affluence and Influence: Economic Inequality and Political Power in America*. Princeton, NJ: Princeton University Press.

Gollust, Sarah E., Rebekah H. Nagler, and Erika Franklin Fowler. 2020. "The Emergence of COVID-19 in the U.S.: A Public Health and Political Communication Crisis." *Journal of Health Politics, Policy and Law* 45 (6): 967–981.

Gollwitzer, Anton, Cameron Martel, William J. Brady, Philip Pärnamets, Isaac G. Freedman, Eric D. Knowles, and Jay J. Van Bavel. 2020. "Partisan Differences in Physical Distancing Are Linked to Health Outcomes during the COVID-19 Pandemic." *Nature Human Behaviour* 4 (11): 1186–1197.

Goren, Paul, Christopher M. Federico, and Miki Caul Kittilson. 2009. "Source Cues, Partisan Identities, and Political Value Expression." *American Journal of Political Science* 53 (4): 805–820.

Goya-Tocchetto, Daniela, Aaron Kay, Heidi Vuletich, Andrew Vonasch, and Keith Payne. 2022. "The Partisan Trade-Off Bias: When Political Polarization Meets Policy Trade-Offs." *Journal of Experimental Social Psychology* 98 (January): 104231.

Graham, Matthew, and Shikhar Singh. 2023. "An Outbreak of Selective Attribution: Partisanship and Blame in the COVID-19 Pandemic." *American Political Science Review*. https://doi .org/10.1017/S0003055423000047.

Graham, Matthew, and Milan Svolik. 2020. "Democracy in America?: Partisanship, Polarization, and the Robustness of Support for Democracy in the United States." *American Political Science Review* 114 (2): 392–409.

Gramlich, John. 2020. "20 Striking Findings from 2020." Pew Research Center, December 11. https://www.pewresearch.org/fact-tank/2020/12/11/20-striking-findings-from-2020/.

Green, Donald P., and Bradley Palmquist. 1990. "Of Artifacts and Partisan Instability." *American Journal of Political Science* 34 (3): 872–902.

Green, Donald P., Bradley Palmquist, and Eric Schickler. 2002. *Partisan Hearts and Minds: Political Parties and the Social Identities of Voters*. New Haven, CT: Yale University Press.

Green, Donald P., and Paul Platzman. Forthcoming. "Partisan Stability during Turbulent Times: Evidence from Three American Panel Surveys." *Political Behavior*. https://doi.org/10.1007/s11109-022-09825-y.

Green, Jon, Jared Edgerton, Daniel Naftel, Kelsey Shoub, and Skyler J. Cranmer. 2020. "Elusive Consensus: Polarization in Elite Communication on the COVID-19 Pandemic." *Science Advances* 6 (28): eabc2717.

Grillo, Edoardo, and Carlo Prato. 2023. "Reference Points and Democratic Backsliding." *American Journal of Political Science* 67 (1): 71–88.

Groenendyk, Eric. 2013. *Competing Motives in the Partisan Mind: How Loyalty and Responsiveness Shape Party Identification and Democracy*. New York: Oxford University Press.

———. 2018. "Competing Motives in a Polarized Electorate: Political Responsiveness, Identity Defensiveness, and the Rise of Partisan Antipathy." *Political Psychology* 39 (1): 159–171.

Groenendyk, Eric, Erik O. Kimbrough, and Mark Pickup. 2023. "How Norms Shape the Nature of Belief Systems in Mass Publics." *American Journal of Political Science* 67 (3): 623–638.

Groenendyk, Eric, and Yanna Krupnikov. 2021. "What Motivates Reasoning?: A Theory of Goal-Dependent Political Evaluation." *American Journal of Political Science* 65 (1): 180–196.

Groenendyk, Eric, Michael W. Sances, and Kirill Zhirkov. 2020. "*Intra*party Polarization in American Politics." *Journal of Politics* 82 (4): 1616–1620.

Grofman, Bernard. 2022. "Prospects for Democratic Breakdown in the United States: Bringing the States Back In." *Perspectives on Politics* 20 (3): 1040–1047.

Grumbach, Jacob. 2022. *Laboratories against Democracy: How National Parties Transformed State Politics*. Princeton, NJ: Princeton University Press.

———. 2023. "Laboratories of Democratic Backsliding." *American Political Science Review* 117 (3): 967–984.

Guay, Brian, and Christopher D. Johnston. 2022. "Ideological Asymmetries and the Determinants of Politically Motivated Reasoning." *American Journal of Political Science* 66 (2): 285–301.

Gusmano, Michael K., Edward Alan Miller, Pamela Nadash. and Elizabeth J. Simpson. 2020. "Partisanship in Initial State Responses to the COVID-19 Pandemic." *World Medical & Health Policy* 12 (4): 380–389.

Gutmann, Amy, and Dennis Thompson. 2012. *The Spirit of Compromise: Why Governing Demands It and Campaigning Undermines It*. Princeton, NJ: Princeton University Press.

Haberman, Maggie. 2020. "Trump Has Given Unusual Leeway to Fauci, but Aides Say He's Losing His Patience." *New York Times*, March 23.

Hall, Andrew B. 2019. *Who Wants to Run?: How the Devaluing of Political Office Drives Polarization*. Chicago. University of Chicago Press.

Hamilton, Alexander, James Madison, and John Jay. (1787–1788) 1961. *The Federalist Papers*. New York: Mentor Books.

Harbridge, Laurel, and Neil Malhotra. 2011. "Electoral Incentives and Partisan Conflict in Congress: Evidence from Survey Experiments." *American Journal of Political Science* 55 (3): 494–510.

Harbridge, Laurel, Neil Malhotra, and Brian Harrison. 2014. "Public Preferences for Bipartisanship in the Policymaking Process." *Legislative Studies Quarterly* 39 (3): 327–355.

Hart, P. Sol, Sedona Chinn, and Stuart Soroka. 2020. "Politicization and Polarization in COVID-19 News Coverage." *Science Communication* 42 (5): 679–697.

Hart, William, Dolores Albarracín, Alice H. Eagly, Inge Brechan, Matthew J. Lindberg, and Lisa Merrill. 2009. "Feeling Validated versus Being Correct: A Meta-Analysis of Selective Exposure to Information." *Psychological Bulletin* 135 (4): 555–588.

Harteveld, Eelco, Lars Erik Berntzen, Andrej Kokkonen, Haylee Kelsall, Jonas Linde, and Stefan Dahlberg. 2022. "The (Alleged) Consequences of Affective Polarization: Individual-Level Evidence & a Survey Experiment in 9 Countries." Unpublished Paper, University of Amsterdam.

Haslett, Cheyenne. 2020. "Tensions with Trump: Dr. Anthony Fauci on Telling the Truth." ABC News, March 24. https://abcn.ws/3sU5qBe.

Heise, David. 1969. "Separating Reliability and Stability in Test-Retest Correlation." *American Sociological Review* 34 (1): 93–101.

Helmke, Gretchen, Mary Kroeger, and Jack Paine. 2022. "Democracy by Deterrence: Norms, Constitutions, and Electoral Tilting." *American Journal of Political Science* 66 (2): 434–450.

Hersh, Eitan. 2020. *Politics Is for Power: How to Move beyond Political Hobbyism, Take Action, and Make Real Change.* New York: Simon & Schuster.

Hetherington, Marc J. 2001. "Resurgent Mass Partisanship: The Role of Elite Polarization." *American Political Science Review* 95 (3): 619–631.

Hetherington, Marc J., and Thomas J. Rudolph. 2015. *Why Washington Won't Work: Polarization, Political Trust, and the Governing Crisis.* Chicago: University of Chicago Press.

Hiaeshutter-Rice, Dan, Fabian G. Neuner, and Stuart Soroka. 2023. "Cued by Culture: Political Imagery and Partisan Evaluations." *Political Behavior* 45 (2): 741–759.

Hibbs, Douglas. 1989. *The American Political Economy: Macroeconomics and Electoral Politics.* Cambridge, MA: Harvard University Press.

Hill, Seth J. 2017. "Learning Together Slowly: Bayesian Learning about Political Facts." *Journal of Politics* 79 (4): 1403–1418.

———. 2022. *Frustrated Majorities: How Issue Intensity Enables Smaller Groups of Voters to Get What They Want.* Cambridge: Cambridge University Press.

History.com editors. 2020. "Al Gore Concedes Presidential Election." https://www.history.com/this-day-in-history/al-gore-concedes-presidential-election.

Hobolt, Sara B., Thomas J. Leeper, and James Tilley. 2021. "Divided by the Vote: Affective Polarization in the Wake of the Brexit Referendum." *British Journal of Political Science* 51 (4): 1476–1493.

Hohmann, James. 2022. "Why One Race in West Virginia Proves Biden's Theory of the Case Has Failed." *Washington Post*, May 11.

Holbrook, Allyson L., Matthew K. Berent, Jon A. Krosnick, and Penny S. Visser. 2005. "Attitude Importance and the Accumulation of Attitude-Relevant Knowledge in Memory." *Journal of Personality and Social Psychology* 88 (5): 749–769.

Holland, Paul. 1986. "Statistics and Causal Inference." *Journal of the American Statistical Association* 81 (396): 945–960.

Homola, Jonathan, Natalie Jackson, and Jeff Gill. 2016. "A Measure of Survey Mode Differences." *Electoral Studies* 44 (December): 255–274.

Hopkins, Daniel J. 2018. *The Increasingly United States: How and Why American Political Behavior Nationalized.* Chicago: University of Chicago Press.

———. 2023. "Stable Views in a Time of Tumult: Assessing Trends in US Public Opinion, 2007–20." *British Journal of Political Science* 53 (1): 297–307.

Hounshell, Blake, and Leah Askarinam. 2022. "Republicans Sharpen Their Message on Ukraine." *New York Times.* March 4.

Hout, Michael, and Orestes P. Hastings. 2016. "Reliability of the Core Items in the General Social Survey: Estimates from the Three-Wave Panels, 2006–2014." *Sociological Science.* https://doi.org/10.15195/v3.a43.

Howe, Lauren, and Jon Krosnick. 2017. "Attitude Strength." *Annual Review of Psychology* 68 (1): 327–351.

Huddy, Leonie, and Alexa Bankert. 2017. "Political Partisanship as a Social Identity." In *Oxford Research Encyclopedia of Politics*, edited by William Thompson, May 24. New York: Oxford University Press. https://doi.org/10.1093/acrefore/9780190228637.013.250.

Huddy, Leonie, Liliana Mason, and Lene Aarøe. 2015. "Expressive Partisanship: Campaign Involvement, Political Emotion, and Partisan Identity." *American Political Science Review* 109 (1): 1–17.

Hughes, Adam. 2019. "A Small Group of Prolific Users Account for a Majority of Political Tweets Sent by U.S. Adults." Pew Research Center. https://www.pewresearch.org/fact-tank/2019/10/23/a-small-group-of-prolific-users-account-for-a-majority-of-political-tweets-sent-by-u-s-adults/.

Ingber, Rebecca. 2017. "The 'Deep State' Myth and the Real Executive Branch Bureaucracy." *Lawfare* (blog), June 14. https://www.lawfareblog.com/deep-state-myth-and-real-executive-branch-bureaucracy.

Iyengar, Shanto. 2021. "The Polarization of American Politics." In *The Routledge Handbook of Political Epistemology*, edited by Michael Hannon, and Jeroen De Ridder. London: Routledge EBooks.

Iyengar, Shanto, and Masha Krupenkin. 2018. "The Strengthening of Partisan Affect." *Political Psychology: Advances in Political Psychology* 39 (S1): 201–218.

Iyengar, Shanto, Yphtach Lelkes, Matthew Levendusky, Neil Malhotra, and Sean Westwood. 2019. "The Origins and Consequences of Affective Polarization in the United States." *Annual Review of Political Science* 22:129–146.

Iyengar, Shanto, Gaurav Sood, and Yphtach Lelkes. 2012. "Affect, Not Ideology: A Social Identity Perspective on Polarization." *Public Opinion Quarterly* 76 (3): 405–431.

Iyengar, Shanto, and Matthew Tyler. 2022. "Testing the Robustness of the ANES Feeling Thermometer Indicators of Affective Polarization." Unpublished Paper, Stanford University.

Iyengar, Shanto, and Sean J. Westwood. 2015. "Fear and Loathing across Party Lines: New Evidence on Group Polarization." *American Journal of Political Science* 59 (3): 690–707.

Jacobson, Gary C. 2015. "It's Nothing Personal: The Decline of the Incumbency Advantage in U.S. House Elections." *Journal of Politics* 77 (3): 861–873.

———. 2019. *Presidents and Parties in the Public Mind.* Chicago: University of Chicago Press.

Jacobson, Louis. 2016. "Yes, Donald Trump Did Call Climate Change a Chinese Hoax." Politifact. https://www.politifact.com/factchecks/2016/jun/03/hillary-clinton/yes-donald-trump-did-call-climate-change-chinese-h/.

Jamieson, Kathleen Hall, and Bruce Hardy. 2012. "What Is Civil Engaged Argument and Why Does Aspiring to It Matter?" *PS: Political Science and Politics* 45 (3): 412–415.

Jamieson, Kathleen Hall, and Doron Taussig. 2017. "Disruption, Demonization, Deliverance, and Norm Destruction: The Rhetorical Signature of Donald J. Trump." *Political Science Quarterly* 132 (4): 619–650.

Jamieson, Kathleen Hall, Allyson Volinsky, Ilana Weitz, and Kate Kenski. 2017. "The Political Uses and Abuses of Civility and Incivility." In *The Oxford Handbook of Political Communication*, edited by Kate Kenski and Kathleen Hall Jamieson, 205–218. New York: Oxford University Press.

Jenke, Libby. 2023. "Affective Polarization and Misinformation Belief." *Political Behavior*. https://doi.org/10.1007/s11109-022-09851-w.

Jensen, Nathan. 2017. "Job Creation and Firm-Specific Location Incentives." *Journal of Public Policy* 37 (1): 85–112.

Jin, Rongbo, Alexander Cloudt, Seoungin Choi, Zhuofan Jia, and Samara Klar. 2023. "The Policy Blame Game: How Polarization Distorts Democratic Accountability across the Local, State, and Federal Level." *State Politics & Policy Quarterly* 23 (1): 1–25.

Johnson, Blair T., and Alice H. Eagly. 1989. "Effects of Involvement on Persuasion: A Meta-Analysis." *Psychological Bulletin* 106 (2): 290–314.

Johnson, Victoria, Reese Butterfuss, Jasmine Kim, Ellen Orcutt, Rina Harsch, and Panayiota Kendeou. 2022. "The 'Fauci Effect': Reducing COVID-19 Misconceptions and Vaccine Hesitancy Using an Authentic Multimodal Intervention." *Contemporary Educational Psychology* 70 (July): 102084.

Jonas, Eva, and Dieter Frey. 2003. "Information Search and Presentation in Advisor–Client Interactions." *Organizational Behavior and Human Decision Processes* 91 (2): 154–168.

Jost, John T. 2021. *Left and Right: The Psychological Significance of a Political Distinction*. New York: Oxford University Press.

Jost, John T., Delia S. Baldassarri, and James N. Druckman. 2022 "Cognitive-Motivational Mechanisms of Political Polarization in Social-Communicative Contexts." *Nature Reviews Psychology* 1: 560–576. https://doi.org/10.1038/s44159-022-00093-5.

Kahan, Dan M. 2010. "Fixing the Communication Failure." *Nature* 463 (January 20): 296–297.

———. 2015. "Climate-Science Communication and the Measurement Problem." *Political Psychology* 36 (1): 1–43.

———. 2016. "The Politically Motivated Reasoning Paradigm, Part 1: What Politically Motivated Reasoning Is and How to Measure It." In *Emerging Trends in the Social and Behavioral Sciences*, edited by Robert Scott, and Stephen Kosslyn, 1–16. Hoboken, NJ: John Wiley & Sons.

Kalla, Joshua, and David E. Broockman. 2016. "Campaign Contributions Facilitate Access to Congressional Officials: A Randomized Field Experiment." *American Journal of Political Science* 60 (3): 545–558.

Kalmoe, Nathan P. 2020. *With Ballots and Bullets: Partisanship and Violence in the American Civil War*. New York: Cambridge University Press.

Kalmoe, Nathan P., and Lilliana Mason. 2020. "Most Americans Reject Partisan Violence, But There Is Still Cause for Concern." Democracy Fund Voter Study Group, May 7. https://www.voterstudygroup.org/blog/has-american-partisanship-gone-too-far.

———. 2022. *Radical American Partisanship: Mapping Violent Hostility, Its Causes, and the Consequences for Democracy*. Chicago: University of Chicago Press.

Kam, Cindy D. 2007. "Implicit Attitudes, Explicit Choices: When Subliminal Priming Predicts Candidate Preference." *Political Behavior* 29 (3): 343–367.

Kamarck, Elaine, and Norman Eisen. 2022. "Democracy on the Ballot—How Many Election Deniers Are on the Ballot in November and What Is Their Likelihood of Success?" *Brookings*,

October 7. https://www.brookings.edu/articles/democracy-on-the-ballot-how-many-election
-deniers-are-on-the-ballot-in-november-and-what-is-their-likelihood-of-success/.

Kang, Yong-Soon, and Paul M. Herr. 2006. "Beauty and the Beholder: Toward an Integrative
Model of Communication Source Effects." *Journal of Consumer Research* 33 (1): 123–130.

Kapucu, Naim, and Donald Moynihan. 2021. "Trump's (Mis)management of the COVID-19
Pandemic in the US." *Policy Studies* 42:592–610.

Karl, Jonathan. 2014. "Obama's Long-Lost Campaign Promise." ABC News, February 17. https://
abcnews.go.com/blogs/politics/2014/02/obamas-long-lost-campaign-promise/.

Karni, Annie. 2020. "Trump Defends Indoor Rally, but Aides Express Concern" *New York Times*,
September 14.

Katz, Elihu. 1957. "The Two-Step Flow of Communication: An Up-to-Date Report on an Hypothesis." *Public Opinion Quarterly* 21 (Spring): 61–78.

Keith, William, and Robert Danisch. 2020. *Beyond Civility: The Competing Obligations of Citizenship*. University Park: Pennsylvania State University Press.

Kelly, Amita. 2016. "McConnell: Blocking Supreme Court Nomination 'About a Principle, Not
a Person.'" *National Public Radio*, March 16. https://www.npr.org/2016/03/16/470664561
/mcconnell-blocking-supreme-court-nomination-about-a-principle-not-a-person.

Kenen, Joanne, and Meredith McGraw. 2021. "Trump's Former Aides Say He Whiffed on Vaccination Legacy." *Politico*, April 20. https://www.politico.com/news/2021/04/20/trump-vaccines
-ex-aides-483387.

Kessler, Glenn. 2020. "Trump Ad Falsely Suggests Biden Supports Defunding the Police." *Washington Post*, July 14.

Kettl, Donald F. 2020. "States Divided: The Implications of American Federalism for COVID-19."
Public Administration Review 80 (4): 595–602.

Kingzette, Jon. 2021. "Partisan Animosity and the Civic Culture: Examining the Causes and Consequences of Affective Polarization in the United States." Ph.D. Dissertation, Ohio State University.

Kingzette, Jon, James Druckman, Samara Klar, Yanna Krupnikov, Matthew Levendusky, and
John Barry Ryan. 2021. "How Affective Polarization Undermines Support for Democratic
Norms." *Public Opinion Quarterly* 85 (2): 663–677.

Klar, Samara. 2013. "The Influence of Competing Identity Primes on Political Preferences." *Journal of Politics* 75 (4): 1108–1124.

Klar, Samara, Yanna Krupnikov, and John Barry Ryan. 2018. "Affective Polarization or Partisan
Disdain? Untangling a Dislike for the Opposing Party from a Dislike of Partisanship." *Public
Opinion Quarterly* 82 (2): 379–390.

———. 2022. "Who Are Leaners? How True Independents Differ from the Weakest Partisans
and Why It Matters." *Forum* 20 (1): 155–167.

Klar, Samara, Thomas Leeper, and Joshua Robison. 2020. "Studying Identities with Experiments:
Weighing the Risk of Posttreatment Bias against Priming Effects." *Journal of Experimental
Political Science* 7 (1): 56–60.

Klein, Ezra. 2020. *Why We're Polarized*. New York: Avid Reader Press.

Krishnarajan, Suthan. 2023. "Rationalizing Democracy: The Perceptual Bias and (Un)Demo-
cratic Behavior." *American Political Science Review* 177 (2): 473–496.

Kruglanski, Arie W. 1989. "The Psychology of Being 'Right': The Problem of Accuracy in Social
Perception and Cognition." *Psychological Bulletin* 106 (3): 395–409.

Krupenkin, Masha. 2021. "Does Partisanship Affect Compliance with Government Recommendations?" *Political Behavior* 43 (1): 451–472.

Krupnikov, Yanna, and John Barry Ryan. 2022. *The Other Divide: Polarization and Disengagement in American Politics.* New York: Cambridge University Press.

Kunda, Ziva. 1999. *Social Cognition: Making Sense of People.* Cambridge, MA: MIT Press.

Lacombe, Matthew J., Matthew D. Simonson, Jon Green, and James N. Druckman. Forthcoming. "Social Disruption, Gun Buying, and Anti-System Beliefs." *Perspectives on Politics.* https://doi.org/10.1017/S1537592722003322.

Lapinski, John, Matthew Levendusky, Ken Winneg and Kathleen Hall Jamieson. 2016. "What Do Citizens Want from Their Member of Congress?" *Political Research Quarterly* 69 (3): 535–545.

Larsen, Bradley, Marc J. Hetherington, Steven H. Greene, Timothy J. Ryan, Rahsaan D. Maxwell, and Steven Tadelis. 2022. "Using Donald Trump's COVID-19 Vaccine Endorsement to Give Public Health a Shot in the Arm: A Large Scale Ad Experiment." National Bureau of Economic Research Working Paper 29896. http://www.nber.org/papers/w29896.

Lau, Richard R., David J. Andersen, Tessa M. Ditonto, Mona S. Kleinberg, and David P. Redlawsk. 2017. "Effect of Media Environment Diversity and Advertising Tone on Information Search, Selective Exposure, and Affective Polarization." *Political Behavior* 39 (1): 231–255.

Lavine, Howard G., Christopher D. Johnston, and Marco R. Steenbergen. 2012. *The Ambivalent Partisan: How Critical Loyalty Promotes Democracy.* New York: Oxford University Press.

Lee, Amber Hye-Yon. 2021. "How the Politicization of Everyday Activities Affects the Public Sphere: The Effects of Partisan Stereotypes on Cross-Cutting Interactions." *Political Communication* 38 (5): 499–518.

Lee, Amber Hye-Yon, Yphtach Lelkes, Carlee B. Hawkins, and Alexander G. Theodoridis. 2022. "Negative Partisanship Is Not More Prevalent Than Positive Partisanship." *Nature Human Behavior* 6 (7): 951–963.

Lee, Byungkyu, and Peter Bearman. 2020. "Political Isolation in America." *Network Science* 8 (3): 333–355.

Lee, Frances. 2016. *Insecure Majorities: Congress and the Permanent Campaign.* Chicago: University of Chicago Press.

Leeper, Thomas J., and Rune Slothuus. 2014. "Political Parties, Motivated Reasoning, and Public Opinion Formation." *Political Psychology* 35 (S1): 129–156.

Lees, Jeffrey, and Mina Cikara. 2020. "Inaccurate Group Meta-Perceptions Drive Negative Out-Group Attributions in Competitive Contexts." *Nature Human Behaviour* 4 (3): 279–286.

Lelkes, Yphtach. 2016. "Mass Polarization: Manifestations and Measurements." *Public Opinion Quarterly* 80 (S1): 392–410.

———. 2018. "Affective Polarization and Ideological Sorting: A Reciprocal, Albeit Weak, Relationship." *Forum* 16 (1): 67–79.

Lelkes, Yphtach, Gaurav Sood, and Shanto Iyengar. 2017. "The Hostile Audience: The Effect of Access to Broadband Internet on Partisan Affect." *American Journal of Political Science.* 61 (1): 5–20.

Lelkes, Yphtach, and Sean Westwood. 2017. "The Limits of Partisan Prejudice." *Journal of Politics* 79 (2): 485–501.

Lenz, Gabriel S. 2012. *Follow the Leader?: How Voters Respond to Politicians' Policies and Performance.* Chicago: University of Chicago Press.

Leonnig, Carol, and Philip Rucker. 2021. *I Alone Can Fix It: Donald J. Trump's Catastrophic Final Year.* London: Penguin Press.

Lerman, Amy E., and Katherine T. McCabe. 2017. "Personal Experience and Public Opinion: A Theory and Test of Conditional Policy Feedback." *Journal of Politics* 79 (2): 624–641.

Lerner, Jennifer S., and Philip E. Tetlock. 1999. "Accounting for the Effects of Accountability." *Psychological Bulletin* 125 (2): 255–275.

Levendusky, Matthew. 2009. *The Partisan Sort: How Liberals Became Democrats and Conservatives Became Republicans*. Chicago: University of Chicago Press.

———. 2010. "Clearer Cues, More Consistent Voters: A Benefit of Elite Polarization." *Political Behavior* 32 (1): 111–131.

———. 2013. *How Partisan Media Polarize America*. Chicago: University of Chicago Press.

———. 2018. "Americans, Not Partisans: Can Priming American National Identity Reduce Affective Polarization?" *Journal of Politics* 80 (1): 59–70.

———. 2023. *Our Common Bonds: Using What Americans Share to Overcome the Partisan Divide*. Chicago: University of Chicago Press.

Levendusky, Matthew, and Neil Malhotra. 2016. "Does Media Coverage of Partisan Polarization Affect Political Attitudes?" *Political Communication* 33 (2): 283–301.

Levin, Mark. 2020. @marklevinshow, August 8. https://twitter.com/marklevinshow/status/12 92269072911147008.

Levine, Marianne. 2020. "McConnell Fends off Accusations of Hypocrisy over Holding Supreme Court Vote." *Politico*, September 21. https://www.politico.com/news/2020/09/21/mcconnell -pushes-back-hypocrisy-supreme-court-419569

Levitsky, Steven, and Daniel Ziblatt. 2018. *How Democracies Die*. New York: Crown Publishing Group.

Levy, Ro'ee. 2021. "Social Media, News Consumption, and Polarization: Evidence from a Field Experiment." *American Economic Review* 111 (3): 831–870.

Lewis, Michael. 2021. *The Premonition: A Pandemic Story*. New York: W. W. Norton.

Lieberman, Robert, Suzanne Mettler, Thomas Pepinsky, Kenneth Roberts, and Rick Valelly. 2019. "The Trump Presidency and American Democracy: A Historical and Comparative Analysis." *Perspectives on Politics* 17 (2): 470–479.

Lindaman, Kara, and Donald P. Haider-Markel. 2002. "Issue Evolution, Political Parties, and the Culture Wars." *Political Research Quarterly* 55 (1): 91–110.

Lipsitz, Keena, and Grigore Pop-Eleches. 2020. "The Partisan Divide in Social Distancing." SSRN Working Paper, May 8. https://dx.doi.org/10.2139/ssrn.3595695.

Little, Andrew and Meng, Anne. 2023. "Measuring Democratic Backsliding" *PS: Political Science & Politics*. http://dx.doi.org/10.2139/ssrn.4327307.

Lodge, Milton, and Charles S. Taber. 2013. *The Rationalizing Voter*. New York: Cambridge University Press.

Long, Elisa F., M. Keith Chen, and Ryne Rohla. 2020. "Political Storms: Emergent Partisan Skepticism of Hurricane Risks." *Science Advances* 6 (37): eabb7906.

Lord, Charles G., Mark R. Lepper, and Elizabeth Preston. 1984. "Considering the Opposite: A Corrective Strategy for Social Judgment." *Journal of Personality and Social Psychology* 47 (6): 1231–1243.

Lupia, Arthur, and Mathew D. McCubbins. 1998. *The Democratic Dilemma: Can Citizens Learn What They Need to Know?* New York: Cambridge University Press.

Luttig, Matthew D. 2017. "Authoritarianism and Affective Polarization: A New View on the Origins of Partisan Extremism." *Public Opinion Quarterly* 81 (4): 866–895.

Madison, James. 1792. "A Candidate State of Parties," *National Gazette*. https://founders.archives .gov/documents/Madison/01-14-02-0334.

Malhotra, Neil, and Jon Krosnick. 2007. "The Effect of Survey Mode and Sampling on Inferences about Political Attitudes and Behavior: Comparing the 2000 and 2004 ANES to Internet Surveys with Nonprobability Samples." *Political Analysis* 15 (3): 286–323.

Margolis, Michele. 2018. *From Politics to the Pews: How Partisanship and the Political Environment Shape Religious Identity*. Chicago: University of Chicago Press.

Martin, Gregory, and Steven Webster. 2020. "Does Residential Sorting Explain Geographic Polarization?" *Political Science Research and Methods* 8 (2): 215–231.

Mason, Lilliana. 2016. "A Cross-Cutting Calm: How Social Sorting Drives Affective Polarization." *Public Opinion Quarterly* 80 (S1): 351–377.

———. 2018. *Uncivil Agreement: How Politics Became Our Identity*. Chicago: University of Chicago Press.

McCarty, Nolan. 2019. *Polarization: What Everyone Needs to Know*. New York: Oxford University Press.

McCarty, Nolan, Keith T. Poole, and Howard Rosenthal. 2006. *Polarized America: The Dance of Ideology and Unequal Riches*. Cambridge, MA: MIT Press.

McClosky, Herbert. 1964. "Consensus and Ideology in American Politics." *American Political Science Review* 58 (2): 361–382.

McConnell, Christopher, Yotam Margalit, Neil Malhotra, and Matthew Levendusky. 2018. "The Economic Consequences of Partisanship in a Polarized Era." *American Journal of Political Science* 62 (1): 5–18.

McCoy, Jennifer, and Murat Somer. 2019. "Toward a Theory of Pernicious Polarization and How It Harms Democracies: Comparative Evidence and Possible Remedies." *Annals of the American Academy of Political and Social Science* 681 (1): 234–271.

McCright, Aaron M., and Riley E. Dunlap. 2011. "The Politicization of Climate Change and Polarization in the American Public's Views of Global Warming, 2001–2010." *Sociological Quarterly* 52 (2): 155–194.

McGregor, Shannon C. 2019. "Social Media as Public Opinion: How Journalists Use Social Media to Represent Public Opinion." *Journalism* 20 (8): 1070–1086.

Merkley, Eric, Aengus Bridgman, Peter John Loewen, Taylor Owen, Derek Ruths, and Oleg Zhilin. 2020. "A Rare Moment of Cross-Partisan Consensus: Elite and Public Response to the COVID-19 Pandemic in Canada." *Canadian Journal of Political Science / Revue Canadienne de Science Politique* 53 (2): 311–318.

Merkley, Eric, and Dominik Stecula. 2020. "Party Cues in the News: Democratic Elites, Republican Backlash, and the Dynamics of Climate Skepticism." *British Journal of Political Science* 51 (4): 1439–1456.

Mernyk, Joseph S., Sophia L. Pink, James N. Druckman, and Robb Willer. 2022. "Correcting Inaccurate Metaperceptions Reduces Americans' Support for Partisan Violence." *Proceedings of the National Academy of Sciences* 119 (16): e2116851119.

Milfont, Taciano L., Laurel Evans, Chris G. Sibley, Jan Ries, and Andrew Cunningham. 2014. "Proximity to Coast Is Linked to Climate Change Belief." *PLOS One* 9 (7): e103180.

Milita, Kerri, John Barry Ryan, and Elizabeth N. Simas. 2014. "Nothing to Hide, Nowhere to Run, or Nothing to Lose: Candidate Position-Taking in Congressional Elections." *Political Behavior* 36 (2): 427–449.

Milosh, Maria, Marcus Painter, Konstantin Sonin, David Van Dijcke, and Austin L. Wright. 2021. "Unmasking Partisanship: Polarization Undermines Public Response to Collective Risk." *Journal of Public Economics* 204 (December): 104538.

Mimms, Sarah, and *National Journal*. 2014. "Michele Bachmann Wants to Sue Obama over His State of the Union Speech." *Atlantic*, January 28. https://www.theatlantic.com/politics/archive /2014/01/michele-bachmann-wants-to-sue-obama-over-his-state-of-the-union-speech/450366/.

Molden, Daniel C., Robin Bayes, and James N. Druckman. 2022. "A Motivational Systems Approach to Investigating Opinions on Climate Change." *Thinking & Reasoning* 28 (3): 396–427.

Molden, Daniel C., and E. Tory Higgins. 2012. "Motivated Thinking." In *The Oxford Handbook of Thinking and Reasoning*, edited by Keith J. Holyoak, and Robert G. Morrison, 295–318. New York: Oxford University Press.

Montgomery, Jacob M., Brendan Nyhan, and Michelle Torres. 2018. "How Conditioning on Posttreatment Variables Can Ruin Your Experiment and What to Do about It." *American Journal of Political Science* 62 (3): 760–775.

Moore-Berg, Samantha, Lee-Or Ankori-Karlinsky, Boaz Hameiri, and Emile Bruneau. 2020. "Exaggerated Meta-Perceptions Predict Intergroup Hostility Between American Political Partisans." *Proceedings of the National Academy of Sciences* 117 (26): 14864–14872.

Morisi, Davide, John T. Jost, and Vishal Singh. 2019. "An Asymmetrical 'President-in-Power' Effect." *American Political Science Review* 113 (2): 614–620.

Moskowitz, Daniel J. 2021. "Local News, Information, and the Nationalization of U.S. Elections." *American Political Science Review* 115 (1): 114–129.

Muirhead, Russell. 2014. *The Promise of Party in a Polarized Age*. Cambridge, MA: Harvard University Press.

Mullinix, Kevin J. 2016. "Partisanship and Preference Formation: Competing Motivations, Elite Polarization, and Issue Importance." *Political Behavior* 38 (2): 383–411.

Murphy, Joe. 2021. "Biden Pledged 200 Million Covid Vaccinations in 100 Days. The Country Hit That Goal with a Week to Spare." NBC News, April 22. https://www.nbcnews.com /politics/white-house/150-million-vaccinations-tracker-biden-goal-n1255716.

Murray, Mark. 2022. "Poll: 61% of Republicans Still Believe Biden Didn't Win Fair and Square in 2020." NBC News, September 27. https://www.nbcnews.com/meet-the-press/meetthepress blog/poll-61-republicans-still-believe-biden-didnt-win-fair-square-2020-rcna49630.

Murray, Stephanie. 2021. "Suburban Dems Flee from 'Defund the Police.'" *Politico*, October 14. https://www.politico.com/news/2021/10/14/democrats-suburbs-lets-fund-the-police-515966

Mutz, Diana. 2011. *Population-Based Survey Experiments*. Princeton, NJ: Princeton University Press.

Newport, Frank. 2020. "Infrastructure Action Should Be a No-Brainer." *Gallup*, December 11. https://news.gallup.com/opinion/polling-matters/327587/infrastructure-action-no-brainer.aspx.

Nicholson, Stephen P. 2012. "Polarizing Cues." *American Journal of Political Science* 56 (1): 52–66.

Nir, Sarah Maslin. 2021. "A Fourth of July Symbol of Unity That May No Longer Unite." *New York Times*, July 4.

Norris, Catherine J. 2021. "The Negativity Bias, Revisited: Evidence from Neuroscience Measures and an Individual Differences Approach." *Social Neuroscience* 16 (1): 68–82.

O'Keefe, Daniel J. 2016. *Persuasion: Theory and Research*. 3rd ed. Los Angeles, CA: Sage.

Olson, Mancur, Jr. 1965. *The Logic of Collective Action: Public Goods and the Theory of Groups*. Cambridge, MA: Harvard University Press.

Orhan, Yunus Emre. 2022. "The Relationship between Affective Polarization and Democratic Backsliding: Comparative Evidence." *Democratization* 29 (4): 714–735.

Orr, Lilla V., Anthony Fowler, and Gregory A. Huber. 2023. "Is Affective Polarization Driven by Identity, Loyalty, or Substance?" *American Journal of Political Science* 67 (4): 948–962.

Orr, Lilla V., and Gregory A. Huber. 2020. "The Policy Basis of Measured Partisan Animosity in the United States." *American Journal of Political Science* 64 (3): 569–586.

Osmundsen, Mathias, Alexander Bor, Peter Bjerregaard Vahlstrup, Anja Bechmann, and Michael Bang Petersen. 2021. "Partisan Polarization Is the Primary Psychological Motivation behind Political Fake News Sharing on Twitter." *American Political Science Review* 115 (3): 999–1015.

Paluck, Elizabeth Levy, Hana Shepherd, and Peter M. Aronow. 2016. "Changing Climates of Conflict: A Social Network Experiment in 56 Schools." *Proceedings of the National Academy of Sciences* 113 (3): 566–571.

Panetta, Grace. 2020. "Trump Says Many of the U.S. Coronavirus Cases Are Just People Who 'Have the Sniffles.'" Business Insider, July 19. https://www.businessinsider.com/trump-says -coronavirus-patients-have-sniffles-many-cases-shouldnt-be-cases-2020-7.

Paris, Celia. 2017. "Breaking Down Bipartisanship: When and Why Citizens React to Cooperation across Party Lines." *Public Opinion Quarterly* 81 (2): 473–494.

Pasek, Michael, Lee-Or Ankori-Karlinsky, Alex Levy-Vene, and Samantha Moore-Berg. 2022. "Misperceptions about Out-Partisans' Democratic Values May Erode Democracy." *Scientific Reports* 12: 16284. https://doi.org/10.1038/s41598-022-19616-4.

Patashnik, Eric, Alan Gerber, and Conor Dowling. 2017. *Unhealthy Politics: The Battle over Evidence-Based Medicine.* Princeton, NJ: Princeton University Press.

Paul, Rand. 2022. "COVID Lockdown Lessons Learned—Fauci Amendment Would Mean No More Health 'Dictator in Chief.'" Fox News, March 14. https://www.foxnews.com/opinion /covid-lockdown-lessons-fauci-amendment-sen-rand-paul?cmpid=fb_fnc

Peirce, Charles Sanders. 1877. "The Fixation of Belief." *Popular Science Monthly* 12:1–15.

Pelosi, Nancy. 2019. @SpeakerPelosi. March 15. https://twitter.com/SpeakerPelosi/status/109 6444664792694784.

Peress, Michael, and Yangzi Zhao. 2020. "How Many Seats in Congress Is Control of Redistricting Worth?" *Legislative Studies Quarterly* 45 (3): 433–468.

Petersen, Michael Bang, Martin Skov, Søren Serritzlew, and Thomas Ramsøy. 2013. "Motivated Reasoning and Political Parties: Evidence for Increased Processing in the Face of Party Cues." *Political Behavior* 35 (4): 831–854.

Peterson, Erik, and Ali Kagalwala. 2021. "When Unfamiliarity Breeds Contempt: How Partisan Selective Exposure Sustains Oppositional Media Hostility." *American Political Science Review* 115 (2): 585–598.

Petty, Richard E., and John T. Cacioppo. 1986. *Communication and Persuasion: Central and Peripheral Routes to Attitude Change.* New York: Springer-Verlag.

Pew Research Center. 2014. "Report: Political Polarization in the American Public." June 12. https://www.pewresearch.org/politics/2014/06/12/political-polarization-in-the-american -public/.

Pew Research Center. 2019a. "Partisan Antipathy: More Intense, More Personal." https://www .pewresearch.org/politics/2019/10/10/partisan-antipathy-more-intense-more-personal/.

———. 2019b. "Pew Research Center: American Trends Panel Wave 48 [Dataset]." Roper #31116487, Version 2. Ipsos [producer]. Cornell University, Ithaca, NY: Roper Center for Public Opinion Research [distributor]. https://doi.org/10.25940/ROPER-31116487.

Pew Research Center. 2021. "Confronting 2016 and 2020 Polling Limitations." https://www .pewresearch.org/methods/wp-content/uploads/sites/10/2021/04/PM_04.08.21_polling .limitations.pdf.

Phillips, Joseph. 2022. "Affective Polarization: Over Time, through the Generations, and during the Lifespan." *Political Behavior* 44 (3): 1483–1508.

Pierce, Douglas R., and Richard R. Lau. 2019. "Polarization and Correct Voting in U.S. Presidential Elections." *Electoral Studies* 60 (August): 102048.

Pierson, Paul, and Eric Schickler. 2020. "Madison's Constitution under Stress: A Developmental Analysis of Political Polarization." *Annual Review of Political Science* 23 (1): 37–58.

Pink, Sophia, James Chu, James Druckman, David Rand, and Robb Willer. 2021. "Elite Party Cues Increase Vaccination Intentions among Republicans." *Proceedings of the National Academy of Sciences* 118 (32): e2106559118.

Plaks, Jason, ed. 2011. *The Social Psychology of Motivation*. New York: Oxford University Press.

Pope, Jeremy. 2021. "The Trump Era Legacy of Partisanism." *Forum* 19 (1): 143–162.

Pozen, David. 2018. "Hardball and/as Anti-Hardball." Lawfare (blog), October 11. https://www .lawfaremedia.org/article/hardball-andas-anti-hardball.

Prior, Markus, Gaurav Sood, and Kabir Khanna. 2015. "You Cannot Be Serious: The Impact of Accuracy Incentives on Partisan Bias in Reports of Economic Perceptions." *Quarterly Journal of Political Science* 10 (4): 489–518.

Przeworski, Adam. 1991. *Democracy and the Market: Political and Economic Reforms in Eastern Europe and Latin America*. New York: Cambridge University Press.

Quattrone, George A., and Edward E. Jones. 1980. "The Perception of Variability within In-Groups and Out-Groups: Implications for the Law of Small Numbers." *Journal of Personality and Social Psychology* 38 (1): 141–152.

Ramirez, Mark. 2009. "The Dynamics of Partisan Conflict on Congressional Approval." *American Journal of Political Science* 53 (3): 681–694.

Rathje, Steve, Jay J. Van Bavel, and Sander van der Linden. 2021. "Out-Group Animosity Drives Engagement on Social Media." *Proceedings of the National Academy of Sciences* 118 (26): e2024292118.

Redlawsk, David P. 2001. "You Must Remember This: A Test of the Online Model of Voting." *Journal of Politics* 63 (1): 29–58.

Redlawsk, David P., Andrew J. W. Civettini, and Karen M. Emmerson. 2010. "The Affective Tipping Point: Do Motivated Reasoners Ever 'Get It'?." *Political Psychology* 31 (4): 563–593.

Reny, Tyler T., and Benjamin J. Newman 2021. "The Opinion-Mobilizing Effect of Social Protest against Police Violence: Evidence from the 2020 George Floyd Protests." *American Political Science Review* 115 (4): 1499–1507.

Repucci, Sarah, and Amy Slipowitz. 2021. "Democracy under Siege." *Freedom in the World 2021*. Washington, DC. https://freedomhouse.org/report/freedom-world/2021/democracy-under-siege.

Reuters. 2022. "Trump Says He Would Pardon January 6 Rioters If He Runs and Wins." January 30. Reuters. https://www.reuters.com/world/us/trump-says-he-would-pardon-jan-6-ri oters-if-he-runs-wins-2022-01-30/.

Reuters / Ipsos. 2021. "Trump's Coattails." April 2. Press release. https://www.ipsos.com/sites /default/files/ct/news/documents/2021-04/topline_write_up_reuters_ipsos_trump_coattails _poll_-_april_02_2021.pdf.

Rieger, J. M. 2020. "40 Times Trump Said the Coronavirus Would Go Away." Video (2:30). *Washington Post*, November 2. https://www.washingtonpost.com/video/politics/40-times -trump-said-the-coronavirus-would-go-away/2020/04/30/d2593312-9593-4ec2-aff7 -72c1438fca0e_video.html.

Riker, William H. 1980. "Implications from the Disequilibrium of Majority Rule for the Study of Institutions." *American Political Science Review* 74 (2): 432–446.

Ripberger, Joseph T., Hank C. Jenkins-Smith, Carol L. Silva, Deven E. Carlson, Kuhika Gupta, Nina Carlson, and Riley E. Dunlap. 2017. "Bayesian versus Politically Motivated Reasoning in Human Perception of Climate Anomalies." *Environmental Research Letters* 12 (11): 114004.

Rivers, Douglas, and Nancy Rose. 1985. "Passing the President's Program: Public Opinion and Presidential Influence in Congress." *American Journal of Political Science* 29 (2): 183–196.

Roberts-Miller, Patricia. 2017. *Demagoguery and Democracy.* New York: The Experiment.

Robinson, Tim. 2021. "Center for Politics Partnership Probes the Deep Divides in American Politics and Society." *UVA Today,* September 30. https://news.virginia.edu/content/center -politics-partnership-probes-deep-divides-american-politics-and-society.

Robison, Joshua, and Kevin J. Mullinix. 2016. "Elite Polarization and Public Opinion: How Polarization Is Communicated and Its Effects." *Political Communication* 33 (2): 261–282.

Rocco, Phillip. 2022. "Laboratories of What?: American Federalism and the Politics of Democratic Subversion." In *Democratic Resilience: Can the US Withstand Rising Polarization?,* edited by Robert Lieberman, Suzanne Mettler, and Kenneth Roberts, eds., 297–319. Cambridge: Cambridge University Press.

Rodriguez, Cristian G., Shana Kushner Gadarian, Sara Wallace Goodman, and Thomas B. Pepinsky. 2022. "Morbid Polarization: Exposure to COVID-19 and Partisan Disagreement about Pandemic Response." *Political Psychology* 43 (6): 1169–1189.

Rogowski, Jon, and Joseph Sutherland. 2016. "How Ideology Fuels Affective Polarization." *Political Behavior* 38 (2): 485–508.

Rosenblum, Nancy. 2008. *On the Side of Angels: An Appreciation of Parties and Partisanship.* Cambridge, MA: Harvard University Press.

Rothschild, Jacob E., Adam J. Howat, Richard M. Shafranek, and Ethan C. Busby. 2019. "Pigeonholing Partisans: Stereotypes of Party Supporters and Partisan Polarization." *Political Behavior* 41 (2): 423–443.

Rudolph, Thomas J., and Marc J. Hetherington. 2021. "Affective Polarization in Political and Nonpolitical Settings." *International Journal of Public Opinion Research* 33 (3): 591–606.

Ruggeri, Kai, Bojana Većkalov, Lana Bojanić, Thomas L. Andersen, Sarah Ashcroft-Jones, Nélida Ayacaxli, Paula Barea-Arroyo, et al. 2021. "The General Fault in Our Fault Lines." *Nature Human Behaviour* 5 (10): 1369–1380.

Saguy, Tamar, and Michal Reifen-Tagar. 2022. "The Social Psychological Roots of Violent Intergroup Conflict." *Nature Reviews Psychology* 1 (10): 577–589.

Scannell, Leila, and Robert Gifford. 2013. "Personally Relevant Climate Change: The Role of Place Attachment and Local versus Global Message Framing in Engagement." *Environment and Behavior* 45 (1): 60–85.

Schattschneider, E. E. 1942. *Party Government.* New York: Farrar & Rinehart.

———. 1960. *The Semi-Sovereign People: A Realist's View of Democracy in America.* New York: Holt, Rinehart and Winston.

Schneider, Avie. 2021. "Fauci Relishes a 'Hallelujah' Moment." *National Public Radio,* January 23. https://www.npr.org/sections/coronavirus-live-updates/2021/01/23/959949611/fauci-relishes -a-hallelujah-moment.

Scoville, Caleb, Andrew McCumber, Razvan Amironesei, and June Jeon. 2022. "Mask Refusal Backlash: The Politicization of Face Masks in the American Public Sphere During the Early Stages of the COVID-19 Pandemic." *Socius: Sociological Research for a Dynamic World.* https://doi.org/10.1177/23780231221093158.

Settle, Jaime E. 2018. *Frenemies: How Social Media Polarizes America*. New York: Cambridge University Press.

Shabad, Rebecca, and Monica Alba. 2020. "Trump Calls Fauci a 'Disaster' and Says It Would Be a 'Bomb' if He Fired Him." NBC News, October 19. https://www.nbcnews.com/politics/politics-news/fauci-says-he-s-not-surprised-trump-contracted-covid-19-n1243857.

Shmargad, Yotam, and Samara Klar. 2020. "Sorting the News: How Ranking by Popularity Polarizes Our Politics." *Political Communication* 37 (3): 423–446.

Sides, John, Chris Tausanovitch, and Lynn Vavreck. 2022. *The Bitter End: The 2020 Presidential Campaign and the Challenge to American Democracy*. Princeton, NJ: Princeton University Press.

Silver, Laura, Janell Fetterolf, and Aidan Connaughton. 2021. "Diversity and Division in Advanced Economies." Pew Research Center, October 13. https://www.pewresearch.org/global/2021/10/13/diversity-and-division-in-advanced-economies/.

Simas, Elizabeth, Scott Clifford, and Justin Kirkland. 2020. "How Empathic Concern Fuels Political Polarization." *American Political Science Review* 114 (1): 258–269.

Simonovits, Gabor, Jennifer McCoy, and Levente Littvay. 2022. "Democratic Hypocrisy and Out-Group Threat: Explaining Citizen Support for Democratic Erosion." *Journal of Politics* 84 (3): 1806–1811.

Simonson, Matthew D., Ray Block Jr., James N. Druckman, Katherine Ognyanova, and David Lazer. 2024. *Black Networks Matter*. Cambridge Elements series in Contentious Politics. New York: Cambridge University Press.

Sinclair, Betsy. 2012. *The Social Citizen: Peer Networks and Political Behavior*. Chicago: University of Chicago Press.

Skelly, Geoffrey. 2021a. "Is the Presidential Honeymoon Over?" *Five Thirty Eight*, January 26. https://fivethirtyeight.com/features/what-should-we-expect-of-bidens-approval-rating-in-the-first-few-months/.

———. 2021b. "Republicans Really, Really Dislike Biden. But It's Not Just about Him." *Five Thirty Eight*, June 10. https://fivethirtyeight.com/features/republicans-really-really-dislike-biden-but-its-not-just-about-him/.

Skytte, Rasmus. 2022. "Degrees of Disrespect: How Only Extreme and Rare Incivility Alienates the Base." *Journal of Politics* 84 (3): 1746–1759.

Slothuus, Rune, and Martin Bisgaard. 2021a. "How Political Parties Shape Public Opinion in the Real World." *American Journal of Political Science* 65 (4): 896–911.

———. 2021b. "Party over Pocketbook? How Party Cues Influence Opinion When Citizens Have a Stake in Policy." *American Political Science Review* 115 (3): 1090–1096.

Small, Raphael, and Robert M. Eisinger. 2020. "Whither Presidential Approval?" *Presidential Studies Quarterly* 50 (4): 845–863.

Sniderman, Paul M., and Edward H. Stiglitz. 2012. *The Reputational Premium: A Theory of Party Identification and Policy Reasoning*. Princeton, NJ: Princeton University Press.

Solender, Andrew. 2021. "Trump Revokes Lobbying Ban He Signed at the Beginning of His Presidency." *Forbes*, January 20.

Stanley-Becker, Isaac, Yasmeen Abutaleb, and Devlin Barrett. 2020. "Anthony Fauci's Security Is Stepped up as Doctor and Face of U.S. Coronavirus Response Receives Threats." *Washington Post*, April 2.

Stecula, Dominik Andrzej. 2018. "Mass Media and Political Polarization in the United States." PhD dissertation. University of British Columbia.

Stolberg, Sheryl Gay. 2022. "Republicans, Wooing Trump Voters, Make Fauci Their Boogyman." *New York Times*, February 7.

Stone, Daniel F. 2023. *Undue Hate: A Behavioral Economic Analysis of Hostile Polarization in U.S. Politics and Beyond*. Cambridge, MA: MIT Press.

Stouffer, Samuel A. 1955. *Communism, Conformity and Civil Liberties: A Cross-Section of the Nation Speaks Its Mind*. New York: Doubleday.

Sullivan, John L., and John E. Transue. 1999. "The Psychological Underpinnings of Democracy: A Selective Review of Research on Political Tolerance, Interpersonal Trust, and Social Capital." *Annual Review of Psychology* 40 (1): 625–650.

Sunstein, Cass R. 2015. "Partyism." *University of Chicago Legal Forum* 2015, art. 2.

Swan, Jonathan. 2020. "Trump: Expect 'Wild Evening' in Tulsa, Mask Optional." *Axios*, June 19. https://www.axios.com/2020/06/20/trump-axios-interview-tulsa-rally.

Taber, Charles S., and Milton Lodge. 2006. "Motivated Skepticism in the Evaluation of Political Beliefs." *American Journal of Political Science* 50 (3): 755–769.

Tajfel, Henri, and Alan L. Wilkes. 1963. "Classification and Quantitative Judgement." *British Journal of Psychology* 54 (2): 101–114.

Tappin, Ben M. 2023. "Estimating the Between-Issue Variation in Party Elite Cue Effects." *Public Opinion Quarterly* 86 (4): 862–885.

Tappin, Ben M., and Ryan T. McKay. 2019. "Moral Polarization and Out-Party Hostility in the U.S. Political Context." *Journal of Social and Political Psychology* 7 (1): 213–245.

Tappin, Ben M., Gordon Pennycook, and David G. Rand. 2020. "Bayesian or Biased?: Analytic Thinking and Political Belief Updating." *Cognition* 204 (November): 104375.

———. 2021. "Rethinking the Link between Cognitive Sophistication and Politically Motivated Reasoning." *Journal of Experimental Psychology* 150 (6): 1095–1114.

Tesler, Michael. 2018. "Elite Domination of Public Doubts about Climate Change (Not Evolution)." *Political Communication* 35 (2): 306–326.

Tetlock, Philip E. 1985. "Accountability: A Social Check on the Fundamental Attribution Error." *Social Psychology Quarterly* 48 (3): 227–236.

Tomz, Michael, and Robert P. Van Houweling. 2009. "The Electoral Implications of Candidate Ambiguity." *American Political Science Review* 103 (1): 83–98.

Truman, David. 1951. *The Governmental Process*. New York: Knopf.

Trump, Donald, and Bob Woodward. 2020. "Trump 'Playing It Down.'" Transcript of Donald Trump and Bob Woodward Covid Conversation. February 7. https://www.rev.com/blog/transcripts/donald-trump-bob-woodward-conversation-transcript-trump-playing-down-coronavirus.

Tufekci, Zeynep. 2020. "Why Telling People They Don't Need Masks Backfired." *New York Times*, March 17.

Tyler, Matthew, and Shanto Iyengar. 2023. "Learning to Dislike Your Opponents: Political Socialization in the Era of Polarization." *American Political Science Review* 117 (1): 347–354.

Tyson, Alec, Brian Kennedy, and Carolyn Funk. 2021. "Gen Z, Millennials Stand Out for Climate Change Activism, Social Media Engagement with Issue." Report. Pew Research Center, May 26. https://www.pewresearch.org/science/2021/05/26/gen-z-millennials-stand-out-for-climate-change-activism-social-media-engagement-with-issue/.

Uscinski, Joseph E., Adam M. Enders, Michelle I. Seelig, Casey A. Klofstad, John R. Funchion, Caleb Everett, Stefan Wuchty, Kamal Premaratne, and Manohar N. Murthi. 2021. "American Politics in Two Dimensions: Partisan and Ideological Identities versus Anti-Establishment Orientations." *American Journal of Political Science* 65 (4): 877–895.

Van Boven, Leaf, Phillip J. Ehret, and David K. Sherman. 2018. "Psychological Barriers to Bipartisan Public Support for Climate Policy." *Perspectives on Psychological Science* 13 (4): 492–507.

Victor, Daniel, Lew Serviss, and Azi Paybarah. 2020. "In His Own Words, Trump on the Coronavirus and Masks." *New York Times*, October 2.

Virgin, Sheahan G. 2023. "The Effect of Core Values on Support for Electoral Reform: Evidence from Two Survey Experiments." *American Journal of Political Science* 67 (1): 239–256.

Visser, Penny S., George Y. Bizer, and Jon A. Krosnick. 2006. "Exploring the Latent Structure of Strength-Related Attitude Attributes." *Advances in Experimental Social Psychology* 38: 1–67.

Voelkel, Jan G., James Chu, Michael N. Stagnaro, Joseph S. Mernyk, Chrystal Redekopp, Sophia L. Pink, James N. Druckman, David G. Rand, and Robb Willer. 2023. "Interventions Reducing Affective Polarization Do Not Necessarily Improve Anti-Democratic Attitudes." *Nature Human Behavior* 7 (1): 55–64.

Voelkel, Jan G., Michael N. Stagnaro, James Chu, Sophia L. Pink, Joseph S. Mernyk, Chrystal Redekopp, Isaias Ghezae, et al. 2023. "Megastudy Identifying Successful Interventions to Strengthen Americans' Democratic Attitudes." Unpublished paper. https://www.strength eningdemocracychallenge.org/paper.

Wallace, Jacob, Paul Goldsmith-Pinkham, and Jason L. Schwartz. 2023. "Excess Death Rates for Republican and Democratic Registered Voters in Florida and Ohio during the COVID-19 Pandemic." *JAMA Internal Medicine* 183 (9): 916–923.

Walsh, Brian. 2020. "The U.S. Divide on Coronavirus Masks." Axios, June 24. https://www.axios .com/political-divide-coronavirus-masks-1053d5bd-deb3-4cf4-9570-0ba492134f3e.html.

Walter, Amy. 2021. "2021 Cook PVI." Cook Political Report. https://www.cookpolitical.com /cook-pvi.

Walter, Barbara F. 2022. *How Civil Wars Start: And How to Stop Them*. New York: Crown Publishing Group.

Washington, Ebonya L. 2008. "Female Socialization: How Daughters Affect Their Legislator Fathers." *American Economic Review* 98 (1): 311–332.

Washington, George. 1796. "Farewell Address, 19 September 1796." National Archive. Founders Online. https://founders.archives.gov/documents/Washington/05-20-02-0440-0002.

Washington Post / ABC News. 2021. "ABC News/Washington Post Poll [Dataset]." Roper #31118174, Version 1. Abt Associates [producer]. Cornell University, Ithaca, NY: Roper Center for Public Opinion Research [distributor]. https://www.langerresearch.com/wp-content/uploads/12 19a2TransitiontoBiden.pdf.

Webber, David, Arie Kruglanski, Erica Molinario, and Katarzyna Jasko. 2020. "Ideologies That Justify Political Violence." *Current Opinion in Behavioral Sciences* 34 (August): 107–111.

Webster, Steven W. 2021. "The Role of Political Elites in Eliciting Mass-Level Political Anger." *Forum* 19 (3): 415–437.

Webster, Steven W., and Alan Abramowitz. 2017. "The Ideological Foundations of Affective Polarization in the U.S. Electorate." *American Politics Research* 45(4): 621–647.

Webster, Steven W., Elizabeth C. Connors, and Betsy Sinclair. 2022. "The Social Consequences of Political Anger." *Journal of Politics* 84(3): 1292–1305.

Weiland, Noah, and Sharon LaFraniere. 2020. "FDA to Release Stricter Guidelines for Emergency Vaccine Authorization." *New York Times*, September 22.

Weingast, Barry R. 1997. "The Political Foundations of Democracy and the Rule of the Law." *American Political Science Review* 91(2): 245–263.

West, Emily, A., and Shanto Iyengar. 2022. "Partisanship as a Social Identity: Implications for Polarization." *Political Behavior* 44 (2): 807–838.

Westfall, Jacob, Leaf Van Boven, John R. Chambers, and Charles M. Judd. 2015. "Perceiving Political Polarization in the United States: Party Identity Strength and Attitude Extremity Exacerbate the Perceived Partisan Divide." *Perspectives on Psychological Science* 10(2): 145–158.

Westwood, Sean J. 2022. "The Partisanship of Bipartisanship: How Representatives Use Bipartisan Assertions to Cultivate Support." *Political Behavior* 44 (3): 1411–1435.

Westwood, Sean J., Justin Grimmer, Matthew Tyler, and Clayton Nall. 2022. "Current Research Overstates American Support for Political Violence." *Proceedings of the National Academy of Sciences of the United States of America* 119 (12): e2116870119.

Westwood, Sean J., and Erik Peterson. 2022. "The Inseparability of Race and Partisanship in the United States." *Political Behavior* 44 (3): 1125–1147.

Wheeler, Russell. 2020. "McConnell's Fabricated History to Justify a 2020 Supreme Court Vote." *Brookings Institution: FixGov Blog.* https://www.brookings.edu/articles/mcconnells -fabricated-history-to-justify-a-2020-supreme-court-vote/.

Wiest, Sara L., Leigh Raymond, and Rosalee A. Clawson. 2015. "Framing, Partisan Predispositions, and Public Opinion on Climate Change." *Global Environmental Change* 31 (March): 187–198.

Wilcox, Clyde, Lee Sigelman, and Elizabeth Cook. 1989. "Some Like It Hot: Individual Differences in Responses to Group Feeling Thermometers." *Public Opinion Quarterly* 53 (2): 246–257.

Wilson, Anne E., Victoria A. Parker, and Matthew Feinberg. 2020. "Polarization in the Contemporary Political and Media Landscape." *Current Opinion in Behavioral Sciences* 34 (August): 223–228.

Wise, Alana. 2020. "Trump Accuses FDA of Playing Politics with COVID-19 Vaccine Guidelines." *National Public Radio*, September 23. https://www.npr.org/2020/09/23/916315311 /trump-accuses-fda-of-playing-politics-with-covid-19-vaccine-guidelines.

Wolak, Jennifer. 2020. *Compromise in an Age of Party Polarization.* New York: Oxford University Press.

Wollheim, Richard. 2016. "A Paradox in the Theory of Democracy." In *Democracy: A Reader*, edited by Ricardo Blaug, and John Schwarzmantel, 179–180. 2nd ed. New York: Columbia University Press.

Woolf, Steven H. 2022. "The Growing Influence of State Governments on Population Health in the United States." *JAMA* 327 (14): 1331–1332.

Yang, Allie, and Meredith Deliso. 2020. "11 Attendees at SCOTUS Nomination Rose Garden Event Test Positive for COVID-19." ABC News, October 5. https://abcnews.go.com/Politics /attendees-scotus-nomination-rose-garden-event-test-positive/story?id=73391378.

Yokley, Eli. 2023. "Red-State Voters Give Democrats Tester, Manchin Opposite Marks ahead of 2024." *Morning Consult*, April 19. https://morningconsult.com/2023/04/19/joe-manchin -jon-tester-approval-rating/.

Yu, Xudong, Magdalena Wojcieszak, and Andreu Casas. 2021. "Affective Polarization on Social Media: In-Party Love among American Politicians, Greater Engagement with Out-Party Hate among Ordinary Users." Working Paper, University of California, Davis.

Zaller, John. 1992. *The Nature and Origins of Mass Opinion.* New York: Cambridge University Press.

Index

Aarøe, Lene, 48
Abramowitz, Alan, 162
Abrams, Samuel L., 162
accountability, partisan animosity and, 161–63
accuracy motivation: COVID-19 consequences and incentives for, 32–33, 98, 208–9, 220n12, 220nn13–15; likability and, 219n10; partisan animosity and, 17, 20–21, 30–33, 97–98
Adamic, Lada A., 218n3
advocacy groups, mobilization by, 175
affective polarization, 6–7, 217n7: hateful partisanship and, 160–64; in- and out-party ratings and, 10; measurement of, 192–94; media coverage of, 39
Affordable Care Act (ACA), partisanship and, 32–33, 66–72
age, as animosity correlate, 51–52
agency rulemaking, 138–39
Ahler, Douglas J., 168–69
Ahmed, Amel, 174
ambiguous politicization, 30: high animosity and, 71–72; partisan animosity and, 36–37, 97–98; party cues and, 65
American Community Survey, 185
American National Election Studies (ANES), 8–10
American Presidency Project, 138
Annenberg IOD Collaborative, 105–6
anti-cues, partisanship and, 29–30, 64–65
antidemocratic attitudes, growth of, 174–75, 228n8
apolitical symbols, partisan animosity and, 102–3
approval: COVID-19 vaccine credit, 110–13; dynamics of, 103; leadership animation and, 98–101; partisan, and gap in, 96–98

assault weapons bans: asymmetric polarization and, 66–67, 70–71; partisanship over, 16
asymmetric polarization: COVID-19 pandemic and, 224n14; party cues and, 64–67, 70–72, 223n3

Bachmann, Michele, 138–39
backsliding of democratic values: executive aggrandizement and, 226n2; partisan animosity and risk of, 5, 140, 149, 156–59, 165, 173–75; state-level policies and, 166, 171–73
Baker, Charlie, 100
Bakshy, Eytan, 218n3
Baldassari, Delia, 217n1
Bankert, Alexa, 25, 28
Bartels, Larry, 156, 174
Bayes, Robin, 32
Bearman, Peter, 30
beliefs: partisan animosity and, 59–61, 170–73; partisanship and confirmation of, 27–28
Beremo, Nancy, 226n1
biases: accuracy motivation and, 30–33, 218n2; demographics and, 164
Biden, Joe, 62, 218n8; anti-violence rhetoric of, 154; approval of, 103–6; COVID-19 pandemic response, 78–79, 84, 86–87, 94, 101–3; election as president, 15, 158–60; executive orders under, 141; Fauci and, 114–15; minimum wage increase endorsed by, 66; nomination of, 13; opposition to defunding police, 65; political animosity toward, 96–101, 207–9; on political compromise, 122–25, 131–32; presidential powers and, 139–40
bipartisanship: partisan animosity and, 161–63; political compromise and, 125–26; skepticism about, 122–25

Bisgaard, Martin, 29

Black Americans: Democratic Party and, 1; protests against police brutality by, 13–15

Black Lives Matter movement, 15, 47–48

Bolsen, Toby, 32

Bond, R., 218n3

Bottoms, Keisha Lance, 100

Boviytz Inc., 185–90

Boxell, Levi, 46

Braley, Alia, 227n8

Brennan Center for Justice, 145–46

Broockman, David, 161

Brooks, David, 2

Brown, Sherrod, 99

Bush, Cori, 65

Bush, George H. W., 113

Bush, George W., 30–31, 113, 138–39, 141

Carlson, Taylor, 163

Carlson, Tucker, 177

causal inference: partisan animosity and, 58–61; partisan animosity and policy outcomes, 161–64

Centers for Disease Control (CDC), 16, 20, 77, 82–83, 98, 116–20, 208–9, 218n10

Centers for Systemic Peace, 157

Chauvin, Derek, 13–15, 65

checks and balances, norm of: executive orders vs., 141–42; partisan animosity and, 21, 36–37, 227n13; protection of democracy and, 172–73

Chen, M. Keith, 220n15

Cheney, Liz, 147

Chick-Fil-A, 103

Christie, Chris, 139

Chua, Amy, 39

church attendance, Republican party alignment and, 1

citizenship for immigrants, polarization over, 66–72

civility, defined, 123–25, 137

Clawson, Rosalee A., 165

climate change: perceptions of consequences of, 220nn14–16; personalization vs. politicization of, 164–67; polarization over, 62–63

Clinton, Hillary, 62, 224n15; unpopularity of, 9–10

collective responsibility: Congress and, 103, 108–9; COVID-19 undermining of, 22; democratic functioning and, 3, 20; out-group spite and, 145; partisan animosity and, 167–68; party cues and, 110

Collins, Susan, 99

Coney Barrett, Amy, 143, 149, 226n4

confirmation bias, 218n2

Congress: apportionment in, 141–42; COVID-19 response of, 109–10; Democratic control of, 15; partisan animosity and approval of, 99–101,

104, 108–10; polarization in, 2, 6; shifting majority in, 5

consequences of actions: accuracy motivation and, 32–33, 97–98, 208–9, 220n12, 220nn14–15; approval of scientific figures and, 98, 118–21; COVID-19 pandemic and, 75–76, 79, 88–93; partisan animosity and, 59–61

conservative values, environmental issues and, 27

Constantino, Sara, 33, 220n16

Coppock, Alexander, 31–32

Coronavirus Task Force, 19–20

COVID-19 pandemic: accuracy motivation and, 33; approval of response to, 103, 223nn9–10; behavioral changes linked to, 4, 60; Congressional response to, 109–10; consequences of and animosity measurement, 5–6, 33, 56, 220n16, 222n13; Delta variant, 94; emergence of, 74–76; panel data regression models on animosity and partisanship, 204–9; partisan animosity and management of, 18–19, 22, 34–37, 113–21; party cues and, 76–79; perceptions of consequences during, 79, 85–87, 88–93, 223nn9–13; policy support and partisan animosity during, 87–89; political figures' reactions to, 19–20, 55–56; political impact of, 13–17; politicization of, 164, 177–78; preventive behaviors, 18–19, 55–56; research during, 8; stability of animosity and, 46–48, 60–61; states' role in health care disparities and, 166–67; survey data on impact of, 5–6

COVID-19 vaccine: approval of, 15; Delta variant and, 94–95; partisan animosity and, 84–85, 110–13, 116–18, 223nn6–7; survey data, 5

Cronbach's alpha measurement, party animosity and, 41–45

data collection and sampling: democratic norms panel for, 214–15; panel data regression models, 204–9; polarization and, 5–6, 185–90

defunding police initiatives, 16, 65, 67

demagoguery, 12

Demagoguery and Democracy (Roberts-Miller), 39

democracy, global decline in, 173–75

democratic accountability: partisan animosity and, 20–21, 96–98; partisanship and, 24–25

democratic collapse: democratic functioning vs., 3–4, 159; global increase in, 173–75

democratic functioning, democratic collapse vs., 3–4, 159

democratic institutions: partisan animosity challenge to, 22–23, 158–78; party cues and, 167–73; public support for, 171–73; states' role in, 165–67

democratic norms: defined, 141–42; on equal political participation, 226n1; executive power and, 138–40; extrasystemic partisan actions, 153–55; panel model for data on, 214–15; partisan animosity and, 36–37, 57–58, 138–57; political context and, 149–53; political parties and, 175; power and, 138–39, 141, 160–63; presidential election of 2020 and, 146–49; shared partisan support for, 171–73; violations of, 146–49, 168–69; voters' commitment to, 226n3

Democratic Party: affective polarization and, 6–8; approval of COVID-19 response in, 102–3; COVID-19 preventive policies and, 18–19, 55–56, 75–81, 86–93; demographic misperceptions of, 168–73; divisions within, 166–67; extrasystemic violence and, 154–55, 227n12; Fauci and, 115–18; gerrymandering opposition and, 145–46; liberal alignment in, 10–12; mask wearing and vaccine support in, 82–85; measuring animosity in, 40–45, 69–72, 191–94, 227nn5; partisan animosity and, 21, 99–101, 196–98; party cues and, 67–72, 221n21; policy issues and, 55–56; political compromise and, 124–25, 132–37; presidential election of 2020 and, 147–49; ratings of, 8–10; scientific figures' support in, 116–18; support for judicial nominees and, 143–46; vote choice and vote intention and, 44–45

demographics: correlates of partisan animosity and, 48, 50–52; data collection and sampling, 185–90; exclusion criteria, 189–90; polarization and, 11; representational biases and, 164

DeSantis, Ron, 100

Dias, N., 217n7

directional goals: accuracy motivation and, 30–33, 219n11; approval based on partisanship and, 96–98; disconfirmation bias, 218n2; leader evaluations and, 98–101; partisan motivations and, 26–28; personal consequences in COVID-19 pandemic and, 88–93

Divided We Fall (French), 39

Dobbs v. Jackson Women's Health Organization, 165

doom loop, 12

Downs, Anthony, 24–25

Druckman, James N., 40, 89, 163, 204

Drutman, Lee, 11

Easton, David, 156

economics, polarization and, 13–17, 47–48

Economist Intelligence Unit, 157

Electoral College, 141–42, 158

elites: citizen identification with, 24–25, 219n7; COVID-19 pandemic and, 35–37, 55–56, 75–76, 86–87; democratic erosion and, 174–75; democratic norms and role of, 36–37, 171–73, 221n20; hateful animosity and, 162–64; mask wearing and vaccine behaviors and, 82–85; partisan animosity and role of, 22, 35–37, 60–61, 222n17; personalization vs. politicization of, 164–67;

polarization and, 10–12, 19, 60–61, 65–67; political compromise and, 126–27

environmental issues, 164–67

executive actions and powers: democratic norms vs., 138–39, 141; partisan animosity and, 21–22, 36–37, 222n15; political context and, 149–53

executive aggrandizement, 226n2

expressive partisanship, 25

extrasystemic partisan actions, 153–55

Facebook, partisanship on, 218n3

Fauci, Anthony: partisan animosity toward, 113–20, 177, 208–9; Trump and, 16, 19–20, 36, 57, 97–99

Federal Emergency Management Agency (FEMA), 110

Federalist Papers, 37, 168

Feeling Thermometer Ratings: likability and, 219n10; partisan animosity measurement and, 8–9, 40–45, 221n7

Feinberg, Matthew, 27, 170–71

"Fight for 15" campaign, 66

Fiorina, Morris P., 162, 170

FiveThirtyEight.com, 96

fixed effects models, 223n5

Floyd, George, murder of, 5, 13–15, 65

flu vaccine, partisan animosity concerning, 118

Food and Drug Administration (FDA), 116–20, 208–9

forbearance, democratic norms and, 226n2

foreign influence: impact of, 227n3; partisan animosity and, 167–68, 177–78

Forthright Panel (Boviytz Inc.), 185–90

French, David, 39

Frey, Dieter, 32

Gamm, Gerald, 166

Garland, Merrick, 142–46

General Social Survey, 46

Gerring, John, 17

gerrymandering, partisan animosity and support for, 143–46

Ginsberg, Ruth Bader, 149

goals: accuracy motivation and, 30–33; political behavior and, 17, 26–28; political compromise and, 126–27

governors: COVID-19 vaccine distribution and, 111–13; partisan animosity and, 100–101

graphical presentations: panel data regression models and, 204–9; partisan animosity impact and, 61, 68–72, 199–203

Green New Deal, 67, 70–71

Grillo, Edoardo, 172

Groenendyk, Eric, 31, 219n11

group belonging: partisanship and, 24–25, 27; polarization and, 220n17

Grumbach, Jacob, 166, 171
Guay, Brian, 218n4
gun rights and gun control, partisanship and, 27
Gutmann, Amy, 125

Harbridge, Laurel, 124–26, 131–32, 136–37
Harrison, Brian, 124–26, 131–32, 136–37
Hart, W., 32
Hastings, Orestes P., 46
hateful partisans: democratic functioning and,
    160; emergence of, 4–5; identification and
    study of, 160–64; norm support and, 140–41;
    relative influence of, 22
health and safety policies, COVID-19 and: ac-
    curacy motivation and, 32–33; criticism of, 177–
    78; establishment of, 74–76; partisan animosity
    toward, 19–20, 60–61, 85–93, 121; political and
    public health failures in, 76–79; politicization
    of, 117–18; states' role in health care dispari-
    ties and, 166–67. See also COVID-19 vaccine;
    masking, during COVID-19 pandemic
Hers, Eitan, 154
Hiaeshutter-Rice, Dan, 102
high partisanship, 176
Hodge, Bubba, 100
Hogan, Larry, 100
hostility, animosity vs., 7
Hout, Michael, 46
Huddy, Leonie, 25, 48
human infrastructure policies, political compro-
    mise, 122–25
hydroxychloroquine, 116

ideological polarization, 6; changes in, 217n1;
    elites and, 10, 35–37; partisan animosity and,
    64–66, 72–73, 163–64; partisan overestimation
    of, 168–73
immigration policies, polarization and, 66–67,
    70–72
information gathering and assessment: accuracy
    motivation and, 30–33; decline of local news
    and, 165–67; partisan motivations and, 26–28
in-party ratings: anti-cues and, 29–30; leadership
    evaluation and, 99–101; partisan animosity and,
    8–10; political compromise and, 127–36
institutional norms, partisan animosity and, 21,
    36–37, 221n20
instrumental partisanship, 24–25, 219n5; accuracy
    motivation and, 31–33
interventions, in partisan animosity, 161–64
ISideWith.com, 65
issues: consequences of polarization on, 97–98;
    partisan animosity and, 18, 49–50, 64–66,
    176–78; personalization vs. politicization of,
    164–67
Iyengar, Shanto, 7–8

January 6th Capitol insurrection, 5, 15, 48, 167–68
Jefferson, Thomas, 175
Jin, Rongbo, 100
Johnson, Ron, 99
Johnston, Christopher D., 25, 218n4
Jonas, Eva, 32

Kalla, Joshua, 161
Kingzette, Jon, 226n1
Kinzinger, Adam, 147
Klar, Samara, 27, 191, 228n1
Klein, Ezra, 39
Kousser, Thad, 166
Krishnarajan, Suthan, 171
Krupnikov, Yanna, 31, 219n11
Kunda, Ziva, 33

Lau, Richard R., 28
Lavine, Howard G., 25
Lee, A., 102, 218n4
Lee, Byungkyu, 30
Leeper, Thomas, 191, 228n1
legislative process, political compromise and,
    126–27
Lelkes, Yphtach, 217n7
Lerman, Amy, 32–33
Levendusky, Matthew S., 8–9, 40, 163
Levin, Mark, 139
Levitsky, Steven, 141, 221n20, 226n2
liberal alignment, social issues and, 217n1
likability, out-party animosity and, 219n10
lobbying ban, 66, 69–70, 223ch4n4
local news, decline of, 165–67
local officials: partisan animosity and approval of,
    100–101, 103, 106–8; personalization vs. politici-
    zation and, 164–67
LOESS regression, 43, 221n5
Long, Elisa F., 220n15
Lupia, Arthur, 219n10

Madison, James, 2, 5, 11–12, 168, 175
Malhotra, Neil, 124–26, 131–32, 136–37
Manchin, Joe, 99
masking during COVID-19 pandemic, partisan
    animosity and, 82–85, 95, 116–18
Mason, Lilliana, 11, 48, 154
mass media: decline of local news and, 165–67;
    partisan animosity coverage in, 16, 39, 65,
    83–85, 170–73, 227n6; party cues in, 28–30;
    perceptions of consequences in, 220n15
mass polarization, 172–73
mayors, partisan animosity and approval of, 100–
    101, 103, 106–8
McCabe, Katherine T., 32–33
McConnell, Mitch, 110, 142–46
McCubbins, Mathew D., 219n10

McLain, Audrey, 163
measurement of animosity, 17, 39–45, 191–94
Medicare drug pricing negotiations, 32–33, 66, 70
mega-identity, partisanship as, 11
Messing, Solomon, 218n3
Milita, Kerri, 28
Miller, Jason, 114
minimum wage increase: partisan animosity over, 65–67; party cues concerning, 67–72
moderates, data on, 6
Moore-Berg, Samantha, 143, 145
moral values, partisanship and, 27
Moskowitz, Daniel J., 165
motivated reasoning: partisan animosity and, 25–28; party cues and, 63–65
Muirhead, Russell, 176
Mullinix, Kevin J., 28, 32, 220n12
mutual animosity, 11

National Aeronautics and Space Administration (NASA) spending cuts, political compromise on, 124–25, 131–37, 210–13
National Institute of Allergy and Infectious Diseases (NIAID), 19–20, 113
negative campaigning, increase in, 28
negativity bias, out-party ratings and, 27–28
Neuner, Fabian G., 102
Newsom, Gavin, 100
New York Times, 2
Noem, Kristi, 100
nondirectional goals: accuracy motivation and, 30–33, 220n13; partisan motivations and, 26–28, 219n8
nonpolitical figures, partisan animosity and, 19–20
nonpoliticized issues, partisan animosity and, 18, 55–56
nonreligious individuals, Democratic party alignment and

Obama, Barack, 62, 66, 96; democratic norms and, 138–39, 141; party cues and, 221n21; Supreme Court nominations by, 142–46
objective truth: accuracy motivation and, 30–33; partisan animosity and, 161–63
Ocasio-Cortez, Alexandria, 62
Operation Warp Speed, 84, 110
Osmundsen, Mathias, 163
outcomes: partisan animosity and, 58–61; public opinion and, 173–75; states' role in democratic outcomes, 166–67
out-party ratings: accuracy motivations and, 33; anti-cues and, 29; COVID-19 vaccine credit

and, 110–13; leadership evaluation and, 99–101; measurement of animosity and, 41–45, 191–94, 221n7; partisan animosity and, 8–10, 17, 27–28, 219n10; party cue-taking and, 64–65; political compromise and, 127–36; social sorting and, 11–12; stability of animosity and, 46–48

paid family leave, partisanship and, 66
panel data, regression models, 204–9
parental identity, partisanship and, 27
Paris Climate Accord, 62
Park, Barum, 217n1
Parker, Victoria A., 170–71
partisan animosity: accuracy motivation and, 31–33; causal inference and, 58–61; causes of, 217n6; challenge to democratic functioning, 22–23, 158–78; climate change and, 62–63; correlates of, 48–52; COVID-19 pandemic and, 18–19, 33, 56–57, 75–76, 79–88, 220n16, 222n13; data collection and sampling, 185–90; defined, 7; democratic institutions and, 173–75; democratic norms and, 138–57; density plot of, 41–42; effects of, 5; evaluation of leaders and, 96–98; evolution of, 8–10; exogeneity of, 28, 45–48, 78–79; extrasystemic partisan actions and, 153–55; ideological polarization and, 64–66, 72–73; impact of, 39–61; increase in, 10–12; institutional norms and, 21, 36–37; instrumental aspects of, 219n5; intraparty animosity and, 166–67; issue positions, 18; leader evaluations and, 98–101; measurement of, 17, 39–45, 191–94; motivations and, 26–28; panel data regression models, 204–9; party cues and, 33–37, 63–65, 67–72; party reform and, 176–78; polarization and, 6–8, 62–73; policy support and, 17–18, 87–88; political accountability and, 20; political attitudes and, 33–37; political behavior and, 17; political compromise and, 124–37; political figures and, 19–20; research methodology on, 12–13; stability of, 45–48; team mindset and, 12; theory of, 3; timeline for, 14–17; undemocratic practices and, 142–49
partisan animosity, political context and, 149–53
partisanship: approval based on, 96–98; climate change and, 62–63; COVID-19 pandemic and, 75–76; democracy and, 37–38; local officials and, 100–101; measurement of, 40–45, 191–94; party reforms and, 175–78; political compromise and, 124–25; positive and negative aspects of, 218n4; research on, 24–25; shared democratic norms and, 171–73
partisan social identity scale, 48–52, 205–9
partisan violence: political consequences of, 3–4; rise in, 2–3. *See also* violence
partisan vitriolic rhetoric, increase in, 28
party competition, policy decisions and, 166–67

party cues: accuracy motivation and, 31–33; approval of leaders and, 109–10; availability of, 4; climate change and, 62–63; COVID-19 masking and vaccine policies, 82–85; COVID-19 pandemic and, 76–81; definitions of, 219n6; democratic functioning and, 159–60, 167–73; history of, 222n2; ideological polarization and, 163–64; leadership evaluation and, 99–101; partisan animosity and, 28–30, 33–37, 63–65, 67–72, 99–101, 199–203; from presidents, 106; in recent administrations, 221n21; scientific advisers approval and, 113–18

party reforms, 175–78

party switching, party animosity and, 43–44

Paul, Rand, 177?

Pelosi, Nancy, 110, 141

perceptions of citizens: misperceptions of opponents, 168–73, 227n4, 227n7; partisan animosity and, 101–3, 163–64;

personalization, politicization vs., 4, 160, 164–67

persuasion: accuracy motivation and, 32; likability and, 219n10

Peterson, Erik, 11

Pew Research Center, 2, 125–26, 218n3, 221n4

Pierce, Douglas R., 28

pluralism: democratic functioning and, 37, 168–73; partisan animosity and, 11–12

polarization: animosity as fuel for, 62–73; contemporary partisan animosity and, 6–8; defined, 6; hateful partisanship and, 160–64; increase in, 10–12; labels for, 7; mass polarization, 172–73; over-time changes in, 217n2; political compromise and, 123–25; recent trends in, 1–2; timeline in United States for, 13–17. *See also* ideological polarization

policymaking: COVID-19 pandemic and support for, 79, 87–93; partisan animosity and, 17–18, 34–37, 55–56, 60, 217n7; party cues and, 28–30; political compromise and, 122–25, 126–27

policy preferences and beliefs: partisan animosity and, 162–64; partisan identity and, 10, 24

political compromise: defined, 125–26; partisan animosity and, 36–37, 52–55, 57, 60, 124–37; testing support for, 131–36, 210–13; voters' attitudes concerning, 123–31

political correlates of animosity, 48–52

political decision-making: motivational theory of, 25; nationalization of politics, 165–67; partisan animosity and, 38

political leaders. *See* public figures

Political Tribes (Chua), 39

politicization: ambiguous politicization, 30; of COVID-19 pandemic, 76–79; partisan animosity and, 220n19; party cues and, 28–30; personalization vs., 4, 160, 164–67

popular vote, Electoral College and, 1

power: democratic norms and, 138–39, 141; executive aggrandizement and, 226n2; misperceptions of opponents and, 171–73; partisan animosity and, 21–22, 36–37, 222n15; political context for, 149–53; presidential powers, 138–40

Prato, Carlo, 172

predictive validity of animosity measures, 42–45, 191–94

presidential election of 2020, 5, 146–49; animus toward leaders in, 96–98; vote choice and vote intention in, 44–45

presidential impeachment trials, 5, 13

preventive behaviors, COVID-19 pandemic, 78–79; partisan animosity and, 18–19, 79–81, 89–93

prior attitude effect, 218n2

Przeworski, Adam, 147

public figures: animus and evaluations of, 96–121; COVID-19 pandemic and, 18–19, 22, 34–37, 56–57, 76–79, 222n12; COVID-19 vaccine credit and, 110–13; hateful partisans' influence on, 164; partisan animosity and politicization of, 52–55, 60, 97–101

public opinion: hateful partisanship and, 163–64; partisanship and, 26–28; system outcomes and, 173–75

Putin, Vladimir, 177–78

racial sorting, as animosity correlate, 51–52

Rathje, Steve, 28

rational choice partisanship, 24–25

Raymond, Leigh, 165

Redfield, Robert, 116

regression analysis: experimental data, 210–14; panel data regression models, 204–9; partisan animosity impact and, 61, 68–72, 199–203

reliability estimates, stability of animosity and, 46–48

religion, as animosity correlate, 50–51

Republican Party: accuracy motivation and, 30–31; affective polarization and, 6–8; conservative alignment in, 10–12; COVID-19 preventive policies and, 18–19, 55–56, 75–81, 86–93, 224n14; demographic misperceptions of, 168–73; divisions within, 166–67; on executive power, 138–39; extrasystemic violence and, 154–55; Fauci and, 115–18; gerrymandering opposition and, 145–46; mask wearing and vaccine resistance and, 83–85; measuring animosity in, 40–45, 191–94, 221n4, 227n5; partisan animosity and, 21, 99–101, 196–98; party cues and, 67–72; policy issues and, 55–56; political compromise and, 124–25, 131–37; politicization of COVID-19 pandemic and, 20; presidential election of 2020 and, 147–49; ratings of, 8–10; scientific figures animosity in, 116–18; state government control and, 166, 171; support for judicial nominees and, 143–46; support for Russia in, 177–78; vote choice and vote intention and, 44–45

reputation: partisan animosity and, 18; party cues and, 73; political compromise and, 127–36, 210–13

respect for institutions, democratic norms and, 151–53

Roberts-Miller, Patricia, 39

Robison, Joshua, 191, 228n1

Rocco, Phillip, 165

Rodriguez, Cristian G., 220n16

Rohla, Ryne, 220n15

Ryan, John Barry, 28

Ryan, Paul, 139

sacrifice, political compromise and perceptions of, 131–36

Sanders, Bernie, 70, 218n8

Scalia, Anthony, 142

Schattschneider, E. E., 177

scientific figures: COVID-19 pandemic and, 74–75, 84–85, 113–18; health consequences and evaluation of, 118–21; partisan animosity toward, 19–20, 57, 97–98, 115–18; politicization of, 164

Scott, Phill, 100

Senate, partisan animosity toward, 99–101

separation of powers, partisan animosity and, 21

Settle, Jaime E., 102

severity metric, COVID-19 responses and, 88–93

Simas, Elizabeth N, 28

60 Minutes (television program), 114

Slothuus, Rune, 29

social distance questions, 40–45

social identity (social sorting): as animosity correlate, 48, 50–52, 169–70, 205–9; hateful partisanship and, 163–64; partisan motivated reasoning and, 26–28; partisanship and, 24–25, 218n1, 218nn3–4, 219n9; polarization and, 10–11

social media: extrasystemic violence and, 154; negative campaigning in, 28; partisan expression on, 170–73, 218n3

social networks, mobilization by, 175

social psychological partisanship, 25

social relationships, partisan animosity and, 37–38, 220n18

Sood, Gaurav, 168–69

Soroka, Stuart, 102

stability of animosity, 45–48

state public leaders: partisan animosity and approval of, 100–101, 103, 106–8; personalization vs. politicization and, 164–67

Steenbergen, Marco R., 25

Supreme Court (U.S.): election rulings by, 1–2, 158–60; judicial nominees to, 142–46, 149

symmetric polarization: COVID-19 pandemic response, 78–79; issue positions and, 65–67; party cues and, 64–65, 223n3

Tappin, Ben M., 29

terror management theory, partisanship and, 220n16

Tester, John, 99

Thompson, Dennis, 125

time, partisan animosity over, 59–61

trait ratings, partisan animosity measurement and, 40–45

Truman, Harry S., 175

Trump, Donald, 62–63: animosity toward, 9–10, 96–98, 207–9; COVID-19 response, 56–57, 74–75, 77, 97–98, 101–3, 116–18, 222n12, 223nn2–3; COVID-19 vaccine credit and, 84, 94–95, 110–13, 223n8; executive orders of, 139, 141; extrasystemic violence and, 154; Fauci and, 20, 36, 97–98, 113–18; party cues and, 221n21; presidential election of 2020 and, 146–49; Putin and, 177–78; Republican trust of, 99–101; stolen election claims of, 15, 158–60, 218n9; voter approval of, 103–6

trust questions, partisan animosity measurement and, 40–45

Uncivil Agreement (Mason), 154

undemocratic processes and politicians, partisan animosity and support for, 12–13, 21–22, 52–55, 57–58, 142–49, 161–64, 226n7

United States: COVID-19 reaction in, 34–37, 56–57, 75–76, 78–79, 97–98; declining quality of democracy in, 157; downgrading of democracy in, 173–75; extrasystemic partisan actions in, 153–55; partisan animosity and politicization in, 101–3; partisan views of, 29–30; political tumult in, 13–17

unlimited campaign donations, 66, 69–70

urban tax incentives for business, 66, 69–70

U.S. Constitution: democratic norms and, 141–42; Electoral College rules in, 1

vaccinations, partisan animosity concerning, 118, 223n6

Van Bavel, Jay J., 28

van der Linden, Sander, 28

Varieties of Democracies project, 173–75

V-DEM, 157

violence, lack of support for: democratic norms and, 153–55; partisan animosity and, 22, 57–58, 168–73, 227n8, 227n10

Voelkel, Jan G., 161

voters: approval gap and partisanship among, 99–101; attacks on Fauci by, 114–18; COVID-19 pandemic response evaluation by, 80–81, 101–3; gerrymandering opposed by, 145–46; mask wearing and vaccine behaviors and, 82–85; partisan animosity and, 23; party cue-taking by, 63–65; personalization vs. politicization in

voters (*cont.*)
 motivation of, 164–67; political compromise
 and attitudes of, 123–31; political parties and
 mobilization of, 176–78; political perceptions
 of, 101–3; presidential election of 2020 and,
 147–49; representational biases and, 164; state
 government restrictions on rights of, 166,
 171–73
voting restrictions, state laws on, 15

Walensky, Rochelle, 94
Washington, George, 2, 5, 167, 175

Washington Post, 114
Webber, David, 154
Webster, Steven W., 162
Westwood, Sean J., 11, 161
white Americans, Republican party and, 1
Why We're Polarized (Klein), 39
Wiest, Sara L., 165
Willer, Robb, 27
Wilson, Anne E., 170–71
Wolak, Jennifer, 123, 137

Ziblatt, Daniel, 141, 221n20, 226n2